Country towns in pre-industrial England

Themes in Urban History

General editor: Derek Fraser

Country towns in pre-industrial England

edited by PETER CLARK

Leicester University Press   1981

First published in 1981 by Leicester University Press
First published in the U.S.A. by St Martin's Press, Inc., New York

Copyright © Leicester University Press 1981

Designed by Arthur Lockwood
Phototypeset in Linotron Times and printed
in Great Britain by Redwood Burn Ltd, Trowbridge
Bound by Butler and Tanner Ltd, Frome

British Library Cataloguing in Publication Data
Country towns in pre-industrial England. –
  (Themes in urban history)
  1. Cities and towns – England – History
  I. Clark, Peter   II. Series
  942'.00973'2   HT133
  ISBN 0–7185–1175–1

FOREWORD

Urban history is an expanding field of study, sustained by a considerable volume of research. The purpose of this series, originally conceived by the late Jim Dyos, is to open a new channel for the dissemination of the findings of a careful selection from that research, providing a conspectus of new knowledge on specific themes.

For each volume in the series, each of the contributors is invited to present the core of his work: the essays, originating in theses but now specially written for this volume, are combined under the control of the editor, who writes an introduction setting out the significance of the material being presented in the lights of developments in that or a cognate field.

It is hoped that in this way the fruits of recent work may be made widely available, both to assist further exploration and to contribute to the teaching of urban history.

In this, the second volume of the series, Peter Clark has drawn together research which demonstrates clearly that urban development was as characteristic of pre-industrial England as massive urbanization was of the Industrial Revolution. This volume adds authoritative weight to the argument that modern English urban history must begin not with the industrial city but with the country and market towns of early modern England.

Derek Fraser
University of Bradford

CONTENTS

Foreword   page v
List of illustrations   ix
List of tables   x
List of abbreviations   xi
General note   xii
Notes on the contributors   xiii

Introduction: English country towns 1500–1800   1
PETER CLARK

The social problems of an Elizabethan country town: Warwick, 1580–90   45
A. L. BEIER
1   Introduction   46
2   Economic problems   48
3   The dimensions of poverty   54
4   Charity   64
5   Poor relief   73
6   Conclusion   78
    Bibliography   79
    Notes   79

Economic structure and change in seventeenth-century Ipswich   87
MICHAEL REED
1   Introduction   88
2   The seventeenth-century town: an overview   89
3   The occupational structure   99
4   The structural and spatial distribution of wealth   115
5   The role of the corporation in the urban economy   120
6   Continuity and change in seventeenth-century Ipswich   126
    Appendix 1: the Ipswich Hearth Tax returns, 1664 and 1674   131
    Appendix 2: civic rents, prices and wages, 1601–1700   134
    Bibliography   136
    Notes   136

Winchester in transition, 1580–1700   143
ADRIENNE ROSEN
1   Introduction   144
2   The local setting   146
3   Manufactures and markets, 1580–1640   148
4   Economic and social problems, 1580–1640   155
5   The Civil War and Interregnum   162
6   Expanding markets, 1660–1700   170
7   Catering to the gentry   176
    Bibliography   184
    Notes   187

Bath: the rise of a resort town, 1660–1800   page 197
SYLVIA MCINTYRE
1 Introduction   198
2 The emergence of the spa   199
3 The growth of the town   204
4 The town and its inhabitants   214
5 The corporation and the building of Bath   222
6 The corporation and the government of Bath   237
   Bibliography   243
   Notes   245

Index   251

LIST OF ILLUSTRATIONS

1 Warwick in the reign of James I   page 49
2 St Nicholas parish, Warwick: baptisms and burials, 1540–1680   55
3 St Nicholas parish, Warwick: baptisms and burials, 1540–1680, by decades   56
4 St Mary's and St Nicholas parishes, Warwick: baptisms and burials, 1650–80   56
5 The ages of the poor (Norwich, Warwick and Ipswich) compared to the ages of
   the general population (Ealing and Lichfield)   63
6 The liberties and parishes of seventeenth-century Ipswich   90–1
7 Town plan of Ipswich in 1778   93
8 Baptisms, marriages and burials in Ipswich, 1538–1740   95
9 The locations of friends and relatives of Ipswich testators, 1603–1714   98
10 Rural properties of Ipswich testators, 1603–1714   100
11 Migration to Ipswich, 1603–1714   101
12 Sixteenth-century houses on the corner of St Nicholas Street and Silent Street,
   Ipswich   111
13 17, St Stephen's Lane: plan   113
14 Markets and major roads in seventeenth-century Hampshire   153
15 Poor relief paid by Winchester corporation through St John's Hospital, 1580–
   1658   159
16 Serle's House, Winchester   183
17 Bath in the early seventeenth century   205
18 Rowlandson's 'The Comforts of Bath': the King's Bath   207
19 Bath at the end of the eighteenth century   213
20 Bath: corporate revenues and debts, 1684–1800   227

LIST OF TABLES

1	Improvement Acts for provincial towns, 1690–1799	page 21
2	Occupations in Tudor Warwick	52
3	Values of testators' goods in Tudor and early Stuart Warwick	53
4	Places of origin of itinerants arrested in Warwick, 1580–7	57
5	The social structure of St Mary's parish, Warwick, 1582	58
6	Harvest failure and the poor: St Mary's parish, Warwick, 1582 and 1587	59
7	The incidence of poverty in St Mary's parish, Warwick, 1544–5 and 1582	64
8	Charity to Warwick's poor in probate records, 1501–1650	70
9	Forms of charity to the poor in Warwick wills, 1480–1650	73
10	The cost of poor relief at St Mary's parish, Warwick, 1582 and 1587	76
11	The occupational structure of seventeenth-century Ipswich	102
12	Professional and salaried occupations in Ipswich in 1702	112
13	Ipswich probate inventories, 1583–1714	116
14	Population change in Hampshire market towns, 1603–76	175
15	Hearth Tax information for Bath, 1664	203
16	Transport facilities in Bath, 1684–1800	209
17	Bath: the census of 1801	214
18	Occupations of Bath inhabitants in the eighteenth century	215
19	Bath lodging houses	218
20	Numbers of chairmen in Bath, 1714–99	220
21	Occupations of members of Bath corporation in the eighteenth century	224
22	Corporation revenue, expenditure and bond debts, 1690–1800	226
23	Bondholders of Bath corporation	235

ABBREVIATIONS

Note Places of publication are given only for works published outside the United Kingdom. In abbreviating less frequently cited periodical titles, commonly accepted abbreviations such as *J.* for *Journal, Rev.* for *Review* have been used; other abbreviations are listed below.

Add.	Additional
AgHR	*Agricultural History Review*
AO	Archives Office
APC	*Acts of the Privy Council*
BIHR	*Bulletin of the Institute of Historical Research*
BL	British Library
Bodl.	Bodleian Library
C	Chancery Records, Public Record Office
CRO	County Record Office
CSPD	*Calendar of State Papers, Domestic*
DNB	*Dictionary of National Biography*
E	Exchequer Records, Public Record Office
EcHR	*Economic History Review*
EHR	*English Historical Review*
ESRO	East Suffolk Record Office
HMC	Historical Manuscripts Commission
HRO	Hampshire Record Office
NNRO	Norfolk and Norwich Record Office
P & P	*Past and Present*
PRO	Public Record Office
RO	Record Office
SP	State Papers Domestic, Public Record Office
TRHS	*Transactions of the Royal Historical Society*
VCH	*Victoria County History*

GENERAL NOTE

Spelling, capitalization and punctuation have been modernized in quotations. In the dates the year has been taken to begin on 1 January. The original £ s.d. currency has been retained.

NOTES ON THE CONTRIBUTORS

A. L. BEIER undertook his doctoral research at Princeton University and is at present Lecturer in Modern History at the University of Lancaster. He has just finished a large-scale study of vagrancy in Tudor and Stuart England.

PETER CLARK has written or edited a number of books, mainly on towns and provincial society in early modern England.

SYLVIA MCINTYRE completed her doctoral work at Oxford in 1973. She has helped prepare (with G.H. Martin) *A Bibliography of British and Irish Municipal History* (Leicester, 1972) and now teaches history at the West Midlands Institute of Higher Education at Walsall.

MICHAEL REED was a post-graduate in the Department of English Local History, Leicester University, and took his Ph.D. in 1973. He is currently Senior Lecturer in Library Studies at Loughborough University.

ADRIENNE ROSEN worked for her D.Phil. thesis at Oxford under the supervision of Dr Joan Thirsk. She was an Assistant Editor of the Victoria County History from 1971 to 1974 and now teaches at St Mary's College of Maryland.

Introduction:
English country towns
1500–1800

PETER CLARK

Introduction:
English country towns
1500–1800

PETER CLARK

In that crucial process by which England became an urban nation nobody would question that the most spectacular roles were played by London, its population soaring from 40,000 in the early sixteenth century to over half a million by the mid-eighteenth, and by the great new industrial cities of the Midlands and the North – Birmingham and the Pottery Towns, Manchester, Leeds and Sheffield.[1] Yet it is increasingly clear that the early modern period also saw significant changes in the function and importance of old-established provincial or country towns. Though they frequently experienced economic and social dislocation during the Tudor and early Stuart periods, by the early eighteenth century many of the larger and medium-rank country towns (as well as some of the smaller ones) had developed as bustling service, marketing and transportation centres. Quite often they boasted vigorous specialist industries. In the case of some of the more important towns they served as social amphitheatres for county landowners, helping both to urbanize the nation's ruling elite and to integrate town and countryside. Indeed it is arguable that the older provincial towns were not just bit-players in the unfolding drama of urban change but performed a central part in the development of a modernizing and industrializing society.[2]

The purpose of the present volume is to examine through detailed case studies some of the major changes and problems that affected English country towns between the Reformation and the Napoleonic wars. The first essay, by A.L. Beier on Warwick, explores the mounting social difficulties of urban society in the late sixteenth century; two more, by Michael Reed and Adrienne Rosen, examine the varying ways in which towns like Ipswich and Winchester reacted to and overcame economic decay; the last, by Sylvia McIntyre, charts the rise of the first English leisure resort, the precursor of a new race of urban communities, Georgian Bath. All these studies deal essentially with middle-rank provincial centres: below the regional importance of a half-dozen or so provincial capitals with populations of 10,000 or more by 1700, but standing above the multitude of small, mainly unincorporated market towns, with clusters of about a thousand inhabitants. This focus on second-rank county towns has been determined in part by the recent pattern of research, but it also reflects their vital importance in pre-industrial England, as the backbone of urban society in the provinces.

1

In this introduction we attempt to put our case studies into perspective and to relate their findings to evidence for other provincial towns, regional and market centres as well as county towns. We must also consider how the studies contribute to the current debate on the structure and difficulties of early modern towns. Areas and topics which require further research will wherever possible be identified. The first part of our survey examines the century or so up to and including the English Revolution, analysing in turn the general structural problems of country towns, the fluctuating fortunes of particular places and those decades of especial stress. The second part uses a similar approach to investigate the period after the Restoration.

Over the last decade a great deal of attention has been paid to English towns in the sixteenth and early seventeenth centuries. In a modest way the subject has become controversial, producing pessimistic and optimistic views of urban trends. In the introduction to *Crisis and Order in English Towns 1500–1700* (1972) Paul Slack and I argued that the sixteenth and seventeenth centuries as a whole, and the pre-revolutionary era in particular, 'witnessed a major collision of continuity and change', with serious and disruptive consequences for the economic and social structures of towns. A revised and amplified version of this argument appeared later in our *English Towns in Transition 1500–1700*.[3] That change not continuity was the main characteristic of urban development at this time is likewise emphasized by John Patten in a recent study.[4] More specifically, Charles Phythian-Adams has argued the case for a deep-seated demographic and economic crisis in provincial towns at the close of the fifteenth and start of the sixteenth century, a view supported by David Palliser and others in several local studies.[5] Less pessimistic, Penelope Corfield has highlighted the economic difficulties of particular towns during the sixteenth and seventeenth centuries but has also drawn attention to signs of expansion in other, mainly larger, urban communities.[6] The most optimistic profile of urban conditions before the Civil War has been sketched by Alan Dyer, who claims that the period was dominated not by urban crisis or difficulty but 'by a continual undulation within the urban sector' with the 'relative decline of a number of towns and the rise of a roughly similar number to replace them'.[7] There is no space here to explore in depth these divergent interpretations. However, it may be useful to review the main demographic, economic and social developments affecting Tudor and early Stuart towns, both in the light of our case studies and other recent work.

Fundamental to the state of English country towns before the Civil War was demographic change. For the early sixteenth century Phythian-Adams has presented a considerable array of urban data showing population stagnation or even in some cases sharp decline, but subsequent decades appear to have been marked by general demographic expansion, affecting both large and small towns.[8] The precise scale and nature of this growth is still rather shadowy because of the deficiencies of parish register data in multiple parish communities and the absence of large-scale family reconstitution studies for provincial towns. Some of the expansion was due to natural population growth, particularly in smaller and medium-sized centres.[9] But a vital factor in the demographic equation was immigration. At Ipswich, according to Michael Reed, a third of the town's expansion stemmed from the inflow of outsiders. The larger the town the more important the contribution of immigration. Like London, most major provincial towns had recurrent deficits of burials over baptisms for at least some part of the period; immigration was thus essential to make good the demographic shortfall and provide the propulsion for growth.[10]

Epidemic disease, increasingly localized to towns, was the main killer though subsistence crises may also have taken their toll, notably in smaller towns, during depressed decades like the 1590s. Epidemics (especially of plague) not only caused high mortality but helped distort the demographic structures of towns. Detailed work on early Stuart Cambridge suggests that while the wealthier central parishes, often relatively free of infection, maintained large households with numerous children and servants, the poorer outer districts, most prone to attack, tended to be dominated by small, broken households of below average size, by rapid rates of population turn-over and by large numbers of immigrants.[11]

Immigration was in fact the life-blood of many urban communities before the mid-seventeenth century. Almost certainly the majority of inhabitants in any provincial town had not been born there. Some migration to towns was structural: the regular and traditional inflow of apprentices and servants from the hinterland to labour in workshops and better-off households, sometimes to move up the urban escalator to civic prominence and office, more often to learn a craft, marry, and then to return to the home locality. But the largest number of incomers before 1640 were not these traditional betterment migrants, but poor folk driven to town, often from long distances, by over-population, unemployment and shortage of housing in the countryside.[12] As A. L. Beier shows below, 113 vagrants are known to have been arrested at Warwick between 1580 and 1587. While the majority had come from within 50 miles, considerable numbers had travelled from much further afield, frequently from the Highland Zone. The Warwick data is amply confirmed by evidence from other towns. Above 600 vagrants were expelled from Salisbury between 1598 and 1638, of whom roughly 20 per cent had tramped more than 100 miles. Even small market towns suffered from high levels of pauper immigration. Up to a point towns were serving as dumping grounds for the demographic and social problems of rural society, though as we have said the influx was almost certainly stimulated by the spasms of high urban mortality.[13] Overall, as Beier's Warwick study demonstrates and as recent work on Yarmouth has suggested, it would be unwise to conclude that demographic increase was a reliable indicator of economic growth in provincial towns at this time. Rather the situation may be analogous to that observed by students of cities in present-day developing countries where demographic growth is seen as increasingly detached from economic development.[14]

What do we know from other sources about the changing economic fortunes of country towns in this period? Regrettably, hard, quantified evidence is still lacking on various aspects of the urban economy during the sixteenth and early seventeenth centuries. As Dyer has recently suggested, much more work needs to be undertaken on probate records, freemen rolls and the like.[15] Nonetheless, certain points can be made.

Looking at industry first, a number of towns were clearly affected by the decay of their staple industries, usually but not invariably textiles. Early casualties were York, Canterbury and Winchester; the decay of their cloth trades as a result of rural competition probably began in the fifteenth century, and accelerated thereafter.[16]

4

At Gloucester and Salisbury textile contraction was most marked in the Elizabethan and early Stuart period, as their clothiers lost out to Stroudwater weavers and Wiltshire medley-makers respectively. Such problems were not unique to English towns: in France, Italy and other parts of Europe urban industry was suffering from the expansion of manufactures in the countryside, which was boosted as in England by the large pool of cheap rural labour created by demographic expansion.[17] Nonetheless, rural competition was not the only factor in urban industrial decline: changes in the pattern of overseas trade and in consumer taste also had their effect. Capping, for instance, which had flourished at Bristol, Lichfield, Gloucester and Coventry in the early sixteenth century, was swept aside by the growing preference for hats, many of which were imported from London, emerging now as the arbiter of English fashion.[18]

A minority of towns combated their industrial difficulties by developing specialist manufactures. Norwich, badly affected by the decay of its old worsted trade, revived from the 1570s with the influx of substantial bands of Dutch and Walloon refugees with skill in the New Draperies. Colchester likewise prospered from the bay-making industry established by Flemish immigrants. Not all such industrial transplants were quite as successful, however. The New Draperies established by Walloons at Canterbury in the 1570s failed to maintain their initial impetus, though the silk-weaving which subsequently developed was more profitable.[19] At Worcester, city clothiers specialized in the production of high quality broadcloths and buttressed their manufacture by securing a statutory ban (in 1533) on rural weaving in the shire. Further north, Shrewsbury's textile finishing crafts, which employed many inhabitants, depended heavily on the monopoly of Welsh cloth, controlled by the civic drapers' company.[20]

Nonetheless, such urban success stories were the exception rather than the rule. Most established towns, bereft of their old staple industries, struggled to survive with a miscellany of secondary manufactures, including tanning and other leather trades, metalware and malting. Tanning was already well established in medieval towns, so that its apparent rise in the sixteenth century may be something of an optical illusion, reflecting the contraction of the clothing trades. As we shall see at Warwick, there is little evidence that tanners and other leather traders were wealthy men capable of pulling urban industry up by its boot-straps. At Canterbury probate evidence suggests that leather craftsmen did moderately well in the late sixteenth and early seventeenth century, their inventorial wealth doubling during the period while that of their counterparts in the clothing trades stayed roughly the same. But mercers, grocers, and others involved in distributive trades did much better; by the early seventeenth century they possessed on average two and a half times the inventorial wealth of leather workers.[21] Metalware producers also tended to be small masters with limited capital. Even the maltsters who achieved notoriety in many towns by engrossing barley in years of dearth may have enjoyed only limited wealth before the late seventeenth century.[22]

All this raises the question: where was urban capital invested if not in town-based industry? Some of it doubtless percolated into rural industries, though the latter's rudimentary organization probably precluded large-scale investment. In ports such as Ipswich some went to buy shipping shares. Another possibility was money-lending.[23] But probably the main share was diverted into rural property ownership. Investment in land was hardly a new phenomenon, of course. Successful townsmen had always sought to consolidate family and economic ties with the adjoining countryside in this way. However, the level of investment may well have increased during the Tudor and early Stuart period, partly because landownership was an essential prerequisite for the gentle status to which so many town magnates now aspired, but also for sound economic reasons. With rising food prices and rents, land virtually guaranteed a profitable return on capital. At Gloucester in the late sixteenth century well over half the aldermanic bench and over a quarter of the common councillors are known to have held land outside the city. At York between 1525 and 1600 at least 15½ manors were held by aldermen.[24] The urban property market was another attractive investment option from the mid-Tudor period. As populations expanded and country folk flooded into town, house rents probably rose markedly. Though some new houses were built (mainly for the well-to-do), the most lucrative strategy for property owners was the sub-division of existing houses and the crowding of as many poor people as possible into the same building.[25] At Norwich in 1572 over a third of the 396 private houses listed as accommodating the poor were owned by members of the corporation (some civic leaders owned up to seven houses); and a number of properties lodged over 20 people at a time. Less information is available for other towns, but at Gloucester well over half the corporation during the late Elizabethan period controlled substantial property there. Complaints of high rents and overcrowding were legion.[26]

Another outlet for urban investment was the distributive sector, probably the most prosperous sector of town economies in the Tudor and early Stuart period. Freemen lists indicate that by about 1600 many towns had a large contingent of mercers, grocers and the like. At Norwich the number of grocers rose from 27 in 1525 to 150 in 1569, making them one of the leading occupational groups in the city. At Gloucester distributive traders formed the largest specific occupational grouping in the city in 1608, while mercers held nearly a quarter of the common council seats between 1580 and 1600. Distributive traders were also prominent at Oxford, Exeter, King's Lynn and other towns.[27]

We still know less than we should like about the precise pattern of urban marketing and internal trade during this period. The evidence of market and fair tolls, where it survives, is clearly highly vulnerable to the distortion of under-registration on one hand and rack-renting (to swell civic revenues) on the other. Nonetheless, toll records provide our most solid data on the trend of marketing activity. Fair tolls for Shrewsbury, which survive from the fifteenth to the seventeenth century, and which have recently been tabulated by William Champion, suggest a generally low and unstable level of marketing in the early sixteenth century followed by a period of sustained growth from the 1580s up to 1640. What the figures cannot tell us, however, is to what extent Shrewsbury was exploiting and benefiting from a general expansion of inland trade in the area during Elizabeth's reign and how far its success was at the expense of other established towns such as Ludlow and Bridgnorth.[28]

Competition between market centres was an important variable in urban economic fortunes at this time. Scarborough, for instance, blamed its decline in the seventeenth century on the rival market attractions of nearby Seamer, which had encouraged many of the former's traders – bakers, drapers and victuallers – to leave the town. According to Dyer, one reason for the minor role of the distributive sector in Tudor Worcester was the competition of other market towns. Sixteenth-century Thaxted suffered from the commercial rivalry of Saffron Walden and Maldon. The level of competition probably varied a great deal from region to region according to the density of market centres. In Leicestershire the seven main market centres –

Leicester, Loughborough, Melton Mowbray, Market Harborough, Lutterworth, Ashby-de-la-Zouch and Hinckley – each controlled a fairly extensive and populous catchment area; most of the small markets never seem to have flourished after the economic recession of the late Middle Ages. But in East Anglia and southern England market towns, with their small and frequently overlapping marketing zones, were constantly jockeying for position. During the sixteenth century the problem was compounded by the fact that most towns offered the same limited array of trades and occupations. In East Anglia, for instance, there were 40 or so lesser towns with at most 25 separate occupations, many of them of a basic, non-specialist character. Even county towns supplied a limited range of specialist goods outside their fairs. Generally speaking, it was only during the seventeenth century that county towns acquired a set of permanent retail shops. The same period witnessed mounting specialization in the commodities sold at market.[29]

Also vital in influencing a town's economic fortunes were changes occurring in its hinterland. Agricultural specialization or improvement might boost the incomes of substantial farmers and encourage them to indulge in conspicuous expenditure in town. It might also change the pattern of demand among husbandmen and labourers, making them less self-sufficient and more dependent on provisions from urban markets or shops. Where large-scale agricultural change took place, as for example the widespread enclosure which affected parts of Leicestershire during the late sixteenth and early seventeenth centuries, there might be a mass exodus of smallholders and labourers into neighbouring market centres, creating new pressures on the urban economy.[30]

Good communications (or the lack of them) might also determine urban prospects. As Adrienne Rosen shows in her account of Winchester before the Civil War (pp. 154–5), the city's economy was blighted by its isolation from the Great West Road which traversed the county. In Warwickshire poor roads limited competition between the larger urban centres. Relatively little action seems to have been taken by corporate towns to improve the roads – or bridges – in their areas. To some extent this was because of the exiguous state of civic finances, but it also stemmed from the recognition that improvement would need the support of local gentry, most of whom were hostile to any move which smacked of urban expansionism. Similar problems arose with regard to river navigation: thus Droitwich's stagnation during the sixteenth century can be ascribed to the lack of adequate river communication. Even when towns stood on good navigable rivers (as at Gloucester), tolls on goods landed or trans-shipped might lead to protracted legal disputes between townsfolk and outsiders and serious interruptions of trade.[31]

In the context of civic regulation of economic activity it is perhaps surprising that so much attention has been lavished on the gilds, despite their general decline in importance from the mid-sixteenth century, while other aspects of civic control have been largely ignored. More systematic work is required on the incidence of market and fair tolls and the exemptions granted to traders from privileged communities; on freedom fines and other levies on outsiders setting up business in towns; on the effectiveness of prosecutions of non-free traders; on the regulation, often through special officials, of the prices and quality of commodities sold at open market. At present one can only speculate about the impact of such measures, but it seems likely that while they were never enforced in this period with any sustained vigour, they did create a climate of uncertainty which may have retarded the large-scale expansion of trade.[32] At the same time, market towns with their less elaborate apparatus of supervision were possibly less affected than the larger corporate towns.

As for the particular commercial problems of ports, our information is patchy, with most research confined to the larger havens. Everything would suggest, however, that the sixteenth and early seventeenth centuries were a time of serious upheaval for many ports. In the Henrician period London took the lion's share of foreign trade, causing considerable difficulties for its provincial rivals. From mid-century growing diversification in overseas trade promoted the revival of a number of large ports including Hull, Bristol, Exeter, Yarmouth and possibly Chester, though even these experienced recession in the 1590s and 1620s.[33] For other havens the period was one of steadily contracting foreign trade, partly because of the competition of the greater ports, partly owing to the disruptive impact of the European wars, and partly because their merchants increasingly opted for the lucrative and less risky coasting trade. Thus both Gloucester and King's Lynn abandoned direct traffic with the Continent in preference for coastal commerce.[34] This kind of shipping was undoubtedly profitable, but it was not without its problems. Merchants from the larger ports might try and muscle in, while there was often competition from small quays and wharves outside port jurisdiction. Silting and wrecks posed a further threat. No small port could have dreamt of spending the £150,000 which Yarmouth raised for its haven works between 1549 and 1714.[35]

We can see then that if the marketing and commercial functions of most provincial towns probably expanded during the Tudor and early Stuart periods, there was a great deal of local variation in the pace and nature of the growth: communications, the state of the rural hinterland, and the level of competition with other towns were vital determinants. Again caution is needed when we consider the growing importance of towns as social and service centres. While there was undoubtedly some increase in the professional services provided by towns during the sixteenth century, in response to demand from the rural well-to-do, the major expansion had to wait until the next century. In the Tudor period important lawyers, frequently with gentry backgrounds, took up residence on the outskirts of towns or in the adjoining countryside: they rarely took an active part in urban affairs. Ordinary town attorneys were usually minor civic figures. It was mainly in the Stuart period that lawyers became leading townsmen wielding substantial economic and political power.[36] Successful town physicians with large country practices were likewise primarily a seventeenth-century phenomenon while town grammar schools had a rather chequered career before 1640. One definite growth area on the service side involved victualling: inns and taverns were increasingly important from the late sixteenth century, provisioning and accommodating merchants and landowners. But their golden age came only after the Restoration.[37]

What of the role of towns as social centres? The principal developments here occurred after the turn of the sixteenth century. Quarter sessions and other shire meetings had been held in the main county towns since the Middle Ages, but gentry attendance was generally low and erratic. It was only towards the end of Elizabeth's reign, with the landed classes' growing sense of a county community and of quarter sessions as the local parliament, that large numbers of justices and gentry flocked to shire meetings in town. By 1640 approximately two dozen nobles and gentry owned houses in York; but this was the chief seat of government in the North. Elsewhere gentry residence in provincial towns was probably on a smaller scale, limited to a handful of families.[38] Not that growing urban contact with local magnates was always profitable. The propinquity of the earl of Leicester at Warwick and the Cecil family at Stamford served mainly to stifle initiative in those towns. Worse, outbreaks of political conflict with county justices might lead to the gentry avoiding town and the loss of valuable social traffic.[39] Even when there was no open conflict, county gentry, hyper-conscious of their new importance in provincial society, often treated urban communities with a mixture of hostility and contempt.[40]

Deprived of wealthy industrialists, town elites tended to be dominated by distributive merchants. Little comparative work has been undertaken on urban rulers during this period, but an investigation of Gloucester in the late sixteenth century would suggest that town magnates were narrow and conservative in their attitudes, unable to provide strong or imaginative economic leadership. At Gloucester and elsewhere such limitations probably reflected the fact that many magnates were city-born or recruited from neighbouring villages and had risen slowly to power through the traditional *cursus honorum* and manipulation of civic patronage networks.[41]

During the sixteenth and early seventeenth centuries small cliques of leading townsmen probably controlled a rising proportion of urban wealth. What effect this had on the demand for urban goods and services is open to question. At Ipswich, for instance, Reed suggests that few of the well-to-do indulged in large-scale conspicuous consumption at this time. At Canterbury data from probate inventories indicates that in the early Stuart period distributive traders, one of the wealthiest groups of inhabitants, invested on average about 10 per cent of their personal wealth in luxury furnishings, plate and apparel. Even so, many of those luxury or specialist items mentioned in the inventories were probably imported from London or abroad rather than produced by local craftsmen. More advantageous to the urban economy was substantial expenditure by the elite on house building.[42]

If the role of the upper classes in the urban economy remains far from clear, that of the middling ranks – the ordinary masters, shopkeepers, dealers and the like who comprised with their families rather more than a third of the population of the typical town – is shrouded in almost total darkness. One or two shafts of light are supplied by detailed studies of individuals, such as Ronald Berger's valuable account of the small Coventry apothecary Thomas Atherall c.1590–1637. Despite working in a moderately prosperous trade, Atherall made only limited economic and social headway during his lifetime, failing to accumulate much capital or acquire more than a modest array of household goods.[43] However, for general illumination we need extensive, systematic research on probate records. Work on the personal wealth of a small sample of middling traders and masters at Canterbury between 1560 and 1640, as recorded in inventories, implies that their true economic position, when price inflation is taken into account, stagnated during the period (although real estate is not recorded in inventories there is little indication from their wills of substantial investment in this direction).[44]

Many middle-rank townspeople were squeezed between sharply rising food costs and more slowly increasing prices for the goods they made or sold. As freemen they had to bear the mounting burden of town taxes, while as respectable parishioners they paid escalating rates for poor relief. The poor created problems in other ways: many semi-trained migrants poured into towns and set up business in competition with established masters, and impoverished traders came from neighbouring villages to poach clients. Middling inhabitants came under severe pressure in bad harvest decades like the 1590s, 1620s and 1630s as food prices soared, demand for goods and services slumped, and paupers multiplied. At Nantwich even a quite substantial mercer like Thomas Minshull noted after the dearth year 1597 that: 'all the gain of my shop was spent but £5 by reason of the dearth and great charges I lived at and giving away to the poor'. The town's parish register recorded for the same year 'many poor people were afamished and sundry of good account were utterly impoverished'. At Leicester about this time we hear of craftsmen who 'were wont to live well' growing unable 'many times [to] take so much in their shops as they are enforced to spend', and thus more in need of poor relief than fit to pay. It is doubtful whether small craftsmen and traders offered any large or expanding market for urban goods and services.[45]

Finally, what of the poor? In Elizabethan Warwick one in nine of the town's families in good years and as many as one in four in bad were recorded as poor. The situation before 1640 was equally critical at Salisbury, Norwich, Gloucester, Canterbury, Sandwich, Ipswich, Cambridge, Shrewsbury, Ludlow, Southampton, Leicester, Coventry, Winchester, and many other established towns.[46] Poverty was also widespread in small communities such as New Romney in Kent, Dursley in Gloucestershire and several of the Leicestershire market centres. In 1638 the judges at Leicester assizes spoke of 'the great increase of poor people within the towns' of the shire, especially at Melton Mowbray. At Ashby-de-la Zouch approximately 38 per cent of the inhabitants were in receipt of poor relief in the period 1624–38.[47] The poor had no common face in pre-Revolutionary England. Some were widows, orphans and the sick – the so-called impotent poor. Many were unemployed or under-employed labourers or artisans, frequently with children. Quite often such people were recent immigrants. One-tenth of Warwick's relieved poor were newcomers and the total number of these people in the community was doubtless much higher. At Southampton in 1582 the court leet protested: 'this town is marvellously oppressed with under-tenants and daily do increase more and more which for the most part are so poor as daily they lie at men's doors for their relief . . .' Suburbs in particular were often overwhelmed with incomers as at Shrewsbury where the peripheral districts of Frankwell and St Chad's were thronged with crowds of destitute who had only been in the town for a few weeks.[48] In addition to the impotent, labouring and immigrant poor, there were also many 'marginal' poor, listed at Warwick as 'ready to decay', small craftsmen who were able to get by without needing relief in favourable years but who were highly vulnerable to dititution if the harvest were bad or trade, local or overseas, were disrupted. Plague outbreaks, concentrated in lower-class areas with their endemic overcrowding and inadequate sanitation, might also deal a serious blow to the precarious position of the marginal poor. After the 1593 plague at Leicester we hear of 500 or 600 poor 'at the least' who 'have sold and gaged all that they have to maintain themselves'. In the dreadful harvest year of 1586–7 there was a landslide of impoverishment at Warwick forcing all groups onto the bread line, desperate for subsistence.[49]

Poverty on this scale was hardly an advertisement for urban economic growth and prosperity in Tudor and early Stuart England. Admittedly, part of the problem was created by subsistence immigration, by towns importing the social problems of the countryside. But urban poverty was also very much a function of the failure of urban economies to keep pace with population increase. Whatever the cause, it is difficult to accept the view that widespread poverty and destitution had only a marginal impact on urban communities. Beier's study below and other recent work suggests that poverty had a wide-ranging ripple effect on towns, depressing demand, undermining the position of lesser tradesmen and generating social tension, political conflict and administrative strains.[50]

As for poor relief, traditional forms came under growing pressure in the pre-Revolutionary period. Neighbourly relief, mostly geared to assisting the elderly and the sick, was unable to cope with the massive increase in labouring and immigrant poor. As Beier shows in detail for Warwick, established charitable relief was badly disrupted by the Reformation, while new-style philanthropy of the type discussed by W. K. Jordan had only a limited effect and was probably less crucial than the continuance of traditional testamentary doles for the poor. Schemes to set the poor to work were generally unsuccessful. In consequence the main burden of relief had to be borne by statutory poor rates combined with sharp discrimination about those who actually received relief. Often there was considerable resistance to rates and lesser traders found their own precarious position threatened by levies. The agencies of relief thus provided only minimal aid for the massed ranks of the urban poor. At best they prevented starvation, at worst they may have exacerbated the economic and social stresses within towns.[51]

One striking manifestation of the deteriorating position of the urban lower orders was the proliferation of alehouses in the century before the Revolution. In some towns every tenth house became a tippling den. Such establishments provided the poor with cheap liquid refreshment (and a narcotic); they sold food in small quantities on credit, when the poor could not afford to go to market; they offered the tramping poor somewhere to sleep before going begging in the town or taking once more to the road. Their function as a refuge for the poverty-stricken and destitute was underlined by the squalid facilities of many alehouses, in a back kitchen or down a cellar, frequently in a shack on the edge of town. Victuallers, like their customers, tended for the most part to be drawn from the lowest classes, often under-employed or workless artisans or labourers struggling to make ends meet by selling ale or beer.[52]

From the preceding analysis of the demographic, economic and social structure of country towns in the sixteenth and early seventeenth centuries we must conclude that many urban communities felt recurrent stresses and shocks, sometimes approaching crisis dimensions. In many respects the problems disrupting towns were more acute than those which confronted rural communities during the same period. Nonetheless, we have also seen that not all towns were defeated by their difficulties: while some decayed, others staked a claim to relative prosperity. The next section will endeavour to identify the 'winners' and 'losers'.

2

Looking at country towns in general, the major regional centres, the provincial capitals, appear to have weathered the storms of the sixteenth and early seventeenth centuries rather better than lesser communities. Admittedly, during the late medieval and early Tudor periods Newcastle, York and Norwich all suffered economic upheavals;[53] but from the mid-sixteenth century they all staged a modest recovery. Newcastle's economy burgeoned as a result of strong metropolitan and foreign demand for coal (though the salt trade was also important after 1600); Bristol merchants advanced into the lucrative Mediterranean and Atlantic trades; Exeter profited from trade with France; and Norwich and York expanded their distributive functions, serving as regional markets for high-quality London and imported wares. York also developed as an administrative and judicial axis under the patronage of the Council of the North and the High Commission for the Northern Province.[54] With their economies moderately buoyant, the provincial capitals managed to ride out the storm of social distress. Even so, the situation was often tense during the 1590s and 1620s, while the Civil War caused major problems, with severe disruption at Bristol and Newcastle.[55]

In the case of middle-rank towns the picture is more variegated, as one can see from the detailed studies which are beginning to appear. Some of the larger ports clearly did well. Hull, after some problems in the early sixteenth century, grew steadily thereafter, importing grain, timber and naval supplies and exporting West Riding cloth to the Baltic. Yarmouth shook off the problems caused by haven silting and prospered after the 1560s from trade with Iberia, France and the Baltic; it also functioned as the largest fish market in Western Europe. More modest, King's Lynn profited from coastal shipments of coal and grain. On the west coast Liverpool (and to some extent Chester) exploited Irish as well as coastal traffic.[56] Nevertheless, a number of ports were in decay, including Sandwich, Boston, Dunwich, Orford, Barnstaple, Grimsby, Southampton and Rye. Some had been on the way down since the late Middle Ages; several suffered from the physical deterioration of their harbours. At Ipswich the port functioned as an important station in the East Coast colliery trade and as the leading export outlet for the cloth industry along the Suffolk-Essex border, shipping its products to the Baltic. From the 1620s, however, as Reed shows, Ipswich's trade was badly damaged by the disruption of the Thirty Years War and the run-down of cloth-making in its hinterland.[57]

Among inland county towns one finds a number of urban success stories. As we noted earlier, Shrewsbury, Colchester and Worcester did well as specialist textile centres, though the first at least suffered from massive poverty and unemployment during the 1590s, 1620s and 1630s. Oxford and Cambridge took advantage of the upsurge in university populations from Elizabeth's reign with the resultant influx of large numbers of gentry; Oxford, in particular, concentrated on the provisioning and entertainment of university members.[58] But a significant majority of medium-sized corporate towns were less fortunate, victims of recurrent economic and social dislocation during the Tudor and early Stuart periods. A hard core of centres including Winchester, Lincoln and Stamford had already started to contract in the later Middle Ages as they lost their markets for staple commodities such as wool and cloth. But their problems were now greatly exacerbated by renewed population pressure and mounting poverty, as we find at Winchester. By the late 1630s, as Rosen shows, the collapse of the cloth trade and large-scale unemployment and pauperization had brought this city to its knees.[59]

More county towns, particularly those in the East and South, ran into severe economic difficulty at the end of the fifteenth and the beginning of the sixteenth centuries. In the most spectacular case, that of Coventry, the population may have fallen by half in the early sixteenth century, leaving parts of the city uninhabited and economic and social organization on the verge of collapse. Other centres adversely affected at this time, though to a lesser extent, included Canterbury, Bridgwater, Ripon, Sandwich, and Bury St Edmunds. In a number of cases the plight of the local economy was aggravated by the Reformation. Although the late sixteenth century saw some limited revival in the fortunes of these towns, the foundations of their recovery were shaky, and severe difficulties again became evident during the 1590s and 1620s.[60]

For a number of county towns like Gloucester and Salisbury which had avoided decay in the early sixteenth century, economic and social crisis was only deferred. The cloth-making industries of these towns began to disintegrate from Elizabeth's reign, with the industrial run-down accelerating in the third and fourth decades of the seventeenth century. At Salisbury the collapse of the cloth industry, combined with harvest failure and the outbreak of plague, precipitated a full-scale crisis during the late 1620s.[61]

If the Tudor and early Stuart period was a time of upheaval and dislocation for the majority of county centres, how did the ordinary market towns fare? A major problem here is that of documentation. Since most small towns were unincorporated their records are scanty or non-existent. It seems unlikely that we shall ever obtain detailed knowledge on more than a small minority of the 500 or 600 simple market towns of the pre-Revolutionary era. However, from only a handful of case studies and some general surveys of marketing activity we can identify the main contours of market town development before the mid-seventeenth century.[62] Firstly, in contrast with the later Middle Ages when their incidence declined, the number of market centres rose from the sixteenth century as old markets regained their urban identity and new ones were established. Secondly, marketing activity apparently expanded. Thirdly, population levels increased. At Ashford in Kent the number of inhabitants probably doubled in the hundred years after 1570, while there was a 50 per cent increase at Ashby-de-la-Zouch between 1563 and 1603.[63] Of course, as we know, demographic growth is hardly a reliable indicator of economic expansion. However, if we assume that there was at least some economic growth in these lesser towns before 1640 or so, how do we explain it? Among the causal factors which are usually cited are: the general expansion of inland trade and marketing in response to demographic increase and agrarian specialization; rising living standards among respectable villagers fuelling demand for goods and services; the higher overheads and more rigid regulations of the larger towns; and the more stable political climate under the Tudor régime. Obviously these were all influential to some degree. On the other hand, it would be wrong to underestimate the crucial importance of the agricultural function of many small towns. Their leading townsmen were frequently farmers with only minor urban interests. As John Goodacre has shown, at Tudor Lutterworth the principal force for economic change was the growing involvement of town leaders in livestock farming which helped stimulate associated trades like butchering and tanning.[64] Market towns did not simply benefit at second hand from landed improvement; they shared directly in the process of agrarian change.

Not that all small towns had a blank cheque for prosperity in this period. There were losers as well. The minor market towns of Fransham and Thorpe in Tudor Norfolk were in decline, as perhaps was Waltham-on-the-Wolds in Leicestershire. Lesser clothing centres such as Winchcombe and Dursley in Gloucestershire and Wilton in Wiltshire also decayed in the sixteenth century. During the early Stuart period the growing concentration on particular commodities by more important market centres may have begun to pose a serious threat to lesser, general markets.[65] Before 1640, moreover, market towns were confronted with a serious poverty problem. At Ashby-de-la-Zouch in Leicestershire, for example, over a third of the population was classed as poor in the early seventeenth century, with many of the paupers immigrants.[66]

In sum, both winners and losers can be detected at most levels of the urban hierarchy at this time. Yet there can be little question that the highest casualty rate was among the middle-tier county towns. Probably the majority of these were afflicted by severe and recurrent economic and social difficulty.

3

While a sizeable proportion of provincial towns were prone to structural instability between the late fifteenth and the mid-seventeenth centuries, it is possible to distinguish particular periods when long-term problems were exacerbated by short-term difficulties creating major crises. One such crisis occurred in the early years of the Tudor period. According to Phythian-Adams, over 70 provincial towns exhibited signs of economic depression and decay at that time, with the 1520s as the low point: provincial capitals and county towns were worst affected. The same period also saw demographic, economic and social disorder threaten many German and other Continental cities.[67]

In early Tudor England the urban crisis was precipitated by a conjunction of pressures – heavy royal taxation, trade disruption, bad harvests and epidemics – compounding the underlying weakness of established corporate centres. In addition, it seems likely that from the 1530s the Reformation served to prolong and accentuate the depression. Though little research has so far been undertaken on the urban impact of the religious changes of the Henrician and Edwardian era, the signs are that the consequences were serious. In the case of Warwick discussed below (pp. 66–8), the dissolution of monasteries, hospitals and the collegiate church of St Mary's deprived the town of a large share of its charitable revenue, thereby helping to undermine both civic finances and the community's long-term ability to overcome its mounting economic and social problems. At Oxford the suppression of religious houses caused upheavals at the parish level, economic dislocation, unemployment and vacant housing.[68] Bury St Edmunds, Coventry and other towns suffered from the loss of their valuable religious traffic, while at Peterborough and Abingdon the suppression of the local abbey was a serious blow to trade.[69] Attempts by townsmen, as at Canterbury, to exploit the Dissolution to rejuvenate the local economy were defeated by growing religious factionalism. Some cities, like Bristol, did manage to acquire Dissolution land which provided a valuable civic nest-egg against future rainy days. But too often moves to buy monastic or chantry property ended in expensive and fruitless litigation.[70]

The next period of urban crisis came towards the end of the sixteenth century. From the mid-1580s until about 1604 established towns faced a tidal wave of difficulty: commercial depression due to foreign wars and privateering; large-scale and repeated attacks of epidemic disease; heavy financial, military and other levies by the Crown; and a high number of bad harvests, which boosted grain prices, caused severe malnutrition, suffocated demand, and sent floods of poor migrants into the towns. Economic decay, disruption and shortages affected Bristol, Yarmouth, Gloucester, Canterbury, Sandwich, Bath, Leicester, Salisbury, York and other towns.[71] Large-scale poverty was reported in numerous communities, while high mortality owing to starvation and starvation-related diseases ravaged Barnstaple, Crediton, Tamworth, Reading and Salisbury. Rioters appeared on the streets at Canterbury, Gloucester, Basingstoke, Cranbrook and Maldon.[72] All in all, the crisis of the 1590s ruthlessly exposed the continuing structural weaknesses of English provincial towns and the dangers implicit in their dependence on an unstable rural economy.

Critical conditions returned again during the 1620s and persisted, on and off, into the 1640s. Once more a series of dearth harvests were of crucial importance, causing food shortages, verging on famine in the Highland Zone, and reducing marketing activity. Urban trade and industry were further disrupted by plague outbreaks, which led to the flight of respectable citizens and the isolation of the infected town from its hinterland. John Ivie's account of the Salisbury plague of 1627 describes a community besieged by marauding bands of the unemployed and destitute, demanding relief from a paralysed magistracy and threatening to destroy the houses of the elite. Overseas commerce fell back sharply as a result of the Thirty Years War, with dire consequences for the older clothing towns, while the contraction of the cloth trade had severe repercussions for towns not directly involved in its manufacture.[73]

The precise impact of the Civil War on urban society has still to be assessed. However, it is arguable that the economic and social implications were considerable. Immigration into the larger walled towns accelerated as activists fled from the enemy and ordinary villagers sought refuge from armed conflict. Foreign and inland trade became erratic as troops seized main roads, demolished bridges and played military musical chairs with unfortified towns. Sieges brought traffic to a halt and frequently caused widespread physical damage. Invading forces killed large numbers of defenders and gutted shops and houses. Citizens had to pay heavy national and local levies, often of dubious legality, to the marauding forces. Rosen's account of Winchester during the Civil War shows a town assailed by the repeated attacks of royalist and parliamentary armies. A small town like Ashby-de-la-Zouch suffered severe physical damage and high mortality with disastrous long-term effects on the urban economy.[74] Among other provincial towns which are known to have sustained considerable economic and physical loss during the 1640s were Lincoln, Penzance, Lancaster, Minehead, Torrington, Stafford, Leicester, Bradford, Birmingham, Gloucester, Bolton, Liverpool, Colchester, Banbury, Cirencester, Worcester and Droitwich.[75] Not all parts of the country were equally affected, of course: most East Anglian towns, under the protection of the Eastern Association, escaped fairly lightly. Overall, the impact of the English Civil Wars was relatively modest by comparison with the devastation wrought by contesting armies in Germany during the Thirty Years War.[76] But coming hard on the heels of two decades of economic and social difficulty for many established centres, the military conflicts of the 1640s marked the nadir of urban fortunes in Stuart England.

Urban change in the sixteenth and early seventeenth centuries was certainly not unilinear. Recent work reveals a kaleidoscope of variations between communities both in their pattern of development and the factors which influenced it. Nonetheless, there are good grounds for reiterating that the underlying trend was one of serious demographic, economic and social instability, particularly for the middle-rank county centres. While this century and a half saw some decades of modest urban prosperity, structural and short-term problems repeatedly fused and interacted to generate major crises during the early sixteenth century, the 1590s, and the reign of Charles I. Set beside the general urban prosperity of the post-Restoration era, the economic and social performance of English country towns in the preceding period seems desultory and erratic, often verging on failure.

4

In contrast to the current flurry of publications on provincial towns during the Tudor and early Stuart periods, interest in urban development in the century or so prior to the Industrial Revolution has been slow to surface.[77] One important reason for this neglect relates to the sources available. Although town archives often survive in greater profusion for the later period, they are frequently uninformative and intractable, while major series of national government records remain uncatalogued and inaccessible.[78] Yet the lack of work on post-Restoration towns belies the importance of the subject. As we shall see, urban communities were an increasingly powerful force in provincial society from the late seventeenth century onwards and though the most exciting growth centres were undoubtedly the new industrial and dockyard towns, major changes transformed the face of established country towns as well.

After an era of sustained demographic growth, the post-Restoration period saw noticeably slower rates of increase among country towns. It is true that some of the provincial capitals and great ports expanded rapidly. Bristol's inhabitants multiplied from about 20,000 in the 1670s to about 45,000 in the 1730s, while the populations of Norwich and Newcastle increased by 60 and 100 per cent respectively between the mid-seventeenth and early eighteenth centuries. Certain county towns which developed important new specialist industries, such as Leicester and Nottingham, also enjoyed a substantial demographic advance.[79] But the general rule for county and market towns was little or no growth, as for example at Winchester, Salisbury, Gloucester, and elsewhere. Some towns actually lost inhabitants, as for instance Yarmouth, Stafford and (later) Oxford.[80] Up to a point this demographic slow-down reflected the diminished inflow of subsistence migrants. In the countryside agricultural production was at last moving ahead of demand as population growth slackened, while institutional restraints such as the settlement laws and improved poor relief at the village level tended to keep the lower orders more at home. There was no great exodus now from the Highland Zone to the towns of southern England, as had occurred in the years before the Civil War.[81]

Another factor in the reduction in immigration may have been the decreased incidence of epidemic disease that had so often decimated urban populations in the preceding period, necessitating wholesale recruitment of outsiders to replenish the community. Plague of course disappeared from the 1660s and other diseases like smallpox inflicted less devastating mortality. By the mid-eighteenth century there is evidence of natural population growth in some larger cities like Nottingham, although elsewhere a constant inflow of migrants was still necessary to maintain or boost urban populations. While the highest rates of growth occurred in the new industrial communities, a definite upward trend is visible for many country towns as well.[82]

If the decades following the Restoration witnessed a lower level of population increase than in the previous century and a half, it was by no means a time of economic stagnation, at least for the larger and medium-sized centres. English tourists visiting provincial towns and cities during the later Stuart period frequently drew attention to their bustling trade and vivacious social traffic. Thomas Baskerville described Bury St Edmunds in the 1680s as a 'town full of rich shops and tradesmen, the streets spacious and the houses well built', much frequented by gentry, while in the next decade Celia Fiennes declared Coventry 'to be a thriving good trading town and is very rich'.[83] Nor were these tributes simply inspired by a natural delight at seeing handsome houses and paved streets after a hard day in the saddle. For many larger towns there is solid evidence of economic resurgence from the late seventeenth century.

One vital pillar of renewed urban prosperity was industrial growth. In the earlier period important industries such as textiles had often become centred in low-cost rural areas: only a few towns which had specialized or secured a monopoly in the production of particular products managed to prosper. In the later Stuart period, however, rising real wages in the countryside made urban industry once more competitive while a growing number of towns began to concentrate on the manufacture of particular goods: Northampton became famous for boots; Gloucester for pins; St Albans for tankards and pots; Witney for blankets; Woodstock for fine steel ware; Kidderminster for carpets; Leicester and Tewkesbury for stockings; Maidstone for papermaking; Macclesfield for buttons and later silk; Stockport for hats; Colchester for clocks; Coventry for ribbons and watches; Bridport for ropes and nets; Banbury for plush; Devizes for serge. The list is almost endless.[84]

Yet it would be wrong to view the revival of urban industry in terms of a continuing battle between town and countryside in which towns had now regained the whip hand. What is striking about the new industrial developments of the late seventeenth and early eighteenth centuries is the increasing degree of integration between urban and rural industry. Instead of towns attempting as in the past to beat down country craftsmen through statutory action or litigation, excluding village producers from their markets, the growing emphasis was on co-operation. As Alan Everitt has rightly stressed, a number of middle-rank towns became the predominant centre of organization of 'occupational regions'. Exemplifying the new trend was a petition of about 1674 by a group of Leicester stocking-makers who claimed to keep 2,000 poor people at work there and in the adjoining villages. Attacking attempts by a group of town freemen to engross the trade and confine it to Leicester, the petition proclaimed that 'it is not the curious making of a few stockings, but the general making of many that is most for the public good, for that sets more people on work, as well children as others, and when the stockings are made up and sorted there are amongst them some for all sorts of people . . .' Clearly the cheaper, coarser country products are seen as complementary to better-quality town stockings, with the former appealing to the growing lower-class market and the latter sold to the well-to-do. A similar pattern of product specialization is also evident in the Sheffield area where town craftsmen concentrated on high-class metalwares while the neighbouring villages produced cruder metal goods. Above all, there was a flowering of specialist crafts in towns.[85]

Urban industry was further boosted by other factors. In the first place there was a major expansion of overseas trade, particularly with the colonies. Although as we shall see London and the great ports still predominated in this area, valuable spin-offs occurred for other provincial towns. Thus many of the commodities that Bristol merchants exported to Africa and the West Indies were supplied by the smaller towns of its hinterland, including hosiery from Tewkesbury and pins from Gloucester. During the Hanoverian period industries, whether in new or old towns, became progressively export-oriented.[86]

No less vital, however, at least in the late seventeenth century, was the expansion of the home market for manufactured goods. The rising real income of ordinary people, in town and countryside, was fundamental in allowing higher levels of conspicuous expenditure – a point we must return to shortly. Improved communications also stimulated the home market. Coastal shipping, still probably the principal means of transporting commodities for most of the period, continued to expand. According to one estimate, the tonnage of English coastal shipping increased by two-thirds after the Restoration, with further substantial accretions in the eighteenth century.[87] Moreover, the rejuvenation of inland towns was aided by the rapid spread of river navigation, linking them to the sea or the Thames river system. Willan has suggested that the national mileage of navigable waterways nearly doubled between 1660 and the 1730s. The navigation of the Ouse from King's Lynn to Bedford, completed in the 1680s, generated for the latter a valuable trade in coal, malt and other agricultural goods. Toll-books indicate that traffic on the river probably rose twofold in the early eighteenth century. Sylvia McIntyre shows below how Bath's development as a marketing and social centre owed much to the opening of the Avon to navigation in the 1720s.[88] Road communications may also have improved after the Restoration, if the increased number of long-distance coaches is any guide. Bridges were apparently repaired and enlarged in the late Stuart period. However, the major breakthrough in road transportation had to wait until the extension of turnpiking in the early eighteenth century; by the 1740s there were two large turnpike networks in the Home Counties and the West Midlands. Finally, from the 1760s on came the well-known boom in canal building.[89]

Improved transportation not only promoted industrial growth in towns, it strengthened their role as distributive centres. Town traders could now sell all the latest imported or luxury goods shipped or carted from the metropolis, and shops – both general and more specialist – proliferated. Winchester had at least 90 shops by 1704; a little later one of Norwich's most fashionable shopping streets was renamed after the capital. Milliners, watchmakers, perfumers, confectioners, goldsmiths, wigmakers, stationers and booksellers multiplied and flourished. Most county towns had at least two booksellers by the early years of the eighteenth century, while provincial capitals had up to half a dozen.[90] Better communications enabled larger towns to extend their marketing radius and increase the volume of trade on market days. Grants of additional market days were secured to cope with the extra business, new market houses were built and other civic amenities improved. Whether or not there was a significant increase in urban efficiency in the period before 1750, as one or two writers have recently claimed, there can be little question that by the early eighteenth century county towns had re-established their central importance in the urban hierarchy, serving as vital distribution points for smaller towns: thus Georgian Chester serviced many of the simpler market centres in Wales. No less crucial, the earlier trend towards specialized marketing of particular commodities accelerated.[91]

From the start of the eighteenth century the reputation of various larger provincial towns as marketing and shopping centres was broadcast and emphasized by the news coverage and advertisements printed in local newspapers. Early newspapers were published at Norwich (1701), Bristol (1702), Exeter (1704), and Shrewsbury (1705). The distribution network of the *Gloucester Journal*, which first appeared in 1722, by 1738 embraced south Worcestershire, south Wales, parts of Oxfordshire, Herefordshire, Somerset and Wiltshire as well as Gloucestershire itself. In the 1760s the *Cambridge Journal and Flying Mercury* could reasonably claim that 'the circulation of it is so vastly extensive that the number sent weekly to only one town in the county of Lincoln is upwards of 600', while seven newscarriers 'at a great expense . . . convey this paper through the counties of Cambridge, Huntingdon, Bedford, Hertford, Northampton, Leicester, Rutland, Nottingham, Derby and part of Norfolk, Suffolk and Essex . . .'[92] As the content and style of the early provincial press testifies, many of its readers were gentry, professional men and other members of the rural elite, and these no doubt provided much of the clientèle of the specialist shops in the towns. In addition, London and provincial newspapers were frequently available in village inns and alehouses and may have stimulated what was undoubtedly a growing appetite for a wide range of urban goods and services in the middle and lower ranks of rural society, prospering now from falling food prices and rising real incomes.[93]

Towns, particularly corporate towns, benefited from improved relations with their hinterlands during the late seventeenth and early eighteenth centuries. With expanding agricultural production there was less risk of that acrimonious competition between town and country for badly needed food supplies which had had such a divisive effect in pre-Revolutionary England. The disappearance of plague meant there were no longer attempts by town or county to impose blockades to isolate the rural or urban infected – a common source of conflict in the Elizabethan and early Stuart periods. On the economic front, townsmen became less hostile towards rural industries, preferring instead to draw them within the urban marketing network. From Reed's study of Ipswich we can see that with the accelerating decay of trade gilds during the seventeenth century it became easier for outsiders to set up in business in towns.[94] Liberalization was further hastened by the influx of foreign traders during the Civil Wars, by legislation during the Revolution permitting parliamentary soldiers to practice any urban trade without prior qualification, by the general decline of the apprenticeship system, and by the devaluation of the civic freedom, hitherto the main official obstacle to outside traders. From the 1690s the freedom was frequently handed out by the gross to neighbouring gentry and their hangers-on for party political purposes.[95] Market and fair tolls and other customary levies on outsiders survived longer, since towns were reluctant to abolish these because of the revenue they would lose. Nonetheless, by the second and third decades of the eighteenth century the exaction of urban tolls and customary dues was increasingly erratic and subject to growing evasion. Meanwhile civic regulation of market activity was left high and dry by the rising proportion of business transacted in the back rooms of inns and alehouses. In sum, the urban economy was becoming more open to outsiders, less regulated and protectionist. True, there was considerable variation between individual towns in the pace of liberalization; there were campaigns from time to time by special interest groups, to regulate market dealing, to exclude foreign traders, to resuscitate the gilds. But recidivism of this sort was usually short-lived and unsuccessful.[96]

Generally, corporate bodies played a declining role in the management of urban economic life in the decades after the Restoration. At Ipswich the magistracy endeavoured to erect worsted and linen manufactures but these projects, Reed contends, were old-fashioned and abortive, failing to take account of new trends in urban economic development. In the eighteenth century major improvement schemes, such as the building of new docks at Hull, tended to be carried out under the auspices of special bodies, distinct from the corporation.[97]

From the later Stuart period urban economies further benefited from the virtual disappearance of those bitter political wrangles which had so disfigured relations between town and countryside before the Revolution. The Restoration settlement celebrated the triumph of county landowners in national and provincial society. Gentry purged town magistracies under the authority of the Corporation Act (1661) and thereafter interfered repeatedly in civic affairs. Town rulers read the writing on the wall. Instead of going out of their way, as in the past, to assert civic autonomy, corporations often welcomed outside involvement in urban affairs. Large numbers of landowners were made freemen, as at Winchester. County gentry became mayors at Canterbury, Gloucester, Northampton, Liverpool, Pembroke, and St Albans.[98] In 1672 Thomas Isham recorded in his diary that the incoming mayor of Northampton, Thomas Williley, a local landowner, is 'going to give a grand entertainment for having been the first elected outside the borough as chief magistrate ... He has invited all the neighbouring gentry and many from all parts of England, wishing to make himself popular with the inhabitants of Northampton'. Three years later when Northampton was badly damaged by fire the corporation obtained a special Act to rebuild the town with overall supervision granted to a committee packed with gentry.[99]

Civic leaders endeavoured to court the increasingly wealthy and leisured landed classes who were benefiting from the concentration of estates and from agricultural improvement, by helping to create a congenial and stylish urban environment. The physical texture of towns was transformed by the replacement, usually at magisterial insistence, of old-style timber and thatch buildings by ones in more fashionable and less flammable brick and tile. Important changes also took place in the layout of towns. After the conflagration of 1675 Northampton's streets were widened and new public buildings erected in the most fashionable London manner. When Celia Fiennes travelled there in the 1690s she enthused over 'the streets as large as most in London except Holborn and the Strand, the houses well built of brick and stone, some all stone, very regular buildings', while another observer called it 'one of the neatest towns in the kingdom'. Parts of Warwick, rebuilt after a devastating fire in 1694, were likewise designed with gentry patrons in mind. Next century no provincial town could compete with the splendour of the quasi-Palladian houses, circuses and squares of Bath, constructed on the northern and western outskirts of the old town. Here too, as McIntyre explains, the fashionable townscape of Georgian Bath owed much to corporate supervision.[100]

Other towns, lacking the money, opportunity, or initiative to sponsor extensive developments, encouraged more piecemeal building and improvement schemes. At Gloucester the magistrates offered leases of town land on favourable terms to gentlemen willing to undertake rebuilding. In the 1690s Trinity tower in the middle of the city was rebuilt; St John's church was reconstructed in 1733–4 in the classical style, while the old Meal Market was demolished at about the same time; in 1759 the city secured an Improvement Act which authorized the destruction of the high cross, king's board and butter market, all of which had encumbered the main streets. Further Improvement Acts followed in 1777 and 1781 allowing the widening of streets, removal of houses and city gates, and the erection of a new common gaol. Some crude idea of the progress of urban improvement in the provinces is provided by table 1.[101] Not all Acts were implemented at once, of course, and some towns had several bites at the legislative cherry before proposed changes were carried through. Nonetheless the data presented below does indicate the major surge of action in the late eighteenth century, affecting the majority of larger provincial cities.

After 1700, numerous county towns boasted a supply of piped water, at least to the wealthier areas. At the same time, London-style street lighting was introduced, illuminating the main thoroughfares and making them safe for the well-to-do. Every fashionable whim of the landed classes was catered for, with towns copying wholesale the social impedimenta of the capital. If no country town could emulate the myriad statues which graced the metropolis, many had a half dozen ill-assorted replicas gazing down on their streets. Gravel walks were also *de rigeur*, facilitating public display and offering panoramic views of the town and later, with the craze for the picturesque, of the adjoining countryside.[102]

Table 1 Improvement Acts for provincial towns,
1690–1799

	no.	% (n = 254)
1690–9	12	4.7
1700–9	14	5.5
1710–19	3	1.2
1720–9	6	2.4
1730–9	9	3.6
1740–9	10	3.9
1750–9	14	5.5
1760–9	41	16.1
1770–9	38	15.0
1780–9	64	25.2
1790–9	43	16.9

According to Peter Borsay, English provincial towns in the later Stuart period experienced an 'urban renaissance' in their role as social and cultural centres. How far this 'renaissance' had any solid local roots, and how far it depended simply on importing ideas and attitudes secondhand from the aristocratic salons of the capital is problematical. Nonetheless, what is clear is that by the early Hanoverian period many county towns functioned as bustling social amphitheatres for the landed elite. After the triumph of the county community at the Restoration, meetings of quarter sessions and assizes provided the excuse for grand political and social gatherings lasting several days, with balls, concerts, and horse races (the latter sponsored by town and county magistrates). Music festivals were another urban extravaganza: the Three Choirs Festival, founded in the 1710s, rotated (as it still does) between the county centres of Gloucester, Worcester and Hereford.[103]

As well as these glittering social events, which drew throngs of gentry at particular times of the year, larger provincial towns now offered a host of other attractions on a permanent or seasonal basis. By the 1680s every respectable country town had at least one coffee house where the London papers might be read and smart gossip exchanged, while no less indispensable was the bowling green – by 1700 it was the *sine qua non* of urbanity.[104] Also immensely popular with gentle visitors was cock-fighting, with matches between shires held in special pits at the great inns.[105]

Music provided another fashionable divertissement. In addition to the festivals, there were regular subscription concerts, celebrity recitals, and choral societies. Salisbury had 'a Society of Lovers of Musick' in 1701 and Wells one soon after. At Gloucester the meeting of the music club on St Cecilia's Day, 1730, took place 'with the usual ceremonies, the whole concluding with a good concert in the club-room, where all strangers, gentlemen and ladies, may partake of the like entertainment every Tuesday in the month'. Some towns employed their own civic musicians – organists and the like.[106] There were other cultural pleasures too. Just as Norwich became famous for its artistic circle, so most provincial towns cultivated their intellectual life. Public libraries became quite common by 1700, while town booksellers sold the latest London works, published books by local authors, and from the mid-eighteenth century ran circulating libraries.[107] In both large and smaller towns a constellation of historical, philosophical and literary societies flourished, with members drawn from the urban and county elite – a famous example was the Gentlemen's

Society of Spalding, founded in 1709. Indicative of the new intellectual vitality of urban society was the growing stream of town histories published from the 1720s onwards.[108]

The kaleidoscope of urban entertainment also embraced travelling shows by fire-eaters, midgets, acrobats and swordsmen; plays (by the 1750s several towns had their own troupes of actors;[109] public lectures and exhibitions, especially on scientific subjects; horticultural societies and festivals, often with local gentry as stewards[110]; and a multiplicity of civic celebrations, including banquets on election days and royal birthdays, mayoral processions, and firework displays.[111]

If the main focus of social activity in post-Restoration towns was the great inn, from the start of the eighteenth century specialist buildings began to appear – notably theatres and assembly rooms.[112] By this period county towns frequently had their own 'seasons', appealing to those members of the rural upper classes who had neither the cash nor the right connections to cut a figure in metropolitan high society. Some landowners borrowed or rented houses for the occasion; in cathedral cities houses in the close were a favourite residence. However, an increasing number of gentry owned town houses and in larger cities stayed there for a good part of the year, only retreating to the country, or one of the spa towns, in high summer. In the late eighteenth century Shrewsbury may have had as many as 600 town gentry (and dependents) in a total population of about 15,000.[113]

The congregation of county landowners in provincial towns had its drawbacks. Brawls might break out with townsfolk as when Sir Roger Dallison, attending Charles II's Court at Winchester, gave the mayor there two boxes on the ear and had to be committed by the king to the castle dungeon. Party strife between Whig and Tory magnates, increasingly violent from the 1680s, threatened on occasion to engulf a town and damage its reputation as a gentry centre. At Lichfield in 1700 the corporation tried to end bitter electoral disputes by ordering that all future parliamentary elections should be decided by consensus. But in general political factionalism never got out of hand and actually had its bonus points. With county magnates bidding against each other to nominate a town's Members of Parliament, valuable favours might be picked up, even on occasion a new town hall.[114]

As Borsay has argued, the large gentry presence in many corporate towns after the Restoration was clearly beneficial to the urban economy. It provided a major stimulus to the building industry, now busy erecting classical-style brick and tile mansions (or remodelling old ones); this in turn had a powerful multiplier effect, as Nicholas Barbon insisted, on a whole variety of trades.[115] Shopkeepers likewise profited from satisfying the whims and fancies of gentle customers. Even more striking was the expansion of the service sector. Innkeeping, already well established before the Civil War, became one of the leading occupations in later Stuart towns, as at Winchester (p. 173).[116]

Inns not only lodged and lubricated upper-class guests. They were the principal arena for a wide variety of social entertainments and provided a place where merchants could make deals and store wares. Not surprisingly, early specialist shops were frequently opened within the precincts of an inn, while auctions were staged there later in the period. No less important, town inns served as termini and staging-points for local and long-distance carriers, and for coach services. By the early eighteenth century a county town like Gloucester probably had two dozen or more country carriers coming every week to its larger inns; from there a half dozen or so long-distance carriers would travel to London and other major urban centres. About

1750 Bristol had over 90 carriers plying in and out of the city. Just as the carriers' wagons kept the upper classes of town and countryside in touch with the metropolis, so the coach services which proliferated during the late seventeenth century transported gentle and professional folk to London, the spas, and other urban communities. In 1715 there were approximately 900 coach services a week from the capital reaching well over 200 towns.[117]

Along with shopkeepers and innkeepers, professional men too basked in the lucrative warmth of gentry demand. Active on the urban scene before the Civil War, lawyers became powerful figures in post-Restoration towns. At Stafford the office of mayor was held nine times by a lawyer between 1692 and 1715, while at Gloucester lawyers comprised the second largest group on the corporation in the late seventeenth century.[118] As well as becoming indispensable officials in town government, lawyers advised and acted for rural and urban worthies in both local and national litigation, in testamentary cases and the holding of manorial courts. They also wore a large number of extra-legal hats. They were estate agents, land surveyors, and money-lenders. Substantial country folk and retired townspeople, particularly widows, invested money with lawyers to be lent at interest, usually on the security of mortgages. At Gloucester during the 1680s Thomas Pearce was described as 'an attorney at law and ... a great putter forth of money at interest ... very many people both in the city and country having for many years entrusted him with the receiving, placing forth and calling in of their moneys...' In Lancashire we find an active group of money-lending attorneys based at Prescot. By the early Hanoverian period town lawyers had become pivotal figures in the provincial capital market, helping to sustain the growth of trade and industry. Within half a century they were also involved in banking, though more often merchants took the lead here because of the complex deposit and remittance side of the business.[119]

Above all, urban lawyers acted as brokers or intermediaries between urban and rural society. As well as occupying civic offices they frequently held posts in county administration, as clerks and deputy clerks of the peace and under-sheriffs. When turnpike and bridge trusts were founded after the turn of the century, who better to serve on the committee or act as clerk or treasurer than the ubiquitous town lawyer. Though some operated in market towns, the majority, probably a growing share, had their base in county centres or provincial capitals.[120]

Larger towns provided an ideal foyer for another expanding professional group, medical practitioners. According to Reed, Ipswich had at least four university-trained physicians by 1702, offering consultations to well-heeled rural and urban patients. Sometimes, as in the case of James Keill at Northampton, physicians ran branch practices on behalf of famous London doctors such as Sir Hans Sloane. More often they worked on their own, like Claver Morris of Wells who rode to gentry patients up to 30 miles away and earned £300 a year. Surgery, hitherto mainly a crude by-employment for town barbers, became a more specialist skill, and major provincial centres often had three or more surgeons apiece in the years after 1700.[121]

Medical practitioners exploited their new-found social and professional standing to write publicity tracts for spas. Bath, as we shall see, profited considerably from medical 'puffing'. But along with the leading spas most county towns in this period discovered, with the aid of a friendly physician, that they had at least one medicinal spring. Urban doctors also did increasing business from the 1720s offering inoculation against smallpox. An even more important boost to medical fortunes came from the establishment of provincial infirmaries. The first provincial hospital was

23

opened at Winchester in 1736 and by 1800 28 had been established, almost all of them in larger towns. Together with the various physicians and surgeons working at the infirmary, other medical practitioners battened on to the town's new reputation as a centre for medical care. Private mental asylums were opened near by, and para-medical services like dentistry became available in the town.[122]

School teachers were further beneficiaries of gentry custom. Though old-style endowed grammar schools teaching ordinary town boys were in decline in many places after 1680, those concentrating on instructing and boarding the offspring of the well-to-do, such as the cathedral school at Gloucester, did a handsome business. Equally successful were the smaller but no less exclusive academies and boarding schools which sprang up after the Restoration, catering for the daughters as well as the sons of landowners. In the early eighteenth century Gloucester had over a dozen private academies, one run by the distinguished dissenter James Forbes, another Mrs Shelton's establishment near the cathedral where 'young ladies may be boarded at reasonable rates' and taught social arts and dancing, as well as ordinary literary and household skills. In the later Hanoverian period schoolmasters, hitherto on the margins of the well-to-do, finally achieved professional status. Other new pro-fessional groups at this time included auctioneers, booksellers, printers, surveyors, bankers and architects.[123]

As well as the growing presence of landowners and professional men, larger towns often had a core of salaried government officials, excisemen, salt officers, and (in ports) customs men – as we find at Ipswich (p. 114). The accession of these groups affected not only the economy but the social structure of county towns. Urban elites, hitherto often narrow and insular, were enlarged and strengthened: they may have become more open. They acquired a more outward-looking attitude and an enhanced awareness of the value of ties with county society (symbolized perhaps by the wholesale assumption of the title of gentleman by respectable townspeople – traders, innkeepers and professional men). More prosperous than their predecess-ors, the new cadres of town rulers provided a valuable source of local capital and, as Reed stresses, generated substantial demand for urban goods and services.[124]

Nonetheless, the urban elite no longer completely dominated the pattern of in-ternal demand in towns. The middling ranks of urban society, modest shopkeepers, ordinary masters, and dealers, were progressively important. At Winchester trades-men provided some of the impetus for the urban building boom after the Restora-tion. In Ipswich we find respectable townspeople furnishing their houses with a growing array of comforts. Business at this economic level always remained some-what precarious. Heavy drinking, negligent servants, bad debts, fire, illness, or a profligate wife could all spell bankruptcy; the turnover of tradesmen was high.[125] However, shopkeepers and masters might try to reduce the risk of downfall by mem-bership of benefit and other societies, and of dissenting congregations, which in some degree afforded collective help for those in difficulty. Records of Georgian fire insurance companies suggest that a considerable proportion of those townspeople taking out policies came from the middle tier of urban society.[126]

Turning finally to the lower orders, one can discern a distinct improvement in their economic and social position. No longer were they overwhelmed by grinding poverty. Agreed, the number of poor remained fairly high. At Winchester in the 1660s as many as a quarter of households inside the city and a half of those in the eastern suburb were listed as exempt from the Hearth Tax on account of poverty. At Ipswich exemptions from Hearth Tax were as high as 60 per cent in some areas, though running at less than half this rate in better-off central parishes. Elsewhere in both large and small towns we find a heavy incidence of poverty after the Restoration. Unfortunately, we have no comparable statistics for the later period. One has the impression, however, that the incidence of poverty remained fairly stable into the mid-eighteenth century, that there were no great tidal waves of impoverishment such as had repeatedly threatened to inundate corporate towns before the English Revolution. Even during difficult harvest decades like the 1690s there is little evidence of a major leap in the level of urban destitution. A number of factors helped improve the situation. One was the reduced inflow of long-distance, subsistence migrants, which we noted earlier. Another was the growing effectiveness of urban relief. The machinery of parish relief became more formalized and bureaucratic and in some towns was strengthened by the amalgamation of small parishes. From the 1690s a considerable number of larger towns centralized relief through Corporations of the Poor. In addition, there was a significant level of philanthropy with old and new endowments seconded by neighbourly relief and *ad hoc* subscription funds to deal with particular emergencies. So far as one can see, *per capita* poor relief in towns was probably rising in the late seventeenth and early eighteenth centuries. At a time of falling food prices this would imply that even those townspeople dependent on parish doles or other forms of relief may have enjoyed a modest increment in their disposable income. For once those archetypal upper-class complaints that recipients of relief were living in idle comfort at the ratepayer's expense may have contained a modicum of truth.[127]

The position of labourers, journeymen and artisans actually in work was probably even better. Real wages rose steadily in the later Stuart period and, given the briskness of trade, the level of involuntary unemployment or under-employment was doubtless lower than in the preceding century. Skilled artisans in towns did especially well. As in most developing societies a considerable part of the increased income of wage-earners was devoted to an improved diet, including extra meat and vegetables (hence the spread of market gardens around towns), and to drink. As the London commentator Thomas Manly remarked in 1669 about rising wages: 'the men have just so much the more to spend in tipple.' Ordinary townspeople not only began to drink more alcohol, but a wider variety of liquors, from expensive strong ales to spirits. Old-style alehouses, squalid boozing kens, with the bare minimum of facilities, gave way to fairly substantial and better equipped establishments, able to satisfy the more sophisticated and expensive tastes of their lower-class customers. To spend extra time at the alehouse and in other leisure pursuits artisans and others may have worked fewer days. But not all the increased purchasing power of the lower orders was dissipated by a high leisure preference and enlarged appetite for food and drink. With the multiplicity of consumer goods now displayed in town shops and advertised in newspapers and broadsheets, skilled workers and their wives picked up the habit of purchasing wares which had once been regarded as luxuries.[128] More systematic work is still needed on the condition of the lower orders in post-Restoration England, particularly in towns. Nonetheless, the signs are that those labouring and artisan classes whose earlier plight had served as a major obstacle to sustained economic growth were now affording a valuable stimulus, through increased demand, to urban trade and industry.

5

As one might expect, not all towns benefited from the more buoyant economic climate of the late seventeenth and early eighteenth centuries. Among the older provincial centres, ones which tended to prosper most were those which developed specialist activities. Urban specialization was already being noted by Baskerville during the 1670s and 1680s and was pronounced enough by the turn of the century for Defoe to exclaim that whereas there are some 'towns which are lately increased in trade and navigation, wealth and people, while their neighbours decay, it is because they have some particular trade or accident to trade which is a kind of nostrum to them . . .'[129] The trend is evident at all levels of the urban hierarchy.

In the case of the provincial capitals the years 1660 to 1750 probably marked the peak of their prosperity and importance in the pre-industrial period. At Norwich, as Corfield has pointed out, there was 'a considerable degree of functional specialization' in the worsted weaving industry and this was the principal factor in the city's dynamic economic performance in the post-Restoration era, with exports particularly important during the eighteenth century. But Norwich had a valuable economic second string: its role as the leading social and distributive centre in East Anglia.[130] The least successful provincial capital, York, had to rely almost wholly on its distributive and service sectors. Defoe remarked in the 1720s that 'there is abundance of good company here and abundance of good families live here'. Many of them resided in the fine neo-classical houses which were erected in the city and its outskirts from the end of the seventeenth century. Overall York's population and economy generally stabilized in the post-Restoration period.[131]

The prosperity of the other provincial capitals depended to a major extent on their function as ports. Newcastle's coal trade with the capital was the proverbial golden goose which continued to lay large profitable eggs until the mid-eighteenth century, with secondary activities like shipbuilding and the salt trade developing under its wing. Not only the city's commercial and shipping interests prospered; Newcastle became an important shopping and professional centre, serving the needs of the wealthy mine-owning landowners of the North-East. In competition with Durham it developed as a lively social forum with many gentry keeping town houses in the western part of the city. Little wonder that Newcastle's population probably doubled between the 1660s and the 1730s (to about 29,000).[132]

Exeter's fortunes in the late seventeenth century were closely linked to the dyeing, finishing and export of serges, which had been manufactured in the towns and villages of its hinterland. Shipments were mainly directed to the Dutch market, though with useful sales to Germany and the Iberian peninsula. Major improvements to the city canal and quay in the 1680s and 1690s helped boost exports to a peak in Anne's reign, though the following decades were a time of stagnation before renewed growth during the late eighteenth century. Yet as Defoe commented, Exeter was 'full of gentry and good company' as well as 'full of trade and manufactures' – 'two things which we seldom find unite in the same town'. After the Glorious Revolution the city had a host of great inns, a gentry quarter in the south-east of town, an exchange, assembly rooms, and at one time three provincial newspapers.[133]

For Bristol the colonial trades were of paramount importance. Its merchants' involvement in the tobacco, sugar and slave trades with the West Indies and Africa yielded enormous dividends. At the same time, its overseas commerce was underpinned by an extensive coastal and river trade stretching into south Wales, the West

Country, and, increasingly vital, up the Severn to the industrializing centres of the West Midlands. This hinterland trade not only provided markets for Bristol imports but furnished industrial goods to be shipped abroad. As with Exeter, moreover, Bristol had an important role as a social and regional centre, its coffee houses, shops, elegant assembly rooms and Georgian streets and squares (Prince and Orchard Streets, Queen Square and Dowry Square) serving to amuse both upper-class visitors and a large contingent of resident gentry. After the turn of the seventeenth century it even had its own spa or hot-well at Clifton, while the neighbouring Gorge was a growing attraction for a new generation of well-to-do captivated by visions of the romantic and picturesque.[134]

If the great regional centres set a smart pace in urban growth after the Restoration, county towns followed steadily behind. Some, as we have already seen, acquired vigorous industrial sectors. As well as those producing manufactured goods, a number of county towns developed profitable agriculture-based industries. Reading, Derby, Stratford-on-Avon, Abingdon, Henley, Mansfield, Stamford and Ipswich became notable malting towns,[135] while Burton, Lichfield, Dorchester, Plymouth, Nottingham, Bridgnorth and Shrewsbury were famous for their locally brewed beers.[136]

One has to see these new industrial specialisms of the old county towns in perspective. While they may have employed a growing proportion of the urban work force they never dominated the economy on the scale found in the industrializing centres of the North and Midlands. At Northampton, for instance, the shoe industry was balanced by a busy service and professional sector.[137] Nonetheless, there can be little question that specialization of this sort provided an important boost to the economic welfare of numerous county towns during late seventeenth and early eighteenth centuries.

Other middle-rank towns channelled their energies in different directions. A sizeable number concentrated on enlarging their social function. We can see from Rosen's work on Winchester how that city exploited its loyalist reputation gained during the Civil Wars, as well as Charles II's patronage, to become one of the leading social centres in southern England. By the early eighteenth century Lichfield played a similar role in the West Midlands. Too close to Birmingham and the Staffordshire industrial townships to resuscitate its old crafts, Lichfield made a virtue of necessity and dedicated itself to the servicing of fashionable traffic travelling down the Watling Street, and to the social entertainment of county gentry. As its favourite son Samuel Johnson brusquely declared: 'we are a city of philosophers; we work with our heads and make the boobies of Birmingham work for us with their hands'. Other well-known gentry towns were Stamford, Warwick, Preston, Lewes, Bury St Edmunds, Chelmsford and Shrewsbury.[138]

A small group of county towns became leisure resorts *par excellence*. The supreme example was Bath. As McIntyre argues later in this volume, Bath clearly faced an uphill struggle if she wanted to expand her distributive and industrial functions, because of competition from Bristol and the clothing townships in the area. But she had the tremendous asset of the Roman baths. With royal patronage, a vociferous medical press and transport improvements, Bath could soon claim to be the principal spa town in the kingdom. Before 1700 the town's permanent population was only about 2,000, with great seasonal invasions of visitors during the summer months as aristocrats, London tycoons and other socialites came to take the waters, bathe, and patronize the coffee houses and other fashionable entertainments. But the eighteenth century, particularly the second half, witnessed a growing resident population of middling landowners, professional classes, retired manufacturers and military men: by 1801 the total population was about 33,000. To service the well-to-do there was a major expansion in the tertiary sector: food and drink traders, lodging house keepers, retailers of luxury wares, builders, all flourished. Scarborough was another medium-sized centre, a decayed port in the early seventeenth century, which gained a reputation after the Restoration as a spa. From the mid-eighteenth century it also developed as a watering-place, leaping on to the new bandwagon of sea-bathing. Two more decayed ports which revived as seaside resorts during George III's reign were Weymouth and (to a lesser extent) Southampton.[139]

As in the case of the provincial capitals, overseas commerce created prosperity for various middle-rank towns in the post-Restoration period. On the east coast Hull exploited Newcastle's preoccupation with the coal trade to become the principal port engaged in commerce with the Baltic, mainly exporting cloths from the expanding West Riding woollen industry. However, after about 1700 Hull's links with the interior stretched well into the industrializing Midlands, as a result of the navigation of the rivers Trent, Calder and Aire. With such an enormous trading network, providing both a large market for imports and also supplying a multifarious range of exports, Hull's economy surged ahead; from a population of about 6,000 in the early eighteenth century, the figure had risen to 13–14,000 in the 1770s. Further south, Yarmouth's position tended to stabilize after the preceding period of high growth. Adversely affected by the loss of its French trade, the decline of its fishery and haven, the port turned away from long-distance commerce towards coastal traffic, especially the coal trade, and the export of grain to the Netherlands. Yarmouth's Achilles' heel may have been its failure to develop close relations with Norwich, whose rapidly expanding cloth trade was mainly conducted via London.[140]

Ipswich likewise cut its coat according to the new commercial cloth. Reed demonstrates how the problems caused by the decay of the Suffolk cloth industry were compounded in the late seventeenth century by the loss of the colliery trade to Yarmouth. To compensate, Ipswich expanded its general coastal business with London, particularly in Suffolk dairy products. At the same time, it sought to buttress the urban economy by emphasizing its social function, parading its attorneys, physicians, stationers, coffee houses and library for the service and delectation of the gentry.[141]

On the south coast the fortunes of middle-rank ports were also mixed. Portsmouth and Plymouth expanded rapidly from the late Stuart period to become substantial urban communities: Portsmouth and Portsea had 10,000 or so inhabitants by the 1740s; Plymouth up to 14,000 at about the same time. In both cases the impetus for growth came from heavy Crown expenditure on their dockyard activity, particularly during the wars with the Dutch and French. Though less important, Deal was another naval base which benefited from the expansion of the British fleet.[142] However, other ports like Rye, Southampton, Chichester, Totnes and Lyme stagnated or decayed. Intense competition from London and the leading ports aggravated the problems caused by primitive harbour facilities and the growing tonnage of merchant ships, though some may have found solace in the black economy of smuggling.[143]

Turning finally to the west coast, prospects were brighter almost everywhere. Not only was Bristol expanding rapidly on the back of colonial trade, but Liverpool, already growing in the earlier period, was now set fair to develop as one of the leading ports in the kingdom. Taking a large share of commerce with the West Indies and Ireland, serving as the principal outlet for the burgeoning Lancashire textile industry and Cheshire salt trade, Liverpool rapidly outpaced its old rival Chester and by 1773 had a population of over 34,000.[144] Further north, Whitehaven (founded by Sir John Lowther in Charles II's reign) and Lancaster both prospered in varying degrees from Atlantic commerce; Whitehaven was also active in the coal trade. Indeed, the Hanoverian period marked a golden age for the west coast ports as English trade shifted its principal focus away from Europe. One of the few exceptions was Chester, crippled by haven decay, though even here the town enjoyed a modest success, expanding its marketing radius in west Cheshire to become a major distribution centre, and exploiting its role as a cathedral city to attract a polite coterie of county gentry.[145]

In the case of second-rank inland towns, prosperity was by no means the universal rule. Stafford, for instance, stagnated badly during the late seventeenth century. The principal problem was the community's failure to discover a suitable specialist role which might give an edge to its general function as an old-style county town. It was unable to compete with nearby Lichfield as a fashionable social centre, while the rise of new industrial communities like Birmingham, Wolverhampton and Walsall denied Stafford any real hope of becoming a specialized manufacturing town. In counties where there were two or more middle-rank towns, the period after the Restoration tended to see one centre triumph at the expense of the rest. Thus in Kent the long-standing rivalry between Canterbury and Maidstone for the title of principal shire town was finally decided in Maidstone's favour in the later Stuart period. Even the attractions of the cathedral close could not stop county gentry preferring the modish company at Maidstone.[146]

In the case of medium-size towns, however, even those one might judge losers in the post-Restoration steeplechase lived to run another day. Southampton, for instance, whose economy was contracting by 1700, recovered some impetus in the late Hanoverian period as a smart seaside resort. Inland towns like Lincoln, which had never won fashionable acclaim among the gentry after the Restoration, prospered from the later agricultural expansion. By contrast the difficulties which many market towns faced between the mid-seventeenth and late eighteenth centuries often proved terminal: resurrection would have to wait until the trumpet blast of the railway or the motor car.[147]

Of those market towns which did prosper at this time most had acquired an important speciality. On the marketing side the concentration on particular commodities was already well under way by the Civil War, as Everitt has stressed, and accelerated in the following decades. Small towns which maintained no more than a general market came under intense pressure from more specialist markets in other towns, from the general stores which sprang up in larger villages, and from middlemen and pedlars buying and selling from door to door in the countryside. At the close of the seventeenth century there was considerable agitation against pedlars who were blamed for the decay or urban trade, doubtless in the smaller places. Even a specialist market offered no certainty of economic prosperity or urban survival, particularly since the majority dealt mainly in wheat and other cereals, commodities which suffered now from over-production and falling prices. Markets concentrating on livestock had an easier time: Watlington, for instance, a small town in Oxfordshire, gained a profitable reputation for veal, while Penkridge in Staffordshire became renowned for its sales of fine-quality horses.[148]

Aping larger urban centres, certain market towns built up their craft specialisms. At Tewkesbury there was a tradition of woollen hosiery manufacture in the area from the seventeenth century, but in the following decades production of cotton stockings was increasingly centred in the town with sales down-river to Bristol. Again in Gloucestershire, woollen cloth manufacture in the villages of the Cotswold slopes became more urbanized, with Stroud in particular developing as a major manufacturing and marketing nexus for high quality, richly-dyed broadcloth. In the East Midlands Hinckley benefited from its location in an area of pastoral farming (with the usual stimulus to by-employments) and supported an expanding hosiery industry. At Kettering an ample supply of long-stapled wool and the entrepreneurial skills of a number of incoming weavers fostered the growth of a thriving worsted weaving industry which employed roughly half the town's adult males up to the 1770s. In the same period lace-making flourished at nearby Wellingborough and also in the market towns of north Buckinghamshire.[149] In the West Midlands and parts of the North the industries which sprang up in various market towns during the seventeenth and eighteenth centuries eventually overwhelmed their economies and transformed those centres into sprawling industrial cities. But elsewhere the industrial sector of market towns usually remained more limited, though crucial for their prosperity.

One final type of specialization needs mention here. A handful of market towns followed the example of Bath and became leisure resorts. In Gloucestershire Cheltenham, still small and backward in 1700, was well on the way by the 1770s to becoming a leading spa town, helped by the patronage of the royal family. In Kent the undistinguished market town of Tonbridge provided the springboard for Tunbridge Wells, though here the spa was located two or three miles away and eventually became a separate community.[150]

Specialization of various sorts proved the salvation of numerous small market centres after the Restoration. But for others the situation was bleak. They were badly affected by competition from county towns busy extending their marketing radius, and from specialist market towns. They often suffered from poor communications, since improvements were generally focused on the main towns. They turned into economic and social backwaters. When the postal routes were organized across the country from the 1680s, the principal links were always between county towns; the most a small place could hope for was to have a branch service. Tardy postal deliveries, as the townsfolk of Lyme complained in Charles II's reign, might have a disastrous effect on trade. Frequently these lesser centres became little more than overgrown villages both in their services and atmosphere: a visitor to Berkhamsted in the 1770s commented, 'the people are so countrified as in any town is I know. They will stare at you as if they had never seen no-one before'.[151] Not surprisingly, a substantial proportion of these small market centres disappeared off the urban map. Data on the incidence of market towns at any particular time is notoriously difficult to evaluate. Juggling with the numbers of market grants, without any attempt to discover whether the putative centres ever gained an urban identity (many new market settlements in the late seventeenth century failed in this vital respect), is as useful for our understanding of early modern urban history as attempts to illuminate agrarian change before the Revolution through the now discredited counting of manors. However, if we employ a fairly conservative approach and exclude from our analysis the more obvious notional centres, that is ones without any significant urban function, we can discern a general contraction of market towns from the late seventeenth into the eighteenth century. According to the detailed findings of John Chartres, the decline was least marked in areas close to the capital and most pronounced in the West Country. Taking England and Wales overall, the number of market centres may have fallen by a fifth between 1640 and 1720. There can be little question that the period after the Revolution was marked by the reorganization and rationalization of the marketing network throughout the kingdom.[152]

6

During the late seventeenth and early eighteenth centuries one detects few of the recurrent spasms of depression and dislocation which blighted urban development in the preceding era. Even during the 1690s, a decade of repeated harvest failure, foreign war, heavy taxation and severe financial upheaval caused by the Recoinage of 1696, there is little evidence of widespread urban recession and social distress. After 1700 we find cases of depression and unemployment following the decline or disruption of particular foreign markets. But the problems were mostly cyclical and localized, as with the decay of certain West Country clothing towns during the 1720s and 1730s. It was this stable climate which encouraged urban communities to dismantle their old civic protectionism; which helped towns and their leaders to become more extrovert, concerned to improve relations with the countryside, to begin to view the economic development of their community in a broader regional and possibly national context. By the mid-eighteenth century and sometimes before town leaders were taking an energetic role in urban improvement and transport innovation.[153] County towns and small centres, as well as provincial capitals, acquired new industrial specialisms or marketed the specialist manufactures of adjoining areas. They became gentry towns or leisure resorts, serving as showcases and engines of demand for the latest manufactured products. Old-established country towns had clearly made an important contribution to the first phase of modernization and industrialization in Hanoverian England.

Yet from the mid-eighteenth century the prospects of country towns were starting to look less bright. Renewed demographic expansion imposed growing strains on their economic and social structures, squeezing wages, creating unemployment and poverty. Meanwhile the rapid industrial and later technological advance of the new manufacturing cities of the Midlands and North posed a mounting threat to the crafts of older towns, invading their home and overseas markets. Many suffered economic difficulty and social distress in the 1750s, 1760s and again in the 1780s and 1790s as a result of foreign war and harvest difficulties.[154]

From the end of the eighteenth century it is arguable that the specialist industrial functions of county and market towns were under severe pressure; such communities were being pushed to the economic sidelines of industrial Britain. As we have already seen and as the following case studies will demonstrate in greater detail, there was nothing predictable about the progress of urbanization in the early modern period.

Acknowledgments

I am grateful to the Social Science Research Council for its generous support of my project on Gloucester and its Region 1550–1800, findings from which are incorporated in this survey. I am also indebted to Penelope Corfield for reading and commenting on the piece in draft.

NOTES

1 Despite their importance in this period neither London nor the new industrial centres have attracted any large-scale systematic research in recent times. For London the best general account is still M. D. George, *London Life in the Eighteenth Century* (1925), though specific problems are considered in a series of provocative essays by F. J. Fisher: 'The development of the London food market, 1540–1640', *EcHR*, O.S.v (1934–5), 46–64; 'The development of London as a centre of conspicuous consumption in the sixteenth and seventeenth centuries', *TRHS*, 4th ser. xxx (1948), 37–50; 'London as an "Engine of economic growth"', in *The Early Modern Town*, ed. P. Clark (1976), 205–15; see also E. A. Wrigley, 'A simple model of London's importance in changing English society and economy 1650–1750', *P & P*, xxxvii (1967), 44–70. For industrial towns there is a good short survey by P. Corfield, 'The industrial towns before the factory, 1680–1780', in *The Rise of the New Urban Society* (Open University, English Urban History Course, 1977), 75–103; on particular aspects of individual centres see R. G. Wilson, *Gentlemen Merchants: The Merchant Community in Leeds 1700–1830* (1971) and J. Money, *Experience and Identity: Birmingham and the West Midlands 1760–1800* (1977). Apart from T. S. Willan's *Elizabethan Manchester* (1980) we have little on that city.
2 For some discussion of the contribution of towns to economic growth in the eighteenth century see P. Abrams and E. A. Wrigley (eds.), *Towns in Societies* (1978), chs. X, XII. E. L. Jones and M. E. Falkus have recently stressed the importance of established provincial centres in the context of urban improvement in 'Urban improvement and the English economy in the seventeenth and eighteenth centuries', in *Research in Economic History*, iv (1979), 194–8.
3 P. Clark and P. Slack (eds.), *Crisis and Order in English Towns 1500–1700* (1972), 4–41; P. Clark and P. Slack, *English Towns in Transition 1500–1700* (1976).
4 J. Patten, *English Towns 1500–1700* (1978), 16 *et passim*.
5 C. V. Phythian-Adams, 'Urban decay in late medieval England', in Abrams and Wrigley, *op.cit.*, 162–85; also his *Desolation of a City: Coventry and the urban crisis of the late Middle Ages* (1979), esp. pts. II and V; D. Palliser, 'A crisis in English towns? The case of York, 1460–1640', *Northern History*, xiv (1978), 113 *et seq.*; *idem*, *Tudor York* (1980), ch. 8 (Dr Palliser kindly allowed me to read the typescript of his book); A. F. Butcher, 'Rent and the urban economy: Oxford and Canterbury in the later middle ages', *Southern History*, i (1979), 42–3.
6 P. Corfield, 'Urban development in England and Wales in the sixteenth and seventeenth centuries', in *Trade, Government and Economy in Pre-Industrial England*, ed. D. C. Coleman and A. H. John (1976), 214–47.
7 A. Dyer, 'Growth and decay in English towns 1500–1700', *Urban History Yearbook 1979* (1979), 60–72; for a refutation of some of Dyer's 'errors' see C. V. Phythian-Adams, 'Dr Dyer's urban undulations', *ibid.*, 73–6.
8 Abrams and Wrigley (eds.), *op. cit.*, 170–2, 180; Clark and Slack, *English Towns*, 83–4.
9 Clark and Slack, *English Towns*, 85–6.
10 See p. 94; Clark and Slack, *English Towns*, 86–7; e.g. Southampton: T. B. James, 'The geographical origins and mobility of the inhabitants of Southampton 1400–1600'

(Ph.D. thesis, University of St Andrews, 1977), 49; even in a small market town like Lutterworth immigration played a crucial role: J. Goodacre, 'Lutterworth in the sixteenth and seventeenth centuries' (Ph.D. thesis, University of Leicester, 1977), 85–6 (I am grateful to Dr Goodacre for allowing me to refer to his thesis).

11 P. Slack, 'Mortality crises and epidemic disease in England 1485–1610', in *Health, Medicine and Mortality in the Sixteenth Century*, ed. C. Webster (1979), 35–7; also D. Palliser, 'Dearth and disease in Staffordshire, 1540–1670', in *Rural Change and Urban Growth 1500–1800*, ed. C. W. Chalklin and M. Λ. Havinden (1974), 70 1; N. Goose, 'Cambridge in the early seventeenth century' (paper read to the Leicester University Early Modern Town Group, May 1979).

12 P. Clark, 'The migrant in Kentish towns 1580–1640', in Clark and Slack (eds.), *Crisis and Order*, 134–8; also Patten, *op.cit.*, 236.

13 See p. 57; P. Slack, 'Vagrants and vagrancy in England 1598–1664', *EcHR*, N. S. xxvii (1974), 361, 369; see also J. F. Pound, 'Tudor and Stuart Norwich 1525–1675' (Ph.D. thesis, University of Leicester, 1974), 193, 200; Goodacre, *op.cit.*, 85–6, 89–90.

14 A. R. Michell, 'The port and town of Great Yarmouth and its economic and social relationships with its neighbours . . . 1550–1714' (Ph.D. thesis, University of Cambridge, 1978), xii; cf. T. G. McGee, *The South-East Asian City* (1967), 17.

15 Dyer, 'Growth and decay', 70.

16 J. N. Bartlett, 'The expansion and decline of York in the later Middle Ages', *EcHR*, N. S. xii (1959–60), 27–32; Palliser, *Tudor York*, 208–10; Butcher, 'Rent and the urban economy', 42–3; see pp. 148–50.

17 P. Clark, '"The Ramoth-Gilead of the Good": urban change and political radicalism at Gloucester 1540–1640', in *The English Commonwealth 1547–1640: essays in politics and society presented to Joel Hurstfield*, ed. P. Clark, A. G. R. Smith and N. Tyacke (1979), 170–1; P. Slack, 'Poverty and politics in Salisbury 1597–1666', in Clark and Slack (eds.), *Crisis and Order*, esp. 171; P. Deyon, *Amiens: capitale provinciale* (Paris, 1967), 205 15; P. Goubert, *Beauvais et le Beauvaisis de 1600 à 1730* (Paris, 1960), 130–1; D. Sella, *Crisis and Continuity: the economy of Spanish Lombardy in the seventeenth century* (1979), 98–100; R. Scribner, 'Economic and social problems of German towns in the early sixteenth century' (paper read to Conference on Towns in Pre-Modern England, London, November 1979).

18 G. Unwin, *Industrial Organisation in the Sixteenth and Seventeenth Centuries* (2nd edn, 1957), 71–2; H. Thorpe, 'Lichfield: a study of its growth and function', *Staffs. Hist. Collns.* (1950–1), 176–7; Clark *et al.* (eds.), *English Commonwealth*, 171; Phythian-Adams, *Desolation of a City*, 217.

19 Pound, 'Tudor and Stuart Norwich', 88 *et seq.*; G. Martin, *The Story of Colchester* (1959), 49; F. W. Cross, *History of the Walloon and Huguenot Church at Canterbury* (1898), ch. XVII.

20 A. D. Dyer, *The City of Worcester in the Sixteenth Century* (1973), 93–118; J. Hill, 'A study of poverty and poor relief in Shropshire, 1550–1685' (M. A. thesis, University of Liverpool, 1973), 152 *et seq.*

21 W. G. Hoskins, *Provincial England* (1963), 108; Pound, 'Tudor and Stuart Norwich', 30; Clark *et al.* (eds.), *English Commonwealth*, 171; for Warwick see p. 52; the Canterbury inventories used in this analysis are in Kent AO, PRC:10/1–72; 11/1–7; 27/1–8; 28/1–20. But tanners may have been wealthier in East Midland towns; see Hoskins, *Provincial England*, 69.

22 Patten, *op.cit.*, 179; e.g. at Leicester: *VCH Leics.*, IV, 97; see maltsters at Stratford in 1595: Warwicks. RO, Warwick Castle Muniments, MS2663.

23 See p. 117, also at Chester: D. M. Woodward, *The Trade of Elizabethan Chester* (1970), 115; Willan, *Elizabethan Manchester*, 89.

24 James, *op.cit.*, 23; W. G. Hoskins, 'The Elizabethan merchants of Exeter', in

Elizabethan Government and Society, ed. S. T. Bindoff, J. Hurstfield and C. H. Williams (1961), 176; for the Gloucester data see my forthcoming paper on 'The civic leaders of Gloucester 1580–1800'; Palliser, *Tudor York*, 103; *VCH Oxon.*, IV, 113–14.

25 Hoskins, *Provincial England*, 77–8; Hill, 'Shropshire', 207; *VCH Oxon.*, IV, 89–90, 112; Michell, *op.cit.*, 275.

26 J. F. Pound (ed.), *The Norwich Census of the Poor* (Norfolk Rec. Soc., XL, 1971), 14–15; Clark, 'Civic leaders'; D. G. Teall, 'The corporation and tradesmen of Stamford 1461–1674' (Ph.D. thesis, University of Leicester, 1975), 292–3; F. J. C. and D. M. Hearnshaw (eds.), *Southampton Court Leet Records: III* (Southampton Rec. Soc., I, 1907), 386–7.

27 J. F. Pound, 'The social and trade structure of Norwich 1525–1575', in Clark (ed.), *Early Modern Town*, 134, 137–8; Clark *et al.* (eds.), *English Commonwealth,* 171; *VCH Oxon.*, IV, 109; W. T. MacCaffrey, *Exeter 1540–1640* (2nd edn, 1975), 162–3; V. Parker, *The Making of King's Lynn* (1971), 15; but note their apparent unimportance at Worcester: Dyer, *Worcester,* 88.

28 W. Champion, 'A late medieval urban crisis? The case of Shrewsbury 1450–1550' (paper read to the Conference on Towns in Pre-Modern England, London, December 1978).

29 J. B. Baker, *The History of Scarborough* (1882), 318–22; Dyer, *Worcester,* 88; R. Tittler, 'Incorporation and politics in sixteenth-century Thaxted', *Essex Archaeology and History,* 3rd ser., VIII (1976), 225; Patten, *op.cit.*, 254, 266–9; T. S. Willan, *The Inland Trade* (1976), ch. III; A. Everitt, 'The marketing of agricultural produce', in *The Agrarian History of England and Wales,* IV, ed. J. Thirsk (1967), 490–1.

30 Goodacre, *op.cit.*, 42–3, 48, 52, 80–6.

31 See p. 50; P. Clark, *English Provincial Society from the Reformation to the Revolution: religion, politics and society in Kent 1500–1640* (1977), 246; P. Large, 'Droitwich in the seventeenth century' (paper read to the Early Modern Town Group, Leicester, January 1980); PRO, E134/4 Charles I/Trinity 9; but note the Mileways Act (1576) for improving roads near Oxford, and the navigation of the Thames to the town in the early seventeenth century: *VCH Oxon.*, IV, 285, 291–2.

32 For work on the gilds see S. Kramer, *The English Craft Gilds* (New York, 1927); also D. Palliser, 'The trade gilds of Tudor York', in Clark and Slack (eds.), *Crisis and Order,* 86–116. The varying ratio of freemen to total urban populations is briefly considered by D. M. Woodward, 'Freemen's rolls', *Local Historian,* IX (1970–1), 91–3; for tolls causing friction at Cambridge see M. C. Siraut, 'Some aspects of the economic and social history of Cambridge' (M.Litt. thesis, University of Cambridge, 1978), 59–61; for the problems of controlling foreign traders see Coventry RO, Leet Book, MS A 3(b), pp. 164–5; C. G. Parsloe, 'The growth of a borough constitution: Newark on Trent 1549–1688', *TRHS* 4th ser., XXII (1940), 189.

33 R. Davis, *The Trade and Shipping of Hull 1500–1700 (East Yorks. Local History Ser.,* XVII, 1964), 6 *et passim;* J. M. Vanes, 'The overseas trade of Bristol in the sixteenth century' (Ph.D. thesis, University of London, 1975), 18, 22, 391–2; MacCaffrey, *op.cit.*, 161 *et seq.*; Michell, *op.cit.*, 38; Woodward, *op.cit.*, 57–65, 125–6.

34 Clark *et al.* (eds.), *English Commonwealth,* 170–2; Parker, *op. cit.*, 11–13; Liverpool turned to Irish trade: Woodward, *op.cit.*, 126.

35 MacCaffrey, *op.cit.*, 131–5 (for Exeter's dispute with Topsham); Michell, *op.cit.*, 6.

36 Dyer, *Worcester,* 145–6; Clark, 'Civic leaders'; for the low incidence of attorneys in the Tudor provinces see C. W. Brooks, 'Litigants and attorneys in the King's Bench and Common Pleas, 1560–1640', in *Legal Records and the Historian,* ed. J. H. Baker (1978), 54.

37 Dyer, *Worcester,* 146–7; though there were over 70 medical practitioners in Norwich 1570–90, only a small minority were professionally trained: M. Pelling and C. Webster, 'Medical practitioners' in Webster (ed.), *op.cit.*, 225–6; for more on early town doctors see J. H. Raach, *A Directory of English Country Physicians* (1962); for town schools in Kent, see Clark, *English Provincial Society,* 193–7; A. Everitt, 'The English urban inn,

1560–1640' in *Perspectives in English Urban History*, ed. A. Everitt (1973), 93 *et seq*.

38 Clark, *English Provincial Society*, 118, 146; A. H. Smith, *County and Court: government and politics in Norfolk, 1558–1603* (1974), 90; Palliser, *Tudor York*, 21; for Winchester see pp. 161–2.

39 See pp. 50 *et seq*.; Teall, *op. cit.*, 410–11; Clark *et al.* (eds.), *English Commonwealth*, 173, 180.

40 D. M. Palliser, 'A hostile view of Elizabethan York', *York Historian*, I (1976), 20; see also Richard Carew's jibes at Cornish towns: F. E. Halliday (ed.), *Richard Carew of Anthony: The Survey of Cornwall* (1953), 137, 157–8.

41 Clark, 'Civic leaders'; see also Palliser, *Tudor York*, 93–8; J. T. Evans, *Seventeenth Century Norwich* (1980), 25, 30 *et passim*.

42 See p. 117; Canterbury data derived from Kent AO, PRC: 10/1–72; 11/1–7; 27/1–8; 28/1–20; Bindoff *et al.* (eds.), *op. cit.*, 178–83.

43 R. Berger, 'Mercantile careers in the early seventeenth century: Thomas Atherall, a Coventry apothecary' (unpublished paper); I am indebted to Professor Berger for allowing me to see a copy of this study.

44 In a sample of 18 woodworkers, metal processors and service workers at Canterbury 1560–99 the average inventorial wealth (excluding desperate debts) was £41. 1; in a sample of 30 in 1600–39 the average was £44. 6, despite the fact that general price levels increased by a half between the two periods. Data from Kent AO, PRC: 10/1–72; 11/1–7; 27/1–8; 28/1–20; E. H. Phelps Brown and S. V..Hopkins, 'Seven centuries of the prices of consumables, compared with builders' wage-rates', in E. M. Carus-Wilson (ed.), *Essays in Economic History*, II (1962), 194–5.

45 E.g. Leics. RO, Borough Hall Papers, II/18/3/6, 18/4/27; M. D. Harris (ed.), *The Coventry Leet Book*, pt IV (Early English Text Society, 1913), 838; W. H. Stevenson (ed.), *Records of the Borough of Nottingham*, IV (1889), 391–2; J. Hall, *A History of the Town and Parish of Nantwich* (1883), 112–13; Leics. RO, II/18/4/15.

46 See p. 54; Clark and Slack (eds.). *Crises and Order*, 165–189; Pound, *Norwich Census*, 7-20; *idem*, 'Tudor and Stuart Norwich', 192–202; Clark *et al.* (eds.), *English Commonwealth*, 174–5; Clark, *English Provincial Society*, 238–9; J. Webb (ed.), *Poor Relief in Elizabethan Ipswich* (Suffolk Rec. Soc., IX, 1966), 121–40; Siraut, *op. cit.*, 269–70; Hill, 'Shropshire', 170–86, 206; W. J. Connor (ed.), *The Southampton Mayor's Book of 1606–1608* (Southampton Rec. Ser., XXI, 1978), 25 *et seq*.; Leics. RO, II/18/4/4 *et passim*; Coventry RO, MS A 3(b), p. 2 *et seq*.; for Winchester see p. 58 *et seq*.

47 Clark, *English Provincial Society*, 240; W. B. Willcox, *Gloucestershire: a study in local government 1590–1640* (New Haven, Conn., 1940), 9–10; T. North, 'Melton Mowbray town records', *Leics. Arch. Soc. Trans.*, IV (1869–74), 353–4; C. J. M. Moxon, 'Ashby-de-la-Zouch: a social and economic survey of a market town' (D.Phil. thesis, University of Oxford, 1971), 94,97.

48 See p. 53 *et seq*.; F. J. C. and D. M. Hearnshaw (eds.). *Southampton Court Leet Records*, II (Southampton Rec. Soc., I, 1906), 236; Hill, 'Shropshire', 53; also J. C. Cox (ed.), *The Records of the Borough of Northampton*, II (1898), 264–5.

49 See p. 59; Leics. RO, II/18/4/4, 15; see also generally Clark, *English Provincial Society*, 240.

50 Dyer, 'Growth and decay', 67; for the position of Shrewsbury, see Hill, 'Shropshire', 172–5; at Chichester in 1596 it was said that the multitude of poor was driving out the better sort of inhabitants and causing the town's decay: *VCH Sussex*, III, 86.

51 See pp. 65–73; P. Slack, 'Social problems and social policies', in *The Traditional Community under Stress* (Open University, English Urban History Course, 1977), 93–5.

52 P. Clark, 'The alehouse and the alternative society' in *Puritans and Revolutionaries: essays . . . presented to Christopher Hill*, ed. D. Pennington and K. Thomas (1978), 49–61.

53 I. S. W. Blanchard, 'Commercial crisis and change: trade and the industrial economy of the North-East 1509–32', *Northern History*, VIII (1973), 69–84; A. F. Butcher, 'Rent, population and economic change in late-medieval Newcastle', *Northern History*, XIV (1978), 75–6; Palliser, *Tudor York*, esp. ch. VIII; W. Hudson and J. C. Tingey (eds.), *The Records of the City of Norwich*, II (1910), lxx–lxxii; also Abrams and Wrigley (eds.), *op. cit.*, 168. Bristol may have been less seriously affected than other centre: Vanes, *op.cit.*, 390.

54 B. Hall, 'The trade of Newcastle-upon-Tyne and the North-East coast 1600–1640' (M. A. thesis, University of London, 1933), 67 *et passim*; Vanes, *op.cit.*, 391–2; MacCaffrey, *op.cit.*, 148–53, 166–8; Clark, *Early Modern Town*, 137–9; Palliser, *Tudor York*, ch.10.

55 W. B. Stephens, 'Trade trends at Bristol, 1600–1700', *Bristol and Glos. Arch. Soc.*, XCIII (1974), 157–9; MacCaffrey, *op. cit.*, 234, 242–3; see also for Exeter, F. Nicolls, *The Life and Death of Mr Ignatius Jurdain* (1655), 60–2; J. Latimer, *The Annals of Bristol in the Seventeenth Century* (1900), 180–2; R. Howell, *Newcastle-upon-Tyne and the Puritan Revolution* (1967), 195–7, 274.

56 Davis, *op.cit.*, 4 *et passim*; Michell, *op.cit.*, 4 *et seq.*; Parker, *op.cit.*, 11–13; Woodward, *op.cit.*, 66–9, 125–7.

57 Clark and Slack, *English Towns*, 100; N. J. Williams, 'The maritime trade of the East Anglian ports' (D.Phil. thesis, University of Oxford, 1952), 69, 254, 292; E. Gillett, *A History of Grimsby* (1970), 66–7, 98, 104, 120; James, *op.cit.*, 19 *et passim*; see p. 104

58 See above; *VCH Oxon.*, IV, 74–5, 106, 109; Siraut, *op.cit.*; Cambridge was also a major marketing centre for coal and corn.

59 J. W. F. Hill, *Tudor and Stuart Lincoln* (1956), 19, 22; A. Rogers (ed.), *The Making of Stamford* (1965), 50–2, 58–60; see p. 157 *et seq.*

60 Phythian-Adams, *Desolation of a City*, 237; Abrams and Wrigley, *op.cit.*, 162 *et seq.*; P. Clark, 'Reformation and radicalism in Kentish towns c. 1500–1553', in W. J. Mommsen, P. Alter and R. W. Scribner (eds.), *Stadtbürgertum und Adel in der Reformation* (Stuttgart, 1979), 108–9; M. D. Lobel, *The Borough of Bury St Edmund's* (1935), 168.

61 Clark *et al.* (eds.), *English Commonwealth*, 170–1; P. Slack (ed.), *Poverty in Early-Stuart Salisbury* (Wilts. Rec. Soc., XXXI, 1975), 7, 118–29.

62 For the best individual studies see Goodacre, *op.cit.* (Lutterworth); and Moxon, *op.cit.* (Ashby). Thirsk (ed.), *op.cit.*, 467–506; also R. Millward, 'The Cumbrian town between 1600 and 1800', in Chalklin and Havinden (eds.), *op. cit.*, 202–28.

63 Willan, *Elizabethan Manchester*, 67; C. W. Chalklin, *Seventeenth-Century Kent* (1965), 32; Moxon, *op.cit.*, 26; see also population growth at Tonbridge: C. W. Chalklin, 'A Kentish Wealden parish, Tonbridge 1550–1750' (B.Litt. thesis, University of Oxford, 1960), 15.

64 Clark and Slack, *English Towns*, 24–5; Goodacre, *op.cit.*, 203; also Moxon, *op.cit.*, 75, 78, 90, 179. In Gloucestershire, approaching a third of the adult males in many small towns may have been directly engaged in agriculture, as at Berkeley, Painswick and Northleach *(Men and Armour for Gloucestershire in 1608* (1902), 146–7, 265–6, 286–9).

65 Patten, *op.cit.*, 269; ex inf. Dr D. Fleming; J. Thirsk, 'Projects for gentlemen, jobs for the poor: mutual aid in the Vale of Tewkesbury 1600–1630', in *Essays in Bristol and Gloucestershire History*, ed. P. McGrath and J. Cannon (1976), 149; Willcox, *op.cit.*, 9–10; *VCH Wilts.* VI, 15–16.

66 Moxon, *op.cit.*, 94, 97; see also above, p. 10.

67 Abrams and Wrigley, *op.cit.*, 163–83; Phythian-Adams, *Desolation of a City*, 281 *et seq.*; Clark, *Early Modern Town*, 6–7.

68 Clark and Slack, *English Towns*, 102; for the similar impact on charitable relief at York see Palliser, *Tudor York*, 271–2; M. L. Prior, 'Fisher Row – the Oxford community of fishermen and bargemen 1500–1800' (D.Phil. thesis, University of Oxford, 1976), 48–53.

69 Patten, *op.cit.*, 266; Phythian-Adams, *Desolation of a City*, 218–19; W. T. Mellows and D. H. Gifford (eds.), *Elizabethan Peterborough* (Northants. Rec. Soc., XVIII, 1956),

34; *VCH Berks.*, IV, 439.

70 Clark, *English Provincial Society*, 39–43, 64 *et passim*; R. C. Latham (ed.), *Bristol Charters 1509–1899* (Bristol Rec. Soc. XII, 1947), 26, 28.

71 J. Latimer, *Sixteenth Century Bristol* (1908), 99–100; Michell, *op. cit.*, 40, 42, 262; Clark *et al.* (eds.), *English Commonwealth*, 175; Clark, *English Provincial Society*, 233, 252; J. Earle, *Bath: Ancient and Modern* (1864), 126; Leics. RO, Borough Hall Papers, II/18/5/33; Webster, *op. cit.*, 36; York City RO, E40/85–7.

72 See above, p. 10; Webster, *op. cit.*, Chalklin and Havinden (eds.), *op. cit.*, 69–70; Clark and Slack, *English Towns*, 90; P. Clark, 'Popular protest and disturbance in Kent, 1558–1640'. *EcHR*, N.S. xxix (1976), 368, 37–5; W. J. Petchey, 'The borough of Maldon, Essex, 1500–1688' (Ph.D. thesis, University of Leicester, 1972), 248–9.

73 Slack, *Poverty in Early-Stuart Salisbury*, 7, 117–23; B. H. Cunnington (ed.), *Some Annals of the Borough of Devizes . . . 1555–1791* (1925), pt. ii, 81; W. B. Stephens, *Seventeenth-Century Exeter* (1958), 13, 15, 19.

74 See pp. 163–6, Northants. RO, Northampton Assembly Book 3/2, p. 77; HMC, 11th Report App. III, 180–1; Moxon, *op. cit.*, 105–6.

75 Hill, *Tudor and Stuart Lincoln*, 200; R. N. Worth (ed.), *The Buller Papers* (1895), 105; K. H. Docton, 'Lancaster 1684', *Trans. Hist. Soc. Lancs. and Cheshire*, cix (1957), 125, 129; Somerset RO, Quarter Sessions Petitions: Minehead c. 1649–50; I. Rogers, 'Barnstaple, Bideford and Torrington during the Civil War', *Trans. Devonshire Assoc.*, lix (1927), 335–6; K. R. Adey, 'Seventeenth-century Stafford: a county town in decline', *Midland History*, ii (1973–4), 156–7; J. Wilshere and S. Green, *The Siege of Leicester–1645* (1970), 15–17; T. Wright (ed.)., *The Autobiography of Joseph Lister* (1842), 14–26 (Bradford); J. A. Langford, C. S. Mackintosh and J. C. Tildesley, *Staffordshire and Warwickshire, Past and Present*, II (n.d.), 542 *et seq.* (Birmingham); F. A. Hyett, *Gloucester in National History* (1924), 106–17, 128; R. N. Dore, *The Great Civil War (1642–46) in the Manchester Area* (1972), 23 (Bolton and Liverpool); Martin, *op. cit.*, 57–9 (Colchester); *VCH Oxon.*, X, 10 (Banbury); K. J. Beecham, *History of Cirencester* (repr. 1978), 36–7; P. Styles, *Studies in Seventeenth Century West Midlands History* (1978), 232–3 (Worcester); Large, *op. cit.*

76 For the Eastern Association area see C. Holmes, *The Eastern Association in the English Civil War* (1974); for regional variations see also I. Roy, 'England turned Germany? The aftermath of the Civil War in its European context', *TRHS*, 5th ser., xxviii (1978), 132–44; H. Kamen, *The Iron Century* (1971), 42–4.

77 The only recent survey of provincial towns in this period is to be found in C. Chalklin, *The Provincial Towns of Georgian England* (1974), chs. 1–2; for individual centres see the pioneering studies of W. G. Hoskins, *Industry, Trade and People in Exeter 1688–1800* (1935), and J. W. F. Hill, *Georgian Lincoln* (1966).

78 For instance, the invaluable records of the Six Clerks of Chancery (PRO C11–12) cannot be used for the period after 1714.

79 B. Little, *The City and County of Bristol* (1954), 326–7; P. J. Corfield, 'The social and economic history of Norwich, 1650–1850: a study in urban growth (Ph.D. thesis, University of London, 1976), 14–15; J. Ellis, 'The taming of the River Dragon: Newcastle-upon-Tyne in the eighteenth Century', in *Cardiff Studies in Local History*, ed. P. Riden (forthcoming); Chalklin, *Provincial Towns*, 21.

80 See pp. 170–1; *VCH Wilts.* VI, 72; P. Ripley, 'Parish register evidence for the population of Gloucester', *Trans. Bristol and Glos. Arch. Soc.*, xci (1972), 200–1; Chalklin, *Provincial Towns*, 18; Coleman and John, *op. cit.*, 238–9; Michell, *op. cit.*, 14; Adey, *Midland History*, 156–7; *VCH Oxon.*, IV, 76.

81 P. Clark, 'Migration in England during the late seventeenth and early eighteenth centuries', *P & P*, no. lxxxiii (1979), 69–88.

82 A. B. Appleby, 'Nutrition and disease: the case of London 1550–1750', *J. Interdisciplinary History*, vi (1975–6), 12–19; J. D. Chambers, *Population, Economy and*

Society in Pre-Industrial England (1972), 85–106; *idem*, 'Population change in a
provincial town: Nottingham 1700–1800', in D. V. Glass and D. E. C. Eversley (eds.),
Population in History (1965), 334–50.
83 HMC, Portland MSS, II, 265; C. Morris (ed.), *The Journeys of Celia Fiennes* (1947), 113.
84 *VCH Northants.*, III, 29; J. Thirsk, *Economic Policy and Projects* (1978), 82–3; HMC,
Portland MSS, II, 274; J. A. Giles, *History of Witney* (1852), 46–52; F. Kielmansegge,
Diary of a Journey to England in the Years 1761–62 (1902), 93; *VCH Worcs.*, III, 165;
VCH Leics., IV, 168–73; T. Rath, 'The Tewkesbury hosiery industry', *Textile History*, VII
(1976), 141–8; D. C. Coleman, 'The economy of Kent under the later Stuarts' (Ph.D.
thesis, University of London, 1951), 197–8, 202 *et seq.*; S. I. Mitchell, 'Urban markets
and retail distribution 1730–1815' (D.Phil. thesis, University of Oxford, 1975), 24–7;
B. Mason, *Clock and Watchmaking in Colchester, England* (1969), 64 *et seq.*; A. Dyer,
'Warwickshire towns under the Tudors and Stuarts', *Warwickshire History*, III (1977),
123; B. Short, *A Respectable Society: Bridport 1593–1835* (1976), 39–41; *VCH Oxon.*,
X, 64–5; *VCH Wilts.*, X, 256.
85 A. Everitt, 'Country, county and town: patterns of regional evolution in England',
TRHS, 5th ser., XXIX (1979), 94; H. Stocks (ed.), *Records of the Borough of Leicester
1603–1688*, IV (1923), 536–8; D. Hey, *The Rural Metalworkers of the Sheffield Region*
(Univ. Leicester Occ. Papers in English Local History, 3rd ser., no. 5, 1972), 9–11.
86 Rath, *op.cit.*, 148; S. Rudder, *The History and Antiquities of Gloucester* (1781), 179.
87 J. A. Chartres, *Inland Trade in England 1500–1700* (1977), 45–6; see also generally
T. S. Willan, *The English Coasting Trade 1600–1750* (1938).
88 T. S. Willan, *River Navigation in England 1600–1750* (1936), 133; J. Godber, *The Story
of Bedford* (1978), 79–80, 84; T. S. Willan, 'The navigation of the Great Ouse', *Beds.
Hist. Rec. Soc.*, XXIV (1946), 2–28; see also the case of Burton: C. C. Owen, *The
Development of Industry in Burton upon Trent* (1978), 13–16, 32–3; see pp. 210–11.
89 K. H. Burley, 'The economic development of Essex in the later seventeenth and early
eighteenth centuries' (Ph.D. thesis, University of London, 1957), 258; Chartres, *Inland
Trade*, 41; E. Pawson, *Transport and Economy: the turnpike roads of eighteenth-century
Britain* (1977), 129–30, 136–43; Money, *op.cit.*, 26–31.
90 See p. 172; P. Corfield, 'A provincial capital in the late seventeenth century: the case of
Norwich', in Clark and Slack (eds.), *Crisis and Order*, 289; see at Ipswich, p. 123; T.
Fawcett, 'Eighteenth-century Norfolk booksellers', *Trans. Cambridge Bibliographical
Soc.*, VI (1972–6), 6 *et seq.* Francis Ward, a Leicester bookseller who died in 1691, left personal estate worth over £1300 (W. A. Jenkins, 'The economic and social history of Leicester 1660–1835' (M.A. thesis, University of Leicester, 1952), 61.
91 J. A. Chartres, 'The marketing of agricultural produce' in J. Thirsk (ed.), *Agrarian
History of England and Wales*, V (forthcoming). I am grateful to Dr Chartres for
allowing me to see a typescript of his study. Jones and Falkus, *op.cit.*, 196; Mitchell,
op.cit., 29, 32, 117–18. For towns involved in the horse trade see HMC, Portland MSS,
II, 290; J. Macky, *A Journey Through England* (2nd edn, 1724), II, 169; J. Hunter (ed.),
The Diary of Ralph Thoresby (1830), II, 166; for the horse trade generally at this time see
P. R. Edwards, 'The horse trade of the Midlands in the seventeenth century',
AgHR., XXVII (1979)), 90–100.
92 G. A. Cranfield, *The Development of the Provincial Newspaper 1700–1760* (1962),
13–17; Gloucester City Library, NV.26.1; G. A. Cranfield, 'The first Cambridge
newspaper', *Procs. Cambridge Antiquarian Soc.*, XLV (1952), 5–16.
93 E.g. PRO, SP 35/28/15; also Cranfield, *Development*, 175–8.
94 See pp. 122–3; for the decline of trade companies elsewhere see Clark and Slack (eds.),
Crisis and Order, 16; also at Norwich, see Corfield, 'History', 76, 233.
95 Styles, *op.cit.*, 244; Lincs. RO, Brogwen Deposit, QS/1/1, pp. 31, 36–7. 38–9; Clark,
'Migration in England', 62; see p. 167; Woodward, 'Freemen's rolls', 94; Bedford,
Town Minute Book 1664–88, 191 *et passim*.

96 For the breakdown in the attempt to collect market tolls from 'foreigners' at Manchester, see A. P. Wadsworth and J. De L. Mann, *The Cotton Trade and Industrial Lancashire* (1931), 67. Mounting opposition to tolls at Gloucester is evident from Glos. RO,GBR 1382/1457, f. 55; 1383/1458, f. 463. For general opposition to trade regulation at Kingston, see J. Whitter, 'A survey of the economic and administrative life of Kingston-upon-Thames' (M.Sc. (Econ.) thesis, University of London, 1932–3), 204; *VCH Oxon.*, IV, 117; Mitchell, *op.cit.*, 91, 93, 129, 171–2, 282–93.

97 See pp. 125–6. G. Jackson, *Hull in the Eighteenth Century* (1972), 243 *et seq.* In Scotland civic intervention may have been more important for economic growth: e.g., I.C.M. Barnes, 'The Aberdeen stocking trade', *Textile History*, VIII (1977), 80–1.

98 J. H. Sacret, 'The Restoration government and municipal corporations', *EHR*, XLV (1930), 245–59; Clark and Slack, *English Towns,* 138–40; Glos. RO, GBR, 1470, f. 4–8; W. Somner, *The Antiquities of Canterbury* (new edn, 1977), 185; Rudder, *op.cit.*, 148, 150; Cox *op. cit.*, 477; M. Mullett, 'The politics of Liverpool 1660–88', *Trans. Hist. Soc. Lancs. and Cheshire*, CXXIV (1973), 48; B. E. and K. A. Howells (eds.), *Pembrokeshire Life 1572–1843* (Pembrokeshire Rec. Soc., L., 1972), 56–7; A. E. Gibbs (ed.), *The Corporation Records of St Albans* (1890), 293.

99 W. Rye (ed), *The Journal of Thomas Isham* (1875), 64–5; A. Luders *et al.* (eds.), *Statutes of the Realm* (1810–28), V, 798–801.

100 Morris, *op. cit.*, 118; *VCH Northants.*, III, 33; Warwicks. CRO, CR 1618, WA 4; see p. 212 *et seq.*; also R. Neale, 'Society, belief and the building of Bath, 1700–1793', in Chalklin and Havinden (eds.), *op.cit.*, 253–77.

101 Glos. RO,GBR 1384/1459; Rudder, *op.cit.*, iii *et passim*; figures for Improvement Acts derived from *Statutes at Large*; for more on these Acts see Jones and Falkus, *op.cit.*, 208–17.

102 Morris, *op.cit.*, 113; M. Falkus, 'Lighting in the dark ages of English economic history: town streets before the Industrial Revolution', in Coleman and John (eds.), *op.cit.*, 248–71; W. C. Lukis (ed.), *The Family Memoirs of the Rev. William Stukeley, M.D.*, III (Surtees Soc., LXXX, 1887), 303; B. Martin, *The Natural History of England...* (1759–63), I, 354, 356; for London statues, see E. Hatton, *A New View of London* (1708), II, 799–802; H. W. Adnitt, 'The orders of the corporation of Shrewsbury 1511–1735', *Trans. Shropshire Arch. and Nat. History Soc.*, o.s. XI (1888), 204; Hunter, *op.cit.*, I, 391; Hill, *Georgian Lincoln*, 14.

103 P. Borsay, 'The English urban renaissance: the development of provincial urban culture c.1680–1760', *Social History*, II (1977), 581–603; *Gloucester Journal*, 9 March 1731; see at Winchester, pp. 179–81; K. A. MacMahon (ed.), *Beverley Corporation Minute Books 1707–1835* (Yorks. Arch. Soc. Rec. Ser., CXXII, 1958), xxi; G. A. Chinnery (ed.), *Records of the Borough of Leicester 1689–1835*, V (1965), 67; D. Lysons, *Origin and Progress of the Three Choirs* (1895); see also at Salisbury: *VCH Wilts.*, VI, 142.

104 A. Gray, *The Town of Cambridge* (1925), 150–1; Latimer, *Bristol in the Eighteenth Century*, 240–1; Tyne and Wear RO, Newcastle Common Council Book 1656–1722, f. 7; HMC, Portland MSS, II, 263, 265, 267; see also *VCH Bucks.*, III, 472 (Buckingham) and J. O. Halliwell (ed.), *A Descriptive Calendar of the Ancient Manuscripts . . . of Stratford-upon-Avon* (1863), 78 (Stratford).

105 F. M. Martin, 'Cultural and social life in Worcester in the second half of the eighteenth century 1740–1800' (B.A. thesis, University of Birmingham, 1962), 57–8; Latimer, *Bristol in the Eighteenth Century*, 140; *Gloucester Journal*, 7 Dec. 1724 and 15 Feb. 1725.

106 M. Dunsford, *Historical Memoirs of the Town and Parish of Tiverton* (2nd edn., 1790), 58; E. Hobhouse (ed.), *The Diary of a West Country Physician* (1934), 39–42; D. Slatter (ed.), *The Diary of Thomas Naish* (Wilts. Rec. Soc., XX, 1965), 42; *Gloucester Journal*, 1 Dec. 1730; Bedford, Town Minute Book, 1688–1718, fos. 129v–130v; for more on urban music-making see Money, *op.cit.*, 81–2.

107 Everitt, 'Country, county and town', 97; for town libraries at Bedford and Hull: *VCH*

Beds., III, 4; *VCH East Riding*, I, 165. R. P. Sturges, 'Context for library history: libraries in eighteenth-century Derby', *Library History*, IV (1976), 44–52; H. M. Hamlyn, 'Eighteenth-century circulating libraries in England', *The Library*, 5th ser. I (1946–7), 197–222; see also J. H. Plumb, *The Commercialisation of Leisure in Eighteenth-Century England* (1973), 7 *et seq.* For the career of one bookseller-cum-printer see T. Gent, *The Life of Mr Thomas Gent* (1832).

108 W. Moore, *The Gentlemen's Society at Spalding* (1851), 5–10; also W. C. Lukis, *The Family Memoirs of the Rev. William Stukeley M.D.*, I (Surtees Soc., LXXII, 1880), 190, 379; II (Surtees Soc., LXXVI, 1883), 265–6, 285–6, 321–2; for the growth of urban scientific societies from the mid-eighteenth century see A. E. Musson and E. Robinson, *Science and Technology in the Industrial Revolution* (1969), chs. III–IV. P. Clark, 'Urban community and urban consciousness: antiquarians and the English city before 1800' (paper read to the International Urban History Conference Leicester, August 1980).

109 E.g., *Gloucester Journal*, 1722 *et passim*; G. D. Lumb, 'Extracts from the *Leeds Mercury*', *Thoresby Soc.*, XXIV (1919), XXVI (1924), *passim*; D. H. Eshleman (ed.), *The Committee Books of the Theatre Royal Norwich 1768–1825* (1970), 15, 17; P. McGrath (ed.), *Bristol in the Eighteenth Century* (1972), 65 *et seq.*

110 F. M. Martin, 'Worcester', 9 *et seq.*, 63; C. Lamotte, *Sermon Preached in St Martin's . . . Stamford Baron at a meeting of Gentlemen Florists and Gardeners . . .* (1740); A. F. J. Brown, *Essex People* (1972), 58.

111 See p. 184; *Gloucester Journal*, 3 June 1723; F. M. Martin, 'Worcester', 47; Chinnery, *op.cit.*, 71, 77, 92. Coventry instituted Lady Godiva's procession in 1678 (*VCH Warwicks.*, VIII, 219–20).

112 Latimer, *Bristol in the Eighteenth Century*, 63; Thorpe, *op.cit.*, 192n.; N. Boston and E. Puddy, *Dereham* (1952), 51; Hill, *Georgian Lincoln*, 15.

113 D. Defoe, *A Tour Through the Whole Island of Great Britain* (1962 edn), II, 80; G. Davies (ed.), *Autobiography of Thomas Raymond and Memoirs of the Family of Guise* (Camden Soc., 3rd ser., XXVIII, 1917), 144–5; *Gloucester Journal*, 23 April 1722; Everitt, 'Country, county and town', 95; see p. 182.

114 A. Newdigate-Newdegate, *Cavalier and Puritan in the Days of the Stuarts* (1901), 77; Gray, *op.cit.*, 136–8 (Cambridge); Lichfield Joint RO, Lichfield Hall Book 1, f. 104v; W. A. Speck, 'Brackley: a study in the growth of oligarchy', *Midland History*, III (1975), 31–8.

115 Borsay, *op.cit.*, 591–3; for the mechanics of eighteenth-century building development see Chalklin, *Provincial Towns*, 57 *et seq.*; N. Barbon, *A Discourse of Trade: 1690* (ed. J. H. Hollander, Baltimore, 1903), 32, 34.

116 Mitchell, *op.cit.*, 3 *et passim*; Everitt, *Perspectives*, 120–34; for the importance of innkeepers at Chelmsford, see M. R. Innes, 'Chelmsford: the evolution of a county town' (M.A. thesis, University of London, 1951), 363–4; and at Ashby, Moxon, *op.cit.*, 203–4.

117 Everitt, *Perspectives*, 104–113; J. A. Chartres, 'The place of inns in the commercial life of London and western England 1660–1760' (D.Phil. thesis, University of Oxford, 1973), 35, 212 *et passim*; *Gloucester Journal*, 1722 *et passim*; Latimer, *Bristol in the Eighteenth Century*, 288; for the dense network of carriers in Essex, see Burley, *op.cit.*, 214–15, 217; Chartres, *Internal Trade*, 55.

118 K. R. Adey, 'Aspects of the history of the town of Stafford 1590–1710' (M.A. thesis, University of Keele, 1971), 60; Clark, 'Civic leaders'; for lawyers' importance at Sheffield see R. E. Leader, *Sheffield in the Eighteenth Century* (1901), 190.

119 R. Robson, *The Attorney in the Eighteenth Century* (1959), chs. VI–VII; Clark, 'Civic leaders'; PRO, C 7/95/52; B. L. Anderson, 'The attorney and the early capital market in Lancashire', in J. R. Harris (ed.), *Liverpool and Merseyside* (1969), 51–74; for Hull merchants-cum-bankers see Jackson, *op.cit.*, 209–33.

120 Robson, *op.cit.*, ch. VIII; Clark, 'Civic leaders'; *List of Attornies and Solicitors admitted*

in pursuance of the late Act . . . (1729).
121 See p. 112; for physicians at Bury St Edmunds: HMC, Portland MSS, II, 265;
F. M. Valadez and C. D. O'Malley, 'James Keill of Northampton . . .', *Medical History*,
xv (1971), 317–35; Hobhouse, *op. cit.*, 26–7; Clark, 'Civic leaders'.
122 See p. 202; Thorpe, *op. cit.*, 192; P. Razzell, *The Conquest of Smallpox* (1977), 40 *et
seq.*; J. Woodward, *To do the Sick no Harm: a study of the British voluntary hospital
system to 1875* (1974), 147–8; H. Temple Smith, 'The history of the old private lunatic
asylum at Fishponds, Bristol' (M.Sc. thesis, University of Bristol, 1973), 5 *et passim*;
Gloucester Journal, 26 March 1787.
123 B. Simon (ed.), *Education in Leicestershire 1540–1940* (1968), 43–4; *VCH Beds.*, II,
167–8; *VCH Glos.*, II, 331; see also A. Smith, 'Endowed schools in the diocese of
Lichfield and Coventry 1660–99', *History of Education*, IV. 2 (1975), 13–15; *Gloucester Journal*,
11 Feb. 1723; for academies at Salisbury see *VCH Wilts.*, IV, 143; Everitt, 'Country,
county and town', 93.
124 Excise and salt officers formed part of a national service and were regularly rotated:
E. Hughes, *Studies in Administration and Finance, 1558–1825* (1934), 160 *et passim*; see
the opening-up of the civic elite at Norwich: Evans, *op. cit.*, 30–3. For more on the
gentrification of urban elites see A. Everitt, *Change in the Provinces: the seventeenth
century* (1972), 44–6.
125 See p. 182 and p. 107 *et seq.*; J. D. Marshall (ed.), *The Autobiography of William Stout of
Lancaster* (1967), 8 *et passim*; Mitchell, *op. cit.*, 310–21.
126 Dunsford, *op. cit.*, 205; Hill, *Georgian Lincoln*, 59; Jackson, *op. cit.*, 281; J. D. Marshall,
op. cit., 2 *et seq.*; R. Mortimer (ed.), *Minute Book of the Men's Meeting of the Society of
Friends in Bristol 1686–1704* (Bristol Rec. Soc., XXX, 1977), xiv *et passim*;
e.g. S. D. Chapman (ed.), *The Devon Cloth Industry in the Eighteenth Century* (Devon
and Cornwall Rec. Soc., n.s. XXIII, 1978), 3–8.
127 See p. 171 and p. 119; Clark and Slack, *English Towns*, 113–14; Cornfield, 'History',
257–60; D. Marshall, *The English Poor in the Eighteenth Century* (1926), 47, 67 *et passim*;
E. E. Butcher (ed.), *Bristol Corporation of the Poor 1696–1834* (Bristol Rec. Soc., III,
1932); D. Owen, *English Philanthropy 1660–1960* (1965), 74–6; see at Winchester
pp. 171–2; Slack, 'Social problems and social policies', 94–5; e.g. Glos. RO, St Michael's
parish, Gloucester, CWl/41 (May 1681).
128 D. C. Coleman, *The Economy of England 1450–1750* (1977), 101–3; *VCH Oxon.*, IV,
114; J. Thirsk, 'Seventeenth-century agriculture and social change' in *Land, Church and
People*, ed. J. Thirsk (1970), 162–3; D. C. Coleman, 'Labour in the English economy of
the seventeenth century' in Carus-Wilson (ed.), *op. cit.*, 303; R. Dunning, *Bread for the
Poor* (1698), 1–2; anon., *An Impartial Enquiry into the Present State of the British Distil-
lery* (1736), 27–9; anon., *A Dissertation upon Drunkenness* (?1728), 2, 5–6; J. Clayton,
Friendly Advice to the Poor (1755), 13, 17, 20.
129 HMC, Portland MSS, II, 274; Defoe, *op. cit.*, I, 43.
130 Corfield, 'History', 42–63 *et passim*; see also Clark and Slack (eds.), *Crisis and Order*,
276–95.
131 *VCH York*, 207 *et passim*; Defoe, *op. cit.*, II, 230; Macky, *op. cit.*, II, 214–15, 217;
Historical Monuments Commission, York, III (1972), lxxix *et seq.*; IV (1975), 54 *et seq.*
132 Ellis, *op. cit.*; see also E. Hughes, *North Country Life in the Eighteenth Century: the
North-East 1700–50* (1952).
133 Hoskins, *Industry, Trade and People*, 16 *et passim*; Defoe, *op. cit.*, I, 222–3.
134 W. E. Minchinton, 'Bristol – metropolis of the West in the eighteenth century' in Clark,
Early Modern Town, 297–313; Latimer, *Bristol in the Eighteenth Century*, 114 *et passim*;
E. Ralph and M. E. Williams (eds.), *The Inhabitants of Bristol in 1696* (Bristol Rec. Soc.,
XXV, 1968), xxii; W. Ison, *The Georgian Buildings of Bristol* (1952), 21 *et passim*; also
A. Gomme, M. Jenner, B. Little, *Bristol: an architectural history* (1979), 115 *et seq*;
B. Little, 'The Gloucestershire spas', in McGrath and Cannon, *op. cit.*, 170–80.

135 Defoe, *op.cit.*, I, 291; P. Mathias, *The Brewing Industry in England 1700–1830* (1959), 423; J. M. Martin, 'An investigation into the small size of the household as exemplified by Stratford-on-Avon', *Local Population Studies*, XIX (1977), 13; J. Townsend, *A History of Abingdon* (1910), 156; J. S. Burn, *A History of Henley on Thames* (1861), 10; A. C. Wood, *A History of Nottinghamshire* (1971), 224–5; Rogers, *op. cit.*, 71–2; J. Kirby, *The Suffolk Traveller* (1764 edn.), 52.

136 Anon., *A Dissertation*, 5; anon., *The London and Country Brewer: Third Part* (1738), 32, 47; Macky, *op. cit.*, II, 159; R. Cornes, 'A short topographical account of Bridgnorth', *Trans. Shropshire Arch. and Nat. History Soc.*, IX (1886), 198.

137 *VCH Northants.*, III, 29 *et passim*.

138 See p. 170; Thorpe, *op.cit.*, 189–95; Rogers, *op.cit.*, 72–3; *VCH Warwicks.*, VIII, 507, 511–13; H. B. Rodgers, 'The market area of Preston in the sixteenth and seventeenth centuries', *Geographical Studies*, III (1956), 53–4; Macky, *op.cit.*, I, 5–6, II, 132; Burley, *op.cit.*, 352, 357.

139 See pp. 201–2; for Scarborough and Weymouth see S. McIntyre, 'Towns as health and pleasure resorts: Bath, Scarborough and Weymouth 1700–1815' (D. Phil. thesis, University of Oxford, 1973), 180–395; F. J. C. Hearnshaw *et al.*, *A Short History of Southampton* (1910), 112–15. In the 1760s Stratford-on-Avon made a bid to become the country's first provincial tourist town – as Shakespeare's birth-place: L. Fox, *A Splendid Occasion: the Stratford Jubilee of 1769* (Dugdale Soc. Occasional Papers, XX, 1973).

140 Jackson, *op.cit.*, 10 *et passim*; Michell, *op.cit.*, 45 *et passim*.

141 See p. 104 *et seq.*

142 Chalklin, *Provincial Towns* 23–4; J. Laker, *History of Deal* (1917), 240, 260, 346.

143 W. Holloway, *History and Antiquities . . . of Rye* (1847), 364–6; Hearnshaw *et al.*, *op. cit.*, 106–7; *VCH Sussex*, III, 102; P. Russell, *The Good Town of Totnes* (1965), 61; C. Wanklyn, *Lyme Regis* (1927), 94–9; HMC, Portland MSS, II, 287.

144 T. C. Barker, 'Lancashire coal, Cheshire salt and the rise of Liverpool', *Trans. Hist. Soc. Lancs. and Cheshire*, CIII (1952), 83–101; F. E. Hyde, *Liverpool and the Mersey: an economic history of a port* (1971), chs. 1–3; P. G. E. Clemens, 'The rise of Liverpool, 1665–1750', *EcHR*, N.S. XXIX (1976), 211–25.

145 J. E. Williams, 'Whitehaven in the eighteenth century', *EcHR*, N.S. VIII (1955–6), 393–404; J. D. Marshall, *Stout*, 26–30; Mitchell, *op.cit.*, 29, 116–17, 254.

146 Adey, *Midland History*, 164–7; Defoe, *op.cit.*, I, 114–15, 118; Coleman, 'Economy of Kent', 14, 239 *et seq.*

147 Hearnshaw *et al.*, *op.cit.*, 112–15; Hill, *Georgian Lincoln*, 138–9, 146–8.

148 Chartres, 'The marketing of agricultural produce'; Patten, *op.cit.* 218–20; Willan, *Inland Trade*, 89–100; Leics. RO, Finch MSS, PP 159; Mitchell, *op.cit.*; 193–9; Edwards, *op.cit.*, 92–3.

149 Rath, *op.cit.*, 141–8; *VCH Glos.*, XI, 99, 120–30; H. J. Francis, *A History of Hinckley* (1930), 86, 111–12; A. Randall, *The Kettering Worsted Industry of the Eighteenth Century* (n.d.). 4–14; *VCH Northants.*, II, 337; G. F. R. Spenceley, 'The origins of the English pillow lace industry', *AgHR.*, XXI (1973), esp. 85–6.

150 G. Hart, *A History of Cheltenham* (1965), chs. 10–11; also McGrath and Cannon, *op. cit.*, 180–99; M. Barton, *Tunbridge Wells* (1937), 67 *et seq.*; also C. W. Chalklin, 'The making of some new towns, c. 1600–1720', in Chalklin and Havinden (eds.), *op.cit.*, 233–4, 248–50.

151 B. Austen, *English Provincial Posts 1633–1840* (1978), 17–24; Dorset RO, B7/D2/1; M. Yearsley (ed.), *The Diary of the Visits of John Yeoman to London* (1934), 38; for more of these decayed market towns in Suffolk see Kirby, *op. cit.*, 116 *et passim*.

152 For one bad fit of market counting see A. D. Dyer, 'The market towns of southern England 1500–1700', *Southern History*, I (1979), 125–34. The failure of various new markets in seventeenth-century Cumbria to achieve 'take-off' is noted in Chalklin and Havinden (eds.), *op.cit.*, 214–16; Chartres, 'The marketing of agricultural produce'; for

Hampshire see pp. 173–4; for Lancashire, Rodgers, *op.cit.*, 55; for East Anglia, Patten, *op.cit.*, 292–4; see also Michell, *op.cit.*, ch. iv.
153 D. G. D. Isaac, 'A study of popular disturbance in Britain 1715–54' (Ph.D. thesis, University of Edinburgh, 1953), 57–70; Glos. RO, GBR 1386/1461, fos. 181v, 209a; 1387/1462 *passim*; Pawson, *op. cit.*, 180.
154 Corfield, 'History', 293–333; Randall, *op. cit.*, 17; Chapman, *op. cit.*, xix–xx; Rath, *op. cit.*, 148–51; Dunsford, *op. cit.*, 245–9; D. E. Williams, 'English hunger riots in 1766' (Ph.D. thesis, University of Wales, 1978), 32 *et passim*; R. F. Wearmouth, *Methodism and the Common People of the Eighteenth Century* (1945), 24–8, 30–6, 70 *et passim*.

The social problems of
an Elizabethan country town:
Warwick, 1580–90

A. L. BEIER

The social problems of
an Elizabethan country town:
Warwick, 1580–90

A. L. BEIER

1 Introduction

Sixteenth-century states gave unprecedented attention to the problem of the poor. They attempted to suppress beggars, organized indoor relief for the 'impotent' poor, put the able-bodied to work and punished the unruly.[1] The typical laboratory for the control of Europe's poor was the town: from Henry VIII's reign onwards English towns made censuses of the poor, licensed local beggars and expelled 'foreign' ones; after the Reformation towns began to levy taxation to support the local poor.[2] Towns were of course not the sole initiators of action. Parliamentary regulation of begging began in the fourteenth century, surveys of the impotent poor were required by statute in 1531, and taxation for putting vagrants to work was proposed to Parliament in 1536.[3] Towns were in the vanguard, nevertheless, of efforts to control the poor in the sixteenth century.

The study of the urban poor has made great strides in recent years. A start has been made in discovering who they were: hospital, judicial and census records have been used to uncover a wide range of facts about the local and vagrant poor, who as a result are less of a faceless mob than they previously appeared. Historians have also studied the causes of urban poverty in early modern Europe. Le Roy Ladurie singled out the years between 1526 and 1536 as a 'tournant social' in which exceptional famine conditions prompted new measures to deal with the poor, and Pullan's findings for Venice and Davis's for Lyons implicitly confirm this thesis. In England short-term crises similarly triggered official action at Norwich in 1570 and at Salisbury in 1604, 1625 and 1635.[4]

Historians have examined cultural and religious influences upon efforts to control the poor. This research has seen a turn away from older interpretations that stressed the differences between Catholics and Protestants. Broadly speaking, differences in attitudes toward begging and the participation of the state and laity in poor relief are thought to be in degree rather than kind. The prevailing attitude, common to Protestants and Roman Catholics, was an Erasmian humanism, which was critical of begging and favoured lay activism in the control of the poor.[5]

Studies of the urban poor have concentrated on the great cities and regional capitals; not surprisingly, because large towns are usually the best documented. Yet there are points in favour of studying country towns such as Warwick, which had only about 2,500 people in 1580. A town of Warwick's size is more typical of English urban communities of the period than the national and regional capitals. In 1700 almost 90 per cent of England's 800 towns with markets still had fewer than 2,000 inhabitants.[6] Certainly Warwick shared some of the special problems of sixteenth-century towns: a sluggish economy, population growth, immigration, political weakness and financial embarrassment. These conditions meant that Elizabethan Warwick, like many other towns, had a major poverty problem.[7]

The present study began life as part of a doctoral thesis on the poor of sixteenth- and seventeenth-century Warwickshire, which was submitted to Princeton University in 1969.[8] The original aim of the research was to study the poor at local level, on the principle that the problem of the poor, a central issue in sixteenth- and seventeenth-century social history, might be better understood through a monographic approach. Histories of the English poor law were largely compilations of statutes and literary evidence, and no studies existed relating the poverty problem to local economic and demographic conditions.[9] A census of Warwick's poor in 1587 seemed a good basis for a study of the poor in Elizabethan times.[10]

I began research with the ambition of writing a 'total history' of the poor in an English town, inspired partly by historians of the *Annales* school, who had on occasion been remarkably successful in documenting the lives of the mass of humanity.[11] Chastened somewhat by fruitless searches for source materials, I still believe that the effort was worth making: it opened up a wide range of sources, and also made me confront the issue of whether history can be understood without reference to the thoughts of people living it, because however much data I collected for my 'total history' there remained a nagging doubt that I was not answering one vital question; what was worse, that I could not answer it with the data I had assembled. That question was, why were the poor treated as they were in the sixteenth century – the itinerant poor arrested and punished, the local poor discouraged from begging and given indoor relief based on taxation? This treatment of the poor had medieval antecedents, but it was first widely enforced in Europe in the sixteenth century.[12] In the end, because local sources were largely silent on the issue, I had limited success in dealing with this normative question.

Many 'national' studies of course fail to resolve normative issues. One advantage of the local monograph is that it can provide a microcosm of national developments. Thus at Warwick we can see the economic and demographic conditions that created a poverty problem in an Elizabethan country town (Section 2). We can learn something about the lives of the urban poor: their family- and age-structures, and who was most likely to become poor; how harvest failure affected the numbers of the poor; their health and mobility; and where the itinerant poor originated, their occupations and crimes (Section 3). We can observe, too, how the dissolutions of monasteries, almshouses and hospitals during the 1530s and 1540s affected a country town, its finances and poor relief facilities. We can test the argument that the dissolutions were not a major cause of sixteenth-century urban poverty; and we can see how far the new Protestant philanthropy met the needs of the poor, and how different in form was post-Reformation from pre-Reformation charity (Section 4). Finally, we can see how the authorities, including two of Elizabethan England's leading puritans, attempted to deal with the poverty problem, and assess to what extent they had a 'new medicine for poverty' (Section 5).

Ten years have allowed me to make substantial amendments to the original manuscript. The major additional research includes probate inventories and wills, which increase our knowledge of the local economy. I have also attempted to trace all pre-Reformation charitable foundations and have made a study of charity to the poor in Warwick wills of the sixteenth and seventeenth centuries. Finally, material has been added dealing with the itinerant poor, since the authorities were as much concerned with them as with the local poor. The text has been largely rewritten.

2 Economic problems

Elizabethan Warwick faced a poverty problem because of long-term economic and demographic changes. Although it was a major market and political centre in Warwickshire in medieval and early modern times, the town experienced economic decline relative to her West Midland neighbours in the late Middle Ages. In the sixteenth century Warwick's population grew considerably, but the result was severe poverty because the economy remained sluggish. Only after 1660, when the town increasingly became a centre of service trades for the county gentry, was Warwick's economy to prosper.

Warwick was a major military and political centre in the Middle Ages and the early modern period. It was 'in the very navel and midst almost of the whole province [England]', equidistant, as Camden noted, from the Norfolk coast and the west coast of Wales. Warwick and Kenilworth were links in a chain of fortified places in the West Midlands forming a barrier against invasion from the north and west. Warwick was also the county town. As the administrative centre of the shire since the thirteenth century, Warwick regularly witnessed the concourses of quarter sessions and the assizes. Although never a front-rank town like Coventry and Worcester, Warwick remained the leading town in the county, politically and socially, in the sixteenth century.[13]

Warwick's economic performance never equalled its political and social pre-eminence in the Middle Ages, and at the end of the period the town was in decline economically. In the thirteenth century it seemed hardly to grow, in contrast to other urban centres in the West Midlands. While Coventry, Birmingham, Gloucester, and Worcester experienced nascent industrial development, Warwick saw little or none. The 20 occupational surnames in the Hundred Rolls of 1279 suggest no significant growth in industry. The town was apparently unattractive to immigrants in the period, drawing but one-quarter of its recorded population from elsewhere, while at Stratford-on-Avon, Coventry, and Bristol the proportion was between one-third and a half. The number of moderately well-to-do persons assessed for the 1332 lay subsidy seems to have been smaller at Warwick than at Stratford-on-Avon. There were signs of cloth, cord, and iron manufacture in the thirteenth century, but the industries were of no lasting importance.[14] Warwick's economic fortunes declined during the fourteenth and fifteenth centuries. There was some trade in cloth after 1350 and possibly some fulling mills on the Avon, but the trade remained small compared with Coventry's or even Birmingham's. By 1413 a three-day fair at Michaelmas had to be transferred to St Bartholomew because it conflicted with neighbouring fairs and yielded no profits.[15]

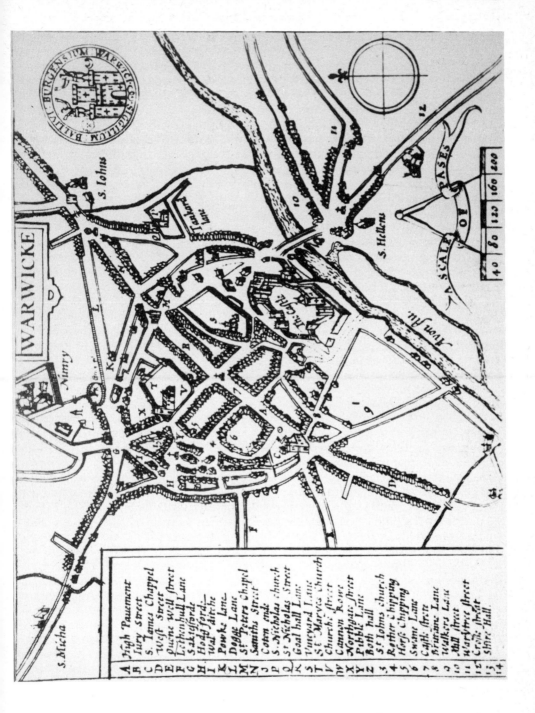

Figure 1. Warwick in the reign of James I (from John Speed's map).

In the sixteenth century Warwick was an important market town in the county, because it was located between two distinct agricultural areas, the wood/pasture Arden to the north and the mixed-farming Felden to the south. In the bad harvest of 1586–7 Warwick was the entrepôt for the grain trade from the Felden to north Warwickshire and Worcestershire towns and villages. In 1656 the town's horse fair drew buyers and sellers from Worcestershire and Oxfordshire. On the other hand, most visitors to its fairs and markets came from the county itself, and Warwick never developed into a great cattle or grain mart as did Market Harborough and Shrewsbury.[16] Moreover, the town had none of the advantages of communications of her rivals in the West Midlands – no navigable river, as had Gloucester and Worcester, and no proximity to major roads, as had Birmingham, Stratford-on-Avon and Coventry. The Avon was not navigable to Warwick until the eighteenth century, and the nearest main arteries lay at some distance – a disadvantage still complained of in the 1630s.[17]

A further possible reason for Warwick's economic stagnation was that it was surrounded by large estates: the Castle estate with over 500 acres in the vicinity of the town by the early fourteenth century, as well as 200 houses in the town itself; the estate of the priory of St Sepulchre which after dissolution remained intact in private hands until the mid-nineteenth century; and St Mary's college, which held lands in the suburbs as well as 50 houses in the town. Although the earls of Warwick had sought to boost the town's economy since the thirteenth century, the continued existence of their own and other large estates probably hindered the growth of independent craft and industrial elements in Warwick.[18] When growth came in the seventeenth century, it was significantly in the professional and service sectors of the economy. Already in 1599 we find county gentry families keeping rooms at the Swan. By the mid-seventeenth century one or two families had had town houses built in Warwick. The movement of gentlemen and the professions into the town, especially noticeable when it was rebuilt after the fire of 1694, transformed Warwick's society. A community made up formerly of husbandmen, mercers and tradesmen became a gentleman's town.[19]

Warwick's economic weakness was reflected by a long history of political subservience, to its earls and then to the local gentry. From the thirteenth through to the sixteenth century Warwick was almost continuously run by its earls.[20] The town's weakness vis-à-vis the landed classes was augmented by the loss of its church lands in the dissolutions of the 1530s and 1540s. In 1545 there was a flicker of independence when the town was incorporated, at a time, significantly, when the earldom was in abeyance. But with the advent of the Dudleys under Edward VI and Elizabeth, Warwick slipped easily into its old subservience again. For the Dudleys held the recordership, which included the power to chose burgesses and the final word in local affairs. They had a steward and a bailiff to represent them in the town, nominated their kinsmen for Parliament, and were consulted over financial problems. They visited the town in lordly array and, after a small affront in 1571, bullied the corporation into granting them its burgesses' hall. When the family's leading Elizabethan scions, Robert, earl of Leicester, and his brother Ambrose, earl of Warwick, died without legitimate heirs in 1588 and 1590, the town was briefly free of patrons. In the following decades it became the gentry's town. From having one master Warwick came to have many, who turned the town into their political battleground in the seventeenth century.[21]

In the 1570s, only a generation after its incorporation, Warwick had had to resort to Robert Dudley, earl of Leicester, the queen's favourite, for help with the town's serious economic difficulties. Warwick's problems were in the first instance financial, but they stemmed partly, as the burgesses acknowledged, from the lack of any local economic thrust. The major problem was the cost of maintaining at borough expense the local ecclesiastical establishment, the legacy of the Reformation and incorporation in 1545. The borough's chance to gain a patron came in 1571 when Leicester was given authority to set up a hospital at Warwick or Kenilworth. In their anxiety to have the hospital at Warwick, the burgesses almost bungled the job. They put themselves at an immediate disadvantage when they failed to meet Leicester upon his arrival in the town in early September.[22] In comic disarray, amidst profuse apologies, they were obliged to grant their own burgesses' hall (formerly the Guild of Holy Trinity and St George) to Leicester for the hospital. At a meeting in November they wrote him a letter granting the hall and at the same time requesting his aid in shoring up the town's finances. John Fisher, the earl's steward, who was a Dudley minion, the deputy recorder, a principal burgess, sometime M.P. and bailiff, was to deliver the letter and 'to impart unto your Lordship not only our poor estate, but also some ways how by your most honourable means the same may be relieved'. The burgesses clearly wanted a *quid pro quo* for their hall; nor was their plea of poverty baseless.[23]

In November, Fisher personally took the letter to Leicester at Greenwich, and their conversation shows Warwick in the doldrums. After a discussion of town finances and the clergy, Leicester 'asked what good trade there was in the said town whereby men gained, and how the poor were relieved'. Fisher's response was in dark tones: 'the number of the poor was great and they were relieved only by the charitable devotion of the inhabitants'. There were weekly collections in the church under the Act of 1563 and 'meat and drink at diverse persons according to every man's ability', but this relief was proving insufficient. From Fisher's remarks it appears that the poor were already a problem in 1571.[24]

Fisher's account of the local economic situation suggests that Warwick had not progressed much since the fifteenth century: 'touching any great trade there was none to be reckoned of, but the most part of men were provided of corn and had some husbandry, which was the chiefest maintenance of their poor housekeeping'. Warwick's distributive traders apparently did not prosper greatly from the general expansion of inland trade during the period. The most important were the mercers, who dealt in spices, and the drapers, in the linen cloth trade. But these trades were centuries old at Warwick and no longer expanding. Next in importance was malt-making, presumably for beer, 'whereby of late years good gains have arisen, though now not so profitably'. Leicester seized upon the idea of malt-making and cited the example of an Essex town where four or five entrepreneurs had specialized in the trade, enriched the place and were each worth £1–2,000 a year. But Fisher's comment that this trade was now declining scotched that idea.[25]

Next the earl suggested that the town establish a 'special trade' to employ the poor, such as cloth- or cap-making, and offered financial assistance. Fisher replied that several townsmen had indeed attempted to manufacture cloth, but had failed because of lack of capital and skilled labour. Now the cloth trade was 'not greatly enjoyed because of the damp and stop of intercourse', which was an accurate statement in 1571 judging by the depressed levels of London exports.[26]

John Fisher's picture of the economy of Elizabethan Warwick is corroborated by other sources. Probate records, although not normally including the poor, apprentices and servants, confirm Fisher's impressions of a country town with little commercial and industrial development. Husbandry accounted for almost a third of the occupations in inventories and wills (see table 2). Next in importance were leather-workers (glovers, shoemakers, tanners, skinners, saddlers, curriers), making up roughly a fifth, followed by victualling, cloth-making mercers and drapers, and miscellaneous trades. Lists of craftsmen in the town in 1586–7 confirm the importance of leather-workers, showing them far in the lead with almost half of the work-force.[27]

Table 2   Occupations in Tudor Warwick*

OCCUPATIONS	1543–70		1571–1602	
	no.	%	no.	%
husbandry	24	30.8	23	27.4
leather trades	17	21.8	18	21.4
woodworking	3	3.8	2	2.4
mercers and drapers	6	7.7	9	10.7
metalworkers	5	6.4	1	1.2
victualling	9	11.5	11	13.1
cloth-making	7	9.0	8	9.5
furnishing	2	2.6	3	3.6
building	0	0.0	4	4.7
professions and services	3	3.8	0	0.0
labourers	0	0.0	3	3.6
servants	2	2.6	2	2.4
	78	100.0	84	100.0

Sources: Warwick wills in PRO; wills and inventories in Hereford and Worcester RO, Worcester.
*'Yeomen' and 'gentlemen' have not been included unless clearly engaged in an occupation.

Warwick's economy stagnated for much of the period up to 1660. The leather crafts reached their outward limit of expansion in the early Elizabethan years, possibly because of competition from other Midlands towns. In 1571 'certain poor men' petitioned the burgesses to relax entrance into leather trades, but thereafter the industry ceased to grow. The most numerous group, the tanners, lived in the poorest wards by this time.[28] Husbandry continued to be the town's leading occupation up to 1602, judging by wills and inventories, whereas at neighbouring Leicester the evidence of inventories shows the numbers of husbandmen falling by 40 per cent after 1560, while the numbers of textile-workers were rising considerably. There was no shift of equivalent proportions at Warwick.[29]

What Warwick's stagnation meant in practice is seen in the values of inhabitants' goods when they died. For much of the sixteenth century, especially from 1544 to 1584, the value of their goods rose little or even fell, depending upon whether the mean average or median is used. In real terms, because of price inflation, the value undoubtedly fell (table 3).[30] Over the period from 1544 to 1652 it is doubtful whether the value of inhabitants' possessions, which included agricultural produce and livestock as well as less inflation-prone household goods, kept pace with price rises. Compared with some Arden parishes, Warwick's economy performed badly. In the mid-sixteenth century, town inventories were worth on average 50 per cent more than those of Arden peasants, but by the end of the century the values of Arden inventories were as high as or higher than the town ones.[31]

Warwick did not remain in the doldrums forever. Three new fairs more than doubled the number of fair days in the town in the seventeenth century. In the late seventeenth and eighteenth centuries the town became a social and service centre for the gentry and professions, and the economy became more diversified. In 1660 there were about 30 trades represented in the town, by 1694 there were 50, and by the late eighteenth century almost 90. Even its rejuvenation in this 'urban renaissance' was inspired, significantly, by the landed classes rather than by local industrial growth. Industry came late to Warwick and then only briefly.[32]

Warwick's economic stagnation in the sixteenth century meant that the people supposed to relieve the poor were losing ground. In addition, a stagnant economy could not keep the poor employed. As the population grew and the traditional means of relief diminished, poverty accelerated.

Table 3 Values of testators' goods in Tudor and early Stuart Warwick

decade	no. testators	mean average value*		median value	
		£	s.	£	s.
1544–53	35	27		19	10
1554–63	78	28		19	10
1564–73	27	26	10	17	
1574–83	38	32	10	13	
1584–93	39	41		31	10
1594–1603	44	48		27	
1604–13	39	37	10	25	
1614–23	32	58	10	38	10
1624–33	42	42		33	10

Source: Warwick inventories in Hereford and Worcester RO, Worcester.
*Rounded to nearest 10s.

Warwick contained about 1,700 inhabitants in 1544, which was not many more than were recorded in 1086. But the town grew considerably in the sixteenth and seventeenth centuries. By 1563 the population was close to 2,000, by 1586 it was 2,500, in 1670 over 2,800, and in 1730 above 4,300. If the town roughly doubled in population from 1500 to 1700, almost half of that growth was concentrated in the 40 years from 1544 to 1586. This remarkable expansion can be documented at parish level. Warwick contained two parishes, St Mary's, which lies within the walls, and St Nicholas, outside. St Mary's was the larger and faster growing of the two. Its population may have increased by over two-thirds from 1544 to 1586. In 1544 St Mary's had perhaps 1,100 inhabitants (230 households); in 1563 it had about 1,400 (288 households) and in 1586, 1,900 (398 households). Even if the 1544 figure, which is the most suspect, were on the low side by 200 inhabitants the parish's growth from 1544 to 1586 would still approach 50 per cent. From 1563 to 1586 alone, when the sources are better, the increase was close to 40 per cent.[33]

Warwick's growth was partly fuelled by immigration: almost one in ten of the poor in 1587 were recent arrivals. But natural increase was also important. St Nicholas' parish registers show baptisms continually in excess of burials from 1540 to 1556, which was the longest such run between 1540 and 1680. The decade of 1541–50 had the greatest surplus of baptisms for the period to 1680 and the fifth highest total in the 14 decades. Since St Mary's was the healthier of the two parishes when comparable records exist in the next century, we can assume that the central parish, too, experienced natural increase at this time (figs. 2–4).[34]

The pattern of growth of Warwick's population can partly be explained by national events. It is thought that England's population rose by as much as a fifth between 1522 and 1545 and by another third from 1545 to 1603, despite major set-backs in the 1550s and 1590s.[35] A major mortality crisis hit the country in the late 1550s, caused it seems by a severe influenza epidemic, and at Warwick mortality in the years 1557–9 was more than double the average for 1547–56: 44 burials, per annum as against 18 per annum in St Nicholas parish (fig. 2). In the diocese of Worcester, in which Warwick was located, the mean number of wills proved during the years 1556–8 was four times the average of the previous five years.[36]

The population recovered in the following decades on the wings of long runs of good harvests and infrequent epidemics: the 1560s were an improvement on the 1550s, the 1570s on the 1560s, and the 1580s on the 1570s.[37] Without the intervention of crises of mortality, of which there is no sign in Warwick in the 1560s and 1570s, the population burgeoned. The increase in St Mary's households between 1563 and 1586 is evidence of this growth; so is the rising number of baptisms over burials from 1571 to 1576. The dissolutions of religious houses, too, may have hastened growth by putting property on the market and making more housing available. Warwick saw a steady trickle of leases and sales of former church properties to local people after the initial grants and sales of the 1530s and 1540s. But in the 1570s and 1580s population growth created severe economic and social problems in the town.[38]

3   The dimensions of poverty

Sixteenth-century legislation divided the poor into those who would not work – vagrants, 'sturdy beggars' or 'masterless men' – and those who could not. The former, usually 'foreign' to a place, were to be punished, sent away, and put to work in their home parishes; the latter, the local beggars, should be provided with indoor relief by public subscription or taxation. Though sixteenth-century practice never followed rigorously these legal definitions, they do have a broad validity for Warwick in the 1580s.[39]

Warwick was only a middle-sized country town in the sixteenth century, but its poverty problem still reached dimensions that required official intervention. In the 1580s the authorities took action against the vagrant poor who came to the town and against local paupers who begged in the street. Wanderers from the four corners of England were arrested, and hundreds of local paupers – one in nine of the town's families in good times and one in four in bad – were cleared from the streets, enumerated in censuses, and ordered to be relieved in their homes from public rates.

There were 113 itinerants arrested at Warwick from 1580 to 1587. Although an average of less than 20 a year, they should not be dismissed lightly. They are unlikely to represent the whole itinerant population that came to the town, because there are gaps in the records and because magistrates probably arrested only the most trouble-some and suspicious. Certainly it is doubtful whether officials caught all offenders, who were defined in the following, broad terms: 'all and every person and persons being whole and mighty in body and able to labour, having not land or master, nor using any lawful merchandise, craft or mystery whereby he or she might get his or her living, and can give no reckoning how he or she does lawfully get his or her living.'[40]

The vagrant poor came to Warwick from all points of the compass. The largest numbers came from neighbouring Midland counties and the majority from within 50

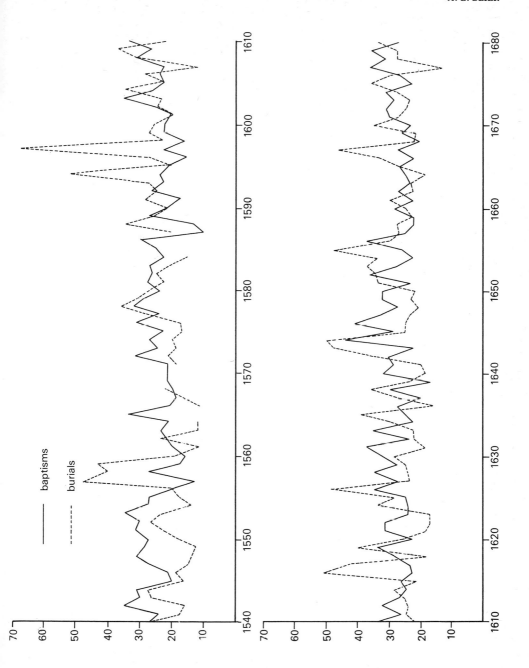

Figure 2. St Nicholas parish, Warwick: baptisms and burials, 1540–1680.

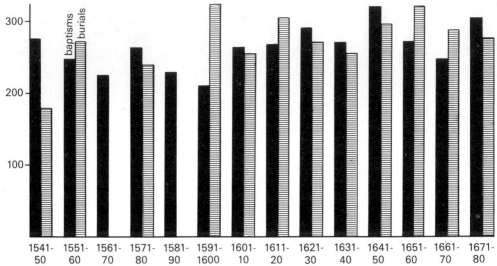

Figure 3. St Nicholas parish, Warwick: baptisms and burials, 1540–1680, by decades.

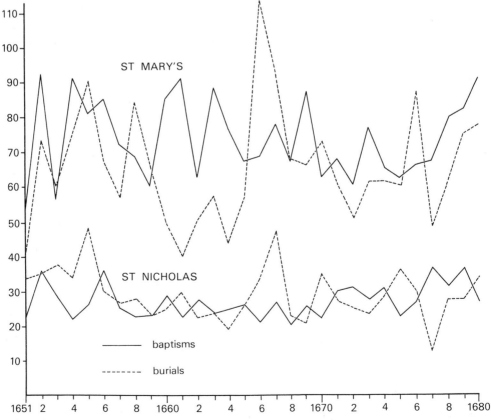

Figure 4. St Mary's and St Nicholas parishes, Warwick: baptisms and burials, 1650–80.

miles of the town as the crow flies; but considerable numbers also came from the North-West, South-West and South-East, some originated in London, Berwick-upon-Tweed and Wales, and a few had been abroad to Ireland and Flanders (table 4): The 74 vagrants who reported their wanderings in detail to magistrates, although averaging only about two miles a day, had recently covered over 8,000 miles.[41] Fewer than two-fifths could lay claim to any permanent 'home', and a number of these had last lived in service rather than in a family of their own. Warwick's vagrants, if not foreign to the area, were clearly footloose.

*Table 4   Places of origin of itinerants arrested in Warwick, 1580–7**

SOUTH-EAST†	no.	%	NORTH-WEST	no.	%
London and Middx.	4		Lancs.	11	
Herts.	2		Cheshire	4	
Surrey	1		total	15	13.3
total	7	6.2			
			SOUTH-WEST		
SOUTH AND WEST			Somerset	3	
Oxon.	4		Devon	3	
Bucks.	4		total	6	5.3
Glos.	11				
total	19	16.8	EAST ANGLIA		
			Cambs.	1	
EAST MIDLANDS			Norfolk	1	
Warwicks.	28		total	2	1.8
Northants.	4				
Leics.	1		EASTERN ENGLAND		
Notts.	1		Lincs.	1	
total	34	30.0	Yorks.	6	
			total	7	6.2
WEST MIDLANDS					
Worcs.	7		NORTH-EAST		
Salop	2		Northumb.	2	1.8
Herefords.	3		IRELAND	1	0.9
Staffs.	3				
Derbys.	3		WALES	2	1.8
total	18	15.9	grand total	113	100.0

Source: T. Kemp (ed.), *The Book of John Fisher, 1580–88* (n.d.), *passim*.
*Places of birth or last residence.
†The regional breakdown here follows roughly that in J. Thirsk, 'The farming regions of England' in *The Agrarian History of England and Wales*, IV, *1500–1640*, ed. J. Thirsk (1967).

Vagrancy in the sixteenth century was a serious matter. Before 1572 vagrants were whipped and had their ears bored. From 1572 repeat offenders were felons without benefit of clergy. Vagrants, including women, were occasionally hanged for the offence.[42] The authorities saw vagrancy as a Pandora's Box. A royal proclamation of Henry VII's reign blamed an increase in murders, robberies, theft, and the decay of tillage on 'idleness; and specially of vagabonds, beggars able to work'. To Edmund Dudley, writing in 1509, idleness was 'the very mother of all vice . . . , and lineal grandame of poverty and misery, and the deadly enemy of this tree of common-wealth'.[43]

The Warwick authorities accused itinerants of a myriad of offences large and small

– not only vagrancy and roguery but also theft, vandalism, drunkenness, brawling and recusancy. Almost half of those arrested were never charged because nothing could be proved against them, and there is little evidence of the gangs of vagrants portrayed in the contemporary 'rogue literature'. The largest group numbered six or seven persons, but they were not a permanent gang. Nor were they engaged in crimes other than wandering. A majority of itinerants claimed to have occupations. To magistrates, though, they fitted the stereotype of 'masterless men': unemployed, employed in dubious trades as tinkers or pedlars, unsettled and disorderly.[44] When a Bedworth collier got drunk in the town on a Saturday night in 1581, the disorder was obvious. But it was also the masterless man's *perceived potential* for disorder that led to his arrest. Contemporaries considered the able-bodied unemployed to be dangerous. The masterless man was synonymous with all imaginable disorders, a metaphor for chaos in the minds of social and political thinkers from Edmund Dudley to Thomas Hobbes. Local authorities were hostile to vagrants because they might commit crimes, or stay and burden the town's poor rates, but that was only part of the story.[45]

Elizabethan Warwick also faced a disturbing growth in the local pauper population. Private charity proved insufficient to relieve them, and there was a major crisis in the corporation before public action was taken. The problem first emerged in John Fisher's account of the town's poverty in his meeting with the earl of Leicester in 1571. A decade later in 1582 a poor rate was levied in St Mary's parish, and one in every nine families was given relief. During the harvest failure of 1586–7 one in every four may have needed relief (tables 5, 6).[46]

Table 5   The social structure of St Mary's parish, Warwick, 1582*

| WARDS | NUMBER OF FAMILIES | | | |
	paying poor rate	maintaining selves; unable to help others	ready to decay into poverty	given relief
High Pavement	24	14	0	1	
Castle Street	12	15	7	1	
Jury Street	11	10	5	1	
Market Place	36	44	22	17	
Saltisford	3	41	26	8	
West Street	13	40	8	12	
Friar Lane	0	0	0	2	
totals	99	164	68	42	373
share of total parish families (%)	26.5	44.0	18.2	11.3	100.0

Source: T. Kemp (ed.), *The Book of John Fisher, 1580–88* (n.d.) 81–94.
*A total of 373 families for St Mary's parish in 1582 is on the low side, considering that the parish had 398 *households* in 1586 (p. 53 above). The disparity is possibly explained by faulty recording in 1582. Whatever the case, the 1582 figure is adopted above in reckoning proportions of poor families on the grounds that it has the merit of arising from evidence dealing with the poor.

Warwick's example shows the difficulties of counting the poor. For one thing, those given relief were not the only poor people in St Mary's parish in 1582. They were simply the poorest. Eleven per cent of the parish's families received relief, but another 18 per cent were listed as 'ready to decay' into poverty. The latter were considered able to support themselves at a low standard in good harvest years such as 1582 (table 4).[47] But some of them slipped into poverty and required the town's assistance when the harvest failed in 1586. Taken together, those on relief and those 'ready to decay' formed the ranks of the poor in 1582, making up almost a third of all families in St Mary's.

Table 6   Harvest failure and the poor: St Mary's parish, Warwick, 1582 and 1587

WARDS	NUMBER OF FAMILIES	
	given relief 1582	in census of poor, 1587
High Pavement	1	0
Castle Street	1	3
Jury Street	1	1
Market Place	17	22
Saltisford	8	32
West Street	12	22
ward uncertain	0	13
Friar Lane	2	0
totals	42	93

Source: T. Kemp (ed.) *The Book of John Fisher, 1580–88* (n.d.), 93–4, 165–72.

Above the poor on the social scale were a middle group accounting for 44 per cent of St Mary's parish who were 'thought able to maintain their households without help of others' relief [and] upon their own labours', but unable to give relief to the poor. They were the town's small craftsmen, shopkeepers and husbandmen, its largest economic group. The families who could contribute to the poor rate in 1582 accounted for 26 per cent of the total. They were the parish's wealthy mercers, grocers, haberdashers, successful craftsmen and traders (table 5).

Another difficulty in counting the local poor is that their lives were so unstable. Half of the poor of 1582 had disappeared by 1587 through death and migration. Economic crises swelled the numbers of paupers overnight. In 1586 and 1587 trade depression and harvest failure caused widespread distress in England. At Warwick in 1587 the numbers of pauper families had more than doubled over 1582. There was widespread begging in the streets and possibly high mortality.[48]

Harvest failure was the most devastating element in the crisis of 1586–7 at Warwick. Wheat prices in England at large were 42 per cent above the 31-year moving average for 1586, but the Midlands were harder hit. At Warwick in January 1587, prices for best wheat were 74 per cent above the moving average, while at Stratford-on-Avon the crisis was still more severe, with best wheat 82 per cent above the average. Even worse hit was Nottingham, where in September and October 1586 the best wheat was 96 per cent above the average and where between September 1585 and September 1586 the best wheat rose 140 per cent, from 2s. 6d. a bushel to 6s. a bushel. By contrast, the year-to-year increase nationally was only 31 per cent.[49] One possible result of the harvest failure at Warwick was a mortality crisis, suggested by a fall in baptisms in St Nicholas parish to their lowest level for the entire period from 1540 to 1680.[50]

The Warwick authorities made a census of the poor needing relief in 1587. While in 1582 there were 42 families on relief in St Mary's, now five years later there were

93 in need, of whom 47 had at least one member begging (table 6). Of 240 resident members of these families, 103 or 43 per cent were begging, most of them children. The families who joined the ranks of the needy in 1587 included 13 who had been 'ready to decay' and 11 'thought able to maintain their households' in 1582. Thus some of the marginal and middle groups of the population in normal times became poverty-stricken in bad times. Warwick's example suggests that the numbers of the poor fluctuated greatly from year to year.[51]

Who were the poor? Although the vagrant poor were footloose, it is easier to document their lives than local paupers'. This is because magistrates examined vagrants as suspected felons, inquiring into their places of origin and last residence, family, working and marital histories, crimes, companions and haunts on the road. From examinations one can build up a portrait of the Elizabethan vagrant that has greater verisimilitude than the broad, sensationalist strokes of the rogue literature. The vagrant was usually young and male, typically the product of service or apprenticeship in a town, rootless and cut off from settled family and work, and prone to petty crime, especially theft.[52]

It is more difficult to discover much about the local poor. The census at Warwick in 1587 provides no information about their occupations. Nevertheless, we know something about their comings and goings, family structure, ages, and living conditions. The pauper population of Warwick was volatile. Of 42 families on the relief rolls in 1582, only 22 were left in 1587. Since it is unlikely that they were removed from the relief rolls in a famine year, they must have died or left the town. The turn-over of almost 50 per cent of Warwick's poor in a matter of five years is twice as high as for the seventeenth-century village populations at Clayworth and Cogenhoe, but perhaps not surprising considering that the evidence concerns the most desperate section of the population.[53]

The family structure of the poor appears simple. The 93 families in the survey of 1587 numbered 245 persons, or a mean size of 2.6 persons per family. When household size is calculated, which includes lodgers or 'inmates', the mean is 3.3 persons. The poor household was significantly smaller than households in the community at large. At Poole in 1574 the mean size for the town was 5.3 and at Stafford in 1622, 4.1. As in the rest of the population, there is no sign among poor households of Peter Laslett's 'large joint or extended' families.[54]

But to say that the typical pauper household was small and contained no more than a nuclear family is not to say very much. In fact, the pauper household is more interesting than this. Its small size was a clear indication of poverty. Pauper households were small because they contained fewer servants and children than the rest of the population. The reason was that they could not afford to keep them. Moreover, the authorities positively discouraged the poor from keeping their children by requiring poor youngsters to take up service in better-off households. Thus the incidence of both servants and children rose as one ascended the social scale.[55] Another striking fact about the pauper population is the large number of women. Adult women outnumbered men by two to one at Warwick in 1587 and were in a majority as heads of households. In a 'normal' population in pre-industrial England women were in a bare majority and headed households in only about one in six cases.[56]

Why were women so numerous among the poor? Women paupers may have lived longer than men. One in every eight of Warwick's adult women paupers was a widow (11 out of 84). Women were also abandoned by men: at Warwick the proportion was one in 12 (7 out of 84). Another 13 women paupers had children but no husbands present. All told, over a third of the town's pauper women had been married and/or had children, but were without husbands. By contrast, only one or two men were widowers or wifeless and responsible for children. The conclusion is inescapable that a high incidence of deaths of partners and desertion left considerable numbers of women in poverty and that among the poor far more typical than nuclear families were fragments of families, headed by women.[57]

Another major exception to the nuclear family among paupers were lodgers or 'inmates'. Again, lodgers reflected the poverty of these households: not only could they not afford to keep servants and children, they had to take in lodgers to make ends meet. Censuses of English communities from the sixteenth to the nineteenth century show that almost a tenth of the population were lodgers, and that roughly a fifth of households contained them.[58] Lodgers were common among the urban poor, judging by Warwick's example. About a third of the town's poor were inmates (70 of 233 cases). Nearly a quarter of pauper households had inmates in 1587, and 45 per cent of the poor were inmates or lived in households containing inmates. Thus almost half of the poor belonged to households which included people who were not of their immediate biological family. In the town's population as a whole over three-fifths of the total lived in households containing persons who were not of the immediate nuclear family of parents and non-adult children. The incidence of outsiders was highest in the richest wards, no doubt because of large numbers of servants.[59]

If a majority of the population were members of households in which outsiders were regularly present, some interesting questions arise. What were the relationships between families and their lodgers and servants? Were servants and apprentices treated as members of the family, as Peter Laslett suggests in *The World We Have Lost*?[60] What were the psychological and social effects on young paupers of early departures from their nuclear families? In general, was the transfer a stabilizing or destabilizing force in society?

The differences in household size between the poor and the better-off are explained by the transfer of children from the former to the latter via service and apprenticeship and by poor women being widowed or abandoned. The better-off also transplanted their children to other households, but not usually to poor households except for wet-nursing. By shedding their children, the poor gained some relief from their burdens. The poor shed children, but took in lodgers. With anything up to a dozen persons crammed into one or two rooms, there must have been overcrowding. Taking in lodgers also gave footholds to migrants who might burden the poor rates. Few towns failed to take action against inmates or 'undertenants' in the sixteenth and seventeenth centuries. In 1605 Warwick expelled 36 at one go. Southwark appointed a special official to chase them out in James I's reign.[61]

What happened to the children of the poor after being shifted to the households of the better-off? The ideal was a patriarchal household in which the master, his family, and servants and apprentices lived in harmony. But it is doubtful whether the patriarchal household was harmonious in practice. The frequent appearance of servants and apprentices in judicial records – in conflict with masters and mistresses, in bastardy and vagrancy cases – suggests that the reality diverged significantly from the ideal. At Warwick from 1580 to 1587 almost one in every four vagrants stating occupations had left service and apprenticeship or had been released. Almost three-quarters of the vagrants of metropolitan origin taken into the London Bridewell between 1597 and 1608 were servants and apprentices.[62] It might be argued that because servants and apprentices were large groups in the working population, they were more likely than most occupational categories to appear in the records. But this argument fails to recognize that in theory servants and apprentices were supposed to be securely placed in patriarchal households. One can understand finding large numbers of harvest workers, journeymen and cloth-workers among vagrants; such jobs were never secure. Yet these people were invariably outnumbered by servants and apprentices.[63]

Comparing the ages of the poor and of the general population of a village or town suggests that poverty in the sixteenth century had three main phases. The first was in childhood and early adolescence before the young were placed in service or apprenticeship. At Warwick, Norwich and Ipswich in the Elizabethan period the proportion of the poor aged from one to 15 was consistently as high as or higher than that found in the general populations of Ealing in 1599 and Lichfield in 1695. The second phase of poverty was as a parent, roughly from age 30 to 60, after people married and had children, and before the children left the family for employment. This was also a time in life when many women were widowed or deserted. The third stage was old age. The old were more numerous among the poor than in the general populations of Ealing and Lichfield. The old were far more likely to be poor than other sections of the population, even children and adults with families (fig. 5). Many people aged over 60 in the Warwick census were described as 'impotent' and 'unable to labour'. This was a time in life when the difference in numbers of males and females was greatest: women over 60 outnumbered men by two to one. The only extended period of relief from poverty was in late adolescence and early adulthood. The age-group from 16 to 30 was conspicuously absent from the ranks of the poor compared with the general population, because this was the time in their lives when the young went out to work and before they married and had children. It is hardly surprising then that young adults were leading organizers and participants in festive and riotous activities in pre-industrial society. As well as being *rites de passage* to adulthood, these activities could be interpreted as a celebration of youth itself. It was the one time in their lives when the poor briefly escaped poverty.[64]

Poor and rich families differed in where they lived as well as in the size and composition of their households. As in other early modern towns, the poor tended to live in the suburbs and the rich in the centre of Elizabethan Warwick.[65] The division was an old one. It is clear in the subsidy of 1544–5, when half of the taxpayers in the Market Place, Saltisford and West Street wards were assessed at £1 worth of goods, which is a level of wealth thought close to poverty even in the 1520s (table 7).[66] The central wards of the High Pavement, Jury Street, and Castle Street, by contrast, had only a fifth to a third of their taxpayers assessed at £1. The figures for 1582 show a similar pattern. The poor were clustered in the same wards as the poor taxpayers in 1544–5: 84 per cent of those 'ready to decay' or on relief were huddled in a slum extending from the north side of town, the Saltisford, through the Market Place into the West Street. These wards accounted for 73 per cent of the total families in St Mary's, but had 84 per cent of the poor. It was in these wards that the town's cheap housing was located, with cottages rented out at 2s. to 5s. a year, while houses in the Jury Street and High Pavement cost from 4s. to 30s.[67] The poor made up 34 per cent of the total families in the slum wards, but only 15 per cent in the wealthy wards.

The suburban slums saw the sharpest increase in poor families in the 1580s. In 1587 the greatest rises were in the West Street and Saltisford wards, where the families needing relief almost doubled and quadrupled respectively (table 6).[68] The poor of the suburban slums were most vulnerable in a crisis such as that of 1586–7.

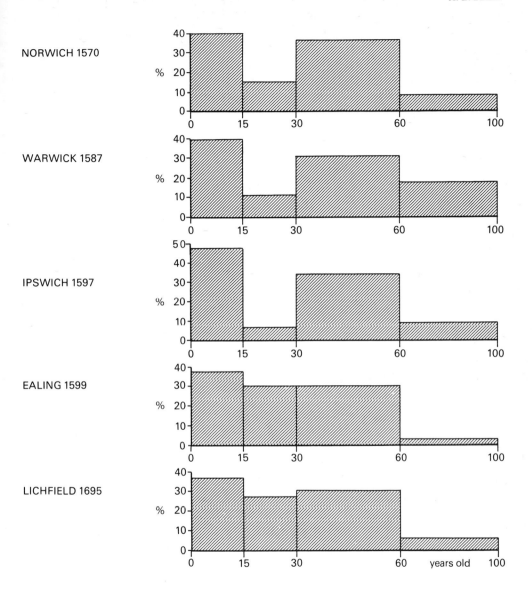

Figure 5. The ages of the poor (Norwich, Warwick and Ipswich) compared to the ages of the general population (Ealing and Lichfield). Sources: *The Norwich Census of the Poor, 1570*, ed. J. F. Pound (Norwich Record Soc., XL, 1971), 95–6; *The Book of John Fisher, 1580–1588*, ed. T. Kemp (n.d.), 165–72; *Poor Relief in Elizabethan Ipswich*, ed. J. Webb (Suffolk Records Soc., IX, 1966), 122–40; K. J. Allison, 'An Elizabethan village "census"', *Bull. Inst. Hist. Research*, XXXVI (1963), 96–103; D. V. Glass, 'Gregory King's estimate of the population of England and Wales, 1695', reprinted in *Population in History*, ed. D. V. Glass and D. E. C. Eversley (1965), 212. Note that age groups for Lichfield are different from the rest by one year at the intervals 15, 30 and 60, though this should not alter the result significantly; and that the data for Warwick and Ipswich have been 'smoothed' to take account of under-reporting of certain age groups.

Twenty-four families appeared in the census of 1587 as poor who in 1582 had been classed as 'able' or 'ready to decay', and all but two came from the three suburban slum wards.

   Another reason for the increase of poverty in the slums was the settlement of poor migrants there. Rents were low in the suburbs, and poor householders took in lodgers. At least three migrant pauper families had footholds in Warwick's suburbs in 1587: one man with two children, a second with four, and a woman with two children who was a lodger in an almshouse in West Street.[69] Little is known about the living conditions of the poor. If, as is likely, they lived mainly in cottages and crofts, conditions must have been crowded and unsanitary. Even allowing that the households of the poor generally had fewer members on average, there were exceptions that must have been hazards to health. In Saltisford ward, for example, the Apswell household included ten people in 1587: Joan or John Apswell and a daughter who was 'foolish and begs'; a lodger, his wife and three children, all of them beggars; a female lodger with her seven-year-old child, both beggars; and a single male lodger.

Table 7   *The incidence of poverty in St Mary's parish, Warwick, 1544–5 and 1582*

WARD	% taxpayers assessed @ £1, 1544–5	% of families poor in ward, 1582*	% total poor of parish, 1582
High Pavement	28	3	1
Castle Street	20	23	7
Jury Street	34	22	5
Market Place	48	33	36
Saltisford	55	27	30
West Street	50	44	18

Sources: PRO, E179/192/153; T. Kemp (ed.), *The Book of John Fisher, 1580–88* (n.d.), 81–94.
* The 'poor' here include both those 'ready to decay' and those given relief (table 5).

This household was untypically large, but it shows the extremes that multi-family households could reach in the Elizabethan slums.[70]

   Crises such as that of 1586–7 made the lot of the poor much worse, but it should not be imagined that their problems were only short-term. Most paupers probably led lives of long-standing, ongoing misery. The causes of this misery can be glimpsed in the census of Warwick's poor in 1587. Censuses of the poor at Norwich in 1570 and Ipswich in 1597 carefully noted whether they were able to work, but unlike the East Anglian towns Warwick had no obvious industry to employ the poor.[71] In Warwick the census-takers instead noted the circumstances of the poor, and their jottings leave no doubt that widowhood, disease and old-age were powerful causes of poverty. Over a third of the town's poor families were afflicted with at least one of these curses. Were the evidence more complete, the proportion would no doubt be higher. In addition, there were women deserted by husbands. Some paupers had more than one problem. For example, 'Anne Isham, wife of Henry Isham, fugitive. She is but young, but has but one leg, and has a child and they both beg'; or, 'Elizabeth, wife of John Nicholls, fugitive. She is of age 70 years. She is almost blind, was born in the town and is lame'.[72]

4   Charity

The traditional means of relieving the poor at Warwick were insufficient by the

1570s, so public rates had to be levied. The shortfall in traditional relief alone did not cause Warwick's poverty problem, which as we have seen resulted from economic and demographic changes, but it meant that extraordinary action was required of the authorities. What caused the shortfall? How far was urban poverty affected by the dissolutions of monasteries, almshouses and hospitals at the Reformation? How far was post-Reformation philanthropy able to relieve the situation?

The history of charity in the sixteenth and seventeenth centuries is full of pitfalls. The evidence is incomplete and, when available, difficult to interpret. Opinion has long been divided, frequently on confessional lines, beginning with contemporaries who debated whether Protestants or Roman Catholics were more generous to the poor. In our day debate still centres on the issue 'how much?' *How much* charity was given to the poor by the pre-Reformation Church? *How much* charity was there in England between 1480 and 1660? *How much* charity was there compared to public poor relief?

Historians have made heroic attempts to answer these questions. Savine concluded that monastic poor relief amounted to only a few per cent of annual income.[73] Current historical opinion appears to be moving towards the view that the relief given in the pre-Reformation period by monasteries, almshouses and hospitals was not inconsiderable, at least when compared with the charity of testators.[74] Another contentious area is indeed charitable bequests in wills. W. K. Jordan argued that there was a massive increase in charity after the Reformation, so great as to make public rates for poor relief unnecessary. He also claimed that charity became increasingly secular and discriminating in its objects. His critics have argued that price inflation meant that charity stagnated and that public rates were more important in relieving the poor than he allowed, and they have reworked Jordan's figures to take into account price inflation and the ongoing yields of endowed charities. Doubts have been expressed, too, about his view that pre-Reformation charity was largely religious and indiscriminate.[75]

In attempting to evaluate charity in terms of £ s. d., historians have made praiseworthy efforts to set aside misleading impressions. But these revisionist studies have themselves serious limitations. At best, they provide us with *minima*, because they are based on incomplete evidence. Monastic charity was listed in the *Valor Ecclesiasticus* (1535) only if it was compulsory, which made it tax free, so that the commissioners were reluctant to record it. 'The Valor Ecclesiasticus does not give a complete idea of monastic charity', Savine warned, because voluntary alms were not recorded.[76] Attempts to measure secular charity are equally fraught with problems. Most studies are based on probate records, which provide incomplete evidence. A great deal of charity remained unrecorded, handed out to passers-by despite statutory restrictions on casual giving.[77] That recorded charity provides evidence only of *minima* may not be important when dealing with long-term levels of giving. But when it comes to deciding whether insufficient charity obliged a town to levy rates, the limitation is a major one because some idea of the *maximum* charity available is necessary to answer the question.

Probate records have other defects in attempting to calculate amounts of philanthropic donations. First, charity continued to be left in kind – loaves of bread, gowns and cloaks for mourners, real estate – to which it is impossible to attach a price. The same point applies to educational and other gifts: how do we cost a university education, or food and clothing for a poor man while in prison?[78] Another problem is how far people received the charity that was left to them. Historians have assumed in cavalier fashion that once a charity was established it was administered. Local studies suggest that it is rarely possible to demonstrate the continuous existence of charities in this period. When evidence is available, it is clear that charities varied enormously in their management. It also appears that no one has resolved the problem of the big donor: should the great upsurges of Jordan's and others' graphs of philanthropy in the years 1501–10 and 1610–30,[79] the results mainly of gifts by a monarch and one or two merchants, be taken as evidence of tidal waves of giving by the population at large? It seems not.[80] Attempts have also been made to calculate how much charity people left as a proportion of their wealth (as recorded in probate inventories after their deaths), but is this a proportion of *total* wealth in all cases? Probably not, because land (including leases and copyholds) was often excluded from inventories, which were limited to household goods and livestock. Where people owned land, the figures are of limited value.[81] Finally, much has been made of a supposed qualitative change in charity from religious to secular objects evident in probate records after 1540. But doubts persist about whether this change was as unprecedented, rapid and profound as Jordan thought.[82]

The early Tudor suppression of religious houses has failed to receive due attention from historians despite a long tradition of dissolution studies. One area of neglect relates to the Edwardian dissolution of chantries, almshouses and hospitals. It is startling to find that there were still about 500 hospitals in existence in England and Wales c.1540 and that they have received no major study since Rotha Mary Clay's in 1909.[83] Even allowing Fuller's point that some pre-Reformation hospitals had 'rickets' because of bad administration and that some were refounded after dissolution, they, together with the almshouses and chantries, deserve further study.[84] Another area of neglect is the impact of the dissolutions upon local communities. Most local studies have concentrated on the redistribution of the lands of the dissolved institutions in 'the great transfer'. Concern with who got what is not surprising, considering that historians have been preoccupied with the distribution of landed wealth as a precondition of the English Revolution.[85] Yet it may also be worth while to examine the impact of the dissolutions upon local communities.

When local communities are studied, the effects of the changes turn out sometimes to have been considerable. Warwick is one case in which the dissolutions revolutionized a town's institutions. At Warwick the effects of the 'great transfer' went deeper than a change of landlord, including the transformation of the town's ecclesiastical establishment, its finances, corporate status and poor relief facilities. In the suppressions of 1536–47 Warwick's losses outweighed its gains, thus setting the scene for the financial difficulties of the Elizabethan years. Warwick's losses suggest a further dimension of 'poverty' in the sixteenth century: the powerlessness of communities in the face of an aggressive state and landed elite.[86]

The Reformation cut a wide swathe through Warwick's religious and charitable institutions. The town had a variety of pre-Reformation foundations. Monastic houses included the Augustinian St Sepulchre's priory and a Dominican friary, numbering about two dozen residents in 1536–8 (including servants). In addition, there was the religious gild of the Holy Trinity and St George, which kept four almshouses; and two hospitals, St Michael's for lepers and St John the Baptist's for travellers, the poor and infirm.[87] The major prize was the collegiate church of St Mary's, one of 18 or so colleges and collegiate churches handed over to Henry VIII in the 1540s.[88] St Mary's was not a large establishment, but it was a wealthy one, accounting for almost three-quarters of the annual revenue of the town's religious foundations in 1535. It was also an important institution in the town. Besides acting as the parish church for the larger of Warwick's two parishes and paying the salaries of a number of village priests, it was a major landowner, ran the local school and doled out alms to the poor. The dissolution of these institutions, especially St Mary's, was therefore a substantial loss. At the very least, someone would have to foot a number of bills if the churches, school and charities were to continue to function. The Protestant zealot, Hugh Latimer, bishop of Worcester, saw the dangers of dissolution in 1538, when he wrote to Cromwell asking him to be 'good lord to the poor college'. He urged Cromwell to prevail upon Henry VIII to award St Mary's 'some piece of some broken abbey, or else I fear they will grow shortly to naught'.[89]

The answer to the question of who would be the new paymaster was the incorporation of the town in 1545. By its first charter the Crown granted the corporation lands that brought in an income of £60 a year, later increased to about £100 a year through further grants. From this total the burgesses had to find salaries for three vicars, the assistant clergy and staff of St Mary's, and a schoolmaster, as well as maintaining local roads and bridges and giving substantial hospitality to visiting notables. Since many of their properties were on long leases at fixed rents in a time of price inflation, the new burgesses faced an uphill struggle.[90]

In the dissolution of local church lands the town of Warwick therefore came off badly. The corporation's grant of £60, later inappropriately called 'Henry VIII's charity', represented less than a seventh of the annual revenue of church lands in 1535. The rest of the properties were scattered in sales and grants to national figures such as John Dudley, earl of Warwick, and the Taverner brothers of London, and to local families such as the Fishers. At one point in 1549 it appeared that the burgesses might even lose their meeting hall, the former guildhall, to the predatory Thomas Fisher, but that event was postponed until the 1570s when, as we have seen, they handed it over to the earl of Leicester.[91]

How much of a gap had the burgesses to fill in the church's relief of the poor? In the *Valor* of 1535 it appears that roughly £50 a year of the gross annual revenue of Warwick's religious foundations was devoted to alms-giving, hospitals and housing, with two-thirds of the total going *ad usum hospicii*, or for 'hospitals'.[92] But the detailed breakdown of charitable objects is not of major importance in assessing the dissolutions' local impact. Nor is the proportion of the annual revenue that went to charity, with which historians have conjured for so long, and which at Warwick was roughly a tenth of the total. More to the point is the issue of the loss of resources in the 'great transfer'. This was what troubled contemporaries, including the politicians Audley and Wriothesley, the Erasmian Starkey, and the Protestants Brinkelow and Lever. They were concerned that church wealth should be used for social and educational reforms, including the relief of the poor.[93] Judging by Warwick's case, their concern was justified.

Historians no longer believe that the dissolutions directly caused the Tudor poverty problem by turning thousands of destitute ex-religious on to the roads, or in totally eliminating the pre-Reformation foundations for poor relief. Many of the ex-religious got jobs and pensions, while some almshouses and hospitals were continued by new owners. But at the end of the day the bulk of church lands were sold into private hands and not used for 'public causes'.[94] In this respect Warwick's experience fits the general pattern.

Some attempt can be made to gauge how much poor relief was lost in the dissolutions at Warwick. The £50 theoretically available from church foundations in 1535 was not insignificant. It is nearly equivalent to the poor rate in a good harvest year in the 1580s, after taking population growth and price rises into account, and it is nearly half the rate in a bad year such as 1587. The dissolutions at Warwick therefore placed at risk a substantial amount of poor relief.

What was the fate of specific institutions? How far was there continuity or re-foundation? The general picture at Warwick is that more foundations were lost than were maintained, despite the fact that purchasers of church lands were supposed to assume responsibility for hospitality and alms-giving.[95] The charity supposed to be given by St Mary's, St Sepulchre's and St John the Baptist, which made up four-fifths of the pre-Reformation total for the town, disappeared without trace. The Stoughton family, who were granted St John's, later built a substantial manor house on the site. Two institutions continued in existence after 1547 – St Michael's hospital and the gild's almshouses in the West Street – but they cannot be said to have made major contributions to the relief of the poor in the post-Reformation years. St Michael's passed into the hands of Thomas Fisher, a protegé of the dukes of Somerset and Northumberland, who was also granted St Sepulchre's priory. Fisher relieved four paupers in the hospital in Elizabeth's reign. The gild almshouses continued to support paupers in the late sixteenth century, but with the aid of public rates by the 1580s.[96]

Where pre-Reformation foundations were continued, the new owners were not magnanimous. Fisher's support of St Michael's amounted to £4 per annum, which was no more than the pre-Reformation total; his successor Sir John Puckering doled out £6 a year, which was a smaller share of the hospital's income (£40 annually by the 1590s) than in 1535. The paupers in the gild almshouses continued to be supported at pre-Dissolution rates, which were worth 50 per cent less by the 1580s because of price inflation. The continuance of these charities obviously helped Warwick in the relief of the poor during the 1580s. But even taking into account another pre-Reformation foundation that remained in existence, the almshouses in Gaol Hall lane founded by the earls of Warwick, these charities gave limited aid to Warwick's poor – certainly no more than a quarter of the relief bill in a good year and a tenth in a bad year. The conclusion is inescapable that Warwick received limited assistance from continuing charities.[97]

The legacy of the 1530s and 1540s to the poor of Warwick was a depressing one. The bulk of the pre-Reformation foundations were destroyed. Although there is limited evidence of pre-Reformation foundations administering relief to the poor, the dispersal of their lands in the dissolutions meant that opportunities for social and educational assistance were lost. Henceforth the poor had to rely on their neighbours and statutory relief.

Neighbourly relief continued to be bestowed on the poor at Warwick in Elizabeth's reign, but John Fisher's remarks to the earl of Leicester in 1571 suggest that it was inadequate by that time. Legislation concerning the poor followed two main lines of development – the suppression of the itinerant poor and the relief of the local poor by public subscription and finally taxation. In some measure, both developments followed logically from (even if they were not caused by) the dissolutions and can be seen in microcosm at Warwick. The Tudor poor laws discouraged the relief of rootless paupers, who, it was thought had proliferated because of the alms they received from religious houses.[98] Post-Reformation legislation made no attempt to revive facilities for the poor itinerant, even though landlords were enjoined to keep 'hospitality'. Instead, he was punished as a vagrant, and new institutions were devised for his incarceration – bridewells and houses of correction. At Warwick the hospital of St John the Baptist, specifically founded to relieve needy travellers, became a gentleman's residence. By the 1580s the town was arresting itinerants in considerable numbers, whereas before the Reformation it had had facilities to relieve them. Even allowing that the pre-Reformation Church was not entirely sympathetic to itinerant beggars, the sixteenth century saw a fundamental transformation of their status.

The relief of the poor by subscription and taxation was a principle of Tudor legislation from the 1530s. At Warwick with the disruption of charities and a rising population in the 1540s, public subscriptions were evidently a necessity. They first appeared in 1547 in the churchwardens' accounts of St Nicholas, the extra-mural parish, when 6s. 6d. was spent to purchase a 'chest for the poor people for the charity of the good people' and over £2 was collected for clothing for the poor. Poor relief by the clergy was required by canon law in the high Middle Ages, but under sixteenth-century English legislation it became a community responsibility. The change was partly inspired by the teachings of Catholic humanists and Protestant divines. At Warwick, where pre-Reformation charities had been largely suspended, there was a clear need for community intervention.[99]

How far did post-Reformation charity fill the gap left by the dissolutions at Warwick? Jordan's studies of philanthropy, which claimed that it bridged any gap (with the volume of charitable bequests rising ten-fold from 1540 to 1660), continue to be debated.[100] At Warwick the picture of charity for the poor is a mixed one that cannot be said to support or refute the argument favouring post-Reformation beneficence. It all depends on how one interprets the figures. Perhaps the most significant result is that in Warwick's case any set of figures is dubious. On one reading, which includes the bequests of the earl of Leicester, charity to Warwick's poor rose by as much as 30-fold between 1540 and 1650, from a mere £20 a decade to over £600, which would support the Jordan argument (table 8). Another reading of the evidence, though, puts the increase at no more than two-fold before 1620 and four-fold thereafter, because it excludes the Leicester legacies. The reason for the vast disparity is uncertainty over whether Warwick's poor drew much succour from these bequests. Since the earl's bequests made up the lion's share of the town's charities for the poor in the period, the issue is an important one.

Leicester's major endowment at Warwick was the hospital that still bears his name and to which he gave £200 a year. There is reason to doubt whether Leicester's hospital was in a healthy state after the earl's death in 1588 and whether it gave much help to the local poor then or in later decades. The earl's will contained a provision that his wife, Lettice, should increase the hospital's endowment with lands from her jointure. This she was loath to do, and although the earl's brother Ambrose Dudley, earl of Warwick, granted £20 per annum out of Leicester's estate, the hospital was soon in a critical condition. After Ambrose's death in 1590, the hospital master, Thomas Cartwright, wrote to Lord Burghley 'concerning the bad state of this hospital' and complained that Lettice withheld the hospital's income, including his salary. The upshot was an Act of Parliament in 1597 to maintain the hospital and a case in Chancery that Cartwright won. In the meantime, though, the hospital suffered. As late as 1611–12 the burgesses wrote that the hospital 'has been of late neglected'.[101]

It is doubtful whether Leicester's hospital gave much aid to the town's poor even

Table 8 *Charity to Warwick's poor in probate records, 1501–1650* (all figures deflated)*

decade	A in dole form		B in endowment form		C 'B' excluding Leicester's hospital		D total 'A' + 'B'		E total 'A + 'C'	
	£	s.	£	s.	£	s.	£	s.	£	s.
1501–10	11						11		11	
1511–20	2	10					2	10	2	10
1521–30			15					15		15
1531–40										
1541–50	21						21		21	
1551–60	14		1		1		15		15	
1561–70	25		1		1		26		26	
1571–80	11		22†		22		33		33	
1581–90	5		654		19		659		24	
1591–1600	5		543‡		14		548		19	
1601–10	14		552		24		564		38	
1611–20	6		504		24		510		30	
1621–30	9		517		37		526		46	
1631–40	12		483§		70		495		82	
1641–50	21		456		66		477		87	

Sources: Warwick wills in PRO and Hereford and Worcester RO, Worcester; *Reports of the Commissioners appointed in Pursuance of Various Acts of Parliament, to enquire concerning Charities in England and Wales, relating to the County of Warwick, 1819–37* (1890), 747–842; E.G. Tibbits, 'The hospital of Robert, Earl of Leicester, in Warwick', *Trans. Birmingham Arch. Soc.,* LX (1936).
* Price data from E.H. Phelps Brown and S.V. Hopkins, 'Seven centuries of the prices of consumables, compared with builders' wage-rates', *Economica,* XXIII (1956), 312–13. All figures above £1 rounded to nearest £. All 'capital' sums (endowments) calculated in terms of annual and decennial yields; cf. J.F. Hadwin, 'Deflating philanthropy', *EcHR,* 2nd ser., XXXI (1978), 110–11.
† The charity of Thomas Oken estimated to yield £6 per annum.
‡ Plus seven houses, 70 acres of land, and £72 for the purchase of four houses.
§ Plus the rents of two houses.

when it was well run. The 'brethren' never numbered more than 12 at a time, which was a small fraction of the urban poor. They were always men, while we have seen that women were the most numerous group of local paupers. Finally, a minority of the brethren were actually from the town, judging by seventeenth-century patents of appointment. Between 1616 and 1680 fewer than half of the brethren were from Warwick when their places of origin were mentioned.[102] We must therefore conclude that Leicester's hospital served the town less than half of the time, that it aided a small number of paupers, and that it was badly run from 1590 to 1610. The example of Leicester's hospital is a warning against assuming that a charity established was a charity administered. It also underlines the problem of the 'big donor'. Without Leicester's bequest recorded charity to the poor of Warwick was tiny, but his bequest makes it appear that there was a great upsurge of philanthropy in the town. Probate data on charitable bequests yield meaningless results, unless there is independent evidence for their effective administration.

If we cannot accept the higher figure for charitable relief at Warwick that includes Leicester's hospital, neither can we adopt the lower one that excludes it. Clearly, the town poor received some relief from the hospital, however exiguous. In addition, there were properties and goods left to Warwick's poor to which it is impossible to attach anything but a notional price tag. What is one to make of vague bequests of 'the residue of my estate', clothing, the unstated rents of houses and bits of land? Figures can be devised for such bequests (and were by Jordan), but they can be no more than guesses.[103]

What can be salvaged from this wreckage of dubious statistics? Even taking the highest figures for recorded charity to the local poor – those that include Leicester's bequests – and admitting that they show a huge increase from 1540 to 1650, their contribution can easily be exaggerated. If reckoned at a maximum of £65 a year in the 1580s, they were less than the value of church lands dissolved from 1536 to 1547, which were worth over £400 annually in 1535, and despite price inflation only just exceeded the value of pre-Reformation expenditure on hospitals, poor relief and hospitality, which ran at £50 a year in 1535. What is more, post-Reformation philanthropy to the local poor hardly surpassed public rates. In a good harvest year such as 1581–2 the poor rate at Warwick was £58 10s., which is almost as much as the maximum figure for charitable relief; in a bad harvest year such as 1586–7 the amount raised by public rates was over 50 per cent higher than that yielded by private philanthropy. Such evidence contradicts the argument that the great volume of charitable relief made rates insignificant except in periods of crisis. This is not to say that philanthropy did not help the poor of Elizabethan and early Stuart Warwick (it obviously did); it is simply to get its contribution into perspective compared with pre-Reformation foundations and the relief levied by rates.[104]

Jordan argued that charity underwent qualitative as well as quantitative changes in the sixteenth and seventeenth centuries. One change was a decline in giving for 'religious' purposes such as masses for the dead and a rise in secular objects such as poor relief and education; a second, the replacement of indiscriminate handouts by endowments that sought out the most worthy cases. Historians have criticized Jordan's quantitative evidence, but have largely accepted the qualitative changes that he posited. Yet the qualitative changes were also central to his conception of philanthropy in the period. To him they marked 'the development of the ethic as well as the institutions of the liberal society' and the transition from medieval to modern times.[105]

Jordan's picture of qualitative changes in charity turns out to be full of distortions when tested in the urban locality. The method used here is to study the forms of charity in over 500 Warwick wills from 1480 to 1650; in particular, the frequency of 'dole'-type gifts versus endowments (and especially of the traditional funeral dole) and the degree to which doles became more discriminating in their objects. First, though, some general criticisms. To think that Protestants had a monopoly of secular giving in the sixteenth century is parochial and whiggish. As noted earlier, Renaissance Venice developed many charitable institutions with secular purposes, including the relief of the poor. At Lyons few masses for the dead were found in bequests from the late fifteenth century, and charities for the poor became more and more numerous about 1600.[106] Another criticism of the Jordan view is that it is doubtful whether pre-Reformation charity was thoroughly religious. J. A. F. Thomson found that differences in charity between pre- and post-Reformation London 'tended to be in extent rather than in kind', while it is easy to forget that the hundreds of medieval hospitals and almshouses dissolved in the early Tudor period had served secular purposes such as the care of the sick, needy, and itinerant. Even the late medieval nobility, often singled out for their indiscriminate largesse in funeral doles, left bequests to the aged and ill, for prisoners and hospitals. Finally, it is incorrect to assume that English Protestants gave charity for secular objects with purely secular aims in mind. Calvinists uncertain about their spiritual election were prone to slip into casuistry in which charity came close to acting as good works. The puritan John Downame wrote in *The Plea of the Poore* (1616) that by giving charity 'we make our calling and election sure' and that 'by these works of mercy we are furthered notably in the way to salvation'.[107]

Jordan's view of charity in England was that before 1540 bequests 'were in the main disbursed as doles, particularly in connection with funerals, for the immediate use of the recipients', and for the religious purpose of aiding salvation. After 1540 'this typical, but on the whole wasteful, if not harmful, form of medieval almsgiving was superseded by endowments most carefully established and regulated' whose objects were overwhelmingly secular.[108] By the term 'superseded' Jordan apparently meant that more money was left in endowments than in casual doles after 1540. At Warwick the post-Reformation years saw an efflorescence of endowed charities which, if Leicester's hospital is included in the reckoning, greatly outstripped doles in £ s. d. (table 8). But cash is not the only, or always the most faithful, measure of social change. If we examine the forms of charity in Warwick wills we find that the dole did not disappear with the Reformation; that in fact it remained the most common type of charity throughout the period; and that funeral doles, although declining in frequency, persisted up to 1640 and far outnumbered endowed charities at most times.

Charity in dole form made up roughly 80 per cent of gifts to the poor in Warwick wills from 1480 to 1650. These doles included gifts to the 'poor men's box' in the church, to the poor at a person's funeral, and many times simply 'to the poor of Warwick'. Even allowing that executors or church officials may have exercised control over who received the doles, donors' wills attempted to qualify doles only to a limited extent: no more than a third selected the 'most needy' or only 'impotent' people for relief; much more common was a blanket gift 'to the poor' sometimes with the specification of a parish or town (table 9). Nor did the proportion of doles that attempted to discriminate among the poor rise sharply in the period, as Jordan's argument implied.[109] Funeral doles declined in frequency from 1560 without disappearing. Over a fifth of total gifts to Warwick's poor between 1601 and 1640 were to be given at the donor's funeral.

The most common charity to the poor at Warwick was not, therefore, an endowment in which the donor's mind was on future generations. Instead, testators were concerned chiefly with the immediate relief of friends and neighbours, and to be remembered by them. The persistence of 'medieval' funeral doles among such diverse social groups as Warwick husbandmen and craftsmen, Sussex gentlemen and London merchants, despite official denunciations, suggests that the notion of good works survived long after the Reformation, possibly encouraged by personal uncertainties about salvation that went with a belief in predestination. Finally, post-Reformation charities often followed the same lines as those before the Reformation with the continued foundation of almshouses and hospitals such as Leicester's at Warwick.[110]

It would be wrong, of course, to conclude that the period witnessed no changes at all in types of charity. The disappearance of pre-Reformation facilities for the relief of itinerants has already been contrasted with the policy of increased severity towards vagrants from Henry VIII's reign. Another new development of the sixteenth century was the belief that work was a cure for poverty. This belief appears in charitable bequests as well as in ideas of social reform such as More's *Utopia* (1516) and in Tudor vagrancy legislation. In their wills people left money to be lent at interest to 'poor tradesmen' and set aside funds for employing and housing the poor.[111] If Warwick's example is at all typical, it appears that the sixteenth century developed new attitudes towards the poor, but without transforming many of the ways in which charity was given.

Table 9   Forms of charity to the poor in Warwick wills, 1480–1650

	A	B	C		D		E		F	
period*	total wills	total gifts to poor	gifts in dole form		doles at death or funeral		qualified doles		endow-ments	
	no.	no.	no.	%†	no.	%†	no.	%‡	no.	%†
1480–1540	39	11	10	90.9	3	27.3	1	10.0	1	9.1
1541–60	112	42	30	71.4	19	45.2	8	26.7	2	4.8
1561–1600	174	111	88	79.3	24	21.6	19	21.6	11	9.9
1601–40	179	113	96	84.9	26	23.0	29	30.2	16	14.2
1641–50	49	23	21	91.3	3	13.0	6	28.6	2	8.7

Sources: Warwick wills in PRO and Hereford and Worcester RO, Worcester.
* Following as far as evidence permits the division in W.K. Jordan, *Philanthropy in England, 1480–1660* (1959).
† As a proportion of 'B', Total Gifts to Poor.
‡ As a proportion of 'C', Gifts in Dole Form.

5   Poor relief

In the 1580s the Warwick authorities attacked the problem of the poor with unprecedented vigour. They regularly arrested and punished the vagrant poor.[112] They ordered a halt to begging, made censuses of the poor, and levied taxation to support them. The authorities acted in part because of events at national level – the poor laws of 1572 and 1576; fears about disorder at a time of invasion threats and plots; and, harvest failure in 1586–7. The 1570s and 1580s also saw the intervention in the town of two leading puritans, Robert Dudley, earl of Leicester, and Thomas Cartwright – who were actively involved in the problem of the local poor. But the steps taken to deal with the poor were also linked to urban conditions, which included a stagnant economy, a growing population, and insufficient private charity, as we have seen. Most important, perhaps, were the corporation's financial troubles, which stemmed from inflation and stingy royal grants at the time of incorporation in 1545. In the 1570s these problems reached crisis-point.

The corporation of Warwick had a turbulent career in the reign of Elizabeth. The Marian charter put the town in the hands of a bailiff and 12 assistants – the 'principal burgesses', of whom John Fisher was one – and provided for a second council of 24 townsmen to serve as assistants to the principal burgesses and to be 'the mouth of the commoners'. There were disputes between the two groups over their respective powers, the assistants claiming 'free speech' at one point, with the result that they were reduced to 12 in the 1570s. J. E. Neale recounts another chapter of Warwick's stormy political history in his study of the parliamentary election of 1586.[113] A third dispute in Elizabeth's reign involved town finance and poor relief. It centred upon local charities and the properties granted to the corporation in 1545. In the 1570s and 1580s these battles produced contentious meetings, ejections of burgesses, a riot and litigation in Chancery. Dissension centred on whether the corporation's property should be used to relieve the poor or whether rates should be levied for the purpose.

John Fisher's interview with the earl of Leicester in 1571 spelled out the town's financial problems. In response to a question about the town's resources Fisher said 'that the town had little land or none but a few beggarly houses and some tithes'. As we saw earlier, the lands granted to the town at its incorporation in 1545 were worth only about £60. By 1571, Fisher explained, this was insufficient to support three vicars and a schoolmaster in a period of married clergy, population growth and price revolution. The legacy of the Dissolution and incorporation was a bitter one. To remedy the situation Fisher hoped that Leicester could get the queen to bestow more tithes on the town. The vicars of St Mary's and St Nicholas should get £40 and £20 a year, respectively, instead of the present £20 and £13 6s. 8d.; the vicar of Budbrooke, £10 instead of £5 3s. 4d.; and the schoolmaster, £10 instead of 20 nobles.[114]

Warwick's financial embarrassment soon centred upon the issue of the relief of the poor. The battle raged from 1576 to 1583. It brought charge and counter-charge about the administration of corporation lands and charities, including £100 left by a local worthy, Thomas Oken, in 1570. The disputes involved the principal burgesses, especially Richard Brookes, a local miller and farmer, and John Fisher. They began when Brookes charged that Fisher and the executors of Oken's will had misappropriated the money. The corporation was split, and the result in Fisher's words was 'brawls'. The wrangling soon spread to other charities, town finances, and in the end to poor relief.[115]

Fisher and Brookes had been at odds since 1576, when there was a pitched battle at Myton over the tithes there. Fisher and his supporters suggested that Brookes was seeking revenge in the subsequent dispute over charities: 'he becomes an open enemy and vows the overthrow and breaking the neck of the corporation'. Local jealousies and rivalries cannot be discounted in the dispute. A quarrelsome streak in Brookes' personality may also have played a part. When he was finally dismissed as a burgess in 1583 his enemies claimed that 'he has been a breeder of many troubles and procurer of great outrages . . . [and] has and yet does maintain and sustain diverse masterless men, brawlers and fighters'. He attended meetings sporadically and then not in civic dress, but 'in garments unseemly for the time and place, as sometimes in a cloak and other indecent apparel, and that of light or whitish colour, betokening him rather to be a miller than a magistrate'. He was cantankerous at the meetings he attended: 'instead of the name of brother, he and his have called some of the principal burgesses gorbellied churls, gouty wretches, crafty knaves, and other names'.[116]

The root cause of these disputes was not personal: it was that Brookes and his supporters were opposed to public taxation for poor relief. The first sign of their opposition came in 1576, when the burgesses met to discuss action to relieve the poor. Nothing was done because a number of burgesses were absent, including Brookes and his supporters, but Fisher and his followers noted that a poor rate was in dispute, so that they meant to decide 'how and what every constable did within every ward of the same town towards the payment of the task . . . wherein many complained themselves to be wronged'. In 1580–1 Brookes mounted an attack upon Fisher and the corporation for ordering the poor to stop begging from house to house. In an apocryphal petition from the poor entitled 'Vox Clamantis', Brookes claimed that the poor would be forced to live off weekly church collections. He stated that the poor were obliged 'most miserably to beg [their] bread from door to door and that if speedy redress be not had herein a number of [them] are like to perish with famine'. Fisher countered that as steward he had put the issue to the court leet and that all the poor were interviewed about possible complaints. There were none, he said, and the commoners and the poor both repudiated Brookes' petition. In 1582–3, when poor rates were levied, the opposition put in a bill of complaint in the Court of Requests. Brookes denounced Fisher for withholding the town's charities, 'thereby the whole town is greatly charged for the necessary sustenance of the said poor people'. Thus taxation for poor relief aroused serious opposition at Warwick.[117]

The town considered and attempted various methods of relieving the local poor before resorting to taxation. Voluntary subscription was one way. In line with parliamentary Acts collections were made in the churches. Neighbourly charity was another method, which traditionally included 'meat and drink at diverse persons' [homes] according to every man's ability'. But by 1571, as Fisher told Leicester, these sources of poor relief were inadequate.[118] The town also considered schemes to put the poor to work. The earl of Leicester proposed an ambitious scheme to the town in 1571. He encouraged the establishment of a 'special trade' such as cloth- or cap-making and cited the success in tapestry-making of the Roman Catholic Sheldons at Beoley. Such a trade, he thought, 'should be not only very profitable, but also a means to keep your poor from idleness'. Cloth or cap manufacture was a useful remedy for poverty because it could employ great numbers: 'workmen and women and such may therein be employed as in no faculty else, for though they be children they may spin and card; though they be lame they may pick and fray wool and do such things as shall keep them from idleness, and whereof some commodity may grow.' A more complete solution to Warwick's poverty problem is hard to imagine.[119]

The earl's scheme included offers of capital and skilled labour to train the poor, though it was not without an element of self-interest. He himself would supply the capital 'if he might understand it be well used', but if he got the money together and it were refused 'then he could not like of it'. He referred to the town of Beverley where he and some local gentlemen had offered £2,000 to the town, but had been refused. In that instance the earl and his consortium were driving quite a hard bargain – the loan to be repaid annually in wool or cash within six years 'at reasonable price', that is, with interest. Leicester told Fisher that the burghers of Beverley had since regretted their lost opportunity.[120]

Fisher replied diffidently to the earl's offer. Trade was bad, he had no commission from his fellow burgesses to take up such an offer, although he was very grateful for it and would put it to them. There is no evidence, however, that the town accepted the offer, or even considered it. After all, it would have added economic mortgage to the already existing political one. Even though the earl had his allies among the burgesses, it is doubtful whether the majority would have accepted the 'thraldom' of which Thomas Oken, the town's leading citizen, had warned earlier that year.[121]

The town again considered putting the poor to work in 1576 by raising a 'stock' in accordance with the statute passed that year, but nothing apparently came of the matter, possibly because of the divisions over poor relief in the corporation.[122] Attempts to relieve the poor by setting them to work therefore foundered at

Warwick. Other towns such as Norwich, which had bridewells and houses of correction, may have been more successful in putting the poor to work and training them in a craft, though certain facts militate against this assumption: first, bridewells and houses of correction seem to have been used mainly for the incarceration and punishment of offenders, much like prisons; second, only a minority of inmates were given sustained training in a craft; third, many institutions had chequered careers, suffering from corruption at the hands of keepers and discontinuous administration.[123]

Censuses and poor rates were the next steps taken to relieve Warwick's poor. The poor rate of 1582 included an attempt at a census of St Mary's parish. Listed were those who could contribute to the relief of the poor; those who could not contribute but were able to maintain themselves without relief; those who were on the verge of declining into need or 'ready to decay'; and those needing relief.[124] The most thorough steps to relieve the poor took place in the crisis years of 1586–7, when the corn supply was closely regulated, a detailed census of the poor was carried out, 'foreign' paupers were expelled, and poor rates were levied at more than twice the cost of 1582 (table 10). Once again, a moving force in the town's relief of the poor was a puritan, the presbyterian Thomas Cartwright, whom the earl of Leicester had made the master of his hospital in 1586.[125]

Table 10   The cost of poor relief at St Mary's parish, Warwick, 1582 and 1587 (per week)

WARD	1582		1587	
	s.	d.	s.	d.
High Pavement	6	3	13	8
Castle Street	1	6	6	8
Jury Street	1	7½	5	2
Market Place	7	7½	13	1
Saltisford		2½		6
West Street	1	4	2	3
Longbridge	*		1	6
totals	18	6½	42	10

Sources: T. Kemp (ed.), *The Book of John Fisher, 1580–88* (n.d.), 81–5; MS version of same, Warwick CRO (unfoliated), relief list for 1587.
* No evidence available.

The reaction to the harvest failure of 1586 was vigorous at Warwick. The town began regulating the corn supply in November, and action continued into the spring and summer months of 1587. On 28 November, searchers were appointed 'to search and view the houses of the inhabitants of this borough for malt done and grain engrossed', and they made returns of their findings. They also reported on barley bought in the market. After the Privy Council's Book of Orders was issued in January 1587, the county JPs gave orders for corn to be brought to the town and for no malt to be made before August 1587. Outsiders from border towns in Worcestershire were 'noted [by two JPs] to do much hurt in the markets' of Warwickshire.[126]

The census of the poor and new poor rate of March 1587, show that market controls were insufficient to relieve the town's poor at this time of harvest failure. The numbers of poor families had more than doubled in St Mary's over 1582 and almost half the parish's poor were begging for a living. The spectre of beggars shocked

Thomas Cartwright and spurred him to action, with the result that we have an excellent example of puritan social activism.[127] It was Cartwright, together with a leading local layman, John Dafferne, who pushed the burgesses into conducting a census of the local poor in March 1587. It was after 'many exclamations and complaints made and set forth by Mr Cartwright and Mr Dafferne touching the disorder of beggars' that constables conducted a house-to-house survey in which all members of poor families were listed – their lodgers, ages, whether they begged and their living conditions.[128]

Cartwright and Dafferne were instrumental in the follow-up to the census. Dafferne had personally participated in the census, but now both he and Cartwright took part in the decisions about who got relief and how much they received.[129] These decisions show that Cartwright and Dafferne discriminated among the poor to be relieved, refusing relief to some. First of the 245 poor in the census, 22 were expelled from the town.[130] Of the remaining 223 persons in need it is possible that only 127 of them were given relief, or just slightly more than half. Relief was apparently allocated for children, but not parents; for example, 'Thomas Page for three children – 6d.'. In 1582 Page had received a dole of 4d. a week as the head of the family with no mention of the children.[131] Cartwright and Dafferne also discriminated among the poor on the bases of age and fitness and whether these conditions justified their way of life, which meant for a large number begging. Isabell Glover, for example, aged 60, had two sons aged 18 and 16 living with her, plus a small child, and possibly another son and his wife, all of them begging. She was given 8d. per week 'for her and her small child' and nothing for the others.[132] Further examples could be listed of selection within families and the sending away of children to service, which broke up families.

Thomas Cartwright's intervention at Warwick shows a prominent puritan confronting the poor-relief issue. Cartwright had firm ideas on the matter. He had written in 1575 that England had great numbers of beggars and rogues because it lacked a presbyterian system in which deacons took control of such problems. At Warwick in 1587 Cartwright and Dafferne were effectively acting as deacons, even though there is no evidence of a formal presbyterian system in the town.[133] Cartwright was careful to draw the line, though, at what he considered to be the responsibility of magistrates. At the same time as he was organizing poor relief in the town he was at odds with magistrates over the punishment of two of his servants in a bastardy case. The magistrates claimed that the hospital was a separate jurisdiction from the town, but Cartwright insisted that this be waived because he wanted the offenders publicly punished. His reasons for public punishment were that he himself had recently preached against drunkenness and whoredom and that he was certain that the earl of Leicester would not favour 'privilege for sin'.[134]

How far was the puritan intervention at Warwick a 'new medicine for poverty'? Leicester's proposal for industrial development to employ the poor has a modern ring to it, because it proposed 'economic growth' as a cure for poverty. The earl's grasp of the economic situation was inadequate, however, and his thinking traditional. His aim was the long-standing one of Tudor social commentators: to benefit the 'Commonwealth'. The villains were those old bogey-men, self-interested landlords: 'I do grieve that every man is only careful for himself. And I think you be most of you graziers and given as in most places men are to easy trades of life, providing for themselves [and] not having consideration to their posterity, which would not so be.'[135] Leicester's social ideas were reminiscent of his grandfather's, the author of

The Tree of Commonwealth (1509), and of the 'Commonwealth' writers of the 1540s. But unlike some Tudor writers, Leicester ignored the institutional and social conditions behind poverty, such as the dissolution of religious houses from which his family had profited.

Cartwright's contribution was similarly unoriginal. The town had already made a primitive census and levied a poor rate before his arrival. His role was to galvanize the town into action at a desperate time. In the event, his 'new medicine' involved sharp discrimination in the allocation of relief. The reasoning behind Cartwright's intervention at Warwick was as traditional as Leicester's: concern about 'the disorder of beggars'; 'to keep the poor at their own houses without begging'. Like most Tudor social critics, Cartwright was preoccupied with the problem of disorder. He advocated a presbyterian system in order to suppress 'riot, adultery, covetousness, pride, idleness, etc.', which he said caused 'diseases, beggary, translations of inheritance from the right heirs, needless deaths, seditions, rebellions (whereof every one is an engine able to pull down the commonwealth)'. Judging by Warwick's example, puritanism was a less radical force in its approach to the poverty problem than has been imagined. Of course it is true that conservative activists, however unwittingly, can change society as thoroughly as self-avowed radicals.[136]

6 Conclusion

Warwick's example shows how serious a problem urban poverty could be in the sixteenth century. The control and relief of the poor bulked large in the town's records. A. D. Dyer calculates that vagrants were in question in over 60 per cent of cases heard by the town's magistrates in the 1580s; certainly their examinations fill many pages of the corporation records. So do poor rates, censuses of the poor, the magistrates' wrangles over poor relief, and efforts to control the corn trade after the harvest failure of 1586.[137]

Warwick's poverty problem was not simply a matter of punishing vagrants and relieving paupers. It had wider ramifications. Its causes lay in the town's economic decline since the late Middle Ages. When the population grew rapidly in the sixteenth century and the economy responded sluggishly, widespread poverty ensued. Warwick's poverty problem was also political in origin. The town had long been subject to the control of the earls of Warwick, and this influence was continued by the Dudley family after 1540. But the sixteenth century saw the intervention of new outside forces which the local authorities were powerless to resist. The Tudor state dissolved the town's church lands and sold and granted them away, mostly to landed gentlemen. The crown granted Warwick a comparative pittance at its incorporation, which seriously affected the town's fortunes in the long term.

The consequences of Warwick's poverty were severe. Because of its penury, the corporation was subject to a host of further difficulties. It had to call on a new patron, the puritan earl of Leicester, who took the burgesses' hall and founded a hospital that was of limited value to the town. Then he unleashed the presbyterian Cartwright on them. The poor relief issue caused the burgesses to split into factions and to fight bitterly over the administration of corporation lands and town charities. Local gentlemen intervened in the dispute at the behest of the burgesses. Henceforth the gentry became increasingly active in the town's affairs; by the mid-seventeenth century they were the rulers of the town in all but name. The effects of

Warwick's poverty problem upon the poor and the ratepayers who supported them are less certain. The poor clearly received rate-supported relief, but what degree of comfort it afforded them and how ratepaying affected the wealth of the better-off are unclear. Even without answers to these questions, though, a study of Warwick sheds important light on sixteenth-century urban poverty.

BIBLIOGRAPHY

The chief documentary source for the study of social problems in Elizabethan Warwick is 'The Book of John Fisher, 1580 to 1588',[138] which contains the examinations of vagrants, poor rates and censuses used in this study, as well as much incidental information on demographic and economic conditions in the town. Lengthy extracts from Fisher's book were published c.1900 by Thomas Kemp.[139] Kemp's transcriptions are in general accurate, but his omissions (for instance, of the poor rate of 1587) make it necessary to consult the original.

The second major source for the history of Elizabethan Warwick, 'The Black Book of Warwick', also issued from the pen of John Fisher and was again edited for publication by Kemp.[140] The Black Book is valuable for what it shows about the corporation's politics, finances and charities, especially for the disputes over the institution of poor rates in the 1570s. It is also useful for the light it sheds on the town's economy in the same decade and the corporation's weakness *vis-à-vis* the lordship of the Dudley family. Kemp's edition contains extracts, and the editorial standard is not as high as in the edition of Fisher's Book.

A third major source used in this study is probate records of wills and inventories which, in the absence of records of freemen and apprenticeships, provide valuable evidence of the occupations of Elizabethan Warwick. In addition, the values of testators' goods, recorded in inventories, show long-term changes in inhabitants' wealth, while from their wills one can determine the kinds (as well as the amounts) of charity they left. The present study made use of all the available inventories and wills for Warwick in the Public Record Office and the Hereford and Worcester Record Office, Worcester. Of course anyone who uses probate records should qualify his results by saying that the records contain few or no wills and inventories of the poor.

In addition to wills, the study of charity in Warwick is based upon the two great standard collections on the subject – the valuation of church properties of 1535, the *Valor Ecclesiasticus* edited by J. Caley and J. Hunter and published between 1810 and 1834, and the nineteenth-century Charity Commissioners' reports.[141] Additional evidence for monastic properties and later charities is found in surveys of the Elizabethan and Jacobean periods.[142] The fate of dissolved pre-Reformation foundations can be traced in records of the central government, Court of Augmentations, *Letters and Papers of Henry VIII*, chantry certificates, and patent rolls – though this paper chase is not a merry one.[143]

NOTES

Although the ultimate responsibility for this study is mine, I am grateful to the following persons for their advice and encouragement along the way: above all, to Lucinda McCray Beier and Lawrence Stone; but also to Lucia Adams, Peter Clark, Janet LaVerne, Joan Thirsk and Keith Thomas. I must also thank Michael Farr of the Warwickshire County Record Office and Margaret Henderson of the Hereford and Worcester Record Office, Worcester, for many kindnesses.

1 Jean-Pierre Gutton, *La société et les pauvres en Europe (XVIᵉ–XVIIIᵉ siècles)* (Paris, 1974), is the best survey of these developments.
2 C. Phythian-Adams, 'Urban decay in late medieval England', in *Towns in Societies* (1978), ed. P. Abrams and E. A. Wrigley, 181–2 (for criticism of this paper, see A. Dyer, 'Growth and decay in English towns, 1500–1700', *Urban History Yearbook* (1979), 60ff. and 73ff. for a reply); E. M. Leonard, *The Early History of English Poor Relief* (1900), chs. 3, 7.
3 Leonard, *op. cit.*, 3–6; 22 Hen. VIII, c 12, *Statutes of the Realm*, III (1819; repr. 1962), 328; G. R. Elton, *Reform and Renewal* (1973), 123.
4 E. Le Roy Ladurie, *Les paysans de Languedoc* (Paris, 1969 edn), 156–7; B. Pullan, *Rich and Poor in Renaissance Venice* (1971), 240–54; N. Z. Davis, 'Poor relief, humanism and heresy', reprinted in her collection of essays, *Society and Culture in Early Modern France* (Stanford, 1975), 24–6; *The Norwich Census of the Poor, 1570*, ed. J. F. Pound (Norfolk Record Soc., XL, 1971), 8–9; P. Slack, 'Poverty and politics in Salisbury, 1597–1666', in *Crisis and Order in English Towns, 1500–1700*, ed. P. Clark and P. Slack (1972), 171–3; P. Clark, 'The migrant in Kentish towns, 1580–1640', *ibid.*
5 Pullan, *op. cit.*, 223–4; Davis, *op. cit.*, 59–62.
6 P. Corfield, 'Urban development in England and Wales in the sixteenth and seventeenth centuries', in *Trade, Government and Economy in Pre-Industrial England*, ed. D. C. Coleman and A. H. John (1976), 221.
7 Clark and Slack (eds.), *Crisis and Order*, 18–20, and *English Towns in Transition, 1500–1700* (1976), 121–5, for overviews of urban poverty.
8 A. L. Beier, 'Studies in poverty and poor relief in Warwickshire, 1540–1680' (Ph.D. thesis, Princeton University, 1969).
9 Leonard, *op. cit.*; J. Pound, *Poverty and Vagrancy in Tudor England* (1971); S. and B. Webb, *English Poor Law History, Part I: the Old Poor Law* (1927); J. F. Pound, 'An Elizabethan census of the poor', *Birmingham Univ. Hist. J.*, VIII (1962), a partial exception to these remarks.
10 T. Kemp (ed.), *The Book of John Fisher, 1580–88* (n.d.), 165–72; original manuscript (unfoliated), Warwick CRO, W19/1.
11 E.g. Le Roy Ladurie, *op. cit.*
12 M. Foucault, *Folie et déraison. Histoire de la folie à l'âge classique* (Paris, 1961), 67ff.; cf. B. Tierney, *Medieval Poor Law* (Berkeley, 1959).
13 W. Camden, *Britannia* (1610 edn), 562–3.
14 H. A. Cronne, 'The borough of Warwick in the Middle Ages', *Dugdale Soc. Occasional Papers*, no. 10 (1951), 16–17; R. H. Hilton, *A Medieval Society. The West Midlands at the End of the Thirteenth Century* (1966), 174, 184, 199: the population in question were, it seems, burgage holders in 1279.
15 *VCH Warwicks*. VIII (1969), 481.
16 Cronne, *op.cit.*, 7; *VCH Warwicks*. VIII, 505; A. Dyer, 'Warwickshire towns under the Tudors and Stuarts', *Warwicks. History*, III (1977), 124, 126–7; M. J. Kingman, 'Markets and marketing in Tudor Warwickshire: the evidence of John Fisher of Warwick and the crisis of 1586–7', *ibid.*, IV (1978), 17–23.
17 Road maps in *Historical Geography of England before 1800*, ed. H. C. Darby (1936), 260, 342; 'English county maps', Royal Geographical Soc. (1932), sheet 15; Cronne, *op.cit.*, 5–7; PRO, SP16/341/42.
18 Cronne, *op.cit.*, 5–6, 14–17; *VCH Warwicks.*, VIII, 438–9, 483–5, 488.
19 *VCH Warwicks.*, VIII, 511; P. Styles, 'The social structure of Kineton hundred in the reign of Charles II', *Trans. Birmingham Arch. Soc.*, LXXVIII (1962), 101; P. Borsay, 'The English urban renaissance', *Social History* v (1977), 583, 586–8.
20 Cronne, *op. cit.*, 5–6, 19–21; Hilton, *op. cit.*, 220.
21 T. Kemp (ed.), *The Black Book of Warwick* (n.d.), 29–51, 385–99, Warwick CRO, W21/6, Corporation Minute Book, 1610–62, 259–81.

22 *The Black Book of Warwick*, 29–40.
23 *Ibid.*, 32, 41.
24 *Ibid.*, 47; 5 Eliz. I, c. 3, *Statutes of the Realm*, IV. i, 411–14.
25 *The Black Book of Warwick*, 47–8.
26 *Ibid.*, 48–9; F. J. Fisher, 'Commercial trends and policy in sixteenth-century England,' reprinted in *Essays in Economic History*, ed. E. M. Carus-Wilson (1954), I, 153.
27 *The Book of John Fisher*, 158–62, and manuscript version in Warwick CRO (100 of 207 craftsmen were leather-workers).
28 W. G. Hoskins, 'An Elizabethan provincial town: Leicester', reprinted in *idem, Provincial England* (1963), 96, 108; L. A. Clarkson, 'The leather crafts in Tudor and Stuart England', *AgHR*, XIV (1966), 27; *The Black Book of Warwick*, XIX, 43.
29 *VCH Leics.*, IV (1958), 78.
30 Industrial goods and foodstuffs both rose about 80 per cent in price from the 1540s to the 1580s: E. H. Phelps Brown and S. V. Hopkins, 'Wage-rates and prices: evidence for population pressure in the sixteenth century', *Economica*, XXIV (1957), 306; cf. A. D. Dyer, *The City of Worcester in the Sixteenth Century* (1973), 158–60.
31 V. H. T. Skipp, 'Economic and social change in the Forest of Arden, 1530–1649', in *Land, Church and People*, ed. J. Thirsk (*AgHR*, suppl., XVIII, 1970), 103, 105: comparing mean averages for 1530–49 (Arden) and 1544–53 (Warwick).
32 *VCH Warwicks.*, VIII, 506–8; Dyer, 'Warwickshire towns', 125, 128; Borsay, *loc. cit.*
33 Figures based on household estimates: 350 in 1544, 410 in 1563, 520 in 1586, 600 in 1670 and 916 in 1730. Sources: PRO, E179/192/153; BL, Harl. MS 595, f. 212; *The Book of John Fisher*, 86 and communicants list (by household) in MS version, Warwick CRO W19/1, unfoliated; *VCH Warwicks*, VIII, 418 and sources cited there. In 1544 and 1586 we lack information for St Nicholas parish, but I have assumed a figure of 120 households, which was the figure in 1563. A multiplier of 4.75 is used throughout, which was the mean household size determined by P. Laslett, 'Mean household size in England since the sixteenth century', in *Household and Family in Past Time*, ed. P. Laslett (1972), 134. The figure for 1544 is arrived at by assuming that the proportion of untaxed was the same as that for paupers in 1582 and adding it to the taxpayers.
34 Parish Registers, St Nicholas and St Mary's, Warwick, Warwick CRO, DR87, DR97; cf. A. D. Dyer, 'The economy of Tudor Worcester', *Birmingham Univ. Hist. J.*, X (1966), 118, for evidence of natural increase there; *VCH Warwicks.*, VIII, 418, for a slightly different view of population levels.
35 J. Cornwall, 'English population in the early sixteenth century', *EcHR*, 2nd ser., XXIII (1970), 43–4.
36 Parish Register, St. Nicholas, Warwick CRO, DR87; W. G. Hoskins, 'Harvest fluctuations and English economic history, 1480–1619', *AgHR*, XII (1964), 36; F. J. Fisher, 'Influenza and inflation in Tudor England', *EcHR*, 2nd ser., XVIII (1965), *passim*.
37 Hoskins, 'Harvest fluctuations', 37; St Nicholas Parish Register, Warwick CRO, DR87.
38 See wills of Thomas and Agnes Shotswell, 1545 and 1547; Lewis Smart, 1556; John Rey, Sr., 1557, Hereford and Worcester RO.
39 Exceptions to the rule that the able-bodied were not relieved include passers-by who were given doles, and heads of family whose children, at least, were given local relief.
40 14 Eliz. I, c. 5, *Statutes of the Realm*, IV. i, 591.
41 These mileage figures correct those in A. L. Beier, 'Vagrants and the social order in Elizabethan England', *P & P*, LXIV (1974), 18.
42 *Statutes, ibid.*; Leonard, *op cit.*, 70–1; *The Book of John Fisher*, 79–80.
43 *Tudor Royal Proclamations* (1964), ed. P. L. Hughes and J. F. Larkin, I, 32; Edmund Dudley, *The Tree of Common Wealth*, ed. D. M. Brodie (1948), 40; W. R. D. Jones, *The Tudor Commonwealth, 1529–1559* (1970), ch. 7; F. Aydelotte, *Elizabethan Rogues and Vagabonds* (1913), *passim*.
44 *The Book of John Fisher*, 3–7; points also covered in Beier, 'Vagrants and the social

order', 8, 15; cf. J. F. Pound and A. L. Beier, 'Debate', *P & P*, LXXI.
45 *The Book of John Fisher*, 58; M. Walzer, *The Revolution of the Saints* (1966), 199;
   T. Hobbes, *Leviathan* (1651), ed. C. B. Macpherson (1968), 238.
46 *The Black Book of Warwick*, 47.
47 Hoskins, 'Harvest fluctuations', 46; C. J. Harrison, 'Grain price analysis and harvest
48 J. D. Gould, 'The crisis in the export trade, 1586–7', *EHR*, LXXI (1956), 214–16; Hoskins,
   'Harvest fluctuations', 46; Harrison, *op. cit.*, 153–4.
49 Hoskins, 'Harvest fluctuations', 43, 46; Warwickshire prices from PRO, SP12/198/77–I,
   II; Nottingham prices from Beveridge MSS in the London School of Economics and Political Science. For permission to consult and quote these manuscripts I have to thank Pro-
   fessors F. J. Fisher and Theo Barker, and the Librarian. Figures in Harrison, *op. cit.*, do
   not differ significantly from Hoskins'.
50 Hoskins, 'Harvest fluctuations', 37n, 46; St Nicholas Parish Register, Warwick CRO,
   DR87.
51 P. Slack, 'Poverty and politics in Salisbury', 176; cf. H. Kamen, *The Iron Century* (1971),
   388.
52 Beier, 'Vagrants and the social order', 6–13; P. Slack, 'Vagrants and vagrancy in
   England, 1598–1664', *EcHR*, 2nd ser., XXVII (1974), 377.
53 Cf. P. Laslett, *Family Life and Illicit Love in Earlier Generations* (1977), 65–7.
54 Laslett (ed.), *Household and Family*, 130, 154.
55 *Ibid.*, 154.
56 *Ibid.*, 146–7.
57 Cf. O. Lewis, *La Vida* (1968), 40, 43, though note that the proportion of households
   headed by women in a slum in San Juan, Puerto Rico, in the 1960s was much lower than
   in Elizabethan Warwick: one in five as opposed to half.
58 Laslett (ed.), *Household and Family*, 134.
59 Survey of communicants, 1586, in MS version of the 'Book of John Fisher', Warwick
   CRO, W19/1, no foliation. A person with a surname different from the head of the
   household is assumed to be an 'outsider': an in-law, married adult sibling or offspring,
   distant relative, servant, friend, or lodger. Cf. D. V. Glass, *London Inhabitants within
   the Walls, 1695* (1966), xxx, xxxv.
60 (2nd edn, 1971), 1–6.
61 *The Black Book of Warwick*, 401–3; H. Raine, 'Christopher Fawsett against the
62 A. L. Beier, 'Social problems in Elizabethan London', *J. Interdisciplinary History*, IX
   (1978), 214; *The Book of John Fisher*, 27–9, 48–9, 61, 67, 75–6, 80, 99, 104–5, 118, 126,
   177, 179, 181.
63 Beier, 'Social problems', 214–16; further evidence is in the book that I am writing on the
   vagrant poor of Tudor and early Stuart England.
64 For youth groups on the Continent and as *rites de passage*, N. Z. Davis, 'The reasons of
   misrule', *P & P*, L (1971), 55; for England, where there is less evidence of formal groups,
   S. R. Smith, 'The London apprentices as seventeenth-century adolescents', *ibid.*, LXI
   (1973), 149ff; B. Capp, 'English youth groups and *The Pinder of Wakefield*', *ibid.*, LXXVI
   (1977), 127ff.
65 Beier, 'Social problems', 208–9; W. G. Hoskins, 'English provincial towns in the
   1520s', in *idem, Provincial England* (1963), 85. Where the poor infiltrated the city centre,
   their streets were most likely to suffer epidemics: P. Slack, 'The local incidence of
   epidemic disease: the case of Bristol, 1540–1650', in *The Plague Reconsidered* (1977),
   55, 57.
66 PRO, E179/192/153; Hoskins, 'An Elizabethan provincial town: Leicester', 93. By the
   1540s £1 was worth a third less than in the early 1520s because of price inflation:
   E. H. Phelps-Brown and S. Hopkins in *Essays in Economic History*, ed. E. M. Carus-
   Wilson (1962), II, 194.
67 *The Black Book of Warwick*, xxii.

68 The rise from one to three families in the Castle Street ward, while larger than in the West Street, hardly includes enough families absolutely to qualify as a significant increase.

69 *The Book of John Fisher*, 169–70, 172; another 11 immigrants cannot be traced to wards.

70 *Ibid.*, 168. Unfortunately no evidence survives to show how large the Apswell house was.

71 *Norwich Census*, 97–9; *Poor Relief in Elizabethan Ipswich*, ed. J. Webb (Suffolk Records Soc., IX, 1966), 122–40.

72 *The Book of John Fisher*, 167–8.

73 A. Savine, *English Monasteries on the Eve of the Dissolution* (Oxford Studies in Social and Legal History, 1909), I, 238; G. R. Elton, *England under the Tudors* (1955), 149.

74 D. Knowles, *The Religious Orders in England* (1959), III, 264–6; G. W. O. Woodward, *The Dissolution of the Monasteries* (1966), 22; J. F. Hadwin, 'Deflating philanthropy', *EcHR*, 2nd ser., xxxi (1978), 112–13.

75 W. K. Jordan, *Philanthropy in England, 1480–1660* (1959), 240–53, 367–9; W. G. Bittle and R. Todd Lane, 'Inflation and philanthropy in England', *EcHR*, 2nd ser., xxix (1976), 203–10; Hadwin, *op. cit.*; J. A. F. Thomson, 'Piety and charity in late medieval London', *J. Ecclesiastical History*, xvi (1965), 178–95.

76 Savine, *op. cit.*, 228

77 L. Stone, *The Crisis of the Aristocracy, 1558–1641* (1965), 47–8. Vagrants' accounts of their peregrinations leave no doubt that hand-outs were common.

78 A point made by D. C. Coleman, 'Philanthropy deflated: a comment', *EcHR*, 2nd ser., xxxi (1978), 120.

79 Jordan, *Philanthropy in England*, 116–17, cited commissions of enquiry into frauds as evidence that charities were carefully administered, but that evidence is obviously open to the opposite interpretation as well; cf. Hadwin, *op cit.*, 111n; below, the Earl of Leicester's foundation at Warwick; and Clark and Slack (eds.), *Crisis and Order*, 20.

80 W. K. Jordan, *The Charities of London, 1480–1660* (1960), 117–22, 136–7, 151–3, 218, 343, gifts by Henry VII, Thomas Sutton and Henry Smith (the latter two dying without legitimate children).

81 Dyer, *City of Worcester*, 241–2; cf. Hadwin, *op.cit.*, 114; W. G. Bittle and R. Todd Lane, 'A re-assessment reiterated', *EcHR*, 2nd ser., xxxi (1978), 127–8.

82 Thomson, *op.cit.*; cf. Dyer, *City of Worcester*, 241, 243; Bittle and Lane, 'A re-assessment', 127–8.

83 D. Knowles and R. Neville Hadcock, *Medieval Religious Houses, England and Wales* (1971 edn), 310–410, 494; R. M. Clay, *Medieval Hospitals of England* (1909).

84 Fuller quoted in W. J. Ashley, *An Introduction to English Economic History and Theory* (1909), I pt 2, 322; A. G. Dickens, *The English Reformation* (1964), 215.

85 Dickens, *op.cit.*, 147–66; L. Stone, *The Causes of the English Revolution 1529–1642* (1972), 73. (1972), 73..

86 For a similar case, see H. J. Hanham, 'The suppression of the chantries in Ashburton', *Devonshire Assoc. Reports and Trans.*, xcix (1967), 129. Cf. Dickens, *op.cit.*, 154, who states that 'the theory that the suppression of the monasteries was a major cause of urban poverty has nothing to commend it'.

87 Knowles and Hadcock, *op.cit.*, 178–9, 219, 400–1; PRO E301/31/35, 53/4A; *Valor Ecclesiasticus*, ed. J. Caley and J. Hunter (1810–34), III, 83–6, 90; *VCH Warwicks.*, II (1908), 97–117.

88 Dickens, *op.cit.*, 214.

89 A. F. Leach, *History of Warwick School* (1906), 91–4; *VCH Warwicks.*, II, 124–9; *Valor Ecclesiasticus*, III, 83–4: the collegiate church of St Mary's accounted for £334 of £456 annual revenue of religious foundations in the town in 1535; PRO, SP1/133/55.

90 PRO, E318/Box 22/1187; *VCH Warwicks.*, VIII, 490, 495, which contains a dubious figure of £80 p.a. for 1545, but which is otherwise helpful.

91 *VCH Warwicks.*, VIII, 491.

92 *Valor Ecclesiasticus*, III, 83–6. I am grateful to Anthony Tuck and Margaret Bowker for their help with this translation.

93 J. J. Scarisbrick, *Henry VIII* (1971 edn), 659, 670–1; J. Youings, *The Dissolution of the Monasteries* (1971), 168–9; *English Historical Documents, 1485–1558*, ed. C. H. Williams (1967), V, 326–7, 330–1, 358–9.

94 Dickens, *op.cit.*, ch. 7; G. W. O. Woodward, *Reformation and Resurgence* (1963), ch. 6.

95 Woodward, *Dissolution of the Monasteries*, 70–1.

96 BL, Harleian MS 540; Warwick CRO, W21/6, Corporation Minute Book, 1610–62, 39–40; *Reports of the Commissioners appointed in Pursuance of Various Acts of Parliament to enquire concerning Charities in England and Wales, relating to the County of Warwick, 1819–37* (1890), 823–4; poor rate of 1587, in MS version of the 'Book of John Fisher', Warwick CRO, W19/1.

97 BL, Harleian MS 540; *Reports of the Commissioners*, 823–4.

98 *Tudor Economic Documents*, ed. R. H. Tawney and E. Power (1924), II, 301.

99 *The Churchwardens' Accounts of the Parish of St Nicholas, Warwick, 1547–1621*, ed. R. Savage (n.d.), 3; Tierney, *op cit., passim*; S. and B. Webb, *op cit.*, 29–41.

100 Jordan, *Philanthropy in England*, 369; and n. 75 above,

101 E. G. Tibbits, 'The hospital of Robert, Earl of Leicester, in Warwick', *Trans. Birmingham Arch. Soc.*, LX (1936), 130–3; Warwick CRO, W21/6, Corporation Minute Book, 1610–62, 39–40.

102 Leicester made provision in his will for women paupers to be put to work in the town, but there is no evidence this was carried out: Tibbits, *op.cit.*, 130–1; 17 of 38 brethren were from Warwick: Warwick CRO, microfilm, Leicester's Hospital 19/1–71, Bundle 1, 1616–98.

103 Jordan, *Philanthropy in England*, 32.

104 *The Book of John Fisher*, 85, 96 and MS version, Warwick CRO, W19/1, for 1587 rate; Jordan, *Philanthropy in England*, 139; cf. Hadwin, *op.cit.*, 110.

105 Jordan, *Philanthropy in England*, 17.

106 Pullan, *op. cit., passim*; C. Aboucaya, *Le Testament lyonnais de la fin du XVe siècle au milieu du XVIIIe siècle* (Paris, 1961), 99–101.

107 Thomson, 'Piety and charity', 195; also, J. M. Jennings, 'The distribution of landed wealth in the wills of London merchants, 1400–1450', *Mediaeval Studies*, XXXIX (1977), 278–9. J. Rosenthal, *The Purchase of Paradise. Gift Giving and the Aristocracy, 1307–1485* (1972), 109–11; cf. Jordan, *Philanthropy in England*, 119, 146–7, 254–5; John Downame, *The Plea of the Poore. Or a Treatise of Beneficence, etc.* (1616), 186, 217.

108 Jordan, *Philanthropy in England*, 254–5.

109 *Ibid.*, 40.

110 K. Thomas, *Religion and the Decline of Magic* (1973 edn), 75, 718; J. Brand, *Observations on Popular Antiquities* (1813), II, 191–3; A. Fletcher, *A County Community in Peace and War: Sussex, 1600–1660* (1975), 155; Robert Brenner informs me that even these exemplars of progressive philanthropy, the London merchants, also commonly bequeathed doles to the poor in the 1640s and 1650s; see also Repertory 34, f. 102b, Court of Aldermen, Corporation of London Records Office.

111 *Reports of the Commissioners*, 790: see below, the Earl of Leicester's plans to put the poor of Warwick to work.

112 For action against the vagrant poor see Beier, 'Vagrants and the social order in Elizabethan England', 15–16.

113 *The Black Book of Warwick*, 10–14, 108–15; J. E. Neale, *The Elizabethan House of Commons* (1963 edn.), 240–4.

114 *The Black Book of Warwick*, 45–7. For a full survey of the town's financial problems under Elizabeth, see A. D. Dyer, 'The Corporation of Warwick, 1545–1588' (BA. thesis, Birmingham University, 1963), ch. 3.

115 *The Black Book of Warwick*, 319–22, 367; *Reports of the [Charity] Commissioners*, 773–6.

116 *The Black Book of Warwick*, 227ff., 314–15, 371–3. Brookes was also accused of not attending church.
117 *Ibid.*, 218, 322–6.
118 *Ibid.*, 47.
119 *Ibid.*, 48; E. A. B. Barnard, *The Sheldons* (1936), for that family and their famous tapestries.
120 *The Black Book of Warwick*, 49.
121 *Ibid.*, 43.
122 *Ibid.*, 218–19.
123 A. L. Beier, 'Rejoinder', *P & P*; LXXI (1976), 132–3; *idem*, 'Social problems', 217–18; PRO, SP16/285/99; *Surrey Quarter Sessions Records*, ed. H. Jenkinson and D. L. Powell (Surrey Records Soc., XIII, 1934), 55–9; BL, Cotton Titus B 10, 268v; J. S. Furley, *Quarter Sessions Government in Hampshire in the Seventeenth Century* (?1937), 41.
124 *The Book of John Fisher*, 81–94.
125 Cartwright's stay at Warwick is described in A. F. Scott Pearson, *Thomas Cartwright and Elizabethan Puritanism, 1535–1603* (1925), ch. 6.
126 *The Book of John Fisher*, 162–4, 186–7, 194–6.
127 *Ibid.*, 165–72.
128 *Ibid.*, 165. Nothing is known of Dafferne's background except that he was a substantial citizen, among the four paying the highest poor rates in 1582, and having five living-in servants in 1586: *ibid.*, 81 and MS version, Warwick CRO W19/1, survey of communicants.
129 *Ibid.*, MS version, poor rate of 1587.
130 *The Book of John Fisher*, 172.
131 *Ibid.*, 94; MS version, poor rate of 1587.
132 *Ibid.*, 170; MS version, 1587 poor rate.
133 C. Hill, *Society and Puritanism in pre-Revolutionary England* (1966 edn), 280–1; Scott Pearson, *op. cit.*, 294–5; P. Collinson, *The Elizabethan Puritan Movement* (1967), 327.
134 'Book of John Fisher', MS version, Warwick CRO, W19/1, 15 March 1587 (no foliation).
135 The *locus classicus* for Protestantism's supposed new approach to the poverty problem is R. H. Tawney, *Religion and the Rise of Capitalism* (1926), ch. 4, pt iv. Leicester quoted from *The Black Book of Warwick*, 28.
136 Cartwright quoted in Hill, *op. cit.*, 280; cf. A. L. Beier, 'Poor relief in Warwickshire, 1630–1660', *P & P*, xxxv (1966), 100.
137 A. Dyer, 'Warwickshire towns under the Tudors and Stuarts', *Warwicks. History*, III (1977), 30.
138 Warwick CRO, W19/1.
139 Warwick, n.d.
140 Warwick, 1898; original in Warwick CRO.
141 *Reports of the Commissioners appointed in Pursuance of Various Acts of Parliament to enquire concerning Charities in England and Wales, relating to the county of Warwick, 1819–37* (1890).
142 BL, Harleian MS 540 and in Warwick CRO, 21/6, Corporation Minute Book, 1610–62, 39–40.
143 Augmentations records relating to Warwick in PRO, E315, 318; chantry certificates in E301; *Letters and Papers, Foreign and Domestic, of the Reign of Henry VIII, 1509–1547*, ed. J. S. Brewer and J. Gairdner (1862–1910), 21 vols, especially vol. XIII; *Calendar of the Patent Rolls preserved in the PRO, Edward VI, 1547–1553*, ed. R. H. Brodie (1924–9), 5 vols.

Economic structure and change in seventeenth-century Ipswich

MICHAEL REED

Economic structure and change in seventeenth-century Ipswich

MICHAEL REED

1 Introduction

I began research into the history of Ipswich in the seventeenth century in 1967 with the object of attempting as comprehensive an account of a second-rank English provincial town as possible within the confines of a doctoral thesis and the constraints of the sources. The thesis was completed in 1973. Plans to publish it were laid aside when I began work on the Buckinghamshire volume in *The Making of the English Landscape* series. The conclusions that I reached in my thesis on the decline of Ipswich in the latter part of the seventeenth century were based upon the evidence then available, largely published accounts of overseas trade. I deliberately avoided attempting any detailed account of the trade of Ipswich because research was already in progress on just that topic. Now that this research is officially posted as 'abandoned' I have felt free to look at samples of both overseas and coastal Port Books. These make it clear that the decline of Ipswich was relative, not absolute. The picture painted by looking almost exclusively at overseas trade was, I now realize, far too gloomy. Undoubtedly the overseas trade of the town fell away considerably, but, as I hope to show later, the coastal trade continued to prosper. Further evidence of this prosperity has come to light now that the probate inventories in the Public Record Office are accessible. These have provided material relating to wealthy merchants and tradesmen, just that top section of the community for which there was so little evidence when I wrote my thesis.

In what follows, the first section is a summary of my account of the political structure of seventeenth-century Ipswich, its regional setting and its demographic history. I have found no reason for changing my view that in the late seventeenth century the population of the town ceased to grow, or at the most grew only very slowly. The second section, on the occupational structure of the town, has been largely rewritten in the light of the new evidence which I have discussed above. The last two sections, on the spatial and structural distribution of wealth, and on the attempts of the corporation to regulate the economy, have been less affected by the new evidence and so remain largely unchanged, save that they have been reduced in length by the omission of much of the detailed illustration.

2   The seventeenth-century town: an overview

'Ipswich is seated on a falling ground to the southward, by the banks of the river Orwell, or Gipping, hard by the place where its freshwater and salt meet, which (with the tide) gives it the convenience of a quay. For its largeness containing twelve parish churches, its various streets, populousness and trade, it may be ranged in the number of cities'.[1] Thus Richard Blome described Ipswich in 1673, and it is to this meeting of the salt water and the fresh that Ipswich has owed its prosperity in the past as a point of interchange for the produce of its hinterland, the sea and the lands facing it across the North Sea. It has always been, and remains to this day, a commercial and service centre rather than an industrial or manufacturing one.[2]

The town of Ipswich is situated on the northern side of the river Gipping at the point where it joins the saltwater Orwell (fig. 6). The Gipping is no more than 15 miles long, and by the time it approaches Ipswich it has divided into a number of channels so that in the seventeenth century the low-lying ground to the west of the town was marshy and liable to flood. The actual site of the town itself slopes up quite noticeably from the water's edge; St Margaret's church, about half a mile north of the quayside, is almost on the 50ft contour. The liberties of the town, however, extended far beyond the built-up area. They measured 19 miles round and covered 8,450 acres. Within the liberties there were 12 parishes, but liberty and parish boundaries did not coincide, the liberties extending to include portions of six other parishes (fig. 6). Within the built-up area of the town, still largely encompassed by the town ditch, there were four ancient wards which cut across parish boundaries. These conflicting areas of authority often generated acrimonious squabbles and occasionally led to lawsuits.

There is now some evidence to suggest that the first streets of the town were laid out in Middle Saxon times on a rectilinear plan, with Upper and Lower Brook Streets and Tavern Street as the main axes (fig. 7), surrounded with a ditch and rampart.[3] The area within the fortifications filled up only very slowly and rather irregularly, obscuring almost all trace of a gridiron plan. The sites of the medieval religious houses had still not been entirely built over by the seventeenth century, and one of the most remarkable features of the town at this time must have been the large open spaces, taken up with gardens and orchards, in the centre of the town. The effect of this was to divide the town in two. Along the water's edge lay the common quay and customs house as well as many dwellings of merchants and mariners, each with its own private mooring. But the social and commercial centre of the town lay to the north of the river, beyond the open spaces of the former monasteries, in and around the parishes of St Lawrence and St Mary Tower. Here was the heart of the town.

Ipswich is one of the oldest incorporated English towns, having received its first charter from King John.[4] The constitution then established remained fundamentally unchanged until 1835, although there were of course many later additions of rights and responsibilities. For the government of the town in the seventeenth century the most important charter was that of 1463, itself a more elaborate version of that of 1446.[5] Two bailiffs were chosen at a General Court, almost always from the 12

Portmen, on the 8 September each year. These bailiffs in their turn chose four from the remaining Portmen to serve as justices of the peace for the year. The General Court was composed of the Portmen and Twentyfour, together with the whole body of the freemen, and it was usual for 40 or 50 freemen, sometimes over 100, to attend. The General Court elected the bailiffs, coroners, treasurer, chamberlains and clavingers, approved the farming of certain corporation offices and the composition of committees for auditing accounts, admitted freemen, disposed of town charities, and elected the members of Parliament for the town. These were wide powers, but in practice for much of the seventeenth century the General Court was managed by the Assembly. This was composed of the 12 Portmen and 24 Common Councillors, almost always referred to as the Twentyfour. They met together usually about once a month, generally just before a General Court, to settle matters that were to be referred to the Court. The Assembly also administered poor relief, arranged the letting of town property, appointed surveyors of highways, fixed the stipend of the town lecturer and took any legal proceedings that might be necessary to defend the

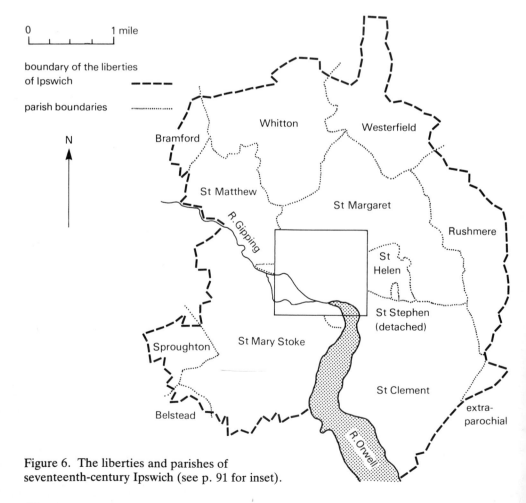

Figure 6. The liberties and parishes of seventeenth-century Ipswich (see p. 91 for inset).

liberties of the town.

The 12 Portmen were chosen for life 'of the wisest and truest of the same town'.[6] and they were almost always chosen from among the Twentyfour. They could be removed from office for neglecting their duties, for what was euphemistically called 'decay in their estates', and on grounds of ill-health and old age. The Twentyfour was composed of freemen chosen for life, and vacancies were almost always filled by the members themselves. This ruling body of 36 men comprised only a small proportion of the well-to-do members of the community, since there were always men of substance in the town who preferred to avoid public life and its burdens. In the early seventeenth century the body of Portmen was dominated to a remarkable degree by a group of families, closely allied by marriage, all either merchants, mercers, or grocers. By 1640 this oligarchy was being broken, and there were a number of factors at work. First of all, several of the families concerned moved out into the neighbouring villages to become country gentlemen (see p. 130). Second, at least one family ended in a daughter and sole heiress. Third and finally, the economic basis upon

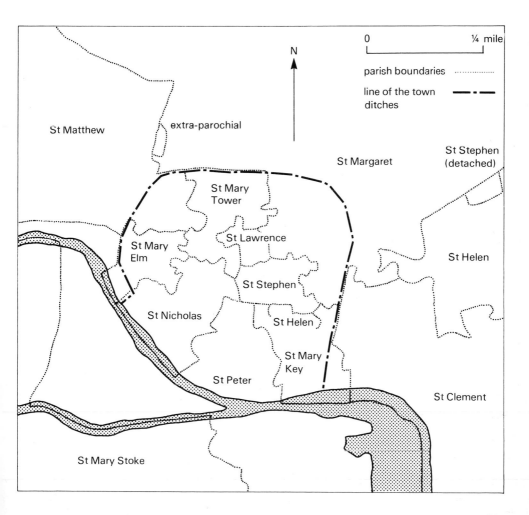

which this oligarchy had been built, namely the Suffolk cloth industry, was in rapid decline. The Assembly in the latter part of the seventeenth century was much more heterogeneous in its economic and social composition than it had been before 1640. Together with the General Court, it became increasingly preoccupied with national political and religious divisions, largely abandoning that careful concern for municipal administration so characteristic of its deliberations up to 1640, in favour of political in-fighting in which admission to the freedom became but another weapon.

The corporation worked through a wide range of officers and courts. The 12 senior members of the Twentyfour were the headboroughs. Every Whit Tuesday afternoon they kept a Court Leet and View of Frankpledge which all male inhabitants between 12 and 60 were required to attend. They had jurisdiction over nuisances and encroachments. The General Court elected a town clerk every year, but in practice the same man filled the office for many years together. There was a Court of Pleas in the town with unlimited jurisdiction in civil cases. Only four attorneys were admitted to practise in this court, and they had to be freemen. The treasurer was elected by the General Court, usually from among the Twentyfour. He was the principal financial officer of the corporation, drawing his receipts from three main sources: rents from property, fines from admission to the freedom, and a number of small miscellaneous items. In addition he received any surplus from the chamberlains, and he had to make up any deficiencies on their accounts. The two chamberlains were elected by the General Court. Their receipts came from four sources: rents of property, rents of office, profits of courts, and a group of miscellaneous items. Other corporation officers included a water bailiff, sergeants at mace, town meters, porters and carters, town waits or musicians, high steward, town counsel and recorder, a town gaoler, three clavingers and even a town trumpeter and drummer. The formal constitution of seventeenth-century Ipswich was complex, sophisticated, self-conscious and, in spite of its ostentatious conservatism, quite different at the end of the century from what it was at the beginning.

The 1603 ecclesiastical return of communicants[7] is the first evidence upon which to base an estimate of the population of Ipswich. It survives for only 9 of the 12 parishes in the town. By taking 2.7 as the number of communicants to a household, and by taking 40 per cent as the proportion of households in the three missing parishes to the number in the town as a whole, it is possible to arrive at the figure of 4,300 as the likely population of Ipswich in 1603. The Hearth Tax of 1664 records 2,016 households in the town, and that of 1674 lists 1,640 (see Appendix 1). A multiplier of 4.75 gives, in round numbers, populations of 9,100 in 1664 and 7,400 in 1674. A brief note of parochial totals of men and women made in 1695 pursuant to the Marriage Duty Act of that year yields, again in round numbers, a population of 8,000.[8]

In order to provide any plausible links between these estimates of the total population of the town at these four points in time it is necessary to turn to the parish registers. The registers of the 12 Ipswich parishes survive with widely varying degrees of completeness. The origins of parish registers have often been described and their deficiencies lamented, and those of Ipswich share all the characteristics which have been noted of others. Not until 1709 is there registration in all 12 parishes of all three vital events. Nonconformity played an unknown but at times possibly considerable role in under-registration. Brownists were present in the town early in the seventeenth century and it was noted in 1606 that some were refusing to have their children baptized.[9] At the very end of the century the register of St Mary Tower notes four burials in the Quakers' yard as well as seven Quaker births. How many more

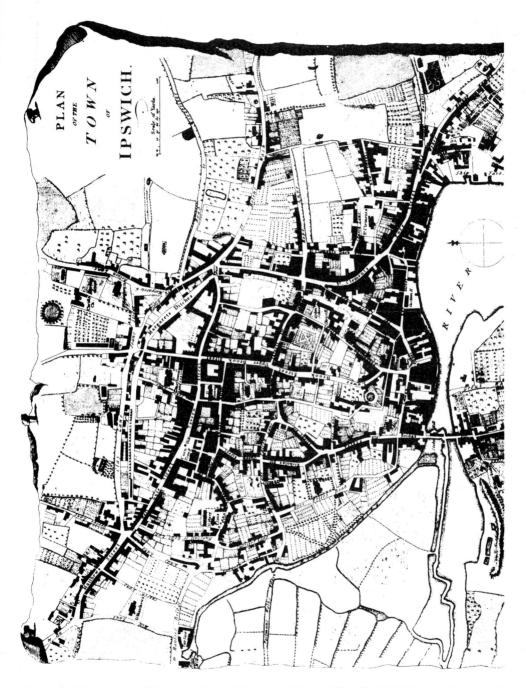

Figure 7. Town plan of Ipswich. A simplification of Joseph Pennington's large-scale printed map of the town issued in 1778, and published as part of Joseph Hodskinson's map of the county of Suffolk in 1783 (reproduced, with permission, from D. P. Dymond's edition of Hodskinson, Suffolk Record Society XV, 1972).

escaped notice altogether it is impossible to judge. Registers generally speaking were poorly kept during the years of the Commonwealth and in more than one parish it is 1663 before numbers of entries inspire any confidence in the completeness of registration. Aggregative analysis of all surviving registers for the town has revealed certain broad trends in its demographic history (see fig. 8). The manifest deficiencies in the registers may mean, however, that these trends have no validity beyond the terms of the records themselves. This must be constantly borne in mind when reading the following paragraphs.

The population in the last third of the sixteenth century was certainly growing rapidly. The total number of registered events in eight parishes grew from 1,002 in 1561–5 to 1,317 in 1586–90, an increase of 31 per cent, or not quite 1½ per cent a year, at which rate the population would double in 47 years. The last quinquennium of the century was marked by high mortality, especially in the years 1597–8, and the excess of baptisms over burials in the quinquennium 1596–1600 was only 77 compared with 256 in the previous one, and over 300 in each quinquennium back to 1576–80.

In the period 1601–5 there were 1,812 registered events, and this period included the severe plague epidemic of 1604. In 1636–40 there were 2,822 registered events, an increase of 55 per cent over 30 years, or 1½ per cent per annum. This is a very crude line of approach but it does suggest that in spite of periods of very high mortality – 1603–4, 1616–17, 1622–3, 1624–7, 1631, 1638–40 – the population of the town continued to grow substantially in the first part of the seventeenth century, and may have reached about 7,400 by 1640, with perhaps as much as a third of the increase coming from immigration. Geographical mobility was certainly very pronounced at this time. The Leet list for the East Ward for 1637 contains 182 names. That for the same ward for 1647 contains 200 names.[10] Of these 200 only 57 would appear to be the same as in 1637, whilst a further 32 have the same surname but a different first name. In other words, in ten years there has been a turnover of more than two-thirds of the adult males in the ward. Of 296 boys apprenticed to the maritime trades between 1596 and 1651, only 110 (37 per cent) were from Ipswich. Of the others, 134 came from Suffolk and 62 from elsewhere in England, including Westmorland and Wiltshire.[11] In the parish register for St Nicholas for the years 1601–20 there were 344 baptisms to 211 families, 63 per cent of which occur only once, and only eight families recorded more than four baptisms during this 20-year period. Mobility of this kind has made family reconstitution impossible for seventeenth-century Ipswich.

It is likely that the rate of demographic growth was beginning to slacken by 1640. The biggest surplus of baptisms over burials came in the quinquennium 1631–5 but the fertility rate, calculated by dividing the number of baptisms by the number of marriages for every quinquennium, reached its peak in 1621–5, at 5.7; thereafter it fell regularly to 3.3 in 1636–40. Registers are defective for almost all Ipswich parishes for the period 1640–60 and it is impossible to obtain any clear or accurate picture of population trends in the town during these years.

The most serious demographic crisis for the town for the whole of the seventeenth century came in 1665–6, and it was caused entirely by an outbreak of plague. Burials began to rise in May 1665. The months of September, October and November saw the highest numbers of burials ever recorded in any months in the town in the seventeenth century, 251, 283 and 128 respectively, and these relate to only nine of the 12 parishes. Altogether there were 1,248 recorded burials in these nine parishes

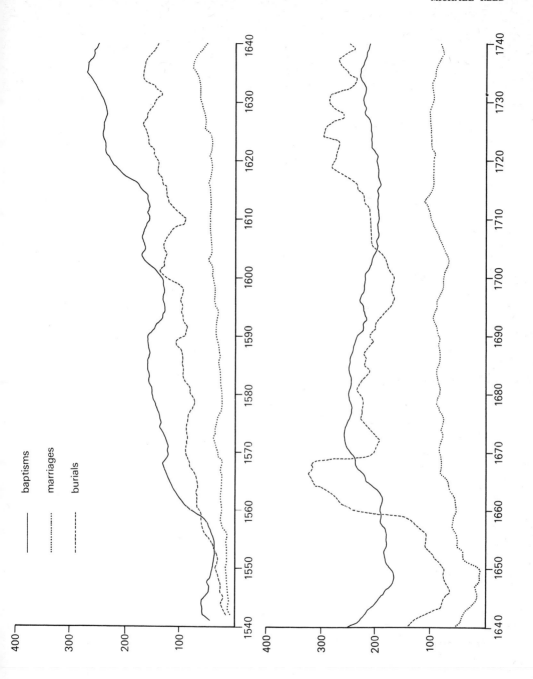

Figure 8. Baptisms, marriages and burials in Ipswich, 1538–1740: nine-year moving average.

between May 1665 and October 1666, perhaps 15 per cent of the population, and at least three in five of these deaths were from the plague. Social and economic dislocation was severe. The port was closed for much of the period. Poor rates could not be collected because, it was said, the major part of the inhabitants were out of town – 109 empty houses are recorded in the chamberlains' accounts. The markets and fairs were prohibited, and even the weekly Lectures were reduced from two a week to one. This was the severest crisis of mortality in the town for the whole of the century, nearly three times as severe as the next, that for the period July 1638 to May 1639.

The loss of at least 15 per cent of the population in the years 1665–6 would have taken ten years to replace, even at a growth rate of 1½ per cent per annum. Demographic recovery after 1666 was, however, slow and uncertain. In the quinquennium 1666–70 there were 92 more burials than baptisms, and in the period 1667–73 there were in all only 322 more baptisms than burials, so that the drop in the estimated population of the town, from 9,100 in 1664 to 7,400 in 1674 – about 18 per cent – is by no means improbable. Between 1675 and 1694 there was an overall surplus of baptisms over burials of 527, only about half of the surplus for a similar period before 1640. There were high mortality peaks in 1678–80, and again in 1689–90. The plague can no longer be blamed for the high death rates of these years, but there were plenty of other diseases ready to take its place. There are, for example, clear references to smallpox in the town in the 1680s. By this time, however, it is apparent that at least one register, that for St Margaret, one of the most populous parishes in the town, is being kept very badly, and so too much credence cannot be attached to population trends based upon parish register totals. One final point needs to be made about crises of mortality in seventeenth-century Ipswich. All seem to have been the consequence of epidemics of uncontrollable disease, not of harvest failure. As far as the parish registers allow, it has proved impossible to identify with certainty a pure crisis of subsistence in the town at any time in the seventeenth century.

By the beginning of the seventeenth century Ipswich was at the centre of a complex region. A region has been defined as an area homogeneous in respect of some particular set of associated conditions, whether of land or people, and the central factor in the creation of a region is to be found in the functions of a nucleated settlement as a regional centre. One of the chief problems in defining a region is the selection of suitable criteria, and the larger the centre the more complex the structure of the area boundaries. The problems become even more acute when the attempt has to be made to define the regional functions of a town at some point in its past, since the evidence is often fragmentary and cannot be quantified. Nevertheless the attempt must be made, because no town is a discrete entity, and its relationships with the region explain much in its history. Such functions may be classified under the three broad heads of administrative, economic and cultural, although it is sometimes difficult to distinguish clearly between them. Each in its turn frequently gives rise to distinctive building forms.[12]

A considerable number of regional administrative functions had come to be centred on Ipswich by the early years of the seventeenth century, although their importance fluctuated during the course of the century, and it is often difficult to give precise expression to the value attached to each one at a given moment in time. The corporation had its own Court of Quarter Sessions with exclusive jurisdiction, but the town was also the site for one of the four quarterly meetings of the Suffolk County Justices. The statute creating a suffragan bishop of Ipswich[13] seems to have been acted upon only once and the town continued to be part of the diocese of

Norwich. However, the registrar of the archdeaconry of Suffolk was to be found in Ipswich, as well as a commissary of the bishop. Ipswich was also a deanery, although the boundaries did not coincide with those of the liberties of the town. The reorganization of the Customs in 1564 led to the creation of a new administrative region based upon Ipswich, which became the head port for no less than 64 ports, creeks and landing places, of which the most important were Colchester and Maldon. This new function led to the building of a customs house on the common quay, not far from the water's edge, at the west end of the common warehouse.

For each of these administrative functions there was a clearly defined boundary, although in fact none of them coincided. The other regional functions of the town lack these precise boundaries and are much more vague and ill-defined. By sea the economic region of the town was enormous. Early in the seventeenth century Ipswich ships were sailing to Greenland, France, Spain, the Low Countries and the Baltic. By the 1630s they were taking emigrants to New England. This long-distance seaborne commerce almost disappeared in the last decades of the century, but the coastal trade retained much of its significance. Ipswich ships played an important part in the Newcastle-to-London coal trade up to the outbreak of the Civil Wars, although after the Restoration they were steadily and inexorably replaced by ships from Whitby, Scarborough and Newcastle. The coastal trade in agricultural produce, grain, butter, cheese and malt continued to be of the first importance, and was stimulated by the ever-rising demands of the population of London for food-stuffs. By land the economic region of the town is equally difficult to define. Simon Cumberland, an Ipswich clothier, was buying wool in Lincolnshire in the second half of the century, [14] and this is but an isolated example of the widespread network of economic links radiating from the town. To add others would not define the region any more clearly. The markets and fairs of the town provided an important focus for the villages and hamlets of the surrounding countryside, although none of them ever acquired any wider significance.

If the economic region of the town is difficult to define at all accurately then its cultural region is even more nebulous. Samuel Ward, town lecturer from 1605 until his death in 1640, exercised a very wide personal influence through much of eastern Suffolk: Henry Dade, the commissary in Ipswich, wrote to Archbishop Laud stating that in his opinion it was Ward's fault that so many were leaving to go to New England.[15] Town lecturers continued to be appointed by the corporation until 1835 but none ever again exercised the kind of personal influence that Ward had. There was a grammar school in the town by 1477 and it received a royal charter in 1566. There is some evidence to show that it drew its pupils from a wide area of eastern Suffolk, but in the absence of admissions registers it is impossible to define this area any more closely. Ipswich was also one of the first towns in the country to have a library. This received many gifts of books and money in its first years, and these are entered in a paper volume presented to the town to serve as a catalogue when the library was founded. Many donors lived in the neighbouring villages, as well as in Ipswich itself.

For all these cultural activities so far discussed, there has been some formal institution which has furnished the starting point. For the last aspect of this function there is not even this. A study of the wills of Ipswich testators has revealed a close network of ties of kinship and friendship over a wide area of eastern Suffolk. This study has also emphasized the importance of the ownership by Ipswich inhabitants of small pieces of property in the same rural hinterland. Marriage licences give the names and

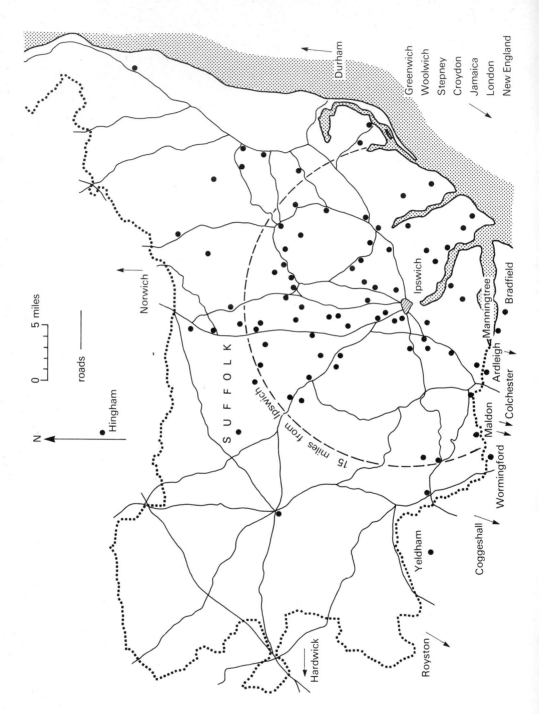

Figure 9. The locations of friends and relatives of Ipswich testators, 1603–1714. Each dot marks a place in which a testator refers to a friend or relative; places outside the county are named.

places of residence of the parties to the ceremony, and thus reveal something of the distance to which people looked for their marriage partners. Settlement certificates were issued to poor would-be migrants, defined as anyone renting property worth less than £10 a year, by their parish of settlement, acknowledging responsibility should they ever need poor relief. Those which have accumulated in Ipswich parish archives date from the 1660s. They provide some indication of the distance travelled by poorer immigrants into the town. Taken together these sources reveal yet further facets of the tightly integrated nexus of personal ties between Ipswich and its hinterland, almost all encompassed within a 15-mile radius of the town (figs. 9, 10 and 11). Finally, by the end of the seventeenth century Ipswich, like so many other county towns, became increasingly important as a centre attracting the country gentry by reason of growing facilities for entertainment and business, and in due course they started buying town houses. This new social function was just beginning to crystallize in Ipswich in the very last years of the century, when there were already attorneys, physicians, a periwig-maker, confectioners, stationers, coffee-houses, a library and a private boarding school in the town; horse-racing was added early in the eighteenth century and a newspaper was established in 1720.

Thus the region of which Ipswich was the centre was of considerable complexity, and the boundaries of its functions, administrative, economic and cultural, even when they can be determined at all precisely, often failed to coincide. The relative importance of these functions changed during the course of the seventeenth century so that the structure of the urban region at the end of the century was quite unlike that at the beginning. For example its economic hinterland had contracted sharply, and the town lecturer of the 1690s exercised nothing of the influence he wielded in the 1620s. Taken together, these changes in regional functions do not of course carry any implications of urban decay; rather they indicate that these particular functions have decayed, to be replaced by others. At the same time they serve to highlight the problems of attempting to define the region of a pre-industrial town.

Seventeenth-century Ipswich fulfils all the criteria required for classification as a pre-industrial town of the second rank.[16] In spite of the changes it experienced during the course of the century it never lost that rank. It is against this background that the economic changes described below must be set.

3   The occupational structure

The analysis of the occupational structure of seventeenth-century Ipswich presents considerable problems owing to the paucity of conventional source materials. No freemen's rolls or registers were kept as such during this period. Probate inventories do not survive into double figures in any one year before 1685 and no parish register records occupations. There are, however, some sources, especially Foreign Fines lists, a Royal Aid of 1661 and an apprenticeship register, which may at least yield pointers as to the direction of economic change in the town.[17] Foreign Fines lists record those non-freemen who paid small dues each year for the privilege of trading in the town. Each contains about a hundred names per annum, and a comparison of the 1674 list with the Hearth Tax returns of that year reveals that those paying Foreign Fines were generally from the lower ranks of the community. Only a rope-maker, three maltsters and a hosier had six hearths, a further nine had five each, and the remaining 112 in the list had four or less. Thus the value of these lists is somewhat

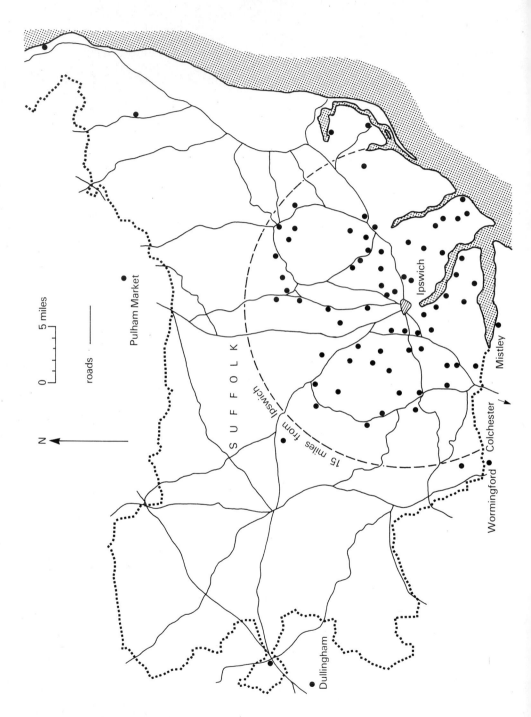

Figure 10. Rural properties of Ipswich testators, 1603–1714. Each dot represents a place in which an Ipswich testator disposed of property; places outside the county are named.

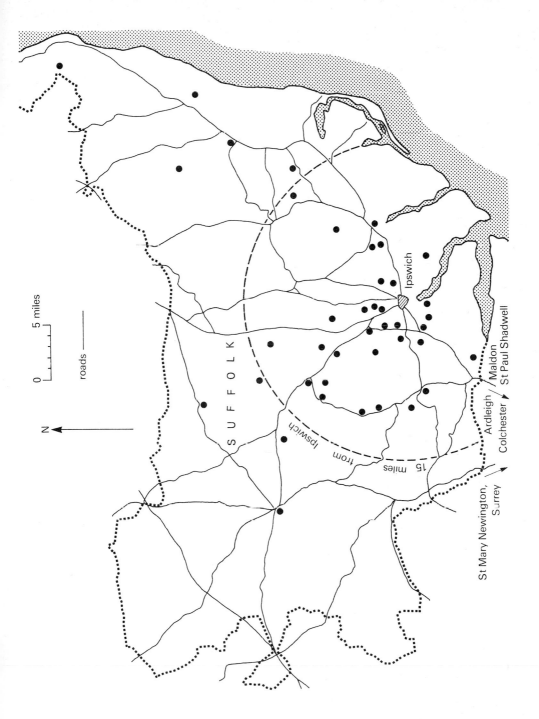

Figure 11. Migration to Ipswich, 1603–1714. Each dot marks a place referred to in a Settlement Order or Renewal Order; places outside the county are named.

limited. The Royal Aid, 'a free and voluntary present to His Majesty' granted by Parliament in 1661, contains, in the record for Ipswich, a list of 241 names and occupations, and provides the longest single list of occupations for the town in the seventeenth century. The apprenticeship register covers the period 1596–1651, but it is very incomplete. The General Court Register contains dozens of admissions to the freedom by service for which there are no apprenticeship indentures enrolled in the register. From its 381 indentures it has proved possible, by eliminating duplicate entries, to recover 187 separate names and occupations. Although evidence of this kind clearly cannot be pressed very far, it is nonetheless likely to indicate broad trends (see table 11).

Table 11   *The occupational structure of seventeenth-century Ipswich**

| | PERCENTAGES | | |
OCCUPATIONAL CATEGORY	1603–60	1661	1662–1714
shipping	18.3	15.6	11.7
distribution and transport	7.1	11.3	8.8
textiles	10.4	8.2	2.4
clothing	11.8	5.4	4.1
leather	15.2	12.2	12.2
metal	8.4	5.7	6.2
woodwork	3.4	2.3	2.8
building	5.4	4.5	5.7
food and drink	6.8	7.9	14.1
professional and salaried	3.6	2.8	5.2
services	0.3	0.9	0.8
gentry	1.9	13.6	6.5
miscellaneous	7.4	9.6	20.7
(sample	1007	353	1196)

*This categorization is based upon that used by J. F. Pound in his 'The social and trade structure of Norwich 1525–1575', *P & P*, xxxiv (1966), 49–69, save that Shipping and Gentry have been made into separate categories and Miscellaneous has been reduced as much as possible. On this kind of occupational categorization generally see J. Patten, 'Urban occupations in pre-industrial England', *Trans. Inst. British Geographers*, N.S. ii (1977), 296–313.

The first column, for 1603–60, is based upon five Foreign Fines lists, 39 probate inventories and 211 wills as well as 187 entries from the apprenticeship register. The second, for 1661, is based upon the Foreign Fines list for that year, containing 132 names, and the Royal Aid. The two together yield a total of 353 names and occupations, since they have only 20 names in common, and they probably account for about 15 per cent of the households in the town. The Royal Aid records 48 occupations and status titles (Mr, gentleman, esquire, yeoman, widow and knight). The Foreign Fines list for the same year yields 43 occupations, of which 27 are not found in the Royal Aid. Thus in 1661 there were 75 different occupations and status titles recorded in the town and this is almost certainly an undercount.[18] They include a surgeon, a schoolmaster, a stationer, a watchmaker, a notary public, two gardeners and a painter. None were truly rural. The last column, for 1662–1714, is based upon five Foreign Fines lists, 118 inventories and 395 wills. Thus the first and last columns are really amalgams of scattered evidence drawn from the entire period covered by each, and so, as well as smoothing out the more violent fluctuations, they also conceal the changes which were taking place over time. Only the second column contains anything approaching a valid sample.

The categories themselves are at times difficult to apply consistently, and each within its very broad terms can conceal the decline of old occupations and the development of new ones. The simple occupational labels which men gave themselves, or were given, can often in practice conceal a wide range of activities. This becomes apparent from the Foreign Fines list of 1661, in which Benjamin Pickas, mariner, was licensed to sell earthenware, tobacco and soap, William Tranham, cordwainer, was licensed to sell pots, and William Thorne, glazier, was licensed to sell butter, cheese and bacon. Nevertheless certain rather nebulous conclusions which may not be valid beyond the terms of this table do emerge: there was no one manufacturing industry of any significance in the town; the textile and clothing trades were declining; leather trades remained important numerically throughout the century; food and drink occupations showed a marked increase; professional, salaried and service groups made some advance.

This analysis of the occupational structure of seventeenth-century Ipswich is scarcely satisfactory. Any account of what it was like to earn a living in the town as a butcher, tailor, clothier or apothecary must be even less satisfactory since, in the absence of business archives of any kind for the period, the single largest body of evidence upon which to rest a description of the economy of Ipswich is that provided by probate inventories. There are 222 of these for the period from 1583 to 1714, but for a number of reasons they are by no means reliable guides. In the first place they give a static view of a man's economic standing at a single point in his career, and since they are concerned with personal possessions they may grossly misrepresent his total wealth because they ignore his real property, which in some cases may have been extensive. Further, several inventories make it clear that certain items of personal property have been deliberately omitted. For example in the inventory of Francis Lucas, merchant, made in 1683, it is stated that he had shares in four ships, but these could not be justly valued because of the hazard of the seas, the said vessels being abroad.[19] Nevertheless a closer examination of surviving probate inventories of those, who, shortly after their death, were said by their neighbours to belong to one of the occupational categories set out in table 11 may reveal at least something of the economy of the town. They give some indication of the scale on which individuals carried on their occupations, although by giving him only one occupational label they may well conceal the very miscellaneous nature of much economic activity. Also, they can provide a rather crude measure of economic success and a fairly clear picture of the resultant life-style. Finally, they sometimes show indirectly those who were employers of labour.

Ship owning, managing, building and the supporting trades were certainly of more importance to the economy of the town in the seventeenth century than any one manufacturing industry. The apprenticeship register already mentioned records 381 indentures. Of these 203 were for mariners and 49 were for shipwrights, figures which give some impression of the importance of shipping to Ipswich. Two surveys of shipping, made in 1582 and in 1702, reveal that tonnage owned in the town multiplied more than six times over that period, and that by 1702 Ipswich ranked third after London and Bristol, having overhauled both Newcastle and Yarmouth.[20] Tonnage growth of this magnitude can be called decline only when seen in relationship to that of London. In 1582 London had six and a half times the tonnage of Ipswich. By 1702 it had over 12 times. There was, however, an important structural change in the industry in Ipswich.

In the early seventeenth century Ipswich-owned ships played a leading role in the Newcastle to London coal trade. A fleet of more than 50 colliers, of between 200 and 300 tons, was engaged in this trade, each ship making about six voyages in the year.[21] Ipswich was also one of the major commercial centres for the East Anglian textile industry, handling about a sixth of the Eastland Company's export trade in Suffolk cloths almost all of which went to Elbing.[22] This meant that the prosperity of Ipswich merchants, shipowners and masters was heavily dependent upon the continued prosperity of the rural textile industry of Suffolk, and this industry was undermined and eventually ruined from two directions. First of all, for much of the sixteenth century, it was concerned with the manufacture of the Old Draperies, heavy woollen cloths, both short and long, coloured and white. During the course of the century the manufacture of the New Draperies was introduced into Colchester by Dutch immigrants, spreading in due course to Bocking, Coggeshall and the towns of the Stour valley. The New Draperies were lighter, cheaper and more varied in texture and colour. The Dutch textile workers in Colchester set a high standard of finish and were rigorous in their maintenance of quality. The New Draperies became increasingly popular in England, in north-west Europe and in Mediterranean countries. Exports multiplied fivefold between 1600 and 1640. In the face of competition of this kind and on this scale the Suffolk Old Draperies industry suffered severely, long cloths disappearing almost entirely from the export trade after 1600.

Secondly, the whole East Anglian textile industry relied heavily upon exports for its prosperity and so was at the mercy of conditions in its overseas markets. The outbreak of the Thirty Years War and the rapid debasement of the Polish and German currencies brought chaos into the Baltic markets. At the height of the slump of 1620–2 it was said that £40,000 worth of Suffolk cloths were unsold and could not be moved. Ipswich merchants, reporting to the Privy Council committee enquiring into the causes for the decay of trade, said that they had hitherto exported between three and four thousand cloths a year, but now they sent less than a thousand, and could not sell even these.[23] There was something of a revival in 1623, and again in 1636–9, but thereafter the collapse of the town's Baltic trade in textiles was almost complete, and this collapse is reflected in the fall in the rents from the cloth hall (see p. 123 and Appendix 2).

In the years after the Restoration the direction and pattern of the activities of Ipswich shipowners and masters changed. The coal trade went increasingly to Great Yarmouth and to rising northern ports such as Sunderland and Whitby, whilst the trade in textiles to the Baltic almost disappeared, the victim of the combined effects of competition from the New Draperies and the chaos wrought by the Thirty Years War. These changes did not however by any means destroy the Ipswich shipping industry, which came instead to concentrate almost entirely on coastal traffic. By the end of the sixteenth century the town was an important exporter of agricultural produce to London, and the continuing growth of London's population provided an alternative opening for Ipswich shipowners and masters as their former interests declined.[24] Suffolk cheese and butter enjoyed a high reputation throughout the century, and Defoe noted the very large quantities of grain being continually shipped off to London.[25] In 1676 alone, 5,527 firkins of butter and 13,857 cheeses were sent by sea from Ipswich, nearly all to London, although some went to Faversham in Kent.[26] At the same time the port continued to fulfil its role as a regional focus by importing a widening range of miscellaneous goods which were then distributed to inland towns such as Debenham, Needham Market and even to Bury St

Edmunds.[27] This coastal trade became of overwhelming importance in the seaborne commerce of the town. In the six months from Christmas 1679 to the end of June 1680, for example, 59 ships left Ipswich – for London (32), Newcastle (15), Colchester (6), Sunderland (2), and Yarmouth, Burnham, Rochester and Dover (1 each).[28] In contrast, for the whole of the year 1680 only 12 ships left the port for foreign destinations – Norway, Rotterdam and Amsterdam – whilst one, the *Employment* of London, took coals for Barbados.[29] Of the ships in the coastal trade, 50 were of Ipswich, 3 of London, 2 were from Harwich, 2 from Lynn, and 1 from Burnham. Of those in the overseas trade only 6 were of Ipswich. The cargoes shipped coastwise included beer, rape cakes and rape oil, flax seed cakes, linseed oil, butter, cheese, calf skins, copperas, wheat, hops, potash, rye, malt, beans, oats, cider in bottles and cordage. The cargoes going overseas included brass, pewter and haberdashery for Barbados, hops and malt to Norway, dressed calf skins to Rotterdam, 26 short Suffolk cloths to Königsberg, and tobacco, custom duty paid inwards from Virginia, to Amsterdam. Ipswich may have lost its position in international trade but as a commercial centre it was clearly of importance, and its relationship with its region as close as ever.

Nevertheless, important as this coastal trade was, there may have been a relative decline even here. In 1625 Ipswich was the destination for 50 coastal shipments from London, the largest number to any outport; Hull was second, with 32. But by 1683 the shipments to Newcastle had more than trebled, to 99, and Ipswich had slipped to fifth place, with 51 – in fact one more than the number of shipments in 1625, emphasizing that the decline in the town's coastal trade was relative, not absolute. In the same year, 1683, Ipswich sent 83 shipments to London, ranking ninth, with Newcastle well to the fore with 1,475. In 1709 Ipswich had 1,098 tons of coastal shipping, ranking fifteenth, after such ports as Scarborough with 21,700 tons and Whitby with 9,140.[30]

Mariners always formed a numerically important section of the community although they very rarely played any part in town government. They tended to congregate in St Clement's parish, thus forming the only discernible occupational clustering in Ipswich in the seventeenth century. A number of their probate inventories have survived. They show that the occupational label could cover a very wide range of economic circumstances, from a poor common seaman to a well-to-do master and shipowner such as William Huggins.[31] His inventory, made in 1685, totalled £172 18s. 2d. His house had at least seven rooms, both the chambers named having hearths in them. He owned a silver porringer, a tobacco-box and a watch, an eighth part of one ship, worth £50, and sixteenths of two others, worth £10 and £6. Lewis Havard, on the other hand, had in 1614 goods in his shop worth £16 out of an inventory total of £27 16s. 6d., and his house of four rooms was only very sparsely furnished.[32]

Other occupations closely connected with shipping include shipwrights, rope- and sailmakers and blockmakers, although unfortunately no inventories survive for any of these occupations. In the early part of the seventeenth century Ipswich was, after London, the most important shipbuilding port in the country. Certainly one of the reasons for this pre-eminence was the close proximity to what Defoe called 'an inexhaustible store-house of timber'. However, by the time Defoe wrote the Ipswich shipbuilding industry had almost disappeared in the face of a combination of competition from London, from Dutch ships captured as prizes, and that silting of the river which was becoming increasing noticeable as the century progressed.[33]

The distributive trades is a category that subsumes a broad spectrum of occupations and attendant economic circumstances. A fundamental distinction must be made between those who were primarily wholesale distributors and those who were chiefly retail. In addition there are those, such as carriers, who were employed solely in transport. It was the first grouping, of merchants engaged in overseas trade, particularly but not exclusively to the Baltic, which dominated the political life of the town early in the seventeenth century. It is likely too, although little hard evidence survives, that they dominated it economically. They must certainly have included some of its wealthiest citizens. It was the collapse of the Baltic trade that undermined the economic basis of their political power, so that the composition of the ruling body after 1660 was much more heterogeneous than it had ever been before 1640. The Portmen and Twentyfour of 1674, for example, included a linen-draper, a stationer, a hatter, a haberdasher, a shoemaker, an ironmonger, two apothecaries, a draper, two grocers and a vintner. The distributive trades were still influential, merchants were still prosperous, but the overseas trade had lost its primacy and the wholesale-retail dichotomy had become blurred, partly because there was in Ipswich no institution such as a Merchant Venturers Company concerned to preserve it.

There survives only one merchant's inventory from before 1663, for Philip Helwys, made in 1611, and it amounted to £18.[34] Helwys actually died at Redgrave, and so he may have been semi-retired. If he really was a merchant then he could have been trading in only a very small way, and he certainly took no active part in town government. After 1660, however, several wholesale dealers' inventories are extant, and they all point to prosperity and occasionally substantial wealth. A tantalizing note on the will of Thomas Wright, merchant, states that an inventory totalling £2,404 9s. 1d. was exhibited in 1681, but unfortunately the inventory itself has not survived. In 1663 Ralph More, merchant, left personal possessions totalling £669 18s. 10d., including £340 in debts good and bad and £105 in shares in shipping. In 1683 Francis Lucas, merchant, left an inventory totalling £649 1s. 10d., including £347 1s. 6d. in debts due, but he was certainly worth more because his shipping shares could not be valued as the ships were at sea. A mercer, Thomas Ives, whose inventory was exhibited in 1662, was clearly very wealthy. His inventory totalled £2,001 8s. 8d., although £567 2s. 7d. of this was in debts good and bad. His warehouses were stuffed with a wide range of cloths, including Padua and Dutch serges, Devon kerseys, Manchester frises, Norwich stuffs, red twills, silks, grograins, bombazines, prunella, even flannel waistcoats.[35]

Only three retailers' inventories survive from before 1660; they are for a chandler, and what were probably an apothecary and a chapman. After 1660, however, a number of inventories are extant and they suggest that retail shopkeepers could be very prosperous. There are three ironmongers' inventories, totalling £309, £400 and £315.[36] One, John Melsupp, had £158 in stock in his shop, including nails, brads, hooks, hinges, horse shoes, locks, ivory and horn combs, fish hooks, curtain rings, door knockers, knives, chisels and gouges, pig rings, fire bellows and handsaws. He had £10 in cash and clothes at the time of his death in 1702, and £95 in debts due out of his total of £309 0s. 3d. Robert Butcher, an apothecary, died in 1708 and his inventory amounted to £626 14s. 9¾d. He had a clock, pictures and window curtains in his parlour, and at least £133 in tobacco in his warehouse, together with sugar, currants, pepper and prunes.[37] A woollen draper, Thomas Wythe, left £111 9s. 10d. in 1685, including £40 in stock in his shop.[38] Shopkeepers who could leave inventories like these must have been among the most prosperous inhabitants of Ipswich in the latter part of the seventeenth century.

There is but one inventory for someone engaged in land transport as opposed to shipping, and that is for Alexander Burton, carrier, who died in 1677.[39] He was clearly retired, and living with his daughter, her husband (a coachman) and their four children in a house which he owned in St Mary Elm parish in Ipswich. He also owned property at Gosbeck, including meadow and an orchard. Almost all of his £58 was in linen, bedding, clothes and household goods, and the inventory gives the impression of plenty – there were 14 pairs of sheets, for example – and of good quality. Carrying must have been one of the more profitable trades of late-seventeenth-century Ipswich (see p. 129).

Representatives of the textile industries were always present in Ipswich but unlike both Norwich and Colchester, where there were large textile industries which owed much to immigrants, the town was never a major manufacturing centre. Instead Ipswich itself was, as we have seen, much more important as a commercial centre and port of export for the rural textile industry of Suffolk. Nevertheless some woollen textiles were manufactured in the town, as the presence of weavers, dyers, shearmen and cloth workers shows, whilst the commercial side was in the hands of clothiers. Linen and canvas were also made, and this branch of the textile industry is represented by linen weavers and poldavis weavers.

Very few probate inventories survive for the textile trades, but they point to a considerable spread of economic circumstance, from the £15 1s. of Stephen Grosse, woollen weaver, of 1590, to the £936 3s. 4d. of George Raymond, clothier, of 1671. Inventory totals considered in isolation are not always very helpful. The will of Stephen Grosse shows that he owned his own house, and it makes bequests of jewellery and plate that are nowhere listed in the inventory.[40] John Wilkinson, cloth worker, left an inventory in 1618 totalling £79 15s., which reveals a large house with at least 13 rooms; his chamber over the hall had a coal fire. He had five tenters worth £10 in his yard, and £4 in teasels. He must have been a master of some substance, employing several assistants. His will shows that he too owned his own premises.[41] John Mixter, weaver, who died in 1685 leaving £50 17s., seems to have been distinctly poorer.[42] Half of his inventory total was made up of debts good and bad. Nevertheless he had a servant to whom he gave his best suit in his will, and who may have helped him with the two looms in his weaving chamber. Thomas Warlters, wool comber, was wealthier. His inventory of 1709 totalled £163 4s.[43] He had in his wool chamber wool in packs and in the fleece worth £54, and more worth £36 out at the spinners. He seems to have done the wool combing on his own premises – he had a combing shop – and then passed it out to be spun. Defoe noted that the poor, in Ipswich and over much of Suffolk generally, were employed in spinning wool for other towns where manufactures were settled.[44]

The two clothiers whose inventories have survived must have been even more prosperous. Michael Osborne died in 1661. His inventory totalled £625 9s. 6d., of which good and bad debts amounted to £263 15s. 11d.[45] He had shears and shearing boards in his shop, wool amounting to £79 in his white wool chamber, £98 in cloths at London, and £54 in cloths at Ipswich. The second clothier, George Raymond, left an inventory in 1671 amounting to £936 3s. 4d., of which £313 was in debts good and bad.[46] He had considerable quantities of wool in various stages of preparation. There were seven packs of white wool in the fleece, worth £35, 198lb of fine white picked wool, as well as weights, scales and 15lb of indigo.

Clothiers, in Ipswich at any rate, appear to have been the most important members of the textile category. They were certainly the wealthiest, and may well have been the most numerous. In 1661 there were more than twice as many of them – 19 – than there were of all other kinds of textile workers put together. Since the function of clothiers was commercial rather than industrial these figures would seem to support the suggestion made earlier (p. 107) that Ipswich was much more significant as a trading centre for the East Anglian textile industry than as a manufacturing centre.

In Ipswich the linen and canvas sector of the textile industry was probably as important as the woollen. In 1574 John Collins, his brother Richard and their apprentices were granted by royal patent the monopoly of making mildernix and poldavis for 21 years within Ipswich and Woodbridge and three miles round them, and John was given for life powers to supervise their manufacture for the navy.[47] Both mildernix and poldavis were used extensively for sail cloth and both were made originally in France. Thus the grant of 1574 has every appearance of an attempt to establish a new industry in England in order to reduce dependence upon imported goods. Locally grown hemp was employed, and further supplies came from Boston and from Lancashire. The industry became well-established, and there was considerable demand from the navy for Ipswich canvas for sails through much of the seventeenth century.[48]

Inventories have survived for two linen weavers and two poldavis weavers.[49] William Cleveland, linen weaver, had two fustian looms at the time of his death in 1606. William Skeete, linen weaver, who also died in 1606, had four linen looms and £6 in linen yard out of his total of £17 15s. Thomas Hawkins, poldavis weaver, had seven looms worth £7 in 1610, and £17 0s. 5½d. in cash, but his house was small, probably with only four rooms, and sparsely furnished. On the other hand, Henry Piper, poldavis weaver, owned his own house in 1615, and two tenements adjoining, one of which was occupied by his son-in-law. He had a tenter yard, a gate-house and at least two workshops containing nine looms, of which five were in use at the time of his death. His inventory totalled £66 9s. Here is another master manufacturer of some standing.

But neither branch of the textile industry, except perhaps that part which was in the hands of clothiers, ever played a leading role in the economy of seventeenth-century Ipswich. Numbers employed in both branches appear to have declined in the latter part of the period, and attemts to revive them from the 1680s (see pp. 125–6 below) were of no permanent effect.

Table 11 shows a steady fall in the numbers in the clothing trades during the course of the century, a category represented almost entirely by tailors. From the six complete inventories which survive for this trade we can see that the occupation covered a wide range of economic conditions, from William Eyreman's personal wealth of £5 8s. in 1589 to Richard Osborne's £162 7s. 5d. in 1619. Richard left £100 to his daughter and property in Ipswich and Stowmarket to his wife for her life and then to the daughter. But of his £162 7s. 5d. no less than £141 1s. 4d. was in debts outstanding.[50]

The leather trades included shoemakers, glovers and tanners. As a category it always seems to have been well represented in the town. For at least two families shoemaking provided the basis for a slow, unspectacular rise over several generations into the professional and gentry classes. John Camplin, the grandson of a shoemaker who was never a freeman of the town, accumulated enough money to be able to buy rural property outside Ipswich and to send his son to Cambridge to become a clergyman. By the time of his death he was sufficiently sure of his social position to call himself gentleman in his will. His son married the daughter of another tradesman-gentleman, a practising house-carpenter, Truth Norris, and his grandson finally made the transition into the country gentry by moving out to Grundisburgh, a village about six miles to the north-east of Ipswich. A cordwainer, John Jeffrey, died in 1685 leaving an inventory totalling £89.[51] He had two sons: one, Francis, died in 1684 leaving £400 to be equally divided among his children; the other, also called John, went as sizar to St Catherine Hall, Cambridge, became archdeacon of Norwich and in due course editor of Sir Thomas Browne's *Christian Morals*.

The metal industries in Ipswich worked primarily for a local market and comprised blacksmiths, pewterers and brasiers, with an occasional nailer, locksmith, gunmaker and goldsmith. In the years after the Restoration a number of watchmakers appear in the Foreign Fines lists but there are no probate inventories for them. Metalworkers seem to have been drawn from the poorer sections of the community if the evidence of their probate inventories is to be relied upon. Even the goldsmith, William Miles, left only £9 in 1588.[52] Unfortunately his will does not survive and so there is no way in which we can penetrate to the truth behind so astonishingly low a total for what was usually a very lucrative occupation. The largest blacksmith's inventory is that of 1712 for Robert Clarke who, although called blacksmith, in fact had far more of his £118 invested in farm stock than in his trade.[53] He had 20 cows and calves worth £43, cheese and butter worth £5 and three acres of turnips worth £4. The other blacksmiths seem to have been purely urban workers but, given the large area of the liberties of the town, the presence of men like Clarke is only to be expected. Indeed it is surprising that we have evidence for so few. There are five further blacksmiths' inventories, three from before 1600 and two after 1660. The largest amounted to £48. The single inventory from a brasier amounts to £19, and that was made for William Rogers in 1692.

In the woodworking category we have only one probate inventory for someone engaged in that trade at his death: for Daniel Mollett, wheelwright, who died in 1709 leaving £12.[54] As our general occupational data in table 11 makes plain, however, there were many more inhabitants practising woodworking crafts in the town at some time in their lives. Some went on to better things, like Luke Jours who began his working life as a turner, added brewing and innkeeping and ended up a gentleman. Probate inventories provide only a refracted image of the real economic world of seventeenth-century towns.

The building trades worked solely for the local market. The chief occupations were masons, carpenters and house-carpenters, joiners, plumbers and glaziers, as well as bricklayers and brickstrikers. All in all they appear to have enjoyed a higher level of prosperity than their brethren in the metal trades. A carpenter, a joiner and a bricklayer each left inventories totalling over £100, and a house-carpenter, Truth Norris, eventually became bailiff and he and his son gentlemen. There must have been some very skilful carpenters, joiners and house-carpenters in sixteenth- and seventeenth-century Ipswich if surviving examples of their work are anything to go by (fig. 12).[55]

The food and drink trades included bakers, maltsters, butchers and victuallers. Bakers and butchers could only have served a local trade, but maltsters may have looked further afield. Their numbers appear to have increased in the latter part of the century, perhaps a consequence of the continued growth in metropolitan demand for malt. Malt was also being shipped overseas in small quantities, to Rotterdam, to Norway and to Hamburg.

As with all of these categories, an occupational label is no accurate indicator of economic success. One butcher, John Denye, had in 1589 an inventory totalling £251. Another, Thomas Bowles, left only £24 in the same year.[56] Bakers may on the whole have fared rather better. Mary Smith, widow, carried on her husband's baking business after his death and her inventory amounted to £364 in 1685, while John Youngs, baker, left an inventory in 1712 totalling £281.[57] Maltsters also seem to have been fairly prosperous, although there are only three probate inventories, ranging from £125 to £210 and all from the latter part of the period.

Innholders and alehouse-keepers were fairly numerous, certainly in the late seventeenth century in Ipswich. From the 1680s the treasurer's accounts record each year those who paid £1 for a licence to keep an inn or an alehouse. The numbers fluctuate from year to year, but generally there were about 70. There is only one innholder's inventory from before 1660, for Robert Smith, who left £76 in 1633. There are, however, ten for the period 1661 to 1714, ranging from the £19 of Robert Pooley in 1712, to the £193 of Daniel Hampshire, who died in the following year. Comparison of the lists of licence holders with the inventories enables a number of inns to be identified. The most famous of all the inns in Ipswich, the Great White Horse, where Mr Pickwick had his encounter with the middle-aged lady, was owned by Martin Shrive. His inventory, made in 1702, totalled £128 13s. 10d., but unfortunately it is not divided up by rooms.[58] Another inn, the Swan, was owned by William Ellis, whose inventory, made in 1703, totalled £118 19s. 10d.[59] The Swan contained hall, parlour, kitchen, pantry, backhouse, brew-house, stable and cellar, shop, parlour chamber, hall chamber, kitchen chamber, shop chamber and wash-house. William owned three butts of stale beer, two more of mild, and a number of empty barrels. His debts, good and bad, amounted to no more than £6. The shop contained a bed and bedding, tables, chairs and a chest of drawers. Other establishments were even better equipped. Thomas Taylor, who died in 1706 leaving an inventory amounting to £100 1s. 2d., had a billiard chamber, with a billiard table, sticks and balls worth £3 10s.[60] His beer was worth £15, and he had 16 dozen bottles of cider worth £5 12s. In the parlour were two tables, 13 leather chairs, seven double mugs, 15 single mugs and three drinking glasses. In his kitchen there was a jack and weights and a pair of bellows, two dozen pewter plates, a mustard pot, a cheese plate, a pie dish and a tinder box.

At 17 St Stephen's Lane, Ipswich, there is a sixteenth-century timber-framed building, now a shop, which had been erected first as a house and then converted into an inn called the Sun (fig. 13). It began as a two-bayed building running north and south, with two rooms over. There was probably at least one other bay on the north. A further, smaller, block extends to the rear on the east side, separated from the main block, which was probably the hall, by a central chimney stack with two back-to-back hearths. There was a yard and carriage entrance on the south, with the gateway on the west. Later, in the seventeenth century, a further extension, jettied and higher than the main building, was added at the east end of the rear block. The rear blocks both have late-seventeenth-century plastered ceilings, and on the outside a pargetted radiant sun. Elizabeth Searles, widow, who owned the Sun at the time of her death in 1668, refers in her will to a parlour chamber and a hall chamber,[61] and she paid tax on five hearths in the 1664 Hearth Tax.

The professional and salaried category includes lawyers, clergymen and physicians, people who clearly enjoyed professional status. There were also a number of barber-surgeons, a calling which occupied a twilight zone between professions and tradesmen. Finally, by the end of the century, there was further a small group of salaried officials. The Poll Tax of 1702[62] taxed salaries and professions, and the surviving record for Ipswich reveals something of the structure of this category (see table 12).

Lawyers were always present in the town throughout the seventeenth century. It seems very likely that they acquired a group consciousness through marriage connections and a shared professional training. While the recorder, the town clerk and the attorneys in the civic Court of Pleas were at the apex of the legal pyramid there was also a small, fluctuating, number of notaries and scriveners in the town. No inven-

Figure 12. A group of houses built in the sixteenth century on the corner of St Nicholas Street and Silent Street, Ipswich. Although rather heavily restored, their façades have comparatively little of the later overlay to be found on so many other houses of the period in the town, and do convey something of what seventeenth-century Ipswich must have looked like (photograph by courtesy of Mrs Sylvia Colman).

tories survive for any member of the legal profession: however, a scrivener, John Walford, gave legacies totalling £270 in his will of 1705, in addition to the considerable marriage portions he had already given to two of his children.[63] Whatever his exact economic position may have been, he was certainly not among the poorer sectors of the community.

Similar niceties of gradation are to be found among the medical practitioners. All four physicians listed in 1702 were doctors of a university. No physicians' inventories survive, but wills show that often they had landed property to dispose of. Surgeons on the other hand were still trained by apprenticeship, had by no means yet thrown off their connections with barbers, and often in fact were almost indistinguishable from shopkeepers. The inventory of Thomas Artis, barber-surgeon, totalled £135 4s. 8d. in 1712, of which £30 was in debts good and bad.[64] His house was comfortably furnished. He had pictures and prints, cane chairs, two bird cages, and a looking glass. His shop window had sashes, shutters and curtains. Outside was a barber's pole and sign. He had ten razors, six blocks for wigs, nine pewter bleeding porringers and three earthen ones, a bleeding staff and a tooth stool, four wigs in curl and some remnants of curled hair.

Table 12   Professional and salaried occupations in Ipswich in 1702

1 registrar of the archdeaconry of Suffolk
5 excise officers
1 town clerk
1 recorder – a part-time post occupied by a sergeant-at-law
4 physicians
2 surgeons
7 Customs officers
1 Officer of the Salt
1 preacher (Mr Langton of the Tacket Street Independent congregation)
6 'for their practice' (almost certainly attorneys and scriveners)

Clergymen may have found themselves in an ambivalent position in seventeenth-century Ipswich. The town lecturer received a house rent-free from the corporation and a stipend of £120 a year, a very considerable salary indeed, but many of the parish clergy appear to have been poorly paid, although in some parishes they received a supplement, not always very regularly, from a compulsory rate on the inhabitants. Religious controversy was at times bitter and a clergyman could find himself adulated by one section of the community and despised and detested by another. These divisions hardened after the Restoration with the growth of dissent. By the early eighteenth century the minister of the Tacket Street Independent congregation was receiving a stipend of £84 4s. from his flock,[65] a fact which the poorly paid Anglican curates who officiated in seven of the 12 parishes must have found galling.

Five probate inventories survive for clergymen. The wealthiest by far was Samuel Golty, whose inventory of 1683 totalled £622 15s. 3d.[66] His library was worth £80, but unfortunately no titles of books are given. John Ward was next, with a total of £346 2s. 1d. in 1662.[67] His library was worth £97 but again no items are specified. His house had at least 13 rooms, and his parlour, with its Russia leather chairs, Turkey cushions and green carpet on the long table, was furnished as a sitting room rather than as a sleeping chamber. The other clerical inventories, all made before 1640, amounted to £75, £59 and £16.

In the seventeenth century clergymen were also sometimes schoolmasters, and schoolmasters were frequently clergymen. The grammar school in Ipswich received a royal charter in 1566, which allowed the salary of the master, £24 6s. 8d., and of the usher, £14 6s. 8d., to be deducted from the fee farm of the borough.[68] No probate inventories are extant for any schoolmasters, but from wills one can see that some at least were men of substance, more especially if they also held a church living. Robert Coningsby, rector of Trimley St Martin and master of the grammar school, made his will in 1709. He left bequests totalling £1,100, all of which, he said, was either out on mortgage or in gold and silver in the house. If his will is to be believed then he had not adopted that method, so common in the seventeenth century, of providing for younger children by charging property left to the eldest with legacies and annuities that must have absorbed the profits for years to come.[69]

There were also other schools in the town during the seventeenth century. They are known only from ecclesiastical visitations and subscription books which yield no more than the name of the schoolmaster, the fact that some masters were un-licensed, and that sometimes the schools were called English schools.[70] There is a will, but again no probate inventory, for one of these schoolmasters. John Mansur was keeping a private school in Ipswich by 1678. He added to his income by drafting wills for his fellow citizens, wills which have their own distinctive diplomatic and script. He died in 1703.[71] He lived in his own house in St Clement, and part of his premises must have been used by his pupils, since his will refers to a livery chest in the further chamber over the school. He gave £50 to his wife in full satisfaction of her dower and

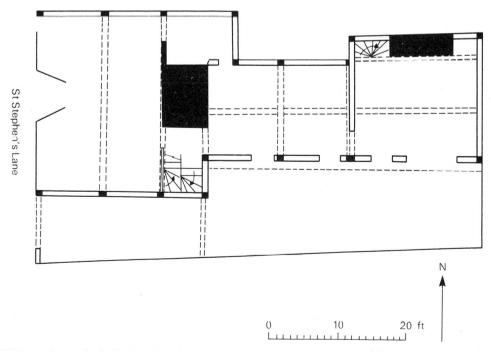

St Stephen's Lane

0   10   20 ft

N

Figure 13. 17, St Stephen's Lane: plan.

third part. If this does indeed represent a third part of the value of his real estate, which included three cottages in St Margaret's parish, then he too was not among the indigent of seventeenth-century Ipswich.

Lawyers, clergymen and schoolmasters were established figures in urban society by the late seventeenth century. It is the Customs, Excise and Salt officers who mark the most significant departure. These 13 men constitute the beginnings of that socio-economic category so characteristic of an industrialized society, the salary earner. Even at an early stage the group shows nice distinctions of status. The Customs Surveyor and Landwaiter had a larger salary than the Boatmen, who in turn received more than the Customs Searcher.

There is next a small group of men who were providing a widening and increasingly specialized miscellany of services, a group which shows a small but significant growth during the period. Before 1660 there were only three; a musician, a painter and a gardener. By the end of the century its members included a periwig-maker, two servants, a fan-maker, a coach harness maker and a bookbinder, as well as two gardeners and an upholsterer. The inventory of Thomas Silsby, gardener, totalled £11 12s. in 1711, and he owned his own gardens and plantations in Ipswich.[72] A coach harness maker, John Peacock, left in 1709 an inventory amounting to just over £19. His shop contained his working tools, cutting board, brass buckles of various kinds, leather traces, brushes, clamps and the body of a calash (a light low-wheeled carriage with a removable hood). His house had six rooms and appears to have been fairly comfortably furnished.[73] These occupations, however, are too varied, and the evidence too slender, for any worthwhile generalizations about their economic standing.

The urban gentry[74] are to be distinguished from other inhabitants of the town by the use of titles of respect: master, gentleman and esquire. Their use was neither governed by any objective criteria nor applied consistently, although it seems clear that the terms, especially Mr, were applied more loosely and indiscriminately in the last half of the century than in the first.

The term 'gentleman' was a status indicator and had quite a different meaning in an urban context from that which it had in rural society. In seventeenth-century Ipswich it was accorded as a term of respect to those few who had acquired a certain level of economic success, but it also conceals what that level was and how it was achieved. The use of the style does not appear to have been the prerogative of any one occupation. Birth alone gave no right to it. Ownership of extensive landed property was not a prerequisite. Many of those called gentlemen were still active in their trades. Only the professional men among them would have been to a university. Thus the urban gentry differed in almost every respect from the country gentry, and outside their urban setting they were of almost no significance.

There are three surviving probate inventories for urban gentry. One illustrates especially well all these points. Luke Jours, gent., died in 1678. His inventory totalled £1,265 5s. 4d.[75] He had £350 in cash in his house. His good debts were worth £272 17s. 3d., and the bad ones amounted to £195 11s. 9d. He had 264 combs of malt worth £105 14s. In addition there were shares in five ships which were not valued for his inventory. Jours must have been one of the wealthiest men in late-seventeenth-century Ipswich, and his wealth was soundly based, with no more than a third in outstanding debts. His will reveals that he owned three victualling houses in Ipswich, the Half Moon, the Rose and the Gun, as well as property in Alderton, Cattawade, Clopton and Grundisburgh. When his son John was admitted pensioner to St John's

College, Cambridge, in 1654 he was described as a turner of St Clement's parish, Ipswich. In that same year he was indicted in the town's quarter sessions for selling beer above the permitted price, and called beer-brewer.[76] By 1661 he had moved to St Peter's, where three years later he paid tax on nine hearths. In the Hearth Tax record he is called Mr. In the Royal Aid of 1661, to which he contributed £20, the same amount that Samuel Pepys paid, he is called gentleman. He served in various municipal offices, being headborough, chamberlain, and bailiff three times. He did not, however, begin at the bottom of the heap. His father, John Jours, died in 1623. According to his will he owned an inn called the Dolphin, and he gave to Luke legacies totalling £110, a not inconsiderable sum with which to begin in the world.

The miscellaneous category in table 11 comprises widows, single men, spinsters, yeomen, and a handful of peripheral townspeople including a gunpowder maker and the town gaoler. By far the largest number were the widows, and inventories survive for no less than 38 of them, making them the largest single 'occupation' in seventeenth-century Ipswich. Ranging as they do from one of the largest, over £1,000, to one of the smallest, no more than £4, and coming from the whole span of the century, they epitomize many aspects of the social and economic history of the town. Widows of merchants were clearly wealthy, living in comfortable circumstances, often with considerable sums of money invested in bonds, mortgages and shipping. Others were residing in only part of a house, which in one inventory is actually called the lodging chamber. Some, if their inventories are anything near complete, must have been living in wretched poverty. Elizabeth Cock, for example, left in 1611 no more than £4 10s. 6d., of which 13s. was in money, 5s. in 'odde Implements', and the rest in clothes.[77] If she ever went to bed, sat on a chair or ate from a plate then they must have belonged to someone else.

The categories listed in table 11 do no more than show the proportions of certain occupational groups in Ipswich during the Stuart period and categorization of this kind often conceals as much as it reveals. It fails to illuminate the variations in prosperity between different trades in an occupational grouping, between branches of the same trade, or between individuals following one craft. Probate inventories can throw some flickering light on these questions but there are too many uncertainties surrounding them for us to be always confident of their findings.

Although the evidence for the study of the occupational structure of seventeenth-century Ipswich is so unsatisfactory, three points do emerge. First of all, very few of the inhabitants of the town appear to have had any direct connection with the land. They must have relied heavily upon markets and shops for the satisfaction of their material needs. Secondly, the century sees the gradual widening of the range of occupations in the town, coupled with increasing specialization. By the end of the century well over a hundred, perhaps 130, occupations were to be found, including such specialized trades as button-maker, fan-maker and bolt-maker. Thirdly, there was almost no change in the patterns of economic organization. Commerce and manufacture remained essentially small-scale, personal and domestic in their management and finance, and as a result they remained very unstable, the prey of disaster of every kind, human, biological and climatic.

4 The structural and spatial distribution of wealth

Probate inventories have up to this point been used to illuminate the economic structure of seventeenth-century Ipswich by arranging them according to occupational categories. However if we aggregate the inventories and rank them by their total valuations then further light is shed both on the town's economy and on its social order.

Table 13 shows that over half of all surviving inventories total under £50, and almost three-quarters are under £100. No less than 28 (12.6 per cent), are under £10, and persons with less than £10 in money, goods, land or chattels were exempt from the Hearth Tax. The implication is a very broadly based socio-economic pyramid with a very steep apex, and even this pyramid cannot, from the nature of the evidence, have included the truly poor. Those with personal wealth over £100 must almost certainly have enjoyed comfort, prosperity and attendant prestige. There was considerable overlapping of economic success between one occupation and

Table 13   Ipswich probate inventories, 1583–1714

	PERCENTAGES			
INVENTORY TOTAL	1583–1600	1601–1660	1661–1714	totals
over £1000			2.1	1.4
751–1000			1.4	0.9
501–750		2.1	3.5	2.7
251–500	3.2	6.4	6.9	6.3
101–250	6.5	12.8	19.4	16.2
51–100	9.7	27.7	15.9	17.6
26–50	16.1	17.0	9.1	11.7
under 25	64.5	34.0	41.7	43.2
(sample	31	47	144	222)

another, and it must be repeated that the use of only one occupational label can be totally misleading. Many men engaged in a wide variety of callings, probably carrying on two or three at the same time. Handicraftsmen were not invariably at the bottom of the pyramid. Mariners, shoemakers, tailors, bakers and bricklayers all have at least one representative over the £100 line. Innkeepers, ironmongers, maltsters and apothecaries seem to have been generally wealthier, and merchants and clothiers still more prosperous. Success seems to have come more frequently to dealers and traders than it did to manufacturers and artisans, although it must also have depended upon non-economic factors beyond the reach of tables and graphs, upon personal traits of thrift and industry, upon a timely legacy or a prudent marriage.

Probate inventories have so far been used to rank individuals and occupations by comparing totals. If we look now at the main components of inventories then it may be possible to learn something of the structure of personal wealth in seventeenth-century Ipswich.[78] Here we can use the broad divisions of debts due to the deceased, stock-in-trade, cash and shares in shipping, and finally purely household and domestic possessions. These divisions are often difficult to apply consistently. In particular the stock-in-trade of the deceased is always difficult to separate from his household effects. Trade and industry were essentially domestic in their organization and the line between occupational and domestic purposes is often impossible to draw with any degree of certainty. Thus any values under this head are minimal.

Of the 222 surviving probate inventories for Ipswich, 27 have more than half in outstanding debts, 14 have over half in stock-in-trade, 2 have more than 50 per cent in cash or shipping, and a further 47 have more than half made up of combinations of two or more of these elements. Altogether 90 inventories are thus accounted for. More significant, however, is the fact that this group includes no fewer than 52 of the 61 inventories over £100, and four of the remaining nine have over 40 per cent of their totals made up in this way. In other words, only one in seven of those people whose inventories reveal some modest economic success had more than half their total personal wealth invested in household and domestic goods. There is almost no indication of lavish or ostentatious expenditure under this head. Indeed total inventorial wealth is not always an accurate indicator of life-style. Mary Huntin, spinster (1686) left £1086, but this included only £37 7s. in household goods, less than Thomas Wythe, a woollen draper (1685) whose inventory total was a tenth of hers. The most expensively furnished house seems to have been that of Mary Bedingfield (1706), where there was £56 7s. 9d. in plate, £30 in a chariot harness and two old horses, and £43 10s. 6d. in linen. The remainder of her £296 10s. 9d. was in household goods, including cane chairs in the dining room, an escritoire in the parlour, some Delft ware and a summer-house in the garden – comfortable perhaps, but scarcely sybaritic.

Thus the major part of the wealth of the 'middling sort' of seventeenth-century Ipswich was to be found spread over bonds, bills, cash, stock-in-trade and shares in shipping, all in varying proportions, although there is no evidence from the inventories of any participation by Ipswich inhabitants in government finance. Economic instability in the seventeenth century would have made risk-spreading of this kind almost essential. Where there is any very marked concentration of wealth into one form of investment then there are often special attendant circumstances. Thus of those with more than half their money in outstanding debts, seven were well-to-do widows or spinsters.[79] A capital sum invested in a good security was clearly one way in which a husband or father provided for dependents. At the other end of the social and economic spectrum were a number of seamen who owned nothing but the clothes they stood up in, together with a promise from an impecunious Admiralty of wages due for service at sea.[80]

However, a low inventory total does not of itself prove definite poverty. A further factor needs to be taken into account when assessing the economic standing of an individual, one which it is usually impossible to quantify. This hidden factor is the ownership of real property. Probate inventories list only the personal wealth of the deceased, and on occasion only that remaining after legacies have been paid and funeral expenses discharged. Land is mentioned only when it is held under a lease. Property, both urban and rural, seems to have been widely owned in seventeenth-century Ipswich, but on a comparatively small scale (see p. 97 and fig. 11). No townsman was a great landowner: acres, when specifically mentioned in wills, are in tens rather than in hundreds, and it is rare for a testator to list more than a dozen properties altogether. Urban artisans, whose inventory totals would seem to imply that they were the poorest of town dwellers, often, on the evidence of their wills, owned their own houses, and cloth and metalworkers, tailors, shoemakers and the like are frequently found disposing of fields and cottages in the countryside around Ipswich.

The study of a number of records relating to this real property within the town enables something to be said about the spatial distribution of wealth, based upon the assumption that the rich lived in large houses and the poor in small ones.

The Hearth Tax (see Appendix 1) reveals that in Ipswich, as in other English provincial towns of this period, central parishes were in general terms occupied by the wealthier sections of the community and suburban ones by the poorer, although it is clear that there is no rigid spatial separation of rich from poor.[81] The Ipswich parishes (see fig. 6) fall into three fairly well-defined groups. The 1664 Hearth Tax is used as the basis for this classification, since the distortions caused by the high mortality of the 1665–6 plague epidemic are still reflected in the 1674 Hearth Tax. At the top are St Lawrence and St Mary Tower, with an average of 4.3 and 3.9 hearths per household respectively. St Mary Tower also has the lowest percentage of households in the 1–2 hearth category and it is likely that the percentage for St Lawrence was also low, though no legible data survives. The next four parishes – St Peter, St Stephen, St Mary Key and St Helen – have an average of from 3.4 to 2.9 hearths per household, still above the average for the town as a whole. They too have between 50 and 64 per cent households with 1–2 hearths although the figures for St Stephen are also missing. Of these four, only St Helen is a suburban parish.

Households in the remaining six parishes all have an average number of hearths below that for the town as a whole, ranging from 2.7 to 2.3. They also have from 65 to 79 per cent of their households in the 1–2 hearth category. Only two, St Mary Elm and St Nicholas, were essentially intra-mural parishes, lying on the river but above Stoke Bridge. This meant that, since ships could not pass the bridge, these areas lacked the attractions of those below the bridge in St Peter or St Mary Key, where many merchants' houses backed on to the river, giving direct access to the seaborne commerce of the town through their own private quays. The other four parishes in this group were primarily suburban, extending well beyond the main built-up area of the town. Here, however, an important qualification must be made. The parish is the smallest unit that can be studied. It may well be that the irregular shapes of the Ipswich parishes do in fact conceal or distort important social and economic divisions, divisions which lie beyond the reach of the surviving documentary evidence.

It is possible to add a further dimension to this aspect of the structure of wealth by comparing two lists showing property owners and occupiers, the first a church rate on eight parishes in 1637, the second an assessed tax record for 1689.[82] The church rate was levied on 1,026 separate houses or premises, of which 219, a fifth, were owner-occupied, although the proportion varied considerably from parish to parish, from 40 per cent in wealthy central St Lawrence to 18 per cent in poor suburban St Margaret. Of these premises, 743, or 72 per cent, were rented, and by a single household. Only 64 of the 1,026 properties covered by this rate were shared, and only five were shared by more than two households. This would suggest that building in early seventeenth-century Ipswich was keeping up with population growth.

The assessed tax of 1689 was levied on 1,250 premises in 12 parishes, and the record reveals a number of remarkable changes since 1637. First of all the total number of houses in all the parishes except St Lawrence shows a marked fall; but too much significance cannot be attached to this because although both assessments exclude the poor, the line in 1637 may have been set lower than in 1689. As in 1637, over three-quarters of accommodation was rented or shared, but there had been a distinct shift in the way this was structured. In 1637 a negligible proportion of owner-occupiers shared their properties with other households; by 1689 this proportion had risen to 10 per cent. Again, while in 1637 72 per cent of households lived in rented accommodation on their own, by 1689 this figure had shrunk to about half: conversely the percentage of shared rented accommodation had risen from 5 per cent to 25 per cent of the total. The obvious explanation is that pressure from the very modest population recovery of the late 1670s and 1680s was being met by subdivision of existing properties rather than by new building. This is confirmed by a comparison of Ogilby's map of the town of 1674 with that of Pennington of 1778. There had been almost no building in the intervening century. A similar phenomenon has been noted for King's Lynn.[83]

There appears to be no clear correlation at parish level between house size and the proportion of houses in owner-occupation or single occupation. Houses are just as likely to be rented or shared in central parishes as in suburban ones. Indeed the lowest proportion of shared houses is in St Mary Stoke, a suburban semi-rural parish lying across the river to the south of the town centre. A high proportion of rented and shared houses may be a normal feature of an urban parish. There is no evidence to show how the Hearth Tax was compiled but in the lists as they survive large and small houses appear in close proximity, so that if in fact the lists represent the approximate order in which the houses were arranged in the streets then there was no marked segregation of rich and poor. However, a study of the Hearth Tax tables in Appendix 1 reveals quite wide variations in the overall distribution of poor and rich as between parishes. In 1664 St Lawrence had only 26.3 per cent of its households exempt from the tax. The next parish with a low percentage was St Mary Tower, with 41.1 per cent. These were the two central parishes in the town. The parish with the greatest percentage exempt from the tax was the suburban parish of St Margaret, with 63.6 per cent. The 1665–6 epidemic appears to have been particularly severe in the poorer parts of the town, so that by the time of the 1674 Hearth Tax St Lawrence had no exempt households, St Mary Tower had 29.7 per cent and St Mary Stoke had replaced St Margaret as the parish with the highest percentage of exempt, 58.4 per cent.

The poor were certainly heavily concentrated in suburban parishes, but were by no means absent from central areas of the town. Indeed it is possible that the Hearth Tax data exaggerate the contrast between wealthy central and poor suburban parishes because an unknown but perhaps significant proportion of the larger houses in the centre of the town would have been inns.

Economic enterprise in seventeenth-century Ipswich was conducted almost entirely upon a domestic, personal scale. Even shipbuilding, the industry making the biggest demands on labour and capital, was organized on an *ad hoc* partnership basis. This means that the structure of personal wealth was intimately connected with the level and scope of economic activity and governed by demographic and social factors. A high mortality rate, coupled with the practice that seems to have been usual in the town of dividing wealth among children rather than passing the bulk of a fortune on to one heir, led almost inevitably to the dispersal of such capital as had been accumulated over a comparatively short working life. At the same time the low level of technology and the lack of permanent business institutions gave a built-in fragility to capital holdings. The only investment with any measure of stability was real property. Its ownership seems to have been widespread in seventeenth-century Ipswich, but the Ipswich evidence fails to make clear whether or not it was a profitable one.

5 The role of the corporation in the urban economy

The urban economy was, to a limited extent, given a framework by the town government. The corporation provided some of the institutions and some of the social investment required, and at the same time acted as the agent of the state in regulating some aspects of economic activity. But these provisions and regulations were highly selective in their application and inefficient and fitful in their operation, their nature and effectiveness changing during the course of the century. The overall pattern is one of decline and decay. Frequently the corporation withdrew from active participation, leaving Ipswich in the last decades of the seventeenth century with a comparatively open and unregulated economic structure. Some institutions were left to run under their own momentum, others declined for reasons external to the town.

a The regulation of the labour supply

The corporation controlled the labour supply in the town by regulating wages and apprenticeship, confining full participation in the town's economy to freemen, and imposing restrictions upon the numbers of immigrants. The regulation of wages was carried out in the town's sessions of the peace pursuant to the Statute of Artificers. Although rates of wages were regularly confirmed, certainly from 1608[84] until 1653,[85] in no case are the actual rates recorded. This may cast some doubt upon the reality of the exercise, and the whole system is not heard of again after 1653. Appendix 2 shows daily wage rates paid to building labourers by the corporation during the course of the century for work on civic property. The evidence is scattered and fragmentary and disappears entirely after 1690. The Appendix also lists prices of building materials, using data which is subject to similar deficiencies. In spite of their obvious weaknesses the figures appear to indicate that wages doubled over the century, but that the bulk of the increase took place in the period before 1660. In any case the wages paid fluctuated within a broad band in any one year. By contrast, prices rose by no more than a third, again with the the bulk of the increase before 1660, and with prices actually paid within any one year also fluctuating within broad limits. In sum, allowing for the limitations of the data, there may have been a modest improvement in real wages in the period after the Restoration.[86]

Full participation in the economic life of the town was a privilege confined to freemen. Freemen were admitted at the General Court, their admission being recorded in its register. The freedom could be acquired by patrimony, by apprenticeship or by purchase. Purchase is not at all common before the very end of the century and then it quickly degenerates into a weapon to be used in political infighting. The son of a freeman was entitled to the privilege provided he had been born after his father was enfranchised. In the case of freedom by apprenticeship the General Court always scrutinized candidates carefully. It made repeated attempts to secure the enrolment of apprenticeship indentures, but the frequency with which ordinances requiring this were passed, repeated and revived suggests widespread evasion.

Only freemen might exercise any trade or manual occupation, sell merchandise or keep open shop, and those other than freemen might earn their living in the town only if they paid a Foreign Fine, which was assessed each year by a committee appointed for the purpose. The economic privileges of freemen were always difficult to preserve and attempts on the part of the corporation to enforce them usually ended in lawsuits which could be costly and were not always successful. The Foreign Fines themselves were often unpaid. Foreigners were also forbidden to buy or sell goods of any other foreigner for resale, a restriction confirmed by the charter of 1519. At the same time freemen were forbidden to act as intermediaries in such transactions, and were liable to be disfranchised if they did.

The effectiveness of these regulations against foreigners is difficult to assess. Some names appear in the Foreign Fines lists for 20 years together, others appear only once. There are occasional orders against foreigners instructing them to shut up shop and depart the town, and some are never heard of again, though others are still to be found in the following years, after what bargaining or pleading, or sheer administrative inefficiency, we cannot tell. Individual freemen[87] sometimes brought a legal action against a foreigner, motivated perhaps more by personal rivalries and jealousies than by an altruistic concern for the ancient liberties of the town. From the viewpoint of many foreigners such regulations, only fitfully and perhaps partially applied, must have been more of a nuisance than anything else.

A corollary to this crumbling of foreigner regulations is to be found in the growing neglect of civic orders against countrymen. In 1575 the General Court ordered that, since a great number of countrybred artificers and handicraftsmen had of late settled in the town, fallen into great poverty and become a charge on the town, no artificer born outside the town was to settle there without licence unless he had been in the town three years before the date of the order. The order was repeated the following year, when the taking of apprentices out of the country was also forbidden, and the Twentyfour were ordered to search out newcomers and expel them from the town. It was repeated again in 1578 and in 1609, when the period of residence in the town was raised to seven years.[88] In 1659 the Great Court revived all previous orders for searching newcomers together with the prohibition against letting houses to them, but this is their last appearance. Actual enforcement of the orders was left to the town Sessions and cases concerning inmates and strangers occur from time to time throughout the century.[89] The disappearance after the Restoration of such sweeping orders calling for the removal of all strangers is probably due fundamentally to an easing of population pressure, although the Settlement Act of 1662 may also have been a contributory factor by providing some immigrants with security against a removal.[90] By the 1680s the corporation was on occasion prepared to welcome newcomers bringing new skills into the town.

b The regulation of trades

The civic fathers also took care to regulate certain occupations in the interests of good order and to protect the consumer: but it is again possible to detect some slackening of purpose in the last decades of the century.

Medieval Ipswich certainly possessed many trade gilds, but these lost much of their separate identity during the course of the sixteenth century. In 1575 the General Court ordered all occupations to be drawn into companies and in 1576 four companies were created by amalgamation. These were Mercers, Drapers, Tailors and Shoemakers.[91] In 1591 new ordinances were approved for the Company of Clothworkers, Shermen and Dyers, which may have been a further amalgamation of the Drapers and Tailors companies. The new ordinances provided, *inter alia*, that no unmarried person should keep any servant, journeyman or apprentice. No craftsman was to take any apprentice born outside the town. Those falling into decay were to be provided for by the company. No householder of the company was to permit any journeyman or apprentice to be absent from church. Anyone who had served an apprenticeship in the town and was unable to obtain work could complain to the warden of his company, who would, upon enquiry, discharge the most recent immigrant journeyman and give his place to the complainant.[92] Almost nothing further is heard of these companies, however.

The Ipswich Clothmakers Company was more notorious. The Company was incorporated by Letters Patent in 1606.[93] The famous *Case of the Ipswich Tailors*[94] was heard in Trinity Term 1613 in King's Bench. The Company brought an action of debt for £3 13s. 4d. against William Sheninge, alleging that one of its regulations required that no person should exercise a trade in Ipswich until he had presented himself before the officers of the Company and proved that he had served a seven-year apprenticeship. Sheninge in reply said that he had served such an apprenticeship and had then entered the household of a gentleman, Anthony Penny, as a domestic servant and made clothes for his master, his wife and children. The court found for the defendant: the law abhors idleness and no man could be prevented from working in any lawful trade, or from exercising several arts.

This decision must have been a severe blow to the Company, but it nevertheless continued its activities until, in April 1618[95] the General Court asked the Assembly to consider what should be done about the Company, which by force of a charter from the king infringed certain liberties of the town. In February 1620[96] the Privy Council heard a petition from the corporation, complaining of the inconveniences caused by the Company. The Council referred it to a committee which reported in March[97] that some principal officers of the town should be joined with the wardens of the Company to correct the faults of the clothworkers, and that the company's ordinances should be viewed by the Justices of Assize. In May[98] the assize judges reported that they had looked at the Company's ordinances, found many that restricted the lawful liberties of the subject and recommended that it should be dissolved and a new company set up. The nomination of searchers was put into the hands of the town bailiffs. There were to be two, one a clothier and the other a merchant, and they could impose fines of up to 10s. for the faulty dressing of cloth. This remodelling left the new Company almost entirely under the control of merchants and employers and all but destroyed it as an organization of small tradesmen and artisans. It is last heard of in 1632, and its disappearance left the town entirely free from any company claiming a monopoly over any branch of manufacture or commerce.

The corporation also attempted to regulate certain other trades, usually with the purpose of protecting the consumer, either from the supplier or from himself. Magistrates checked weights and measures, presenting offenders at the town's sessions of the peace, paying particular attention to bread and making sure that loaves were of the correct weight. The town also made some attempt to control the number of alehouses and the brewing and malting trades. In 1610 the number of alehouses was fixed at 16, and then raised to 24 in 1663,[99] but by the 1680s about 70 inns and alehouses were paying on average £1 a year for their licences, and the money thus raised was a valuable addition to the corporation's faltering finances. Unlicensed alehousekeepers were fined from time to time, as were those who supplied them with their beer and ale.[100]

Closely allied to the regulation of alehouses was the regulation of the selling of wine by retail. That retailers of wine should be licensed by the head officers of corporate towns was first required by statute in 1553, when the number of licences at Ipswich was fixed at three.[101] From the 1570s, however, the granting of wine licences was a monopoly enjoyed by a succession of patentees, until it reverted to the Crown in 1670.[102] There are numerous instances in the early seventeenth century of the corporation granting its three wine licences at the same time as the Receivers General of the Fines for Wine Licences were also issuing them in Ipswich, usually about six a year.[103] After the Restoration the right of the corporation to give its three was questioned on a number of occasions, but without success since rents for the wine licences continue to appear in the treasurer's accounts throughout the century.[104]

The magistrates also attempted to regulate the trade in meat. In 1596 the General Court forbade the selling of meat other than in the Butchery. This order was revived in 1607, when the practice of butchers carrying meat about the town in skips was condemned, as it was again in 1649.[105] Between 1684 and 1697 there were a number of attempts to confine the retail distribution of meat, butter, cheese and fish to the appointed markets and times, apparently without much success.

There are other hints of changes in methods of retail distribution. Glass-fronted shops were to be found in Ipswich at the beginning of the seventeenth century. Up to mid-century the corporation made some attempt to legislate for shopkeepers, especially on the closing of shops on the Sabbath, but abandoned these moves after the Restoration.[106] In the last decades of the century wholesale tailors and salesmen were operating in the town, and some goods were being sold by auction.[107] Retail trading by the end of the century was entirely free from regulation, a consequence of the almost total preoccupation of the corporation with political and factional squabbling. In 1700 John Brome could remark upon the rich shops to be found in the centre of the town,[108] and we can catch a glimpse of some of these shops through those probate inventories of well-to-do shopkeepers described earlier (see pp. 106–7).

c   The provision of services and facilities
The corporation provided premises and institutions which probably facilitated to some extent the functioning of certain occupations and trades. These included a cloth hall, a common quay, butchers' shops, markets and fairs.

The office of cloth hall keeper, as with the great majority of municipal offices, was leased out for a term of years, the lessee paying a fixed annual rent. The hall was provided so that cloths sold in gross might be searched and sealed as a check on quality and to avoid deceitful bargains. All cloths coming to the town for export had to be brought into the hall, where they were stored until shipment could be arranged. The hallage dues were a penny a week on broad cloths and a halfpenny on other kinds of cloth. Clearly the cloth hall and its rents depended upon the prosperity of the textile industry in the Ipswich hinterland, the decline in its rents reflecting the industrial contraction already discussed. By 1630 the hall was in the keeping of a widow, and she was remitted the arrears of her rent on account of her poverty. No rent at all was paid between 1632 and 1635, and then it was reduced from £10 a year to £4. By 1665 arrears totalled £14 and in 1667 the rent was reduced again, to £2 10s a year. From the 1680s 30s of this was being regularly remitted to the lessee (see Appendix 2).

The corporation maintained a common quay and town warehouses. On the quay was a crane, where coal, corn and salt were weighed as they were unloaded. A meter was appointed by the corporation, who took half the dues. The fluctuations in the metage profits received by the chamberlains provide a useful barometer of the state of the seaborne trade of the town (see Appendix 2). They are clearly subject to short-term factors – the effects of the plague epidemic of 1665–6 are immediately obvious – but they show no real evidence of long-term decline, in contrast to the downturn in the rents of the cloth hall. Since merchandise passing through the meter's hands was carried almost entirely by coastal shipping, whilst the cloth hall served the overseas trade, the contrast between metage profits and cloth hall rents underlines our earlier point (see pp. 104–5) about the town's growing dependence on its coastal trade.

The corporation provided a shambles on the Cornhill where about 30 stalls were erected and leased out to butchers for annual rents, which varied from stall to stall, from 53s. 4d. to 14s. a year. In addition further stalls were permitted on the Cornhill on payment of a weekly rent ranging from 1d. to 4d. In the first half of the century these rents yielded between £40 and £50 a year. They first reached £60 in 1654 and thereafter fluctuated quite widely between about £55 and just under £80 a year. No butcher could have more than one stall and they were not permitted to sell their meat elsewhere, though the dreary repetition of this last regulation during the course of the century (see p. 123) may imply growing evasion.

Markets were held in the town on Tuesdays, Thursdays and Saturdays at the beginning of the century. By the early decades of the eighteenth century they were also being held on Wednesdays and Fridays.[109] The principal market place was on Cornhill. Only freemen could erect stalls here, paying 3d. each market day. Stalls could also be erected in the street leading from the Cornhill to Newbargate, provided they were no more than 10 ft long and only one man's wares were on show. These markets were frequented by countrymen from a wide area of eastern Suffolk and enjoyed a reputation for being well-stocked, but they never acquired much more than a regional importance.

The most important fair in the town was Holyrood Fair, held on 14 September and the two following days. It was held on St Margaret's Green and sold a wide variety of goods, including cattle, horses, rope, butter and cheese. Two other fairs were also being held by the beginning of the seventeenth century, St James's and St George's. In October 1656 General Court, without giving any reason, ordered that these last two fairs should be suppressed at once.[110]. In 1670 Assembly resolved that one or two new fairs should be obtained and after consultation with counsel in London it was decided to revive the fairs of St George and St James. In the charter of 1684 cattle fairs on 7 and 8 May and 11 and 12 August were obtained, and these were held on Handford Hall Farm, corporation property lying to the west of the town. By the mid-eighteenth century Holyrood Fair was still transacting a great deal of business, particularly in butter and cheese, and two fairs were still held for the buying and selling of cattle in May and in August. St George's saw toys and lean cattle sold, but St James's Fair, a contemporary wrote, was not worth mentioning.[111]

The corporation also made some attempt to maintain the transport facilities in and about the town. In 1613 and again in 1694 it laid down the charges which the common carriers might make to convey passengers and goods by road to London.[112] It also regularly appointed surveyors of highways and spent considerable sums on the repair of bridges on the approaches to the town. Generally, however, responsibility for paving the streets within the town was imposed by a local Act[113] upon the owners of property, and lessees were permitted to deduct expenditure under this head from their rents. Enforcement was in the hands of the headboroughs, with a penalty of 1s. for every default, plus 8d. for every square yard left unpaved.

Finally, the corporation provided a water supply. In 1614 it was decided to bring the water in lead pipes to the Cornhill and then to St Peter's Church. The corporation bore the adventure of ten fodder of lead from Hull and a cistern was built on Cornhill in the following year.[114] In March 1616[115] the first leases of water were granted, at first to only 40 households. In the beginning the charges were a fine of £5 and a rent of 5s a year, but these were progressively increased during the course of the century. The water was to be used only for household purposes and the lessee was forbidden to give it away or allow it to run to waste. The repair and upkeep of the pipes and cistern was at the charge of the corporation. In 1681 six out of the 12 parishes in the town had piped water, to 139 households, about 8 per cent of the 1,640 households listed in the 1674 Hearth Tax return.[116]

d Civic aid and inducements

From time to time the town leaders made attempts to attract new trades and crafts-men and were prepared to spend money to that end, although none of their efforts was ever of any lasting effect. The corporation also had within its gift a number of charitable funds which may have been an important source of credit for Ipswich tradesmen.

For much of the period up to 1640 efforts were made to establish some kind of staple in Ipswich. In 1605 representatives travelled to London 'to move the Lord Treasurer', Lord Buckhurst, the high steward of the town, for a staple of corn, without success.[117] A committee was set up in January 1619 to consider another staple, and in October 1622 it was proposed to have there a staple 'of all manner of East commodities'. Conditions were agreed and in January 1623 letters were written to the Marquis of Buckingham, but nothing ever came of either of these proposals.[118] In 1632, when a new charter was being discussed, it was resolved to ask for a staple of coal and brank (buckwheat), but the charter of 1635 made no mention of it.[119]

In 1616 the corporation petitioned the Privy Council to be allowed to set up a sugar refinery. It was desired by the grocers, and a certain Paul Tymmerman had offered to run it.[120] But the Privy Council rejected the idea on the grounds that no alien or denizen, which is what Tymmerman seems to have been, should be allowed to carry on this trade. In February 1617 the Council went on to write that this refusal was never intended to debar the king's natural subjects from any lawful course of trade. Nevertheless no-one in Ipswich was to join in partnership with Tymmerman or act as frontman for any stranger.[121] Nothing is heard of the scheme again.

The years after the Restoration saw more elaborate, more expensive but equally unsuccessful attempts to introduce new trades into Ipswich. In 1668 a move was made to settle some Dutch immigrants in the town for the making of linen. The Assembly sent a committee to wait on Lord Arlington, and also wrote to Norwich and Colchester to enquire what advantages, or otherwise, had accrued from their Dutch congregations. It was also decided to consider inviting two or three manufacturers of white pottery ware to settle in the town.[122] Letters were exchanged between the town and Lord Arlington, the town offering a bleaching place for the Dutch, but nothing came of the proposals, save that Lord Arlington was made a free burgess in 1677.

In 1681 the corporation was engaged in two separate enterprises. First of all some Norwich stuff weavers were persuaded to settle in the town. The corporation sent a ship to fetch their belongings in the August, and in the November four men were loaned £200 free of interest for one year. One of their number was still in the town in 1685 when he was admitted to the freedom,[123] but the industry put down no permanent roots.

Much greater efforts were made to accommodate French protestant refugees. In September 1681 the town offered a church, promised to free them from town and parish charges, and began to raise a stock for 20 or 30 looms to make linen. Both Handford and Stoke Mills were considered for their employment, as was the idea of building a fulling mill. One group certainly settled in the town, but they were said to be of the poorest and meanest sort, although they were peaceable enough. Flax and hemp were sown locally and yielded well, but there was a shortage of spinners and so they had to buy foreign yarn to keep the weavers at work. In 1686 the corporation gave £100 to the French, and six linen looms for conversion to woollen weaving. In the following year they were given permission to make hats and open shops to sell them by retail, but as with the Norwich stuff weavers, this community also failed to establish itself.[124]

A further attempt was made in November 1693 to attract foreign immigrants when it was agreed to admit 50 families of French Protestants to weave lustrings. The corporation promised each family 40s. and their expenses in coming to Ipswich, a church and £20 a year for two years for their minister. They were not to be rated or put into office for seven years, and they were forbidden to exercise any other trade. In 1711 the Lustring Company was employing at least 79 weavers in Ipswich, but again the venture never became permanent in the town.[125]

In December 1690 the corporation made a final attempt to settle a linen manufacture in the town, offering to the Incorporation of the Linen Manufacture a workhouse and warehouses free, a bleaching ground at a reasonable rate, and an undertaking that the common hoymen would carry the goods produced at very reasonable rates.[126] In January 1699 the General Court set up a committee to consider the most proper way of bringing a manufacture into the town. In the following month Mr Thomas Dormer, a master weaver from Norwich, came into the town and met the corporation. But there is no further record, either of the linen manufacture, or of the committee, or of Mr Dormer.[127]

The creation of charities by private benefactors for the provision of interest-free loans to tradesmen, especially to young men beginning their careers, may have been of some importance in the seventeenth-century economy.[128] By 1665 a total of £1,001 was available in Ipswich for lending out for periods of up to ten years. These charities were invariably administered by the corporation. The borrower had to provide two sureties for the repayment of the loan, and on occasion these became forfeit and the corporation was put to the expense of a lawsuit to recover the loan.[129] In addition Ipswich was one of the towns included in Sir Thomas White's Charity, with its annual provision to leave £25 each to four young men, preferably clothiers, for 10 years.

Unfortunately there is nothing surviving to indicate how the loans were used or their importance to individual borrowers. In general the funds seem to have been honestly administered during much of the century. It would appear however that in 1675 the corporation took £529 9s. to pay off its debts, and repaid neither principal nor interest. By 1744 forfeited bonds amounted to £566 14s, and by 1835 all had been lost,[130] a not inappropriate gloss upon the failure of the corporation to make any significant contribution to the economy of seventeenth-century Ipswich.

6   Continuity and change in seventeenth-century Ipswich

Ipswich at the beginning of the seventeenth century was one of the leading English provincial towns, perhaps one of the first ten.[131] Its population was probably around 4,300 and growing rapidly. It was an important commercial centre, particularly for the export of woollen cloth to the Baltic, although its merchants also traded to France, Spain and the Low Countries. The coastal trade was almost equally important, particularly since the shipping of coal from Newcastle to London and the trade in agricultural produce to the capital were both growing. Within the town there was comparatively little industry. Although woollen textile manufacture was present, Ipswich was not a leading centre for the industry in the same way that Colchester or Norwich were. The canvas and sailcloth industries were probably as important and certainly lasted longer. The most numerous occupations in the town appear to have been those connected with the sea and shipbuilding. There were many seamen and shipwrights, as well as rope-makers, anchorsmiths and the occasional instrument-maker. The liberties of the town were very extensive but few of its citizens had any direct involvement in agriculture, and instead were dependent upon wages and profits for their livelihood. In the absence of a large leisured group, either of rentiers or landlords, merchants formed the top layer of the social structure. There was no equivalent in Ipswich in the early seventeenth century either to a county stratum or to an extended clerical hierarchy such as was to be found at Exeter.[132] The largest house in the town was Christchurch Mansion, with 32 hearths, but its owners, the Withypolls, themselves of merchant origin, played no part in the town's affairs, and it was 1703 before the owner thought it worth his while to take up the freedom of the town. Occasionally Ipswich merchants prospered sufficiently well to be able to buy a rural estate and become country gentlemen within a couple of generations. But there were only a handful of these. This meant that there were no profound social divisions in the town, no gentry/non-gentry dichotomy in the social structure. Those who called themselves gentlemen were in fact merchants and tradesmen and were considered as such by the world outside.

Although the citizens were almost completely urbanized in the sense that they had no direct involvement in agriculture, the relationship between the town and its hinterland was as intimate and complex as it was in other English towns. Considerable geographical mobility meant that ties of kinship and friendship placed the town at the centre of a network of connections that penetrated deeply into the countryside of eastern Suffolk, occasionally into Norfolk and Essex and sometimes even further afield into London, Newcastle and eventually Holland and New England. The citizens were entirely dependent upon their region for supplies of food, which were bought and sold in the town's shops, markets and fairs. These were visited by countrymen from a wide area of eastern Suffolk, although they did not achieve the national importance of, for example, those at Reading.[133] At the same time the trade and commerce of the town were based upon the woollen industry and the agriculture of the region. But Ipswich was by no means parasitic upon the countryside. It earned its keep by providing services and opportunities which would otherwise not have been available. The demand for agricultural produce from the fairs and markets of the town stimulated agrarian development in the countryside. The greater economic opportunities and social flexibilities of the town encouraged migration from the already densely populated High Suffolk area. The grocers of Debenham and Needham Market brought in their sugar, tobacco and brandy through Ipswich, and the clothiers of East Bergholt and Hadleigh looked to merchants using the port of Ipswich for the 'vent' of their cloths.

The town was an ancient borough with a sophisticated political superstructure. Government of the town was in the hands of an Assembly which was a self-perpetuating oligarchy composed of the more prosperous merchants grouped together by a tightly knit pattern of marriage alliance. Admission to this group was difficult but not impossible, depended upon economic success, and was likely to take two generations. But the attendant burdens of office and the limitations upon the numbers of the Assembly meant that there were always men of substance in the town who were not closely associated with its government and perhaps did not wish to be. Ultimate authority in the town lay with the General Court, which was composed of all freemen. It was here that bailiffs were elected, and although the freemen dutifully chose those whom they were expected to choose through the early part of the century, they were not so amenable during the years of the Commonwealth and the divisions created by the turbulence of those years were not bridged before the end of the century.

The Assembly in the years before 1640 took an active part in the government of the town. A water supply was provided, streets were paved and ordered to be lit; markets were regulated in the interests of purchaser and vendor alike; a grammar school and a town library were maintained at its expense. Its members had some idea of the responsibilities of office as well as the dignities and prerogatives. Attempts were made to provide for the really indigent, particularly children and the old. Christ's Hospital was a municipally administered institution for this purpose, as well as being a house of correction for the recalcitrant. At the same time, parochial churchwardens and overseers of the poor were cajoled and bullied into providing for the poor of their parishes.

One of the most important ways in which the Assembly provided for the poor in the early part of the seventeenth century was by buying supplies of corn and fuel and then selling them cheaply, sometimes at a loss. The actual extent of this is impossible to measure but it must certainly have cushioned the worst effects of a bad harvest and high food prices upon the 'harvest-sensitive' sections of the population. A pure crisis of subsistence seems to have been absent from seventeenth-century Ipswich. Instead crises of mortality were the result of outbreaks of epidemic disease and the death rate was an autonomous factor independent of harvest fluctuations, although high food prices must have exacerbated the misery caused by uncontrollable disease.

But the economic structure of the town was by no means static. Change was continuous and complex, often originating in causes far beyond the town, and with consequences that could penetrate into the remotest niche of the fabric of communal organization. The decline in the town's export trade in textiles to the Baltic was the result of competition from the New Draperies, changing fashions, wars and currency crises in the countries of the Eastland. One of the consequences was the break-up of the political hegemony of the merchant oligarchy which drew its wealth from this trade. Ipswich ships in the last decades of the century were squeezed out of the Newcastle to London coal-carrying trade. The steady increase in the size of ships over the century, coupled with the slow silting of the haven noticeable from the middle of the sixteenth century – although this was not as serious as that at a number of outports, such as Chester and Boston – was sufficient, when joined to severe competition from London, to lead to the decline of the town's ship-building industry.

These changes were apparent to contemporary observers, and to many they seemed to indicate decline and decay. Richard Blome noted that within living memory the town had 140 sail, but in 1673 there were not above 60.[134] Another traveller wrote in 1714 that he wondered why a place 'so well situated for Trade, should be so much neglected.'[135] Defoe thought that when he first visited the town, in about 1668, there were at least 100 ships belonging to it, but that by the time he came to write there were scarcely 40. He attempted some analysis of the causes, blaming competition from the great numbers of Dutch ships captured as prizes, as well as 'the neighbourhood of London, which sucks the vitals of trade in this island to itself'.[136]

Celia Fiennes, on the other hand, blamed the 'disregarded' appearance of the town on the 'pride and sloth' of its inhabitants.[137]

The decline in the town's overseas trade is incontrovertible – the entries in the Port Books, or rather the lack of them, confirm this. But overseas trade was only one aspect of the town's seaborne commerce. The coastal trade came to assume a larger and larger proportion of this commerce, and, although it did not expand at quite the staggering rate of that of Newcastle, it was at least much more stable than the overseas trade had ever been. Loading calf skins and rye may not have seemed very exciting to contemporaries, or even a very good indicator of prosperity, but Ipswich traders and dealers were, from the evidence of probate inventories, clearly doing very well out of it.

The survival of Port Books means that seaborne trade is comparatively easy to study. Trade by land is much more difficult to describe and, in the absence of market toll records for the town, impossible to quantify. There are merely stray hints as to its nature and direction, but sufficient to suggest that it may have been very extensive. Carriers were going regularly to London well before the end of the sixteenth century, and the network of carriers' routes developed considerably during the seventeenth century. In 1694 the town's justices of the peace laid down the rates to be charged by carriers for bringing goods into the town by common waggon, stage coach, carts, or horses from Bury St Edmunds, Eye, Botesdale, Stowmarket, Woodbridge and Colchester.[138] Evidence of the role of the London carrier is to be found in a rather unexpected place. The coastal Port Books record the movement out of Ipswich of goods landed from ships, especially the packet boat from Holland. The Ipswich waggon was going every few days to London carrying goods which had come into the country in this way. One of the chief articles was silk: no less than 582lb weight of silk were loaded into the waggon on 3 May 1680.[139] Other merchandise which appears less often includes paper, maps and books, goshawks, beads and Holland damask. It is no wonder that Alexander Burton appears to have been so well off (see p. 107).

Cheesemongers appear in the Foreign Fines lists after the Restoration. Although there is no evidence of their contribution to the coastal trade in cheese and butter it must have been considerable. Large numbers of cheeses and great quantities of butter had to be brought into the town from the countryside before being shipped to London; this trade the cheesemongers doubtless organized. Defoe writes of upwards of 600 country people on horseback and foot coming into Ipswich with something to sell in the town's markets, besides the butchers and what came in carts and waggons.

By the last decades of the seventeenth century one of the six prime post roads in the country ran through Ipswich from London on its way to Yarmouth. At least two commentators wrote that the streets within the town itself were clean and well-paved,[140] although if the evidence from the Headboroughs' Verdict-Books of rubbish, dead pigs and piles of oyster shells left lying in the streets is to be believed, then these terms must be interpreted liberally. Defoe wrote that one of the advantages of residence in Ipswich was the easy passage to London, the coach going through in a day. Traffic of this kind brought prosperity to the inns of the town, and they were described in 1714 as being very good.[141] The surviving probate inventories of innkeepers (see p. 110) bear witness to this.

The decay and decline of Ipswich in the late seventeenth century can be exaggerated. What must have appeared to contemporaries to be decline was instead a change of direction, away from traditional, prestigious functions, trades and occupations, into newer, more diversified, perhaps more seemingly frivolous ones. The comparatively open economic structure of the town and the absence after the 1620s of any gild with restrictive or coercive powers must have provided opportunities for new trades and crafts to become established and for many inhabitants to combine two or three. That those trades favoured by the corporation, and which it did so much to try to establish in the town, did not in fact take root shows its unhappy knack of backing losers and its inability to appreciate the new direction which the town's economy was taking.

As a commercial and trading centre Ipswich must have been of considerable regional importance. By the last decades of the century it was also developing as a social and services centre. Its facilities for business and pleasure, its stationers and bookbinders, gardeners, periwig-makers, fanmakers, physicians and attorneys, its coffee houses, schools, library and shops were attracting country gentlemen to buy houses in the town. John Ogilby's map of the town, made in 1674, marks the house of Sir William Barker, Viscount Hereford's house, the Lady Leake's house and that of Lady Barkham. Lord Hereford owned Christchurch Mansion, the largest house in Ipswich. Sir William Barker was descended from Robert Barker, merchant, portman and bailiff of the town, who had moved out to Grimston Hall, Trimley St Martin, in about 1591, and into the country gentry. He became a Knight of the Bath, and his son a baronet. When Defoe visited the town he wrote of the very good company to be found in it. Although there were not so many gentry as in Bury St Edmunds, the people, he declared, were persons well informed of the world, and who have something very solid and entertaining in their society. Defoe attributed this to their frequent conversing with gentlemen and masters of ships who had seen more of the world than the people of an inland town. He thought it one of the most agreeable places in England.[142] When Lord Oxford visited the town in 1737 he noted that it was extremely pleasant and healthy, that a great many people who had got money and left off trade resided there, and lived merrily with balls and assemblies.[143]

It is only with hindsight that this new direction can be discerned. It is a gradual process, occupying much of the last 30 years of the seventeenth century, and probably taking a further 20 years to become fully established. The corporation itself seems to have contributed almost nothing to these new developments. Indeed it was probably scarcely aware that they were taking place. From the formal records of the two governing bodies of the town, General Court and Assembly, it would seem that they were almost totally preoccupied with factional quarrels.

This new departure in the town's economic structure must, however, be set against a background of underlying stability. The topography of the town remained almost untouched. There does not appear to have been any great outburst of building in the town between the Restoration and the end of the century, and the only major addition to the townscape seems to have been the Shire Hall, built in 1700. Similarly, the overall social organization of Ipswich remained the same. Although the power of the merchant oligarchy had been broken by 1640 this was due to long-term economic factors, not to any radical change in the nature of society. The stages of social mobility remained almost unaltered, the national evaluation of successful tradesmen only marginally less deprecatory at the end of the century than at the beginning. Again, much of the ancient civic political structure continued. One can detect changes, of course. Some institutions lost their vitality. That concern for the *minutiae* of municipal government characteristic of the early seventeenth century disappeared. Standards of civic administration declined. The corporation ran heavily into debt. The salaries of municipal officers remained unpaid. But there was no breakdown in public order, no collapse of government.

Finally, helping to underpin urban stability, economic organization remained essentially domestic. Commercial and manufacturing enterprises still depended entirely upon the resources of families, individuals and small partnerships, and as a consequence they were still largely at the mercy of the demography and the social values of a pre-industrial community. And yet, in spite of the fragility of economic structure in individual cases, probate inventories make it abundantly clear that during the seventeenth century there was a real rise in standards of comfort and amenity in many households across the community. By the end of the century, houses were furnished with china cups, tea sets, walnut chairs and tables, carpets, curtains, mirrors, clocks, books and pictures. Shops stocked an astonishingly wide range of textiles, hardware, drugs, spices and foodstuffs. Inns demanded large numbers of pots, glasses, mugs, plates, knives, bottles, barrels of beer and hogsheads of sherry. By 1700 urban demand was making an important contribution to the first stages of industrialization.

Appendix 1   The Ipswich Hearth Tax returns, 1664 and 1674

1   Distribution of hearths by household

parish	paying number of hearths per household					exempt			total no. of households
1664	1	2	3–5	6–9	10+	1	2	3+	
St Lawrence	67	numbers missing				8	10	6	91
St Mary Tower	4	10	34	15	9	16	23	2	113
St Peter	1	18	38	17	5	20	27	6	132
St Stephen	44	numbers missing				17	15	7	83
St Mary Key	6	16	31	14	5 +5	39	36	8 +2	162
St Helen	4	1	10	6	1 +2	29	numbers missing		53
St Matthew	16	23	35	15	4 +2	49	26	4	174
St Clement	14	68	85	36	5	80	161	14	463
St Mary Stoke	2	8	9	7	1	45	numbers missing		72
St Nicholas	6	34	22	11	5	48	51	4	181
St Mary Elm	6	25	24	8		28	15	1	107
St Margaret	20	42	44	23	9 +2	245	numbers missing		385
1674									2016
St Lawrence		2	31	24	8				65
St Mary Tower	1	6	28	22	9	4	24		94
St Peter		28	57	21	8	12	50		176
St Stephen		16	24	13	2	6	7		68
St Mary Key	3	18	31	14	7	16	15		104
St Helen	4	1	12	8		4	19		48
St Matthew	8	29	33	19	5	1	29		124
St Clement	1	69	120	38	6	56	107		397
St Mary Stoke	2	7	7	10	1	26	12		65
St Nicholas	1	18	35	12	5	27	34		132
St Mary Elm	1	10	29	8	1	15	6		70
St Margaret	1	42	63	29	10	21	131		297
	22	246	470	218	62	188	434		1640

131

2 Distribution of households

| parish | number of households | | total | percentage exempt |
	paying	exempt		
1664				
St Lawrence	67	24	91	26.3
St Mary Tower	72	41	113	36.2
St Peter	79	53	132	40.1
St Stephen	44	39	83	46.9
St Mary Key	77	85	162	52.4
St Helen	24	29	53	54.7
St Matthew	95	79	174	45.4
St Clement	208	255	463	55.1
St Mary Stoke	27	45	72	62.5
St Nicholas	78	103	181	56.9
St Mary Elm	63	44	107	41.1
St Margaret	140	245	385	63.6
	974	1042	2016	51.6
1674				
St Lawrence	65		65	
St Mary Tower	66	28	94	29.7
St Peter	114	62	176	35.2
St Stephen	55	13	68	19.1
St Mary Key	73	31	104	29.8
St Helen	25	23	48	47.9
St Matthew	94	30	124	24
St Clement	234	163	397	41
St Mary Stoke	27	38	65	53.4
St Nicholas	71	61	132	46.2
St Mary Elm	49	21	70	30
St Margaret	145	152	297	51.1
	1018	622	1640	37.9

3 Distribution of hearths

| parish | number of hearths | | | total number of households | average number of hearths |
	paying	exempt	total		
1664					
St Lawrence	338	48	386	91	4.2
St Mary Tower	379	69	448	113	3.9
St Peter	358	95	451	132	3.4
St Stephen	185	69	254	83	3
St Mary Key	340	140	480	162	2.9
St Helen	99	58	157	53	2.9
St Matthew	363	113	479	174	2.7
St Clement	782	442	1224	463	2.6
St Mary Stoke	109	81	190	72	2.6
St Nicholas	289	165	454	181	2.5
St Mary Elm	196	61	257	107	2.4
St Margaret	538	379	917	385	2.3
	3976	1720	5696	2016	2.8

1674

St Lawrence	390		390	65	6
St Mary Tower	406	52	458	94	4.8
St Peter	496	112	608	176	3.4
St Stephen	237	20	257	68	3.7
St Mary Key	332	46	378	104	3.6
St Helen	109	42	151	48	3.1
St Matthew	405	59	464	124	3.7
St Clement	926	270	1196	397	3
St Mary Stoke	127	50	177	65	2.7
St Nicholas	303	95	398	132	3
St Mary Elm	185	27	212	70	3
St Margaret	694	283	977	297	3.2
	4610	1056	5666	1640	3.5

4 *Proportional distribution of households by number of hearths*

	number of households with				percentage of total of column		
	A	B	C		A	B	C
parish	1–2	3–5	6+ hearths	total			
1664							
St Lawrence	numbers missing						
St Mary Tower	53	36	24	133	46.9	31.9	21.2
St Peter	66	43	23	132	50	32.6	17.4
St Stephen	numbers missing						
St Mary Key	97	39	19 +7	162	59.8	24.1	11.7 +4.4
St Helen	34*	10	7 +2	53	64.1	18.9	13.2 +3.8
St Matthew	114	39	19 +2	174	65.5	22.4	10.9 +1.2
St Clement	323	99	41	463	69.8	21.4	8.8
St Mary Stoke	55*	9	8	72	76.4	12.5	11.1
St Nicholas	139	26	16	181	76.8	14.4	8.8
St Mary Elm	74	25	8	107	69.1	23.4	7.5
St Margaret	307*	44	32 +2	385	79.7	11.4	8.3 + .6
	1262	370	197 +13	1842	68.5	20.1	10.7 + .7
1674							
St Lawrence	2	31	32	65	3.1	47.7	49.2
St Mary Tower	35	28	31	94	37.3	29.8	32.9
St Peter	90	57	29	176	51.1	32.4	16.5
St Stephen	29	24	15	68	42.6	35.3	22.1
St Mary Key	52	31	21	104	50	29.8	20.2
St Helen	28	12	8	48	58.3	25	16.7
St Matthew	67	33	24	124	54	26.6	19.4
St Clement	233	120	44	397	58.7	30.2	11.1
St Mary Stoke	47	7	11	65	72.3	10.8	16.9
St Nicholas	80	35	17	132	60.6	26.5	12.9
St Mary Elm	32	29	9	70	45.7	41.4	12.9
St Margaret	195	63	39	297	65.7	21.2	13.1
	890	470	280	1640	54.3	28.7	17

*Assumes that all exempt households were in this category.
The 1664 Hearth Tax is PRO, E179 257/12. That for 1674 is printed in S.A.H. Hervey (ed.),
Suffolk in 1674 (Suffolk Green Books No. XI, vol. 13, 1905).

Appendix 2   Civic rents, prices and wages, 1601–1700

(Extracted from the treasurer's and chamberlains' accounts)

date	rent of Cloth Hall		metage profits	daily wages (building labourers)		prices per 1000 bricks		tiles	
	£	s.	£	s.	d.	s.	d.	s.	d.
1601				1					
1602								13	4
1603									
1604	3			1					
1605				1	4				
1606				1					
1607				1					
1608			9	1				16	
1609	10		10			16			
1610	5		10	1	4			17	
1611	10		12	1		17		17	
1612			10	1		5	4		
1613			8		10				
1614	8		10	1		17			
1615	8		8	1	6				
1616	8		8	1		16	6	16	6
1617	8		8	1	4				
1618	8		5	1	4				
1619	8		7	1	4				
1620	8			1	4				
1621	8		18	1	6				
1622	8		26			15			
1623	8		16	1	6	15			
1624	8		18	1	6	15			
1625	8		3	1	4				
1626	8		13	1	4				
1627			12						
1628			11	1	6				
1629			14	1	4	16		16	
1630			15			15	6		
1631	10		14	1	4	15	6		
1632			15			15			
1633			22	1	2	15			
1634			17	1	6	15			
1635			15						
1636	4		14	1	7	16			
1637	4		22	1	6	16			
1638	4		17	1	4	16			
1639	4		16	1	3	17			
1640	4		15			17			
1641	4		14	1		16			
1642			14	1		17			
1643									
1644			12	1					
1645			10	1	3				
1646			14	1	6				
1647			17						
1648			21						

date	rent of Cloth Hall		metage profits	daily wages (building labourers)		prices per 1000 bricks		tiles	
	£	s.	£			s.	d.	s.	d.
1649			12	1	6	17			
1650			9			16			
1651			4	1	8				
1652			7						
1653				1	5				
1654			9						
1655	4		10						
1656			11					18	
1657			11						
1658			9						
1659	4		11					17	
1660	4		10	2				18	
1661			12						
1662	4		11	2		20		18	
1663	4		15	1	6	20		18	
1664	4		12	2		18	6		
1665	4		5	1	6			18	
1666	4		6	2		17		17	
1667	2	10	10	1	8	17		18	
1668	2	10		2				18	
1669	2	10		1		18		17	
1670			15						
1671	2	10	14	1	6	17		17	
1672	2	10		1	8				
1673			15						
1674	2	10	17	1	6				
1675			18						
1676									
1677			19						
1678			19						
1679	2	10		1	8				
1680	2	10		1	8	17		17	
1681	2	10		1	8				
1682	2	10	20	1	10	17			
1683			18						
1684	2	10	18	2				17	
1685			16						
1686	2	10	16	1	6	18		18	
1687			19						
1688	2	10	7	1	6	18		18	
1689	2	10	12	1	6	18			
1690	2	10	13	1	8	18		17	
1691			11						
1692			14						
1693			11						
1694									
1695			9						
1696	2	10	10						
1697	2	10	12						
1698			14						
1699	2	10	12						
1700	2	10	20						

BIBLIOGRAPHY

The archives of the corporation of Ipswich are now housed in the East Suffolk Record Office, Ipswich Branch, where there is a comprehensive inventory. A survey of the corporation archives was published as an Appendix to the Ninth Report of the Historical Manuscripts Commission, but its treatment of the seventeenth-century material is perfunctory and often misleading.

For the administrative work of the corporation there are two main series of records, the General Court books and the Assembly books. There are three volumes of General Court books covering the period 1572 to 1704, with a gap between 1634 and 1643. The first volume is written in a crabbed minuscule hand which is particularly difficult to read. Volumes 1 and 2 record the activities of the corporation in minute detail. Attendance at the General Court is scrupulously noted and the lists of names of those present, sometimes over a hundred, are especially valuable for the reconstruction of the political careers of those active in corporation affairs. The one real deficiency is the failure to record the occupations of those admitted to the freedom. The third volume is very much less detailed and is almost entirely taken up with admissions to the freedom and references, more or less oblique, to factional squabbles. The work of Assembly is recorded in four volumes covering the period 1609 to 1726, the last showing the same falling-off in detail so characteristic of the last General Court book.

Financial records are voluminous. Both treasurer's and chamberlains' accounts survive for the whole period from 1603 to 1714, sometimes in duplicate, although there are gaps. There are accounts for the leasing of water from the supply provided by the corporation, and a number of volumes of a miscellaneous nature containing rate assessments and foreign fines. The various institutions in the town concerned with poor relief, namely Christ's Hospital, Smart and Tooley Foundations, also have long series of accounts, ordinances, etc., but again there are lacunae.

Three thick volumes contain detailed records of proceedings in the town's Sessions of the Peace over the period 1602 to 1720, and there is a separate Sessions Indictment Book for the years 1683 to 1686. There are 18 volumes of Petty Court proceedings, 1601 to 1713. These can be very frustrating because it is rare to find a case brought to action and a verdict recorded, but the court also served as a Court of Orphans and the detail on family relationships can often be illuminating.

The records of 10 of the 12 parishes in Ipswich are also in the East Suffolk Record Office, Ipswich Branch. These records include the parish registers, as well as churchwardens' accounts, settlement certificates, removal orders and overseers' accounts. Not all classes of records are to be found for every parish, and there are often considerable gaps. The church-wardens' accounts for St Peter's parish are in the British Library, together with a number of parish register transcripts, including the two not in the East Suffolk Record Office.

Also at Ipswich are the records of the archdeaconry of Suffolk, including wills, both original and register copies, probate inventories, visitation and instance books. The records of the diocese of Norwich are in the Norfolk and Norwich Record Office at Norwich and these include visitation records, wills and probate inventories.

Ipswich Public Library has further parish register transcripts, the Town Library catalogue, the diary of Devereux Edgar, covering the years 1700 to 1709 and largely a record of his activities as a justice of the peace, and a copy of Ogilby's map of the town of 1674.

The principal classes of documents used at the Public Record Office were the Hearth Tax and Lay Subsidy records (E179), the port books (E190), Exchequer depositions (E134) and Exchequer special commissions (E178), as well as the fines and rents for wine licences in E101 and E163, and the wills and probate inventories of the Prerogative Court of Canterbury.

NOTES

I wish to thank my thesis supervisor, Mr Charles Phythian-Adams, for his patience, guidance and the stimulus of his conversation while it was in progress, and Mr Peter Clark, the editor of this volume, for resuscitating it in the first place and for his suggestions and advice on adapting it for publication here. I am also indebted to Mrs Sylvia Colman for allowing me to reproduce her plan of the Sun Inn and supplying the photograph for fig. 14.

1 R. Blome, *Britannia* (1673), 209.
2 C. A. Moser and W. Scott, *British Towns* (1961), 17.
3 S. Dunmore, V. Gray, T. Loader and K. Wade, 'The origin and development of Ipswich: an interim report', *East Anglian Archaeology*, I (1975), 57–67, and S. Dunmore, T. Loader and K. Wade, 'Ipswich Archaeological Survey: second interim report', *East Anglian Archaeology*, III (1976), 135–40.
4 C. Gross, *The Gild Merchant*, I (1890), 6–8.
5 *Calendar of Charter Rolls*, VI, 54–5, 197–9.
6 ESRO, C13/1, f.60.
7 BL, Harleian MS 595, f.167, printed in 'The condition of the archdeaconries of Suffolk and Sudbury in the year 1603', ed. C. H. W. White, *Procs Suffolk Inst. Archaeology and Natural History*, VI (1886), 361.
8 ESRO, C13/1, f.117d. The figures are printed correctly in G. R. Clarke, *The History and Description of the Town and Borough of Ipswich* (1830), 69, but he adds in the column headed 'where of women kind' to give a total population of 12,308 and nearly twice as many men as women.
9 NNRO, VIS/4.
10 ESRO, C7/2/6 (unpaginated).
11 J. Webb, 'Apprenticeship in the maritime occupations at Ipswich, 1596–1651', *Mariner's Mirror*, XLVI (1960), 29–34.
12 See R. E. Dickinson, *City and Region* (1964), esp. chs. 1–4 and 8, and H. Carter, *The Study of Urban Geography* (1972), esp. ch. 6.
13 26 Hen. VIII, c.14.
14 Lincs. RO, MM. 6/5, MM 6/1/5. Cf. B. A. Holderness, 'The agricultural activities of the Massingberds of South Ormsby, Lincs., 1638–c. 1750', *Midland History*, I (1972), 15.
15 *CSPD, 1633–1634*, 450.
16 P. Clark and P. Slack (eds.), 'Introduction' to *Crisis and Order in English Towns, 1500–1700* (1972), 4–5.
17 ESRO, C9/3, PRO, E179.257/7; ESRO, C9/4
18 J. Patten, *English Towns 1500–1700* (1978), 273, has 78 recorded occupations for Ipswich for the period 1600–49.
19 PRO, PROB 4/5827.
20 PRO, SP12/156/45, and CO388/9/73. Cf. R. Davis, *The Rise of the English Shipping Industry* (1962), 35.
21 J. U. Nef, *The Rise of the British Coal Industry*, II (1932, repr. 1966), 26.
22 The following paragraphs are based upon R. W. K. Hinton, *The Eastland Trade and the Common Weal* (1959), D. C. Coleman, 'An innovation and its diffusion: the New Draperies', *EcHR*, 2nd ser., XXII (1969), 417–29, J. E. Pilgrim, 'The cloth industry in Essex and Suffolk 1558–1640' (M.A. thesis, University of London, 1939), W. B. Stephens, 'The cloth exports of the provincial ports 1600–1640', *EcHR*, 2nd ser., XXII (1969), 228–43, and B. Supple, *Commercial Crisis and Change in England 1600–1642* (1959, repr. 1964).
23 BL, Hargrave MS 321, fos. 59d–60d.
24 See F. J. Fisher, 'The development of the London food market 1540–1640', *EcHR*, V (1934–5), 56, and E. A. Wrigley, 'A simple model of London's importance in changing English society and economy 1650–1750', *P & P*, XXXVII (1967), 44.
25 D. Defoe, *A Tour Through England and Wales*, I (Everyman edn 1928, repr. 1948), 45.
26 PRO, E190.609/7. R. Blome, *Britannia* (1673), 207, noted the activity in Suffolk of

Kentish men buying butter and cheese for Faversham market; see also J. H. Andrews, 'The trade of the port of Faversham, 1650–1750', *Archaeologia Cantiana*, LXIX (1955), 125.

27 PRO, E134.4 Anne Mich. No. 19.
28 PRO, E190.610/12.
29 PRO, E190.610/14.
30 T. S. Willan, *The English Coastal Trade 1600–1750* (1938), App. 2 and 7.
31 ESRO, FE1/3 no. 120.
32 NNRO, INV/27A no. 39.
33 Davis, *op. cit.*, 55; Defoe, *op. cit.*, I, 47–8; A. G. E. Jones, 'Shipbuilding in Ipswich 1700–1750', *Mariner's Mirror*, XLIII (1957), 294, and *idem*, 'Shipbuilding in Ipswich 1750–1800', *ibid.*, LVIII (1972), 183; Nef, *op cit.*, I, 174, II, 27 n.8 and 95–8.
34 NNRO, INV/24 no. 46.
35 ESRO, IC/AA/112 no. 51; PRO, PROB 4/2912, 5827, 5778.
36 ESRO, FE 1/4 no. 137, FE 1/5 no. 52, FE 1/6 no. 39.
37 ESRO, FE 1/6 no. 44.
38 ESRO, FE 1/3 no. 79.
39 NNRO, INV/60A no. 95.
40 ESRO, IC/AA1/31 no. 229, FE 1/2 no. 161B.
41 NNRO, 228 Barber, INV/29 no. 206.
42 ESRO, IC/AA1/115/7, FE 1/3 no. 21.
43 ESRO, FE 1/6 no. 142.
44 Defoe, *op. cit.*, I, 45.
45 PRO, PROB 4/2887.
46 PRO, PROB 4/805.
47 *Calendar of Patent Rolls 1572–1575*, 375. Mildernix: a variant of modrinacks, a kind of canvas – the word is of obscure origin (*OED*). Poldavis: a coarse canvas or sacking, formerly much used for sailcloth; it takes its name from Poldavide, Douarnenez Bay, Brittany, where it was made (*OED*, where two of the quotations refer to its being made in Ipswich). ESRO, C9/4, fos. 98d–100d. An Act was passed in 1603 for the regulation of their manufacture: 1 James I, c. 24.
48 G. Unwin, 'Industries', *VCH Suffolk*, II (1907), 271–2, see e.g. *CSPD, 1635*, 139, 238, 258, 373, 560; *1664–1665*, 132, 134, 136; see also J. Thirsk, *Economic Policy and Projects* (1978), 40–2.
49 NNRO, O.W. 100, INV/21 no. 39, INV/21 no. 176, 28 Turner, INV/23 no. 77, 226 Angell, INV/27 File 2 no. 81.
50 NNRO, INV/5 no. 24, 211 Mason, INV/30 no. 151H.
51 ESRO; FE 1/3 no. 99, IC/AA2/75/47.
52 NNRO, INV/6 no. 31.
53 ESRO, FE 1/8 no. 66.
54 NNRO, INV/70 no. 24.
55 See N. Pevsner, *The Buildings of England; Suffolk* (1961), 265–83.
56 NNRO, INV/9 no. 9, ESRO, FE1/2 no. 62.
57 ESRO, FE 1/3 no. 117, FE 1/7 no. 124.
58 ESRO, FE 1/4 no. 56.
59 ESRO, FE 1/4 no. 34.
60 ESRO, FE 1/5 no. 150.
61 S. Colman, 'The timber-framed buildings of Ipswich: a preliminary report', *East Anglian Archaeology*, III (1976), 141–4; NNRO, 37 King.
62 ESRO, K30/2/2.
63 ESRO, IC/AA2/79/167.
64 ESRO, FE 1/7 no. 138.
65 ESRO, FK3/1/11/5, fos. 38–42.

66 PRO, PROB 4/2878.
67 NNRO, INV/50A no. 170.
68 *Calendar of Patent Rolls 1563–1566*, 479.
69 ESRO, IC/AA2/80 no. 204; see M. Spufford, *Contrasting Communities* (1974), 85–7, 104–11.
70 NNRO, VIS/4, 5, 6, 8, 9, VCS/1, 2, 3; E. H. Carter, *The Norwich Subscription Books* (1937), *passim*.
71 ESRO, IC/AA2/78/235.
72 ESRO, IC/AA1/141/55, FE 1/7 no. 55.
73 NNRO, INV/70 no. 245.
74 See, *passim*, L. Stone, 'Social mobility in England, 1500–1700', and A. Everitt, 'Social mobility in early modern England', both in *P & P*, xxxiii (1966), D. Marshall, 'La Structure sociale de l'Angleterre au XVIIe siècle', and G. E. Aylmer, 'Caste, ordre (ou statut) et classe dans les premiers temps de l'Angleterre moderne', both in *Problèmes de stratification sociale* ed., R. Mousnier (Paris, 1968), 101 and 137.
75 PRO, PROB 4/4530, PROB 11/358/51.
76 ESRO, C8/4/8, pp. 37, 42.
77 NNRO, 56 Coker, INV/25 no. 47.
78 See, *passim*, R. Grassby, 'English merchant capitalism in the late seventeenth century. The composition of business fortunes', *P & P*, xLvi (1970), 87, and idem, 'The personal wealth of the business community in seventeenth century England', *EcHR*, 2nd ser., xxiii (1970); 220.
79 See NNRO, INV/5 no. 93, INV/24 no. 220, INV/28 no. 28, INV/68 no. 19, ESRO, FE 1/3 no. 107, FE 1/4 no. 68, FE 1/9 no. 69 and FE 1/9 no. 83.
80 PRO, PROB 4/2885.
81 See, for example, for Exeter, W. G. Hoskins, *Industry, Trade and People in Exeter 1688–1800* (1935, repr. 1968), 116; and for York, G. C. F. Forster, 'York in the 17th century', *VCH County of York, The City of York*, (1961), 165. Cf. also H. M. Spufford, 'The significance of the Cambridgeshire Hearth Tax', *Procs Cambridge Antiq. Soc.*, Lv (1961). 53.
82 ESRO, C9/4 and K30/2/1.
83 V. Parker, *The Making of King's Lynn* (1971), 48–50.
84 ESRO, C8/4/6, f.58.
85 See the list of reissues in W. E. Minchinton, *Wage Regulation in Pre-Industrial England* (1972), 106.
86 See E. H. Phelps Brown and S. V. Hopkins, 'Seven centuries of building wages', *Economica*, N.S. xxii (1955), 196, and their 'Seven centuries of the prices of consumables, compared with builders' wage rates', *Economica*, N.S. xxiii (1956), 296.
87 ESRO, C5/14/4, fos. 37d, 42, C6/1/6, fos. 75, 79; cf. J. R. Kellett, 'The breakdown of gild and corporation control over the handicraft and retail trade in London', *EcHR*, 2nd ser, x (1957–8), 381.
88 ESRO, C5/14/3, fos. 34d, 43, 51d, 269.
89 ESRO, C5/14/4, f. 123, C8/4/7, f. 151, C8/4/8. fos. 75, 487.
90 Cf. P. Styles, 'Evolution of the law of settlement', *Univ. Birmingham Hist. J.*, ix (1963–4), 33.
91 J. Wodderspoon, *Memorials of the Ancient Town of Ipswich* (1850), 174. The relevant pages of the General Court Book (ESRO, C5/14/3) are now missing.
92 ESRO, C5/14/3, f. 152.
93 PRO, C66/1705.
94 11 Co. Rep. 53a.
95 ESRO; C5/14/3, f. 310d.
96 *APC*, 1619–21, 122–3.
97 *Ibid.*, 147–9, and BL, Lansdowne MS 162, f. 208 (195).

98 *APC*, 1619–21, 208–10.
99 ESRO, C6/1/4, f. 55, C6/1/6, f. 294.
100 E.g. ESRO, C8/4/7, pp. 93, 99, 124, C8/4/8, pp. 218, 487.
101 7 Edw. VI, c.5.s.3.
102 15 Charles II, c. 14, 22 & 23 Charles II, c.6. A. L. Simon, *The History of the Wine Trade in England*, III (1906, repr. 1964), 174–5, 189.
103 E.g. ESRO, C5/14/3, fos. 275d, 289, 303, C5/14/4, fos. 91d, 105d; PRO, E101, 526/27 and 639/1.
104 ESRO, C5/14/4, fos. 185d–186, 205d, C5/14/5, f.30d, C6/1/7, fos. 117, 122.
105 ESRO, C5/14/3, fos. 172, 256d, C5/14/4, f. 46.
106 ESRO, C5/14/3, fos. 67, 224d, 256d.
107 ESRO, C5/14/5, f. 98.
108 ESRO, C7/2/5 (unpaginated), under 22 Feb. 16 James I, and 28 July 17 James I. J. Brome, *Travels over England, Scotland and Wales* (1700), 119. For similar developments in Norwich see P. J. Corfield, 'A provincial capital in the late seventeenth century: the case of Norwich', in *Crisis and Order in English Towns 1500–1700*, ed. P. Clark and P. Slack (1972), 263, esp. 269.
109 J. Kirby, *The Suffolk Traveller* (2nd edn, 1764), 53.
110 ESRO, C6/1/6, f.120, C5/14/4, fos. 94d, 99d.
111 Kirby, *op. cit.*, 53, cf. W. Owen, *New Book of Fairs* (rev. edn, 1783).
112 ESRO, C5/14/3, f. 293, C8/4/8, pp. 402–3.
113 13 Eliz. I, c. 24.
114 ESRO, C5/14/3, fos. 298, 303, C6/1/4, f. 140d.
115 ESRO, C5/14/3, f. 305d.
116 ESRO, C9/25 and C9/26.
117 ESRO, C5/14/3, fos. 250, 252d. See R. H. Tawney and E. Power (eds.) *Tudor Economic Documents*, III (1924, repr. 1965), 173, for a similar proposal of 1573.
118 ESRO, C6/1/4, f. 239d, C6/1/5, fos. 37d, 38d, 40d.
119 ESRO, C6/1/5, fos. 108d, and R. Canning, *The Principal Charters which have been granted to the Corporation of Ipswich* (1754), 15.
120 ESRO, C6/1/4, f. 191d.
121 *APC*, 1616–17, 27, 156.
122 ESRO, C6/1/6, fos. 377, 381.
123 ESRO, C6/1/7, fos. 12, 67, C5/15/5, f. 11.
124 ESRO, C6/1/7, fos. 20, 30, 92, 108, 114; *CSPD, 1680–1681*, 437, 570, 629, *CSPD, 1682*, 306; *CSPD, Jan.–June 1683*, 199; V. B. Redstone. 'The Dutch and Huguenot settlements of Ipswich', *Procs Huguenot Soc. London*, XII (1917–23), 183; Baron F. de Schickler, *Les Eglises du Refuge en Angleterre*, III (1892), 303.
125 ESRO, C5/14/5, f.83; Redstone, *op. cit.*, 203–4. The Royal Lustring Company was incorporated in 1692; C. T. Carr (ed.), *Select Charters of Trading Companies* (Selden Soc., XXVIII, 1913), 231, and *CSPD, 1691–1692*, 387.
126 ESRO, C5/14/5. fos. 55d–56d. The Linen Manufacture was incorporated in 1690: see *CSPD, May 1690–Oct. 1691*, 186, 424, Carr, *op cit.*, 212.
127 ESRO, C5/14/5, fos. 119, 120, C6/1/7, f. 198.
128 F. G. James, 'Charity endowments as sources of local credit in seventeenth and eighteenth century England', *J. Economic History*, VIII (1948), 153.
129 E.g. ESRO, C5/14/4, fos. 40, 48, 57, etc.
130 *First Report of the Commissioners of Municipal Corporations in England and Wales*, Appendix pt IV (Parliamentary Papers, XXVI, 1835), 2335; *An Account of the Gifts and Legacies that have been given and bequeathed to Charitable Uses, in the town of Ipswich* (new edn, 1819), 73–87.
131 W. G. Hoskins, *Local History in England* (1959), 174–8. For its significance as a regional centre in East Anglia see J. Patten, *English Towns 1500–1700* (1978), esp. ch. 6.

132 W. G. Hoskins, *Industry, Trade and People in Exeter, 1688–1800* (1935, repr. 1968), 19.
133 C. F. Slade, 'Reading', in *Historic Towns*, ed. M. D. Lobel, I (1968), 8.
134 Blome, *op. cit.*, 209.
135 Anon., *A Journey Through England* (1714), 5.
136 Defoe, *op cit.*, I, 43.
137 *The Journeys of Celia Fiennes, op. cit*, 143–4.
138 ESRO, C8/4/8, 402–3.
139 PRO, E190, 610/12.
140 Blome, *op. cit*, 209, J. Brome, *Travels over England, Scotland and Wales* (1700), 119.
141 Anon., *op. cit.*
142 Defoe, *op. cit.*, I, 46.
143 HMC Portland, VI, 65, 170.

Winchester in transition, 1580–1700

ADRIENNE ROSEN

Winchester in transition, 1580–1700

ADRIENNE ROSEN

1 Introduction

The Oxford doctoral thesis on which this essay is based was written from 1968 to 1975. My choice of a topic evolved gradually; I was interested in the structure and workings of small communities in early modern England, and towns offered more complexity than rural areas as well as better records. I happened to attend a conference on urban archaeology at which Martin Biddle described the Winchester Research Unit's work on the medieval city, mentioning in passing that no one had yet made full use of the early modern archives, and my subject developed from there. In 1968 it seemed to me that early modern urban history was still preoccupied with size and success – the provincial capitals, with their expanding population and flourishing industries, were receiving much more attention than the smaller and poorer towns which far outnumbered them. My thesis on Winchester was therefore undertaken in part as a counter-example, a case study of a town which did not grow significantly and which experienced serious social and economic problems in the sixteenth and seventeenth centuries. Since 1968, of course, much more research in urban history has been published and our overall picture of urban development has become far more sophisticated. Historians are now accused of paying too much attention to crisis and failure, and researchers are invited to look beyond county towns like Winchester – which once seemed so small – to study the even smaller market towns.

In order to trace the long-term changes in Winchester's society and economy, my thesis covered a period of 150 years, from 1520 to 1670. Within that period a broad range of topics was examined. Early chapters covered the state of the city and the structure of its society in the 1520s, using the evidence of lay subsidies, and the impact of the Reformation, which created religious divisions in Winchester and added to the city's economic difficulties by closing two large abbeys and several minor houses. The middle section of the thesis was an analysis of the city's government, society, and economy in the Elizabethan and early Stuart periods. The origins, career structure, wealth and attitudes of the governing class were examined in some detail, using court records, wills and inventories. Less information is available on the lower ranks of urban society, but church court records yielded data on migration and literacy. The chapter on the economy looked at the failing local textile industry and its decline, then turned to the organization of Winchester's markets and fairs, and the growth of the city as a retail centre. Chapter 6 focussed on the problems of the early seventeenth century and the response to urban poverty. Chapter 7 described the impact of the Civil War on the city, and the internal strife engendered by Interregnum politics, and the final chapter surveyed Winchester in the decade after the Restoration when its fortunes were beginning to revive.

Further research on Winchester since completion of my thesis, and the added perspective brought by my work on other subjects, by teaching, and by recent publications, have modified my original rather pessimistic picture of Winchester and its problems. In particular, research on the period after 1670 has revealed a broader recovery than I anticipated, and this essay accordingly continues the story to 1700. Continuation into the eighteenth century would show Winchester's further development into a fully-fledged county social centre, but the exigencies of research time and publishing space have imposed their own limits. Comparison with other towns – in England, Europe and North America – has also become easier in the last decade as more urban history has found its way into print, and recent writing has confirmed that Winchester shared most of its problems with other towns of moderate size. In the interests of brevity I have limited my allusions to other towns, but their parallel histories have helped to shape my interpretation of the evidence from Winchester.

One aspect of Winchester's history I would have liked to have pursued further is the context of the county economy and society, and the changing relationship between county and city. Early modern Hampshire is still, however, a surprisingly neglected area. Many of the most obvious topics of research remain to be investigated: little is available (in print, at least) on demographic change and population distribution in the county, on the rural economy, on the gentry and their allegiances, or on the Hampshire cloth industry. Limited research in printed sources has yielded the information on Winchester's hinterland included in this essay, but a great deal more work on Hampshire is needed.

The essay presented here is based mainly on the last three chapters of my thesis, covering the late sixteenth and seventeenth centuries, with added information on the period from 1670 to 1700. The material has been amplified, reconsidered, and rewritten several times in the light of helpful criticism from examiners, friends, and the editor of this volume. The first sections are devoted to the difficult decades from 1580 to 1640, when Winchester experienced the stresses of epidemics, immigration, and growing poverty, and all these were exacerbated by the rapid decline of the cloth industry which had provided much of the city's employment. At the same time, Winchester's markets and shops, and its service sector, were beginning to expand, though the region was still poor and other Hampshire towns competed with the city for custom. Section 5 examines Winchester's Royalism and describes the havoc caused by the Civil War, followed by increased intervention by outsiders in the city's government. The final sections trace the expansion of Winchester's trade and its facilities for visitors after the Restoration, heralding a revival of the city's economy even though its industry was now insignificant. Winchester was also developing a promising new role as a centre for upper-class county society, aided in the 1680s by Charles II's brief period of patronage. The wealth and prestige enjoyed by Winchester in its medieval heyday as the royal capital were long gone, never to return, but the economic and social transitions of the sixteenth and seventeenth centuries had brought the city's long decline to an end and set it on the road to modest prosperity.

2   The local setting

> I shall hereafter under favour apply myself to . . . that truly ancient city which now hangs down its head and at this day presents herself *tanquam Carthaginis cadaver*, a body without a soul . . . yet heretofore she did march without check, cheek by jowl with the best and bravest cities in this kingdom. But all and every city are subject to one and the same fate, that is to be visible in infancy, flourish in maturity, and decline and droop in decrepit age.
>
> John Trussell of Winchester[1]

When Alderman Trussell wrote those words in the 1640s, neither he nor his readers could doubt that Winchester's 'decrepit age' was well advanced. The signs of decay could be seen all around, in the city's physical deterioration, its reduced population, and the poverty of many of its inhabitants. Every pundit had his theory as to the causes of Winchester's decline – Trussell put forward several, ranging from the moral shortcomings of the city's governors to sheer old age, as expressed above – but everyone also knew that Winchester had once enjoyed fame as a royal capital and one of the chief towns of England. In fact the city's deterioration was of far longer standing than most of its seventeenth-century citizens realized, for Winchester had reached its peak of population and prosperity in the early twelfth century, and its history ever since had been one of gradual decline. It was not until the end of the seventeenth century that Winchester at last found stability, based on its expanding role as the market and social centre for Hampshire. The period covered by this study, from 1580 to 1700, therefore encompasses the final decades of the city's decline, and the gradual emergence of solutions to some of its problems.

Since Winchester's past glories continued to affect the city's fate even in the seventeenth century, a brief review of its history is in order.[2] Winchester had been founded beside the river Itchen by the Romans, who built stone city walls and thus determined the city's comparatively large area (144 acres) and its rectangular shape. The modern street-plan was established by the Saxons, who gave Winchester its High Street, running down the middle of the city from the Westgate to the Eastgate, a smaller street parallel to it on either side, and north-south streets running from the High Street to the city walls. The adoption of Winchester as the royal capital and seat of royal administration brought an impressive cathedral, a royal palace, and the castle on its hill overlooking the town. Furthermore, the city was the seat of the richest bishopric in England and an important ecclesiastical centre, and by the twelfth century the south-east quarter of Winchester contained the large episcopal palace of Wolvesey and two wealthy monasteries as well as the cathedral in its close. A survey compiled in 1148 – when Winchester had already reached its peak of prosperity – shows a highly developed and densely built-up community, with extensive suburbs outside the walls and a total urban population of 8,000 or more.

The long decline in the city's size and status started in the twelfth century, as the superior attractions of London began to draw the royal administration, and the wealth and commerce associated with it, away from Winchester. Prosperity ebbed away gradually, hastened by destructive sieges in 1141, 1216, and 1217, and by the devastating impact of the mid-fourteenth-century plagues. The city's decline was temporarily alleviated in the later Middle Ages by its woollen cloth industry. From the twelfth to the fifteenth centuries Winchester was a centre of cloth manufacture, particularly cloth-finishing, and it was prominent in the international wool trade as a Staple town from 1326 to 1353. But this economic base too was gradually under-mined in the fifteenth and sixteenth centuries, as the cloth industry departed for cheaper locations, and Winchester was left without any significant economic special-ization. Trade in southern Hampshire was depressed still further by the rapid decline of Southampton in the sixteenth century. Winchester's population probably reached its lowest level in the first half of the sixteenth century: in the 1520s there were ap-proximately 1,500 people inside the walls and 1,300 in the suburbs,[3] and the later six-teenth century saw only slight growth to about 1,600 in the city with another 1,500 outside the walls in 1603.[4]

By 1600 Winchester's diminished population was therefore living in a setting de-signed for a community of much greater size and importance. Whole streets had been abandoned since the early Middle Ages. Once a city of 56 parishes,[5] Win-chester by 1580 was using only six city churches and another six in the suburbs. The High Street was the only densely inhabited section of the town, and a visitor in 1635 noticed empty ground inside the walls 'especially on the north and west sides . . . converted into orchards, and gardens, and little pastures'.[6] The dissolution of Win-chester's four friaries and two of its three large monasteries (the cathedral priory became a capitular foundation, with little outward change) added further to the dilapidated appearance of the city and to its economic woes; the effects would have been even more severe without the fortunate survival of Winchester College, the cathedral establishment, and the hospitals of St Cross and St Mary Magdalen.

But the relics of Winchester's past riches were not all so mortifying, for the city continued to enjoy a status determined by its importance in earlier days. Despite the greater size of Southampton, Winchester was the county town of Hampshire, the seat of county government and meetings of quarter sessions and assizes. The ecclesi-astical establishment also brought valuable social and economic benefits. The bishops themselves were usually absent in London, but their interests were repre-sented by a staff of legal officials in Winchester. The most important of the bishops' local rights was their jurisdiction over the Soke, an area covering the suburbs which stretched along the main roads outside Winchester's north, east, and south gates.

The city's political institutions too had developed as a result of its medieval wealth and influence, and by the sixteenth century Winchester had a long tradition of self-government. The governing body was the corporation, consisting of all the freemen, whose numbers fluctuated between 45 and 70 for most of the early modern period. Since the freemen constituted less than 15 per cent of the adult males living inside the walls, to be admitted into the corporation was to enter an elite; but in fact power was concentrated in the hands of a group far smaller than this. Even membership of the Twenty-Four, a select body of senior freemen, did not confer real authority. Only when a man was made an alderman, and finally elected mayor, did he become part of the true ruling group, for from the late sixteenth century onwards political power was increasingly concentrated in the hands of the mayor and his brethren (the ex-mayors), who were usually also the aldermen. All the governing offices and insti-tutions of Winchester, most of them centuries old, were confirmed in 1588 by a charter of incorporation. The city shared with other old-established boroughs an almost fanatical sense of civic pride – no privilege granting independence from the county was too small to be ardently defended, and the elaborate ceremonial laid down for high days and holidays served to display the dignity of the city's governors before the lower orders.

Winchester's place in the hierarchy of English towns in the sixteenth and seventeenth centuries was clearly defined. With its tiny population and limited resources, the city stood far below London or the great provincial capitals. At the same time, no Elizabethan Englishman would have counted Winchester among the small and unsophisticated market towns, though the city's markets were essential to its economic life and its population was comparable to that of some market centres. The city shared most characteristics with the medium-sized county and cathedral towns, which were self-governing and often walled, possessed a variety of small industries, and provided a modest range of goods and services. The fortunes of these middling towns were mixed in the sixteenth and seventeenth centuries: some flourished, but many experienced difficulties similar to Winchester's as their staple industries declined and they developed new specializations or adapted to general distribution as their major function.[7] The cloth industry in particular had been the basis of wealth and employment in many English towns, and changes in types of cloth, and the shifting balance between the regions where they were made, brought painful economic readjustments to many urban centres in the sixteenth and seventeenth centuries. Some regions such as the South-East saw their urban cloth industry disappear for good, and Winchester was not the only southern town struggling to support unemployed clothworkers in the seventeenth century.[8]

By 1700, however, Winchester had found an enduring economic role which was to sustain the city into modern times and restore a limited measure of prosperity to its hard-pressed inhabitants. That transition, from an impoverished cloth town in the late sixteenth century to a thriving social and retailing centre by the late seventeenth, with all the changes in Winchester's economy and society that such a transition implied, forms the theme of this study.

3 Manufactures and markets, 1580–1640

By the late sixteenth century it was abundantly clear that the cloth industry which had been Winchester's economic mainstay in the later Middle Ages was in trouble. In 1581 a subsidy list for the city showed the decline well under way: only nine of the 100 most highly assessed male taxpayers were engaged in the manufacture of cloth, and another two in its sale, as compared to 16 gentlemen and professional men, 15 in food and drink, 12 in general retailing, and nine each in leather-working and the metal crafts.[9] The early seventeenth century brought yet more problems for clothiers and their employees, and the decay of Winchester's staple industry created unemployment which in turn aggravated all the social and economic problems which beset the city in common with many provincial towns before the Civil War. The gradual withering away of textile manufacture, and the failure of any other industry at Winchester to replace it, therefore merit examination as important contributors to the city's malaise in the early seventeenth century.

Most of the cloth produced in sixteenth-century Winchester was Hampshire kersey, a light woollen fabric which had displaced broadcloth as the regional speciality in the fifteenth century. The city was a centre for both production and distribution of kerseys. Spinning was probably done by the poor and by workers in the countryside, but the yarn was brought back to the city for weaving, 17 weavers and 19 fullers were working at Winchester in 1578, in addition to the clothworkers in the Soke.[10] Cloth-finishing, which required supplies of running water, was concentrated at the eastern end of the town where streams ran beside the streets, and along the river in the eastern suburb. Several fulling-mills stood along the Itchen just outside the walls, and the fulled cloths were stretched and dried on racks in gardens and vacant plots before being dyed.

Winchester cloth-dealers sold a few kerseys locally, but the great majority of the kerseys made in Hampshire were destined for export, either from Southampton or from London. Even though Southampton was near at hand, most of the county's output was transported 70 miles by cart and pack-horse to London: in 1565, for instance, 19,432 Hampshire kerseys were exported from London between Easter and Michaelmas, while only 2,794 left Southampton in the same period.[11] More than three-quarters of the combined total in 1565 went to Antwerp, which served as the collection centre for cloth which would eventually be sent on to Italy and thence to the Levant. The collapse of the Antwerp market in subsequent years left France and Italy as the major customers for kerseys, but foreign tastes were changing and the number of kerseys exported fell rapidly in the early seventeenth century.[12] In 1619 only 6,854 Hampshire kerseys were shipped from London and Southampton combined,[13] and by the later seventeenth century southern kerseys had virtually disappeared. Domestic sales through London may have accounted for some of the cloth made in Hampshire, but the evidence of declining production shows clearly enough that by 1640 southern kerseys were no longer in demand either at home or abroad.

The decline of the kersey need not have spelled the end of the Hampshire textile industry – Devon and Norfolk made successful and very profitable transitions from Old to New Draperies – but the new stuffs never flourished in Hampshire as broadcloths and kerseys had done. The new techniques were first introduced in Southampton, by a group of Walloon refugees who settled there in 1567; some were invited to move to Winchester, but they chose to stay close to their church in Southampton.[14] The refugees brought with them a knowledge of the manufacture of serges, and by the early seventeenth century a variety of half-worsteds was being made in Winchester and other Hampshire towns. The occupations of woolcomber, worsted-weaver, and serge-weaver began to appear at Winchester during the reign of James I, and exports from Southampton in 1619 included small quantities of 'Winton cloth rashes' and 'Winton perpetuanoes'. In the early years of the seventeenth century serge manufacturers claimed to employ 3,000 people in Winchester and Southampton, 'besides a multitude of country people, fifteen miles compass', and 3,000 tods of wool were used at Winchester and 10,000 at Southampton each year.[15]

The tentative beginnings of the new industry in Hampshire were soon undermined, however, by the economic crises and wars of the 1620s and 1630s combined with strong competition from other textile-producing regions. A petition of 1618 complained that employment around Winchester, 'indifferent' at the best of times, had fallen off sharply.[16] The volume of wool used in and around the city for clothing had diminished to less than 300 tods a year by 1621, and the Winchester clothworkers petitioned for relief in 1622.[17] Nine years later, the depression of 1631 brought the industry to a complete standstill in the Soke:

Those few that do use clothing within the said liberty are not able to go on with their trading any longer (their stocks being out in cloth and commodities ready made which lieth upon their hands for want of vent or sale), by reason whereof the said poor are most of them ready to famish and perish this hard time of dearth and scantiness.[18]

Even a temporary interruption of trade put severe strain on the smaller cloth-workers who lived from one sale to the next, and poor weavers turned to victualling and other sidelines to survive.[19] The larger entrepreneurs too had been diversifying to protect themselves, and by the early seventeenth century there were no longer any wealthy clothiers at Winchester whose assets and business interests were wholly devoted to the cloth industry, as had been common a century earlier. Even the clothiers in the Soke, who avoided the distractions and expense of civic office-holding, were following the example of their city colleagues by investing in land and marrying their children to the offspring of country gentlemen or cathedral canons.[20] The amount of capital devoted to clothing at Winchester diminished decade by decade, until by 1660 the cloth industry had joined the city's other minor manufactures as a small undertaking serving only local needs. By the late seventeenth century clothing had 'almost disappeared' from south-east England, as the northern and western counties took over leadership in the manufacture of English textiles.[21]

None of Winchester's other industries could replace clothing as a major source of employment, for without exception they were aimed at limited local markets. Hampshire was well supplied with hides and bark, and leather-working prospered at Winchester throughout the sixteenth and seventeenth centuries. Tanning, like cloth-finishing, required good water supplies and produced noxious wastes, and the trade was concentrated in the low-lying north-east quarter of the city and in the eastern suburb. Whereas tanning was confined to a few large workshops owned by men of some substance, the production of leather goods attracted large numbers of poor craftsmen. Sixteen shoemakers and cobblers lived inside the walls in 1580, plus saddlers, collarmakers, curriers, and glovers, and by 1691 the city had 36 leatherworkers of all kinds, an increase slightly greater than the proportional rise in Winchester's population.[22] One unusual form of leather-working was a small parchment-making industry, catering to the city's lawyers and institutions. Metalworking too was undertaken to serve local custom, which was sufficient to support a small group of blacksmiths, plumbers, pewterers, goldsmiths, braziers, cutlers, armourers, gunsmiths, pinmakers and ironmongers throughout the seventeenth century. Small metal wares were also brought into Winchester for sale, and an ordinance of 1576 restricted selling by strangers from citizens' houses to turners, nailmen, and the Hallamshire cutlers.[23] Brewing and malting attracted a disproportionate amount of official attention in the late sixteenth and seventeenth centuries because of their consumption of grain. Malting certainly increased at Winchester before 1640, but court records show that much of it was done by members of other trades as a lucrative sideline, much as brewing had been practised as a part-time occupation in the sixteenth century. It was only in the mid to late seventeenth century that malting as a full-time occupation became prominent at Winchester.

The city's fortunes as an industrial centre before the Civil War were therefore unpropitious. Left without any industrial specialization, Winchester was obliged to fall back on its markets, fairs, and shops, which had proved to be the only enduring element in the urban economy throughout all the vicissitudes of the previous seven centuries. Retailing was to become the basis of the city's wealth, and the expansion of inland trade in the half-century before the Civil War came just in time to strengthen Winchester's marketing sector as its industry crumbled.

By the sixteenth century two markets were held at Winchester each week, on Wednesdays and Saturdays. Most selling occurred in the market-place, an open area next to the cathedral churchyard. There stood the market house, a tiled wooden building rebuilt in 1620, which housed the standard weights and measures and a bell to signal the opening of the market. Close by were the pens from which animals were sold. A few shops stood around the edges of the market-place, but most traders sold from 'standings', spaces 6ft or 12ft long hired from the city bailiffs, where temporary stalls could be set up or wares displayed on the ground.[24] The market-place was often called the cornmarket, and grain was probably the major commodity sold, but records also mention the sale of malt, bread, cheese, butter, eggs, fruit and vegetables, capons, rabbits, geese, firewood and charcoal, and live sheep and pigs. Selling on market days also took place in the High Street around the market cross, a stone edifice mounted on steps which served as display space for country traders and also as the platform for public announcements and proclamations. Dealers in meat and fish from outside Winchester sold from two rows of shambles. In 1585 there were at least 13 butchers trading in Winchester,[25] besides those in the suburbs and country butchers at the markets, and the city's inhabitants and customers must have consumed large quantities of meat to keep them all in business. The Winchester markets showed no signs of specialization during the sixteenth and seventeenth centuries, a feature consistent with the city's function as a centre of general distribution.

The two annual fairs at Winchester, held in February and October, brought craftsmen as well as farmers to the city. In addition to livestock, the usual range of foodstuffs and yarn for the city's weavers, goods were sold at the fairs by turners, coopers, joiners, smiths and nailmen. Foreign craftsmen, who were usually rigorously excluded from the city, were permitted to work there briefly during the fairs.[26] Two more fairs were held on the hills just outside Winchester. St Giles' Fair, once the meeting-place of international merchants, was almost moribund in the seventeenth century, but Magdalen Fair was a flourishing event which drew crowds to Winchester each July. Winchester College bought its cheese at Magdalen Fair in the sixteenth century, and Celia Fiennes described it in the 1690s as 'a considerable fair . . . the traffic mostly hops which that country produceth good and cheese; it's noted for a vast many of wains from several parts especially from the west country'.[27] The observation about custom from the west is confirmed by a record of horse sales at Magdalen Fair in 1623: more than half the sellers came from Somerset, and a quarter of the purchasers from Wiltshire, with smaller contingents from Dorset, Berkshire, Hertfordshire, Sussex, Surrey, and Middlesex.[28]

No records survive to show the distances over which customers travelled to Winchester's markets, and it is therefore impossible to delineate the city's economic hinterland with any accuracy. Markets in southern England generally drew their custom from fairly small areas,[29] and fig. 14 shows the market towns with which Winchester was in competition. Central Hampshire was clearly Winchester's preserve, but the high chalk downs north of the city were lightly populated and there was close competition between markets in the area. In 1593 Winchester despatched lawyers to London to take action against 'the markets erected at Alresford and Waltham to the great prejudice of the city'. Nothing could be done about New Alresford, whose market in 1673 was 'very considerable', but the town was very small and suffered disastrous fires in 1644 and 1690, and its competition constituted an irritant rather than a threat to Winchester. The city's suit against Bishop's Waltham, however, continued for many years, and the new market there either succumbed or was insignificant by the 1670s.[30]

John Taylor's guide to taverns in 1636 provides an approximate ranking of Hampshire market towns, since taverns were among the facilities catering to visitors as well as inhabitants. According to Taylor only three towns had more than three taverns: Portsmouth (6), Winchester (7), and Southampton (8).[31] These communities were the focal points of trade in the county, with two markets each and permanent shops to attract customers throughout the week. Had Southampton been a thriving town its competition would have severely limited Winchester's potential growth, but the port was deep in decline throughout the seventeenth century and Winchester assumed the role of Hampshire's retail centre. Southampton did not relinquish all its inland trade, however. Winchester's proposal to open the river Itchen to navigation in the 1620s met bitter opposition from Southampton, which claimed that as many as two to three hundred men were employed in carrying goods to Winchester and on to Oxfordshire, Berkshire, northern Wiltshire, most of Surrey, and 'all the good towns of Hampshire', and that the navigation would reduce them to six or eight boatmen.[32] Southampton managed to block a series of bills for the navigation during the 1620s, and when the Itchen was finally included in a successful bill in 1664 a clause was inserted at Southampton's insistence limiting the commodities carried to coal and 'the Norway trade', thereby preventing Winchester from becoming a distribution centre for imported goods.[33]

Winchester's status as the administrative centre for the county, and its cluster of church institutions, were nevertheless sufficient to give the city a major advantage over nearby rival towns. County assizes and quarter sessions drew crowds to the city several times a year, and more than 1,000 Hampshire voters were polled at Winchester in the election of 1614.[34] The church courts of Winchester, consistory and archdeaconry, brought suitors who needed to prove a will, settle a neighbours' quarrel, or dispute the parson's claim for tithes. Tenants and petitioners travelled to the city on business arising from the far-flung estates of the bishop, the dean and chapter, and Winchester College, even though stewards regularly journeyed to the outlying manors to hold courts.[35] No other town in Hampshire was the focus of so much public and private business.

The kinds of business that brought visitors to the city frequently required consultation with lawyers, and by the sixteenth century Winchester had long been established as a centre providing a wide array of legal and other professional services. At least 30 lawyers were working in the city in the late sixteenth century and a similar number in the early seventeenth, and nearly all of them held positions serving the bishop, the cathedral, or the College. Acceptance of a civic office other than that of recorder was still uncommon, but lawyers resident in Winchester were on hand to advise the corporation, and also acted for town and country clients. Large numbers of lawyers in addition to the cathedral clergy and the College Fellows gave Winchester a substantial class of educated and relatively wealthy men, and their presence in turn created demand for specialist services including those provided by physicians and booksellers. The city normally had two or three physicians serving the upper classes during the late Tudor and early Stuart periods.[36] Specialized bookshops still lay in the future, but in 1617 the dean 'sent to the booksellers' in search of heretical books,[37] which were probably to be found among the stock of mercers and

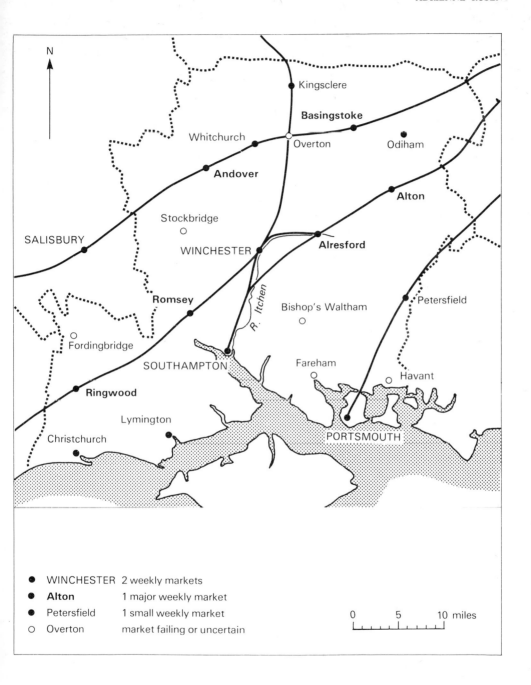

Figure 14. Markets and major roads in seventeenth-century Hampshire.

grocers as well as stationers. Education was naturally dominated by Winchester College. The city grammar school had closed early in the sixteenth century, and the College tried to shut down a new city school in 1629, claiming that it already provided education for 'the youth of all sorts' in Winchester and the surrounding area.[38] Some small Catholic boarding schools also appeared in the early seventeenth century.[39]

The expansion of inns and shops before 1640 suggests that visitors to Winchester were increasing. General retailing by grocers, mercers, and haberdashers was certainly a growth sector, and probate inventories show a handful of wealthy traders with stock worth several hundred pounds and many smaller businesses carrying a wide range of cheap goods.[40] Specialized shops were still rare, but the occupation of stationer first appeared at Winchester between 1550 and 1599, gunsmiths and tobacconists arrived between 1600 and 1649, and a haberdasher's stock in 1625 consisted entirely of hats.[41] While the number of large inns was fairly constant, their custom increased as country gentlemen and the city elite adopted them as congenial meeting-places. The corporation entertained the commissioners of gaol delivery to dinner at the White Horse in 1591, and the Bull was described about 1615 as 'a place of usual resort for the most part of the Justices ... and divers other meetings of gentlemen, whereby a great benefit and profit did arise unto the tenant of the said messuage or tavern by provision of diet and otherwise'.[42] John Trussell, Winchester's antiquarian alderman, wrote proudly that in 1603 Winchester had provided the 'best accommodation and entertainment' for the London law-term when it was moved from Westminster to escape the plague, and that 'neither Hertford, St Albans or Reading could make any indifferent comparison'.[43]

The competition between towns in Hampshire was heightened by the fact that the region which provided their custom was neither rich nor populous in the early seventeenth century. Travellers commented on the emptiness of the countryside, and contemporary head-counting confirms their impressions – median population density in Hampshire parishes in 1603 was 35 per cent lower than in the more highly developed counties of Norfolk and Suffolk.[44] In 1515, while the cloth industry was still flourishing, Hampshire had ranked a poor twentieth out of 34 English counties in lay wealth per 1,000 acres.[45] Furthermore, despite the county's proximity to London, farmers maintained their traditional patterns of agriculture – sheep-corn husbandry on the downlands, and dairying, horse-breeding and the fattening of cattle and pigs in the vales and woodland areas – without developing any strong agricultural specialization before 1640. Traditional crops served well enough, and Hampshire supplied London with corn in years of shortage, but the lack of commercial enterprise in agriculture was typical of this charming but somewhat backward county.[46]

The Hampshire road system promoted trade in those market towns which were favourably placed on major thoroughfares, but Winchester was not among their number – indeed, the cross-county routes actually diverted traffic away from the city. Until about 1400 the Great West Road, the major route from south-west England to London, had passed through Winchester, but as the city declined travellers adopted the shorter route across northern Hampshire, using the valley of the Test and not the Itchen to cross the downs (fig. 14).[47] The increase in private travel during the seventeenth century therefore contributed little to Winchester's trade, while Andover and Basingstoke developed into busy thoroughfare towns. The condition of Hampshire roads provoked frequent complaints from travellers. The corporation of Winchester was not responsible for the upkeep of the highways outside its walls, but in 1660 it reimbursed the mayor for emergency repairs to a major access road which had deteriorated so much that carts and carriages could no longer reach the city.[48]

In spite of all the limitations imposed by its hinterland, its geographical position, and its competitors, Winchester was beginning to see some real growth in its custom before 1640. That growth was still in its early stages, however, and could do little to offset the poverty associated with the city's failing cloth industry. Some visitors in the early seventeenth century found Winchester a bustling county town, but the city's governors and the urban poor – preoccupied alike with seemingly overwhelming problems – would probably not have agreed that Winchester's economic health was improving.

4   Economic and social problems, 1580–1640

The inexorable decline of Winchester's staple industry inevitably created stresses in the city's economy and social structure. Workmen lost their livelihood or were under-employed, thus jeopardizing their ability to support their families. Immigrants to the city could no longer be easily absorbed, and tensions arose between settled inhabitants and newcomers competing for employment and relief. Small clothiers and independent workmen who had previously contributed to taxes and the poor rate became recipients of relief, and the burden on the middle and upper ranks of urban society grew heavier. The decades before 1640 would in any case have been marked by a readjustment to new economic circumstances, but the period also brought a succession of short-term crises which compounded the city's problems and created severe hardship among its poorer citizens.

The evidence for demographic change at Winchester in the late sixteenth and early seventeenth centuries is poor: only one of the six functioning intramural parishes has a surviving register before 1660, and coverage of the six parishes in the suburbs is spasmodic. St Maurice, the single city parish whose register survives, was, however, the most populous of the six, with approximately 27 per cent of the intramural population in 1603, and the parish included both poor and wealthy areas; with appropriate caution its data may therefore be used to suggest demographic trends in the city as a whole. Population in St Maurice was increasing from 1580 until about 1620, though not at a spectacular rate. Baptisms outnumbered burials in two years out of three, even in the 1620s and 1630s, and despite the death-toll of epidemics the parish produced a small net surplus between 1580 and 1640. If St Maurice was typical of the whole city, Winchester was experiencing moderate growth, part of which came from natural increase. Overcrowded housing was not a serious problem – in fact a sixteenth-century petition had denounced 'the joining of houses two, three or four together'[49] – and Winchester may have provided a healthier environment than larger towns.

Nevertheless, the city suffered severely from epidemics in the late sixteenth and early seventeenth centuries. In 1583 the first outbreak of plague for almost 20 years prompted the corporation to issue a list of plague orders, based on those for London which had been printed and distributed by the Privy Council.[50] The number of burials remained above normal levels in St Maurice in 1584 and 1585, though the suburban parishes whose registers survive show no unusual mortality. In 1593 trade was interrupted when plague in London forced the closing of Winchester's gates to strangers, 'especially footmen or such as bring packs', and an alderman was imprisoned and had his shop forcibly closed for receiving merchandise from the capital. The corporation built a pest-house, but registers show only slightly elevated numbers of burials.[51] In 1597 deaths in the northern suburb and in St Maurice again rose to epidemic proportions, perhaps due to famine and related sickness. The next major outbreak of plague spread from London in 1603, reaching Winchester by October and lingering until 1606. As was often the case, the impact of the epidemic differed markedly from one parish to another: burials in St Peter Chesil, outside the Eastgate, rose from three in 1602 to 32 in 1603 and 25 in 1604, while inside the walls St Maurice was hardly affected. Plague must have been present in other parts of the city, however, for officials collected funds for the relief of victims and their families from the city coffer and the chamberlains, with a rate on householders and donations by the mayor.[52] The suburbs, but not apparently the city, were affected in 1609 by another epidemic.[53]

After a lull of more than a decade, plague broke out again in 1625; it was the most catastrophic epidemic at Winchester since the Black Death. Burials in St Maurice had been high since 1623, and in August 1625 a sudden steep rise signalled the beginning of the crisis. In September the corporation petitioned the Privy Council for help, complaining of 'great distress'; all of Winchester's 'principal and wealthiest inhabitants' had fled into the country, and those who remained were short of food because no one would come to the market. The eastern suburb buried four times as many inhabitants in 1625 as in a normal year, and St Maurice was extremely hard hit with 88 deaths, about one-fifth of the parish's population. Relief payments from the city coffer alone came to over £80.[54]

Once again a major epidemic was succeeded by a relatively healthy period, and there is no evidence of widespread sickness again at Winchester until 1637. The London plague of 1636 had reached rural Hampshire, and the disease spread to the towns in the following year.[55] The eastern and northern suburbs and St Maurice were all afflicted – St Bartholomew, outside the Northgate, which had escaped the outbreak of 1625, recorded almost seven times as many burials in 1638 as in a normal year.

Migration into Winchester from the countryside quickly made up the demographic losses caused by epidemics, however, and added significantly to the city's population. Many of the newcomers were destitute and needed immediate relief. Southampton too was overrun with poor immigrants, and the existence of an alternative destination for these migrants in Hampshire may have spared Winchester from the full onslaught of rural-urban subsistence migration. The city was also the target of migrants seeking better employment, whether through the traditional method of apprenticeship or as interloping craftsmen. Immigration had been heavy throughout the sixteenth century, with the result that by 1600 only a third of the city and Soke's inhabitants were natives of Winchester, and John Trussell noted as if it were an unusual occurrence that the two bailiffs and the mayor elected in 1640 had all been born in the city.[56]

The pressure of hundreds of newcomers competing with the settled townspeople for dwindling opportunities for employment provoked an increasingly hostile policy against outsiders. The tailors and hosiers had sought protection as early as 1566 against rural craftsmen who came to the city 'at divers quick times of work and against high feasts', working surreptitiously from inns and alehouses and private dwellings, then leaving with the crowds.[57] Each week the constables presented to the town court any householder who took in lodgers, and from 1611 a charitable apprenticeship fund was restricted to poor children born in Winchester. In 1637 masters were prohibited from taking on any journeyman or servant from outside the city without first giving security for his future support.[58] Though the intent behind such regulations was clear enough, their enforcement depended on the determination of city officials. Thomas Frend set up shop as a goldsmith in Winchester during the 1620s without serving his apprenticeship there or becoming a freeman, and frequent warnings and even the closing of his shop failed to dislodge him. A special ordinance against Frend passed in 1622 proved useless, for two years later he was still trading in Winchester and was alleged to have 'drawn away the custom of the country' from native goldsmiths.[59]

A succession of crises – whether in the form of famine and high food prices, epidemics or trade depressions – forced many more inhabitants than usual to turn to the corporation for relief in the late sixteenth and early seventeenth centuries. In the spring of 1587, after a bad harvest the previous summer, grain supplies in the Winchester markets ran low and the corporation bought wheat and rye for the poor who could no longer afford the high prices. Rent arrears were forgiven for tenants too poor to pay, and the corporation began to include the maintenance of a poor child in the terms of some of its leases.[60] A series of bad harvests in the mid-1590s again threw hundreds of Winchester's inhabitants on the mercy of their fellow-citizens. The corporation bought wheat and rye for the poor in 1594 and 1595, and instituted a register of grain brought to the market. Relief in the 1590s also took the form of supplies of wool and flax for spinning, to enable the poor to earn a pittance for themselves.[61]

The next two decades provided a breathing-space, marred only by the epidemic of 1603 and combined plague and high grain prices in 1609 which again necessitated the purchase of corn for the poor.[62] The worsening state of the local textile industry, however, together with widespread trade depression and the impact of the plague of 1625, made the 1620s and 1630s a period of extreme difficulty. In 1627 a petition estimated the number of recipients of alms within the city at 600, perhaps one-third of the inhabitants.[63] In addition to distributing alms the corporation bought firewood for the poor in 1629, 1630, and 1637, and lent £500 to a clothier in 1630 to create employment.[64] The depression of 1631 affected the Soke particularly severely, and a petition put the number of poor there at 500, again nearly one-third of the population.[65]

Charles I's wars in the 1620s had the effect of adding to the city's problems, not only by disrupting international trade and thus dislocating the domestic economy, but also by impressing local working men for the army and by sending waves of troops to be billeted in Winchester on their way to Portsmouth and Southampton. Two regiments from the West Country were sent to the city in 1626, and another contingent from Dorset arrived in March 1627. By May the soldiers' pay was eight weeks in arrears, and the troops were close to mutiny. Attempts to collect the Forced Loan, which would have provided funds with which to pay the troops, met opposition and excuses. By December the citizens were ready to protest, and when plans were announced for three Irish regiments to be billeted in the city and Soke the corporation drew up a list of its grievances and appealed to the Duke of Buckingham, its high steward. Over £50 had been spent on facilities and supplies for troops billeted in Winchester or passing through. More serious was the effect of soldiers on the city's trade, for the increased demand for food drove prices up in the market, and meetings

157

of assizes and quarter sessions were transferred to other towns, taking with them many of the city's customers. Two more regiments were billeted at Winchester in the summer of 1628 before embarking for La Rochelle, but the deputy-lieutenants appear not to have used the city for billeting thereafter.[66]

Impressment placed an additional burden on individual families and on the public funds which often became their sole means of support. The number of soldiers required from Winchester was generally small, but extra men were often collected in the city to make up the allotted numbers. Over 1,500 soldiers were levied from Hampshire during the 1620s and the deputy-lieutenants had increasing difficulty in meeting their quota.[67] When the city was required to supply 26 men in 1639 to fight the Scots, the corporation petitioned for exemption on account of the

> miserable estate of this poor city, consisting for the most part of poor mechanics who have no other means for maintenance of themselves, their wives and children but what they get by their daily labours; from which if they be taken but for a month or two their families must of necessity perish or be sustained by the revenues of the chamber, which are so small, and the number of the poor thereby at this present relieved so many, that all will not satisfy their necessity, with the continual taxes laid upon the inhabitants in weekly payments upon them.[68]

Winchester's problems of poor relief in the late sixteenth and early seventeenth centuries were shared by every English county town to varying degrees, and the methods adopted by the corporation closely resembled the expedients of other town authorities. The first line of defence was to turn away as many potential paupers as possible: the beadle was paid each year to drive out the beggars who swarmed into the city at the time of assizes and quarter sessions, and any pauper who could plausibly be transferred to another parish was sent away.[69] Not all poor people could be excluded, however, and several hundred impoverished inhabitants turned to public funds for relief. The collection of the weekly poor rate and the distribution of relief were administered by the corporation in the early seventeenth century, and the city parishes seem to have played little part in aid to the poor.[70] Payments of poor relief – usually amounting to between 3d. and 12d. a week to each recipient – were recorded each year in the accounts of St John's Hospital, a medieval foundation which by the reign of Elizabeth was effectively controlled by the corporation: the totals shown in the accounts reveal a sharp increase in the scale of public relief in the 1620s and 1630s, even when adjusted for inflation (fig. 15).[71]

The resources available for poor relief at Winchester were augmented by charity from the institutions in and around the city. Two hospitals just outside the town, St Cross and St Mary Magdalen, housed about 60 respectable aged poor (not all from Winchester), and St Cross distributed bread to 600 poor people six times a year.[72] The dean and chapter made the most valuable contribution, with regular payments of 13s. 4d. a week to the city poor, supplies of wool for spinning in slack times, and apprenticeships for the cathedral choirboys; and both the chapter and Winchester College frequently dispensed casual alms to poor travellers.[73] The absentee bishops, on the other hand, gave little help to their cathedral city, and the corporation accordingly developed much closer relations with the dean and chapter.

Winchester also had the county workhouse, established in the castle in 1579 with the encouragement of Sir Francis Walsingham. As one of the earliest houses of correction, it was intended as a model for others, and ambitious plans were drawn up for its operation. The workhouse was to employ 80 men and women, chiefly rogues but with paupers admitted to make up the number, paying them 'as much as they shall have at any clothier's hand'. Inmates were to work at the manufacture and finishing of kerseys and serges, the making of gloves, knitted stockings, felt hats and nails, and rogues sentenced to labour would provide the power in a mill to full the cloths, draw water, and grind flour and malt. Actual production appears to have been less extensive than originally planned, however, for the new keeper in 1582 envisaged only spinning, carding, grinding corn, and smith's work.[74] At first the corporation held aloof from the county workhouse and maintained its own house of correction in the tower of a disused parish church, but from 1619 city rogues were sent to the county house and the corporation contributed to the keeper's fee.[75]

The corporation's accounting system, divided between St John's Hospital, the coffer and the chamber, makes it difficult to assess actual income, especially since it is evident that money was casually passed from one official to another as needed,[76] but the rapid expansion of expenditure on poor relief in the 1620s and 1630s undoubtedly placed civic finances under severe strain. In these circumstances of great need and limited resources, private philanthropy was a useful addition to public funds for the relief of Winchester's poor. Virtually every alderman left at least some small sum to be given directly to the city's poor, and many set up elaborate charities. Lee Beier has shown that funds bequeathed were not always received, but the Winchester evidence suggests that most bequests by local inhabitants did eventually reach the corporation, though long delays and expensive lawsuits were not uncom-

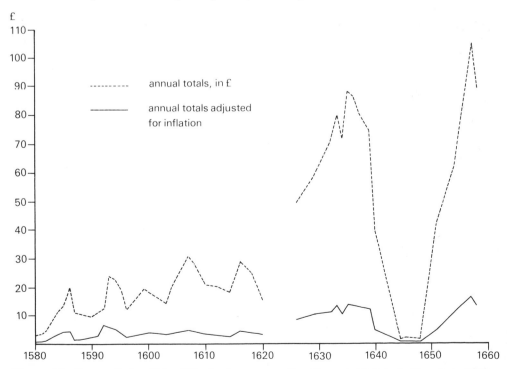

Figure 15. Poor relief paid by Winchester corporation through St John's Hospital, 1580–1658.

mon: it took 20 years, for example, to recover the endowment for an almshouse established by the will of Peter Symondes in 1587, and the house did not open its doors until 1615.[77] The quantification of philanthropy is full of pitfalls, but it is safe to say that major testamentary benefactions to the poor at Winchester between 1580 and 1640 provided at least £400 for direct distribution, plus property and capital to provide £66 a year more, as well as £210 to set the poor to work, £215 for apprenticing poor children, £250 for charitable loans, and a new almshouse and maintenance for 17 almspeople.

Whether this money was used in the best interests of the poor is, however, open to question. Since most benefactions had been given by former friends and colleagues, the leaders of the corporation assumed the right to determine how the money was spent. When the selection of almspeople or recipients of charity was left to the corporation, it tended to choose its own members and their families – Peter Symondes' hospital, for instance, became largely a home for retired and impoverished freemen. The choice of freemen to receive loans from Sir Thomas White's gift, intended for young tradesmen beginning their careers, was also manipulated by the corporation, and some borrowers had been freemen for as long as 20 years.[78] The proprietary attitude of Winchester's governors to the money entrusted to them could also lead to misuse and occasional outright corruption. The coffer accounts record many loans of charitable funds to aldermen or local gentlemen, and repayment dates for influential borrowers were elastic.[79] It is of course possible that such loans represented a convenient form of investment, intended to preserve the funds against inflation, but the corporation's use of the money – such as nine-year loans – was more attuned to the interests of the wealthy than the poor. Funds from two legacies for poor relief were used for legal fees in the suits to recover Peter Symondes' bequests.[80] By the 1660s the corporation was even charging 6 per cent interest on local charitable loan funds and on loans under Sir Thomas White's gift, contrary to the terms of White's will.[81] Yet the Winchester elite was not venal so much as casual with city money, and in times of need mayors and aldermen gave generously from their own pockets. Their identification with Winchester and its interests was so close that the concept of a strict separation between public and private funds was alien to their understanding.

However good their intentions, the city's leaders were unimaginative and ineffective in their attempts to alleviate poverty. The need for relief always outstripped the resources devoted to it, and the assize justices reproved the mayor in 1630 for 'not ordering his poor better'.[82] The galvanizing force behind poor relief in many towns – notably at Salisbury, Warwick, and Norwich – was puritanism, a force which left Winchester virtually untouched before the Civil War. In a period when most towns organized lectureships, the only Sunday lecture in Winchester was provided by the dean and chapter.[83] Such resistance as there was to the Established Church tended towards Catholicism rather than puritanism, and the ecclesiastical census of 1603 found twice as many recusants as nonconformists in Winchester and the Soke. The notable absence of puritanism among members of the oligarchy was fostered by the city's close social and economic ties to the bishop and the cathedral. The bishop's local influence was waning, but it was by no means entirely gone – many of the city's M.P.s in the early seventeenth century, for example, were episcopal kinsmen or allies. More important in the corporation's day-to-day concerns were the dean and chapter, who gave generously for poor relief and other extraordinary expenses. Some of the chapter's clerks and lawyers became mayors of the city, and the canons' families intermarried with leading members of the oligarchy. Puritanism would probably have strained these ties and appeared to threaten the strongly hierarchical outlook of the governing elite. Some junior members of the corporation who staged a minor revolt in 1622 were indeed denounced as men 'troubled with a pruriticall [puritanical] itch of scratching against authority', and accused of holding 'alehouse private conventicles ... to make confederacies against the mayor and his brethren';[84] but the oligarchy was quite strong enough to survive this attack on its power, and protestant nonconformity remained rare at Winchester until the 1640s.

Even if they lacked imagination, the governors of Winchester were not complacent about the state of their city in the early seventeenth century. The writings of John Trussell, the only member of the elite to leave any trace of his private thoughts, show a deep sense of unease at the social changes taking place around him. The pursuit of private gain rather than the public good preoccupied too many elected officials, in Trussell's view, and he accused his fellow magistrates of failing to punish 'licentiousness' and thus encouraging offenders. Begging, bastardy, drunkenness, Sunday trading, and other offences were all rampant, and Trussell blamed their increase on the negligence of the city's leaders.[85] Tougher enforcement of the law was obviously not a sufficient answer to such problems, however, and the corporation tried a number of different schemes in attempts to revive the urban economy.

Winchester had been a textile centre for so long that it was almost impossible for contemporaries to realize that the local cloth industry was finally dying, and not in a merely temporary decline. Efforts to protect and resuscitate clothing accordingly continued into the mid-seventeenth century. The provision of work for the poor most frequently took the form of wool for spinning or carding. Several charitable loan funds were restricted to clothiers or gave preference to clothworkers, and workers in the cloth industry were also exempted from the corporation's annual tax on unfree artificers established in 1563.[86] In the 1590s the corporation decided that the New Draperies were the key to future prosperity, and a scheme was introduced to teach poor children to spin worsted yarn, paying the profits of their labour to their parents.[87] But no amount of protection or ingenuity could save the textile industry in Winchester, which was fading for reasons outside the city's control.

A second initiative, also unsuccessful, was the attempt to open the river Itchen to navigation between Winchester and the sea. Local tradition had it that the river had been used for transport in the Middle Ages and navigation had been regarded ever since as a solution to the city's problems. A previous attempt in the 1530s had failed, but in 1617 the corporation commissioned a survey of the river to determine the feasibility of trying again.[88] Money was raised by means of a lottery, and the corporation appealed to the dean and chapter and the bishop for contributions and support. Throughout the 1620s Winchester's M.P.s introduced bills for the navigation into Parliament, but they always failed – presumably because Southampton's implacable opposition outweighed any support raised in the county – and the idea was dropped until the 1660s.[89]

In the long term the most successful of the policies pursued by the corporation in the early seventeenth century was the encouragement of the county gentry's use of Winchester as a local social centre. Members of the elite who cultivated connections with the gentry were probably motivated more by snobbery than calculated concern for the urban economy, but gentle custom and patronage were to play an important part in Winchester's recovery later in the century. An early sign of upper-class interest was the establishment at Winchester of horse-racing, a sport patronized by the gentry and nobility. In 1591 and 1605, the earliest references to racing at Winchester, the corporation provided refreshments for gentlemen attending the race.[90] The Marquis of Winchester and the Earl of Southampton took an active interest in promoting the races, the Hampshire gentry contributed towards the costs, and civic leaders gave generously to encourage a sport which admirably suited their purpose by attracting gentlemen to the city for pleasure. By the 1630s members of the nobility regularly competed at the Winchester race meeting, which had become an established event in the social calendar.[91] The admission of gentlemen as freemen was another sign of the corporation's desire to forge links with the county gentry and of the gentry's awakening interest in the city. Non-resident gentlemen freemen had been rare in the sixteenth century, but 5 of the 27 freemen admitted between 1610 and 1619 were gentlemen, 10 of 28 in the 1620s, and 16 of 39 in the 1630s. Local gentlemen also received generous loans of city funds in the early seventeenth century, often as much as £100 or £200, paying interest rates of 8 or 10 per cent in accordance with the prevailing rate.[92] The courting of the gentry was not universally popular – discontented junior freemen resented gentlemen who dabbled in urban affairs, and Trussell described their behaviour at corporation meetings:

> If that a gentleman casually chance
> To the society, they straight advance
> And bristle like New Forest hogs: to show
> The small respect they unto gentry owe.[93]

Hostility among the lower ranks of the corporation had little effect on policy, however, and the leaders of the corporation continued to foster their mutually beneficial relationship with the gentry.

Thus the first signs of Winchester's new role catering to an upper-class clientele were gradually appearing by the early seventeenth century. The 60 years before the Civil War had also seen expansion of the city's general marketing and distributive functions, and the foundations of its later economic growth had been firmly laid. But in 1640 the future still looked bleak for Winchester, which had been buffeted by forces which brought poverty to many larger towns. The search for new ways to support its population was moreover to be swept aside by the impact of the Civil War, which added physical destruction and economic upheaval to the problems of the early seventeenth century.

5   The Civil War and Interregnum

Whatever the private sympathies of Winchester's inhabitants may have been, the city was known as a Royalist stronghold from the earliest stages of the war. At first sight this choice of loyalties might seem surprising, for like other towns Winchester had suffered from Charles I's policies: the billeting of troops had been expensive and unpopular, heavy taxation had aroused opposition, and the king's wars had added to the city's burden of poor relief. Yet the traditional leaders of Winchester, on whom the charge of loans, taxes, and philanthropy fell most heavily, were predominantly Royalist, and it was their sympathies which gave the city its reputation to the outside world. Having successfully defended their privileges in the 1620s, members of the oligarchy were instinctively sympathetic to the claims of traditional authority. Winchester had always seen itself, too, as a royal city; Queen Mary had been married in

Winchester cathedral, every Tudor monarch had visited the city, and James I and Charles I had both passed through frequently on their way to hunt in the New Forest.

Perhaps most important in determining Winchester's allegiance were the city's close ties with the Established Church. The diocesan bureaucracy and the cathedral establishment provided jobs, custom, charity, and an educated elite in Winchester, and relations between the citizens and the dean and chapter were close, if not always harmonious. The cathedral clergy also ministered to most of the city churches, so the high Anglicanism of the close directly influenced religious sentiment among the citizenry. The weakness of puritanism in the early seventeenth century has already been noted, while Catholicism remained strong and socially respectable, and religious sympathies inclined Winchester strongly towards allegiance to Charles I.

As events turned out, however, the citizens' opinions had little effect on the city's fate. Situated between the Parliamentarian South-East and the Royalist West, close to Portsmouth and Southampton, and within striking distance of the Great West Road to London, Winchester was too strategically placed for either side to leave it in enemy hands. Between 1642 and 1646 the city was captured and re-captured, sacked and pillaged by armies from both sides, and the mayors could do little but bend with the prevailing wind and try to minimize the damage. Like many local leaders, they were far more concerned with the preservation of their city than with arguments over higher principles.[94]

Winchester became involved in the war a few months after fighting broke out. In December 1642 a small band of Royalists under Lord Grandison was chased out of Marlborough by Sir William Waller and fled to Winchester, a town reputed (according to a Parliamentarian pamphlet) to be 'full of malignant spirits'.[95] The Royalists retreated into the castle, leaving the citizens to defend the crumbling city walls against Waller as best they could. Resistance quickly proved both futile and foolish. The pursuing Parliamentarian troops forced their way into the city and surrounded the castle, which surrendered at dawn the next day, whereupon Waller's unruly men broke loose and stripped their defeated enemies of everything of value.[96] The townsmen too had incurred the troops' anger, but Waller managed to restrain his men while he demanded a £1,000 composition from the mayor. The money was hastily collected, but Waller turned his soldiers loose nonetheless. Seeking out citizens suspected of Royalist sympathies, the soldiers ransacked mercers' and drapers' shops and plundered houses until their anger was appeased. Another group plundered the houses in the close, then moved on to the cathedral where they smashed monuments and windows, broke up the organ, tore service books and vestments, and overturned the caskets containing the bones of Saxon kings.[97]

During 1643 Winchester was constantly harassed by roving bands of soldiers, who would descend on the city and demand food and lodging, plunder the houses of Catholics, take money, horses, and arms, and depart without paying. Often the soldiers rode in on a market day to round up the country people's horses and demand money for their return. Word of these raids soon spread, and the number of sellers bringing produce to the markets fell, causing prices of basic foodstuffs in Winchester to rise beyond the means of many citizens. Meetings of quarter sessions and assizes had ceased in the summer of 1642, and without the normal influx of customers the city's tradesmen and innkeepers struggled to survive – in any case, looting had left them with little to sell. The mayor and aldermen were taken prisoner several times for non-payment of levies and taxes, and it was common practice in both armies to capture local gentlemen and raise money by holding them to ransom.[98] Waller stationed a troop of horse in Winchester in March 1643 and levied £350 from the citizens and £150 from Sir Henry Clerke of Hyde Abbey.[99] In October 1643 the Royalist Sir William Ogle marched into the city and established his winter quarters in the castle. Ogle had lived in Winchester before the war and had been its M.P. from 1640 to 1643, but his troops were no less destructive than Waller's. Ogle was soon joined for the winter by Sir Ralph Hopton; more than 5,000 men were now quartered in and around Winchester, and the tensions between citizens and soldiers were exacerbated by shortages of food and clothing.[100]

John Trussell's poem 'Caerguent's Lament', written in 1644, paints a vivid and harrowing picture of the constant pillage and its effects on Winchester. Trussell was by now an old man in poor health, dismayed by the suffering of his beloved city, and his poem describes the social upheaval brought by the war as well as its material damage:

But when free billet went throughout the town
And no man could be master of his own,
When common soldiers must have bedding found,
When owner, wife, and children on the ground
Chalk out their lodging; when the honest woman
Must be observant to her that is as common
As any barber's chair; when ragged grooms
In every house must have the private rooms
To make them stables for their horse . . .[101]

Now what they said they would do, they have done,
In making poor and rich men's estate all one;
The rich no rent, the poor their houses get,
The rich no money have, the poor no meat,
The poor would raiment have, so would the other,
For scarcely either thereof have wherewith to cover
Their bare; linen and woollen so divided are
That poor and rich thereof have equal share,
Feathers the poor, bed ticks the rich do lack
(With them the troopers clothe their chivalls [horse's] back).
Orchards and gardens unenclosed stand,
Whereof both poor and rich have like command.
There is no wine, the poor and rich I think
Content must be with our own country drink.
The poor and rich may now for company
Travel on foot, for horse there is not any.
The plate is gone, glasses are broke in pieces,
And rich and poor are forced to drink in dishes.
Woe worth the while, what shall become of me
When poor and rich are thus in one degree?[102]

Winchester Castle remained in Royalist hands throughout 1644, but the rest of the city still lay at the mercy of the Parliamentarian forces. On 29 March, Waller won a decisive victory against Hopton at Cheriton, five miles outside Winchester. As the Royalist cavalry fled from the battle Waller followed them to the city; this time the mayor prudently opened the gates, but Waller could not take the castle and withdrew after looting a few houses. A week later, however, he returned and blew open the Southgate while his infantry stormed over the city walls, to plunder the town yet again.[103] By the summer of 1644, Winchester Castle and Basing House were the only two Royalist strongholds left in the South-East, and many Royalists made their way to the city as one area after another fell to Parliament.

Though the garrisons at Winchester and Basing were isolated, their attacks on traffic along the Great West Road were bringing trade between London and the West Country to a standstill, and the western clothiers as well as the Parliamentary army urgently needed a safe route across the southern counties.[104] A siege of Winchester was inevitable, and during 1644 and 1645 Ogle continued his preparations by demolishing houses and felling trees to improve the castle's defences.[105] On 28 September 1645, Cromwell arrived outside the walls and took the suburbs of Winchester without resistance. Ogle decided that the crumbling city walls were indefensible, and he retired into the castle, allowing Cromwell to enter the city without incident. Then for a whole week the Parliamentary guns battered at the castle defences, firing from the high ground north and west of the castle and from houses in the town. Caught in the cross-fire, many buildings around the castle were burned – even the Royalist Peter Heylyn later wrote that Ogle had done more damage in Winchester, in his attempts to silence Cromwell's guns, than all Waller's plundering.[106] On the fifth day of the bombardment Cromwell began to fire mortar grenades, a new and terrifying missile which in one day demolished the roof of the mansion house inside the castle, killed the horses working the horse-mill in the courtyard, and frightened the Royalists into sleeping in the open court instead of the buildings. At last a breach was made in the north wall, and to forestall total defeat Ogle was forced to surrender. One reason for the castle's unexpected fall, according to a member of the Royalist garrison, was that Ogle had rounded up men from the town to supplement his troops. Whenever there was a lull in the firing, the townsmen's wives and children came to the walls and called to their husbands, entreating them to give up the castle and come home, and towards the end of the siege most of the townsmen crept away.[107]

The fall of the castle replaced the Royalist garrison with a Parliamentary one, which remained in Winchester until the following June. In October 1646 the cathedral was raided again: this time the soldiers attacked the chapter house and found the muniments, which they burnt, threw into the river, and scattered over the town.[108] The government remained suspicious of Winchester as a potential centre of Royalist revolt, and troops were quartered there again in 1648 and 1651. The city's military potential was finally destroyed when Parliament ordered the slighting of the castle. The massive medieval foundations proved to be too solid for complete destruction, but enough was pulled down in 1651 to ensure that the castle would never again be of military value.[109]

John Trussell's picture of the disruption caused by the war, both in private lives and in city government, was not exaggerated. From 1642 to 1646 almost every aspect of the city's administration had been suspended. Only the most essential corporation meetings were held, and renewals of leases of city property stopped abruptly after September 1642 and did not resume until May 1646. More serious, the corporation's finances were in disarray. Payments into and out of the coffer had virtually ceased during the war, no chamberlains' accounts had been passed, the bailiffs had not paid the fee-farm, and fines and dues remained uncollected. Rents too had fallen behind during the war, depriving the corporation of a substantial part of its income. Ordinances in 1646 and 1647 threatened legal action against tenants refusing to pay arrears of rent, and the corporation pursued some of its debtors as far as the courts.[110] Not only had the war caused an interruption of income, but the need for expenditure had increased. The city's bridges and streets were in urgent need of repair, and at least £200 was spent on the Westgate, damaged during the siege of the castle. The greatest debt outstanding was the £1,000 levied by Sir William Waller in 1642. The mayor had borrowed from everyone in Winchester who had money to lend, and repayments of small sums were still being made in 1657.

Many of Winchester's wealthier inhabitants had also suffered financially from the war. Some were Royalists who had fought for the king or contributed to his cause, for which they paid heavy fines after the war. Thomas Chaundeler of Hyde Barton, for example, was £2,000 in debt by 1647, and Sir James Phillips, Ogle's stepson, was fined over £600 and had large debts in 1649.[111] Many others suffered losses from the disruption of trade, plundering from houses and shops, and non-payment of rents and debts. The chief desire of anyone with conspicuous wealth was to escape the attention of both sides in the conflict. William Longland, a Winchester grocer, refused in 1643 to buy the lease of a farm on the grounds that 'if it were known that he . . . had any interest either in the said farm or stock it would be more prejudicial to him than the same was worth, he being before taken notice of by the garrison to be a very wealthy and rich man'.[112] Longland was a Royalist, as was the Winchester garrison in 1643, but he obviously felt that his sympathies would not have protected him.

The desire to avoid unwelcome attention led to more movement than usual among the wealthy, both into and out of Winchester. John Trussell noted the flight of most of the 'best able' from their homes and trades at the height of the war,[113] and several gentlemen and leading members of the corporation migrated out of the city to country residences, returning only after 1660. There was also an influx of Royalist gentlemen and their wives into Winchester during the 1640s. Sir William Ogle in 1645 found himself responsible for 'a very great number of noble ladies and gentlewomen of divers countries' who had taken refuge in Winchester, and the castle garrison included 300 Hampshire and Sussex gentlemen.[114] Peter Heylyn was among the refugees, and found in Winchester 'to his heart's delight the sweet enjoyment and conversation of loyal persons'. Winchester's post-Restoration success in attracting the local gentry for business and pleasure may well have owed something to memories of those 'halcyon days' in the 1640s when Royalists gathered in the city to find a congenial refuge among their friends.[115]

The war was also responsible for increased mobility lower down the social scale, and some of the soldiers and other wanderers uprooted by the fighting settled permanently in Winchester. In December 1646 the grand jury presented more than 30 newcomers – including several who later became prominent citizens – and a number of the same men appeared on another list headed 'soldiers married'.[116] These were not vagrants, but respectable craftsmen and tradesmen. In the face of hostility from Winchester's established traders, the newcomers proved themselves flexible in their choice of occupation. The example of William Snow was typical: a soldier who married a local girl, Snow set up business first as a cutler, though he had not served an apprenticeship in that trade. The city's seven established cutlers petitioned against him, so Snow changed his trade and became a linen draper, prospering enough to be elected bailiff in 1653 and 1654.[117] Contemporary commentators viewed the social and economic mobility made possible by the war with mixed feelings – Thomas Fuller, for one, admired the 'improvement' in poor uneducated soldiers acquired by 'conversing with their betters', but regretted their reluctance to return to their original lowly occupations.[118]

Immigration continued at a high level in the 1650s, as measured by the number of unfree artificers taxed by the corporation each year. From a low point of 78 in 1648 and 1651, the totals soared to 95 in 1653, 113 in 1655, and 121 in 1658.[119] Part of the rise can be attributed to the natural reluctance of traders to become freemen in politically troubled times, and to the decreasing number of clothworkers (who were exempt from the annual tax). Nonetheless it is clear that immigration to Winchester was exceptionally high during the 1650s, as enterprising traders seized the opportunity to replace those driven out or ruined by the war. The pre-war ordinance against foreign traders remained on the books and was even re-issued in 1656, but the corporation began to license individual traders in occupations not widely practised in Winchester, beginning with a pinmaker and a watchmaker in 1654 and 1655.[120]

The great ecclesiastical institutions which had provided employment and brought business to Winchester were among the casualties of the Civil War. The cathedral clergy scattered to their country parishes, and Bishop Curle retired. Wolvesey Palace fell into decay, and the most dilapidated buildings in the cathedral close, many of them damaged by looting soldiers, were occupied by poor families.[121] The houses in better repair were assigned to representatives of the new political order. The Committee for Sequestrations, for example, held its meetings in the close in 1649, and the former steward's house became a storehouse for sequestered goods. The two official preachers appointed by Parliament also settled in the cathedral precincts, and Major-General Goffe lodged there in 1656.[122]

The economic impact of the removal of the bishop and dean and chapter was probably severe. The departure of the large wealthy households from the close left their domestic servants without employment and removed valuable custom from Winchester shopkeepers. Most of the officials were also turned out of their jobs: the former keeper of Wolvesey wrote bitterly in 1654, 'I freely forgive all the world all the wrongs I have suffered as the taking away my means and my livelihood and my moneys due [to] me which I hope the guilty consciences of some will return to my executor'.[123] Responsibility for the upkeep of the highways outside Winchester had been assumed by the dean and chapter before the war, and in their absence the major roads deteriorated while neighbouring parishes bickered over who should pay for repairs.[124] Perhaps most detrimental to the city was the loss of an important source of charity, for there is no evidence that the new trustees of the chapter estates continued their predecessors' contributions to poor relief.

Winchester College, by contrast, survived the war and Interregnum virtually unscathed, despite its wealth and its reputation as a centre of recusancy. Its salvation lay in the judicious use of money and influence, administered by Warden Harris. Harris wrote afterwards in his own defence, 'I never parted with any money of the College to the king's use before such time as this city was made a garrison, and if it appear any such thing has been done since, it was only *ad redinendam vexationem*, to keep the College from being made a garrison or being oppressed by the violence of Sir W. Ogle'.[125] The influence was chiefly that of two former pupils of the College, Nicholas Love, the trustee for the bishop's lands, and Nathaniel Fiennes, son of Lord Saye and Sele. In spite of two visitations, the number of ejections and intrusions was small, the buildings were left virtually untouched, and none of the College lands were sequestered.

Military incursions on Winchester's autonomy were succeeded in the late 1640s by political intervention from London. In April 1648 Parliament ordered the disfranchisement of one Winchester alderman and the restoration of another,[126] but the ruling elite was still stubbornly Royalist. When Charles I passed through Winchester as a prisoner in December, on his last journey from the Isle of Wight to London, the mayor and aldermen defiantly went out to meet the king and offered him the mace of the city.[127] Pressure on recalcitrant magistrates intensified in 1649, and in September an Act of Parliament, procured by John Lisle and Nicholas Love, the two M.P.s for Winchester, and Sir Henry Mildmay, effectively replaced the existing corporation by nominating a new mayor, 3 new aldermen, 7 new benchers, and 10 new members of the Twenty-Four.[128]

These men, and the freemen admitted by them, dominated city government in Winchester for the next ten years. Their backgrounds were varied: at least half of them had been in the city by 1642, but some had arrived in Winchester during the war, including the ex-soldier William Snow. Many of the new men were young, in their 20s and 30s. A significant proportion of the group were puritans. The leaders of the new corporation were mostly lawyers and officials, men already active in county government. Membership of the new corporation did not coincide with any pre-existing opposition group in Winchester, but in general it represented the younger and more radical elements in the city which had not committed themselves to the cause of Charles I.

Once in power, the new corporation of Winchester set about governing with great energy but very little originality. Dozens of ordinances were passed, city records were sorted and labelled, and the penalty for absence from assemblies was increased to 10s. Yet the new governors remained preoccupied with the minutiae of street-cleaning and record-keeping, and their close attention to civic ritual suggests that their chief desire was to be treated with as much respect as the old corporation had been.[129] Winchester's economy was recovering naturally in the 1650s from the effects of the war, but the city's new leaders could claim little credit for that. From 1652 onwards the new corporation was in any case preoccupied with internal disputes, which periodically erupted into tavern brawls, riots, and the exchange of insults at corporation meetings.[130]

Perhaps the most difficult problem facing the new corporation, like its predecessor, was poor relief. The war had added to the numbers of widows and children in need of assistance, and impressment of men for Cromwell's campaigns in the 1650s left more families without a breadwinner.[131] An ordinance issued in 1656 set out the corporation's relief policy, which was almost identical to pre-war practices: able-bodied paupers were divided into vagrants and beggars to be driven out, and the deserving poor for whom work would be provided. Alms were restricted to paupers who were sick, the aged, infants, orphans, idiots, the blind or lame, and 'such as are overcharged with children', and the list of recipients was to be reviewed quarterly. A puritan flavour was added by making relief conditional on church attendance, and by emphasizing education in religious doctrine and literacy for poor children.[132] Poverty appears to have been contained more efficiently during the Interregnum than before the war, but the late 1650s taxed the corporation's resources to the limit. In 1656–7 St John's Hospital paid out £104, more even than during the worst years of the 1630s (fig. 15), and the corporation claimed in 1660 that 'above 200 families' at

Winchester were in need of relief.[133]

The money available for poor relief was increased in 1656 by a scheme which neatly combined charity with economic regulation. Complaints had been made that fuel prices in Winchester were being driven up by excessive numbers of alehouse-keepers brewing their own ale and beer. The corporation therefore devised a scheme whereby two 'common brewers' were given a life monopoly of brewing in the city (at a cost of £20 a year each, to be used for poor relief), and alehouse-keepers' licences were made conditional on a £20 obligation not to sell drink brewed by anyone but the two common brewers. The two brewers were prohibited from malting their own grain, and prices for their products were set by city quarter sessions. The recipients of this profitable monopoly were both leading members of the political elite. After only six years in operation, however, the scheme fell victim to politics. The 'oppressed victuallers' of Winchester petitioned the House of Lords against the brewing monopoly at the Restoration, and in 1662 the two brewers were compensated for their investment and the scheme wound up.[134]

The return of Charles II in 1660 was greeted in Winchester with jubilation.[135] Losing no time, the surviving members of the 'old corporation' (those who had been ousted in 1649) petitioned the House of Lords against the intruders, and for the next two years the city's political factions struggled for control.[136] The new corporation's days were numbered, and in August 1662 the arrival of the commissioners for regulating corporations put an end to the political turmoil. Eighteen members of the corporation were expelled for 'disloyalty to the king's majesty that now is, and being nonconformists to the church government', in addition to three men expelled earlier in 1660. In their place, the commissioners recommended the next mayor, 2 new benchers, 5 new members of the Twenty-Four, and 4 new freemen.[137] Of the 21 men intruded by Parliament in 1649, only one remained in the corporation after 1662. Not all the expulsions were permanent, however, for the leaders of the new corporation proved themselves adept at political survival. Four of the eight men who had been mayors during the Interregnum returned to favour in the 1660s and were elected to the mayoralty again. Respect for authority died hard in Winchester, and once a man had joined the political elite his personal status in the city was assured – even the rivalries engendered by the politics of 1649–62 could not dislodge an ex-mayor permanently from the ranks of the city's leaders.

The commissioners' purge of the corporation in 1662, and their 'recommendation' of new officers, set the final seal on Winchester's submission to outside authority. Sir William Ogle as governor of the castle had given orders to the mayor in 1645, and the Interregnum had seen repeated interference, notably the Act remodelling the corporation in 1649. John Lisle, Nicholas Love, and the county committees had ensconced themselves in the cathedral close and intervened in corporation appointments. In every case the agents of intervention in Winchester's affairs were members of the Hampshire gentry, and their participation was to continue and increase after 1662. Far from fighting to preserve its independence from the county, as it had done repeatedly under the Tudors, Winchester submitted willingly after 1660 to the county gentry's involvement in its government.[138]

In 1662 the destruction wrought by the Civil War in Winchester was still plain to see. The castle lay in ruins, some of the houses in the close were past repair, the city walls had been thrown down in several places, and the bishop's palace was unfit for use.[139] Physical damage had been particularly heavy in the south-west quarter, close to the castle; the parish church of St Clement's had been 'miserably ransacked and torn in pieces [by soldiers], rendered useless as a church', and 'most part of the parish' had been burnt during the siege.[140] Civic finances, already under strain, had been weakened further, and individuals and families had suffered all the personal miseries and economic hardships attendant upon war. Coming on the heels of several decades of economic instability, the events of the 1640s seemed only to plunge Winchester further into poverty.

And yet, paradoxically, the Civil War brought the city some benefits which were in the long term to lead to renewed growth. While the city's support for Charles I appeared disastrous in the 1640s and 1650s, a Royalist reputation was a useful asset after the Restoration. Charles II spoke with sympathy of Winchester's sufferings,[141] and his interest in the city was to be of great value in the 1680s. Royalist gentlemen had flocked to Winchester during the war; most of them left the city after 1645, but they returned in large numbers after 1660. Not all the city's social attractions were lost during the Interregnum, for the race-meeting was certainly held in 1647, 1649, 1654, and 1657, and in May 1654 Winchester's inns were crowded with race-goers.[142] Even the physical destruction caused by the war eventually proved useful in clearing large spaces for the building of elegant town houses and a royal palace. However unpropitious they had seemed at the time, Winchester's misfortunes in the Civil War were actually to assist the city's development in the later seventeenth century.

6 Expanding markets, 1660–1700

Between 1660 and 1700 Winchester's fortunes gradually revived. Progress was slow at first; economic growth was temporarily halted by the plague of 1666, and in 1670 the corporation still took the view that the city 'was never in so low and mean condition as now it is'.[143] Many of the city's inhabitants lived in poverty, and Winchester's days as a centre of industry were over. But the provision of goods and services to all classes of Hampshire society was a function with considerable potential for growth, and the city's tradesmen rose to the challenge of expanding demand. In addition, Winchester's development as a meeting-place and shopping town for the gentry and their families added an important new element to the city's clientele. Both traditional and new markets for the city's wares were growing in the late seventeenth century, and both were essential to Winchester's prosperity.

Whereas the troubled half-century before 1640 had seen population grow at Winchester, the post-Restoration economic revival was accompanied by demographic stagnation. Totals of baptisms in the parishes for which registers survive fluctuated with little overall increase, and a surplus of baptisms over burials in one parish was usually balanced by a net loss in another. Estimates of population totals in the 1660s and 1670s also suggest that Winchester's growth over the seventeenth century as a whole had been modest. While the population of mainland Hampshire had increased by 26.2 per cent between 1603 and 1676, and the population of Hampshire towns by as much as 40.4 per cent, Winchester's growth had lagged behind at only 17.8 per cent, or one-quarter per cent a year (see table 14, p. 175). The Hearth Tax list of 1665 shows 410 occupied houses inside the walls, taxed and exempt, and 14 in the cathedral close. Another 290 occupied houses were listed in the suburbs.[144] If we add 10 per cent to the totals of occupied houses for under-registration, adopt a low multiplier of 4.25 people per household,[145] and include estimated figures for the residents of almshouses, Wolvesey Palace, and the College, the population within Winchester's walls comes to nearly 2,100 and the suburban total to almost 1,600. The Compton Census of 1676 yields virtually the same figures for both the city and the Soke,[146] which suggests that the losses caused by the plague epidemic of 1666 had only just been recovered a decade later, probably with the help of increased immigration. Population estimates by the parish clergy in 1725 do, however, point to quickening demographic growth in the early eighteenth century, particularly in the parishes outside the walls.[147]

Without significant natural increase between 1660 and 1700, immigration was the principal source of growth in the city's population. Records relating to movement into the city are sparse, but scattered references show that travellers continued to arrive at Winchester's gates, from Hampshire villages and from further afield. The ordinance against inmates was renewed in 1677, and many householders who took in newcomers were presented at quarter sessions, but the corporation still complained that 'this city is made the common receptacle of . . . wanderers and beggars'.[148] Settlement papers show that those longer-distance migrants who arrived in Winchester came predominantly from the South-West of England, as had also been the case in the sixteenth century.[149]

Demographic gains stemming from immigration in the later seventeenth century were, however, minimized by losses from epidemics, most notably the final outbreak of plague which paralysed Winchester in 1666. Amongst the wealthy the general reaction to the epidemic was flight; the College sent its pupils home or into the country for six months, the cathedral clergy eventually left the city, and civic administration ground to a halt.[150] 'All the town is emptied . . . into the country about', wrote a Hampshire countrywoman in June 1666, and again two months later, 'Winton is as bad as ever considering the small number remaining in it'. The long absence of city leaders encouraged disorder, and in July 'the sick broke out, not for want . . . but to visit the houses of the better sort'.[151] Quarter sessions and assizes were moved to other towns, and the economic impact of the city's long isolation is apparent from the excise farmers' claim that receipts from Winchester had fallen to less than a quarter of their normal total between September 1666 and March 1667.[152] A petition in 1670 asserted that 'many hundreds of the inhabitants' had died of the plague,[153] and the unusually high totals of wills proved and administrations granted in 1666 and 1667, as well as burials recorded in several incomplete parish registers, indicate considerable mortality. In 1668 the farmers of the Hearth Tax cited Winchester as an example of a town in which collections had fallen since the plague due to 'the houses continuing void and the people impoverished'.[154] After 1666 smallpox was the most serious epidemic disease. Winchester was stricken by smallpox in 1684 and burials remained above normal levels until 1686, and there was another severe outbreak in the Soke in 1693–4, aggravated by exceptionally high local grain prices.[155]

Even though most of the external pressures which had reduced so many families to pauperism in the early seventeenth century had disappeared by 1660, the need for poor relief remained. In 1665 a quarter of the households inside the city, and half of those in the eastern suburb, were declared exempt from the Hearth Tax because of their poverty.[156] The corporation distributed about £70 a year through St John's Hospital in the later seventeenth century, and there is some indication that city parishes were now supporting paupers as well.[157] Local institutions, particularly the College, the cathedral chapter, and St Cross, continued to play an important auxiliary role in the relief of the poor. Individuals too gave small sums to the indigent: one former mayor, for instance, ordered his executors to pay 52s each year at the cathedral font to 13 poor people 'as I have given it for the space of four years last past as from a person unknown'.[158] Small sums given to poor citizens 'in their present necessity' frequently appear in the corporation accounts, and such references to casual and occasional alms-giving suggest that a constant flow of small donations from the better-off to the poor took place in towns.

Without new industrial development it was unlikely that Winchester would ever be able to support all its poor inhabitants, for retailing and the service trades which formed the basis for the city's new growth were not labour-intensive, and underemployment persisted throughout the eighteenth century.[159] A variety of minor manufactures made some contribution to Winchester's economy. Woollen and worsted textiles were still made in the neighbourhood, and a number of industries based on wool, such as felt-making and coverlet-weaving, were practised on a small scale in the city. Leather-working was an important secondary industry, and the city's leatherworkers were strong enough to organize petitions to Parliament in 1698–9 against the new duty on leather. New fashions also spawned new trades, and the second half of the seventeenth century found a number of silk-weavers at Winchester, and a small tobacco-pipe manufacture using local clay deposits.[160] All these were aimed mostly at local consumption, however, and Defoe described Winchester as 'a city without trade, that is to say, without any particular manufactures'.[161]

The city's markets, fairs, and shops, on the other hand, were showing unmistakeable signs of vitality. By 1691 congestion in the streets on market days had reached such a pitch that horse-teams were banned from the central stretch of the High Street. The October fair too had outgrown its site and in 1669 separate streets were assigned for the sale of leather, horses, and sheep.[162] Magdalen Fair attracted more traffic every year: £20,000 worth of cheese was sold there in 1696, and the Kingsgate had to be widened in 1713 to protect pedestrians from the procession of heavily laden wagons.[163]

By the late seventeenth century Winchester was also a major shopping centre for its region. At least 90 shops inside the walls were assessed for Land Tax in 1704, and there were others in the suburbs.[164] Custom for shopkeepers came from the city's own residents as well as visitors: inventories show that even middling tradesmen could now afford such luxury items as silver tankards, musical instruments, and pictures to decorate their houses, and wealthy householders owned china and porcelain dishes, large libraries, and coaches. The customers drawn by shops – which had the double attraction of being open throughout the week and of providing goods on credit – in turn encouraged pedlars and dealers who preferred to do business outside the regulated setting of shops and markets. In 1691 two ordinances prohibited selling 'in inns, alehouses, private houses, streets, lanes or any other places', or the sale of grain by sample in alehouses or elsewhere unless the final transaction was to take place at the market; but in reality the corporation could do little to prevent such informal trading.[165]

The development of facilities for visitors to Winchester in the late seventeenth century reflected their growing importance to the city's economy. In 1686 a military survey of stabling and beds for travellers found that Winchester was well provided with accommodation, far surpassing that of any other Hampshire town (see p. 173).[166] Indeed, only six other provincial towns in England had stabling for more than 1,000 horses in 1686: like Winchester, the towns of Cambridge, Exeter, St Albans, Leicester, Bristol, and Warwick were all local centres which regularly attracted large crowds. On county election days, for instance, as many as 4,500 Hampshire voters gathered at Winchester in the early eighteenth century.[167] Whether visitors stayed or

	beds	stabling
Winchester	336	1,048
Andover	212	582
Southampton	179	287
Basingstoke	104	357
Portsmouth	164	87

returned home at the end of the day, the most immediate beneficiaries of their presence were inns and alehouses, which provided shelter and refreshment for travellers and their transport. In 1704 Land Tax was paid on eight major inns, and on 14 other premises with names which suggest the sale of drink and hospitality.[168] Winchester's major innkeepers were now among the city's most prominent citizens. Whereas in the sixteenth century innkeepers had been excluded from the mayoralty 'for the dishonour that might thereof ensue',[169] between 1650 and 1700 seven mayors and bailiffs kept inns, and for the first time some innkeepers were termed gentlemen. In addition to inns, a much larger number of taverns and alehouses offered hospitality to residents and visitors. Larger alehouses provided some of the same facilities as inns, albeit on a smaller scale – beds for guests and stabling for their horses, a meeting-place for chapmen and corn-factors and their customers, as well as drink and conviviality. Seventy-six victuallers were licensed to sell drink in Winchester and its environs in 1684, an increase over the 41 inside the walls in 1631; the corporation continued its complaints about the proliferation of alehouses, but few were actually suppressed in the late seventeenth century.[170]

Most of the customers in taverns and alehouses were local residents and short-term visitors, but a sizeable – if unwelcome – contribution to business also came from soldiers quartered in and around the city. Winchester's convenient proximity to the south coast, and Portsmouth's rapid development under Charles II and William III, drew ever-increasing numbers of troops to the region. The hospital of St Mary Magdalen at Winchester was taken over in 1665 for Dutch prisoners of war, who did so much damage that the almspeople abandoned the building.[171] The French campaigns of the 1690s multiplied the troop movements, as thousands of soldiers marched to and from Portsmouth. The corporation viewed the men as potential trouble-makers, but it supplied them with bedding, fuel, and beer; Winchester victuallers, on whom the troops were billeted, disliked them even more. Army officers, on the other hand, were entertained separately by the mayor, and in the eighteenth century military officers were accepted into the city's polite society.[172] The presence of troops, 'though not agreeable to the whole of [Winchester's] inhabitants' – as an eighteenth-century resident explained – 'is certainly beneficial to the trading part of them',[173] and soldiers undoubtedly contributed to the urban economy.

Winchester's growth as a retail centre in the later seventeenth century owed much of its strength to economic development in its hinterland, both in the towns and in the countryside. Four of central Hampshire's largest market towns – Romsey, Andover, Basingstoke, and Alton – had salvaged specialized textile manufactures from the ruins of the Hampshire cloth industry, and all four towns were prospering. Romsey and Andover produced shalloons, a light worsted used for the lining of men's clothes; Romsey was 'much inhabited by clothiers' in 1673, and Defoe described Andover enthusiastically as 'a handsome town, well built, populous . . . a thriving town'.[174] Basingstoke too had 'fallen into a manufacture' of shalloons and druggets, and at Alton in 1738 500 people were employed making barragons, a corded summer-weight worsted.[175] Industry and fuller employment put money into the pockets of Hampshire consumers, and some of that new wealth was spent in the county town.

Competition between towns within the county was still keen, but the number of markets in Hampshire had decreased over the seventeenth century, and Winchester's status as the county's administrative and ecclesiastical centre ensured the city's continued primacy over other towns. The urban hierarchy in the 1650s and 1660s is illuminated by the distribution of trade tokens issued by retailers.[176] Between 1649 and 1672 traders from 36 towns and villages in mainland Hampshire issued tokens: 27 places had fewer than 5 issuers each, but Ringwood had 6, Gosport, Lymington, and Romsey 7 each, Basingstoke 10, Southampton 14, Andover 15, Winchester with the Soke 16, and Portsmouth 36. Among the inland towns, only Andover, enriched by its position on the Great West Road and its burgeoning cloth industry, could rival Winchester's diversity, though in 1686 Andover had only two-thirds as many beds and half the stabling provided by Winchester. As the county town, Winchester attracted far more visitors, and the new industries in Hampshire market towns complemented the functions performed by the city rather than competed with them.

The widely varying demographic fortunes of Hampshire towns between 1603 and 1676 are shown in table 14.[177] Portsmouth's spectacular growth, following its development as a military port and dockyard, was already exerting a powerful effect on south-east Hampshire. Fareham, Havant, and Bishop's Waltham, the three small market towns closest to the port, had all lost their markets by 1673. Petersfield, the post-town on the road between Portsmouth and London, had nine inns in 1696–7, and towns as far away as Godalming and Guildford derived much of their trade from traffic to Portsmouth.[178] As a distributive centre, however, Portsmouth was poorly situated, and its shopkeepers specialized in catering to the needs of army and naval customers. Southampton too was unlikely to pose any threat to Winchester's trade in the late seventeenth century: the only major town in Hampshire whose population declined between 1603 and 1676, the port appeared to Defoe to be 'in a manner dying with age'.[179] Among the smaller market towns, Fordingbridge, Stockbridge, and Overton as well as the three towns mentioned above had all ceased to hold markets by 1673, in a gradual process of rationalization through competition. Even the small towns whose markets survived were falling behind: traders from Alresford, Alton, and Whitchurch, all of which had markets of their own, brought produce to the Winchester market, finding it more profitable to make the journey than to sell at home.[180]

Important changes in Winchester's hinterland were also taking place in the countryside. Between 1603 and 1676 rural population in Hampshire had grown by almost 20 per cent, an increase greater than in other southern and eastern counties.[181] Agriculture too was showing significant signs of change. Farmers on the Hampshire chalklands, who in the sixteenth and early seventeenth centuries had ignored the experiments which were slowly transforming agriculture in other counties, began in the late Stuart period to try out new ideas.[182] Turnips, sainfoin, clover and ryegrass were introduced, to improve the fertility of the light chalk soils and to provide more fodder for sheep. The new technique of floating water-meadows, ideally suited to the chalk streams of Hampshire and Wiltshire, had been widely adopted by 1700. These innovations made possible the keeping of larger flocks of sheep, which were folded on the light soils; cereal yields improved significantly as a result, and cultivation was gradually extended on land once used only as sheep downs. Despite falling grain prices in the late seventeenth century, Hampshire farmers were able to maintain and even improve their incomes by increasing production, and by exporting grain surplus to domestic needs to southern Europe through Southampton. The adoption of new ideas was a gradual process, beginning in the second half of the seventeenth century and gathering momentum in the early eighteenth, but innovation was sufficiently widespread by 1700 to have brought about a real improvement in the purchasing power of rural landowners and tenant farmers.

Table 14   Population change in Hampshire market towns, 1603–76

	COMMUNICANTS		% change
	1603	1676	
Portsmouth	469	2,560	+445.8
Fareham	485	1,000	+106.2
Petersfield	359	708	+ 97.2
Whitchurch	400	787	+ 96.7
Bishop's Waltham	458	870	+ 90.0
Andover	872	1,557	+ 78.5
Lymington	325	538	+ 65.5
Basingstoke	1,000	1,591	+ 59.1
Alton	700	1,065	+ 52.1
Stockbridge*	416	612	+ 47.1
Romsey	1,317	1,850	+ 40.5
Odiham	502	649	+ 29.3
Winchester and Soke	1,851	2,181	+ 17.8
Ringwood	1,199	1,384	+ 15.4
Fordingbridge	833	943	+ 13.2
New Alresford	342	385	+ 12.6
Kingsclere	913	1,002	+ 9.7
Christchurch	1,236	1,277	+ 3.3
Southampton	2,138	1,921	− 10.1
Havant	451	369	− 18.2
Overton	552	372	− 32.6
all Hampshire towns	16,818	23,621	+ 40.4
rural Hampshire	35,973	42,996	+ 19.5
Hampshire (excl. Isle of Wight)	52,791	66,617	+ 26.2

* with King's Somborne and Little Somborne

The new methods were not labour-intensive, and it is doubtful whether agricultural employment rose significantly, though seasonal work may have increased; but rising gentry incomes created rural employment in other ways, notably through the building of the profusion of late Stuart and early Georgian brick houses which still adorn the Hampshire countryside.[183] Lying at the southern edge of the chalkland, Winchester was ideally placed to benefit from these changes, for increased population and increased wealth at all social levels in the countryside were bound to be reflected before long in the incomes of the city's shopkeepers, craftsmen, and providers of services.

Despite its keen interest in the city's fortunes, the corporation of Winchester had

175

contributed very little to the post-Restoration revival. Changes in the city's hinterland, whether in market towns or in the countryside, were beyond the magistrates' control, and the continued decline of Southampton which removed a potential competitor during the crucial period of Winchester's growth was equally fortuitous. The construction of the Itchen navigation, the project pursued for so long by the corporation, was not completed until 1710 and never fulfilled the expectations of its promoters. It could even be argued that the magistracy impeded growth in the later seventeenth century by maintaining its policy of economic regulation. Enforcement of regulations gradually lapsed in the face of economic reality, but the corporation made determined efforts to retain control. The members of several trades were formed into companies, for the easier supervision of membership and conditions of work: first were the carpenters, joiners, and masons in 1663, followed by the tailors and hosiers in 1672, the butchers in 1678, all the leather-using craftsmen in 1691, and members of the building trades the same year.[184] Fines were still exacted for using a trade without serving an apprenticeship at Winchester. The annual tax on unfree artificers was abandoned in the mid-1670s, but the town continued to require strangers to obtain permission and pay a fee before they set up shop. Applications were not automatically approved – an edgetool-maker was turned down in 1666 even though he found two sureties, and a glover was admitted only on his second application in 1667.[185] Traders without official sanction were presented, fined, and even sued in national courts (at some expense to the corporation), well into the eighteenth century.[186] But the policy of exclusion was probably selective, for the traders pursued most relentlessly were all in occupations widely practised in Winchester and therefore in competition with established businesses, while members of new or rapidly growing trades were accorded more lenient treatment.

The policy followed most enthusiastically by Winchester's elite was encouragement of the Hampshire gentry's interest in their county town. The new visibility of the gentry was also the most conspicuous aspect of the city's renaissance in the late seventeenth century; but the expansion of custom from the lower ranks of society, buying unromantic necessities as well as the new variety of consumer goods, was an equally essential prerequisite to Winchester's revival.

7   Catering to the gentry

The gentry of Hampshire had for centuries met at Winchester for business and politics, but it was the late seventeenth and eighteenth centuries that saw the city's flowering as a centre for county society. Winchester's development was by no means unique, for each county and region needed its social centre, as gentlemen in the provinces began to seek out more sophisticated amusements and a wider range of goods and services.[187] Restoration dramatists writing for London audiences made the tedium and provinciality of country life a comic cliché – young men and women of fashion agreed that 'there is no life but in London', and shuddered at the thought of being 'hurried back to Hampshire';[188] their mockery exaggerated the point, but life in the country could indeed be dull, especially for women and young people. Provincial centres therefore served a useful function, offering the gentry in their own counties a taste of some of London's attractions, without the expense of a journey to the capital. Defoe attributed Winchester's 'good company' and 'sociableness' to the abundance of gentry living in the county,[189] and Hampshire appears to have had plenty of gentlemen who preferred to shop and meet their friends in familiar surroundings rather than venturing to London.

Winchester's attractions were enhanced by the absence of any competing social centre in the area. No provincial capital on the scale of Norwich or Exeter had developed in the South and South-East of England, doubtless because of London's overwhelming competition; only Salisbury, much smaller than most regional capitals, was sufficiently distant from the metropolis to thrive. Portsmouth was by far the largest town in Hampshire by 1660, but it was still a raw dockyard and garrison centre without the social amenities of an old-established city, and its position on an island was thought to be unhealthy. Both Portsmouth and Southampton were to develop their own attractions for polite society in the mid-eighteenth century, based on the new vogue for sea-bathing and drinking salt water, but until about 1740 Winchester had little competition to detract from its custom.[190] Basingstoke had a race-meeting by 1688,[191] and gentlemen seeking the most specialized goods and services might travel to Salisbury or London, but Winchester's shops, inns, and assemblies were quite adequate to meet most of the gentry's needs.

Tradesmen who produced, mended, or sold the luxury goods sought by fashion-conscious gentlemen and their families were conspicuous at Winchester by 1700. Goldsmiths who had long been established in the city, and upholsterers, tobacconists, and gunsmiths whose shops had first appeared there in the first half of the seventeenth century, found their trade increasing in the second half. In 1646 one of the newly settled soldiers was presented for using the trades of a milliner and bookseller,[192] and though he changed his occupation, others followed him in both trades. One bookseller was active in the 1660s, and a grocer was selling sermons by a local clergyman in 1663. Another bookseller, usually termed a stationer, became a freeman in 1679 and was in business at Winchester for at least 20 years thereafter.[193] By 1700 Winchester also had silkweavers, hatters, seamstresses, watchmakers, and coachmen, all catering to wealthy residents and visitors. Service trades patronized by the upper classes also flourished. Work for gardeners increased as the rich added ornamental gardens to their houses. Particularly striking was the proliferation of barbers and tailors: the tailors and hosiers of Winchester, not counting those working in the suburbs, had increased from 14 in 1580 to 23 by 1672.[194]

Winchester's professional 'pseudo-gentry' were thriving too, as the demand for their services expanded. Foremost among professional groups in the post-Restoration period were lawyers. The greatest increase in their numbers had occurred a century earlier, but the 30–40 lawyers practising at Winchester in the late seventeenth century still represented the largest professional cadre in the city, and their influence on the corporation was growing. About 20 lawyers were admitted as freemen between 1660 and 1700, and ten of them became mayors, twice as many as the five lawyers elected to the mayoralty in each of the periods 1560–1600 and 1600–40. Most held offices serving the bishop, the dean and chapter, Winchester College, the county, or the corporation, but private clients from the city and the countryside also represented a lucrative source of employment. Even illiterate farmers might now travel to Winchester to consult a lawyer and initiate a lawsuit, and the gentry made extensive use of legal services in their land-dealings and marriage settlements.[195]

Medical services for the wealthy formed a smaller but growing element in the array of professional services available in the city under the late Stuarts. At least six physicians practised at Winchester between 1660 and 1700, and one of them became mayor in 1695. In 1665, two doctors lived in houses of 15 and 8 hearths respectively, and, like gentlemen, physicians could now aspire to burial in the cathedral, the ultimate social accolade. For the ailments of the lower classes there were apothecaries and surgeons, and their numbers too were increasing.

A few small private schools brought pupils and their families to Winchester, but Winchester College overshadowed all other educational establishments in and around the city. Commoners and scholars attending the College each numbered about 70 in the later seventeenth century; the sons of Winchester's lawyers, cathedral clergy, and College Fellows were well represented among the scholars, but tradesmen's sons were more likely to receive their education as commoners. Gentlemen's sons awaiting entrance to the College were taught privately by senior boys and the schoolmaster. The Warden and Fellows with their families lived comfortably in 'handsome apartments', and the southern suburb of Winchester, clustered around the College and the south gate of the Close, formed a wealthy professional enclave.[196]

Finally, the cathedral clergy constituted another segment of the pseudo-gentry class resident in Winchester. The rebuilding of the canons' houses after the Restoration placed them and their families on an equal footing with the gentry and the urban professional class. A visitor in 1721 described their homes as 'the best houses in Winchester', noting the addition of elegant gardens which were open to visitors, and Winchester's cathedral clergy seemed to Defoe to be 'very rich, and very numerous'.[197] All these professional men – lawyers, physicians, schoolmasters, and clergy – constituted a class that was affluent, highly educated, and more sophisticated than the average citizen, and they played an increasingly important role both in Winchester's economy and its social life.[198] The frequency of inter-marriage between the families of the pseudo-gentry emphasized the distinction between tradesmen and themselves; there were occasional matches between wealthy drapers' daughters and lawyers, but for the most part the pseudo-gentry married among themselves, and maintained their position by passing down offices and professions from father to son.

Among the many forms of business for which gentlemen travelled to Winchester was the arrangement of loans and credit. Under the medieval Statute of Merchants the mayor was empowered to enrol recognizances for debt, and from the 1640s Statute Merchant bonds were entered in the Ledger Books with other officially sealed documents.[199] Between 1640 and 1700 57 bonds were enrolled at Winchester, with a total of 61 debtors and 66 creditors, and an analysis of the bonds throws some light on the city's function as a financial exchange. Ten of the debtors and 23 of the creditors lived at Winchester – people were more likely to travel to the city to borrow or buy than to lend or sell – but eight bonds were drawn up entirely between parties resident outside Hampshire. The only plausible reason for the enrolment at Winchester of a debt between, for example, a Lancashire gentleman and a London merchant, must be that at least one of the parties was in the neighbourhood and the process of enrolment was regarded as a good legal safeguard. The parties to Statute Merchant bonds were virtually all from the ranks of the gentry, professional men, or substantial craftsmen or tradesmen. These were not small or casual debts – most fell between £200 and £600, but 15 of the bonds recorded debts of £1,000 or more. The legal wording gives no clue as to the circumstances of the debt, but some were apparently incurred through wholesale trade, and one bond for £1,000 was part of a marriage settlement. Nor can one tell whether attorneys had acted as intermediaries in arranging loans, as in Lincolnshire.[200] Professional men were particularly active as lenders at Winchester: creditors included two physicians, seven clergymen, and at least five lawyers. Hampshire gentlemen and yeomen were prominent among debtors, and the loans raised at Winchester in the later seventeenth century probably financed some of the agricultural improvement taking place in the county. Gentlemen no longer received loans of corporation funds as they had done before the Civil War, but the wealth of the city's professional class, and of fellow members of the county gentry, was an equally convenient source of capital. The development of county centres like Winchester as meeting-places for the middle and upper classes facilitated trade and business deals as well as social life.

Widows and spinsters with capital to invest have been found among lenders in studies of rural indebtedness,[201] and four upper-class women appeared as creditors in the bonds registered at Winchester. Women played a greater part in the economy as consumers, however, and there is evidence to suggest that they were active customers at the smaller provincial centres. The freedom of a wife to make purchases on her husband's credit in local shops is illustrated by the case of Edmund Clerke of Hyde Abbey just outside Winchester, a gentleman who in 1674 married a young and extravagant second wife. Within 15 months the new Mrs Clerke 'did take up of the drapers and seamstresses and other tradesmen in Winchester divers needless wares and goods . . . fit for persons above [her husband's] degree and quality', to a value of £186. Clerke had to pay the bills, though he prevented further embarrassment by instructing the shopkeepers of Winchester not to deliver goods in future without his written consent.[202] Local social centres could also provide respectable amusements for country gentlewomen. John Macky, who visited Winchester in 1721, observed of the social gatherings organized by the corporation:

> These assemblies are very convenient for young people; for formerly the country ladies were stewed up in their fathers' old mansion houses, and seldom saw company, but at an assize, a horse-race, or a fair. But by the means of these assemblies, matches are struck up, and the officers of the army have had pretty good success, where ladies are at their own disposal; as I know several instances about Worcester, Shrewsbury, Chester, Derby, and York.[203]

Social centres could thus serve also as marriage markets, bringing members of county families together and enabling young people to meet in an approved setting. Upper-class women were especially well served by the development of local centres for shopping and social life.

Another group mentioned by Macky as frequent patrons of Winchester's amusements were the many Catholic gentlemen living in the neighbourhood, 'who being bred abroad, never miss the assembly'.[204] Like women, these Catholics had grown up outside the mainstream of upper-class country life, and their separate education and their exclusion from local government set them apart in county society. Winchester had long been a town sympathetic to recusancy, and its Catholic community grew and flourished in the later seventeenth century. There were three Catholic schools in villages close to the city – the largest, at Silkstead, had nearly 80 pupils in 1696 – from which boys could go on to the English colleges abroad.[205] A number of prominent Catholic families lived in Winchester, 'very quietly and friendly with their neighbours'; they were regularly presented as recusants by the constables, and the Corporation Act prevented their election to municipal office, but a few Catholics did become freemen and there was no persecution. In 1720 the mayor refused to co-operate with the bishop's attempts to drive them out, being 'unwilling to dislodge so many popish families, who by residing here were of great advantage to the city'.[206] Winchester even had a separate catholic cemetery at St James, the site of a former parish church outside the Westgate. After 1660 St James was regularly and openly used for Catholic burials, and the rector of St Thomas, the closest city parish, entered them in his own parish register.[207]

The weekly Winchester assemblies, like those in other towns, began in the very late seventeenth or early eighteenth century. John Macky described their purpose as 'for the young people to get together, and divert themselves', and explained, 'You drink tea and coffee, play at cards, and often country-dances, you pay but half a crown a quarter towards the expense'.[208] Apart from the assemblies and the annual summer race-meeting, however, Winchester in the late seventeenth century still provided very few facilities for entertainment. There were two bowling-greens in the city, and citizens used the Arbour, an open space outside the walls, to 'pass the time in walking and shooting'. Coffee was available, presumably in a coffee-house, in 1684.[209] Travelling actors occasionally performed in the room over the market-house, but there was no permanent theatre in Winchester until 1785. At the George Inn in 1721 Macky encountered a group of travelling tumblers, trumpeters, and rope-dancers, led by a quack doctor, who 'erected stages in all the market towns, twenty miles round'.[210] But late seventeenth-century Winchester had as yet none of the libraries, concerts, or debating clubs that were appearing in larger centres, and there was no Winchester newspaper until the 1740s. Visitors to the city came for business, shopping, and sociability, rather than organized entertainment.

The highlight of the social year at Winchester was the race-meeting. The corporation was eager to promote the races, and in 1664 it announced in the *Intelligencer* its intention of reviving the race as an annual event and presenting a piece of plate for the winner. By 1676 the city, the marquis of Winchester, and a group of gentlemen subscribers each provided a plate to be run for, and the races were spread over two days in August, the time of year when the gentry left London for the country.[211] In 1682 the corporation decided to try for even more exalted patronage, and a notice was placed in the *London Gazette:*

> The inhabitants of this city being ambitious of the honour of His Majesty's presence, and desirous that many of the nobility and gentry of this nation . . . may meet there to attend him, and recreate themselves on their downs . . . [will establish a plate] to be run for at such times as he should think he might most conveniently go thither from Windsor, and divert himself on their downs.[212]

The offer was accepted, and on 30 August 1682 the Court accompanied Charles II to Winchester for the races.

Charles took an instant liking to the city, and within three days of arriving in Winchester he decided to build there.[213] The site of the ruined castle stood conveniently empty, and by Christmas plans had been drawn up by Sir Christopher Wren for a magnificent palace. The corporation of Winchester was overjoyed at the prospect of royal patronage, and showed an almost embarrassing willingness to accommodate the king's every wish. The site of the castle, which the corporation had bought for £260 and used as a source of stone for building repairs, was immediately presented to the king for the token sum of 5s. Prices of food and lodging were strictly regulated during the king's visits, and city leases were granted subject to the king's building plans.[214] The outgoing mayor even suggested in September 1682 that the city voluntarily surrender its charter, but that was too much for his colleagues. Under the influence of the king's continued interest, however, the corporation did agree to surrender the charter in June 1684, hoping in vain that it would be re-granted.[215] This docile submission stands in strong contrast to Winchester's stubborn opposition to James II, after it became clear that the new king was abandoning his brother's plans.

While Charles lived, however, his building progressed with remarkable speed.[216] The foundations of the 'King's House' were laid in March 1683, and that summer Charles brought the Court to Winchester for a month, with another long visit a year later, to watch his palace grow. Wren's design for the building clearly reflected the autocratic style of Versailles, recently remodelled by Louis XIV. The palace itself consisted of an imposing central block with two wings, containing apartments and two chapels for the king and queen and the Duke and Duchess of York. A grand avenue was projected from the palace on its hill above the city down to the cathedral, flanked by houses for the courtiers, and a large area south and west of the city was bought up for an ornamental park. The bricklayers and masons were hard at work and the palace was ready for roofing when Charles died suddenly in February 1685 and construction came to an abrupt halt. James II attended the Winchester races in September 1685, but he showed no interest in completing the palace. The materials were eventually sold or transferred to other royal buildings, and the unfinished King's House stood empty, with intermittent use as a prison and a barracks, until it burned down in 1894.

Winchester's elevation to the rank of a royal resort had ended as suddenly as it had begun less than three years earlier. The full economic benefits of royal residence were never realized, but the city's brief period of fame had already made some impact on the local economy. A total of 352 acres in and around Winchester had been bought for the Crown; the corporation and other landlords exerted pressure on their tenants to settle quickly, but a few held out for higher prices, and £1,250 was paid out in 1683 for the urban properties alone. The land was leased out again in 1691, with a proviso in case the Crown ever decided to finish the palace.[217] Nearly seven million bricks were made from earth from outside the city walls, and large quantities of chalk, lime, and flint were dug from St Giles' Hill. All this activity, plus the construction itself, provided work for hundreds of men. The skilled master craftsmen were all outsiders, but some local men worked on the palace, and there was also an influx of building workers seeking employment: in February 1685, for instance, nine men presented with their families in the town court as 'strangers intruded into the city' included four joiners, three carpenters, and a bricklayer. Their sudden arrival created some problems – as when three London masons were accused of beating and robbing a local man – but the benefits of greatly increased custom for local suppliers far outweighed the problems of keeping order.[218] Each time the king and the Court visited Winchester crowds of people came with them, like the Irishman in 1683 who described himself as 'one that followed the Court', and all these people needed food, lodging, and entertainment. In 1685 James II's election manager at Winchester used the prospect of custom for city tradesmen as an inducement to change their votes, assuring his supporters of 'the custom of all my friends, both now and when the Court comes down'.[219] If Charles II had lived longer, or his successors had shared his liking for Winchester, the city's economic prospects would have been dramatically improved.

Even without royal patronage, however, Winchester remained an important county centre throughout the eighteenth century. The majority of its customers were always visitors, but Winchester was also beginning to attract a number of resident gentlemen, and their new houses gradually transformed the city's appearance. Most houses built by gentlemen in the sixteenth and early seventeenth centuries had been in the suburbs, but after 1660 large mansions began to appear inside the walls (see fig. 16). The first was Eastgate House, taxed on 16 hearths in 1665, which was built for Sir Robert Mason. Sir John Clobery built a large house in Parchment Street about 1670, and other gentlemen followed suit. Eastgate House was the only mansion to be built at the lower end of the town in the later seventeenth century; all the others stood on the higher ground to the west, and they were particularly concentrated in the south-west quarter of Winchester, where Civil War damage had been most extensive.[220] The Hearth Tax list of 1665 shows ten houses in the city (excluding inns) with ten or more hearths; by 1704 there were about 20 substantial private houses, mostly inhabited by gentlemen or professional men. John Macky in 1721 found in the side-streets of Winchester 'the finest houses, with gardens, and some of them as handsome as one can see any where, all sashed and adorned after the newest manner'.[221]

Indeed, the later seventeenth century saw a minor building boom at Winchester. Tradesmen as well as gentlemen took to building, albeit on a more modest scale. Some built new houses, and many older houses were re-fronted by taking in the area under an old-fashioned first-floor jetty. In the cathedral close, repairs were urgently needed on buildings which had been ransacked and neglected during the war and Interregnum; extensive rebuilding proceeded throughout the 1660s and early 1670s, and by 1674 nine of the canons lived in large houses with ten or more hearths.[222] The bishop too was involved in the post-Restoration rebuilding. Bishops Duppa (1660–2) and Morley (1662–84) spent more than £4,000 to patch and repair the dilapidated palace at Wolvesey, and Morley founded a Matrons' College for clergymen's widows in 1674. At Winchester College, a large new building called 'School' for the commoners was added between 1683 and 1687.[223] The prospect of royal residence caused an even greater flurry of building activity in the brief period 1683–5. In 1684 an excise official reported that 'houses are building here about for persons of quality' (adding that alehouses were opening near the new mansions for the benefit of the servants), while Bishop Morley began a small new palace south of the old one in the belief that he and his successors would be spending more time at Winchester.[224]

Apart from Morley, the seventeenth-century bishops of Winchester had largely withdrawn from their cathedral city, and in their absence the Pawlet family, marquises of Winchester, gradually assumed the political and social patronage once wielded by the bishops. After 1660 the marquis or one of his sons often sat in Parliament for Winchester and acted as its high steward, and the corporation willingly accepted their intervention in political affairs. The marquis had no house of his own at Winchester, but the deanery appears to have been at his disposal for entertaining.[225] During the turbulent political changes of the 1680s the Pawlets were first forced to share their patronage, and then supplanted completely, by Bernard Howard, a younger brother of the fifth and sixth dukes of Norfolk and a Catholic. Howard first appeared in Winchester in 1676, and he made himself useful as an ambassador between the king and the corporation during Charles II's brief period of interest in the city. With the accession of James II, Howard became even more influential. He exerted considerable pressure as Court manager in the parliamentary election of 1685, and was named recorder of Winchester in James's abortive charter.[226] But James's fall in 1688 put an end to Howard's influence; he continued to live quietly in Winchester, but the Pawlets, newly created dukes of Bolton, resumed their former role as patrons of the city.

Thus non-resident gentlemen and noblemen became steadily more involved in corporate life at Winchester, and the magistrates offered them every encouragement. Half of the freemen admitted between 1680 and 1700 were of the rank of esquire or higher, and most of them were resident outside the city. Gentlemen rarely attended corporation meetings, but they voted in parliamentary elections, and the mayor welcomed all comers: in 1690 the Duke of Bolton, his son the Marquis of Winchester, and the Earl of Bridgwater were all permitted to vote, and the unsuc-

Figure 16. Serle's House, Winchester. The most imposing of the mansions built by gentlemen at the upper end of the town in the post-Restoration period. The house stands on the site of Sir William Ogle's residence, which was damaged in the Civil War, and Serle's House was probably built for his wife's descendants about 1715 (photograph by courtesy of D. G. Dine, Hampshire County Library).

183

cessful candidate's appeal against non-resident voters was dismissed with the assertion that 'they constantly voted in elections for parliament men, and they were never objected against.'[227] Non-resident gentlemen freemen also came to the city for civic feasts. At least eight times each year the whole corporation gathered at St John's House or one of the large inns for a grand dinner, accompanied by musicians and quantities of wine. More refreshments and entertainments were provided on the reigning monarch's accession day, and on Guy Fawkes' Day. This annual round of ritual conviviality was supplemented by yet more dinners whenever the Duke of Bolton sent the corporation some venison or a visiting dignitary was to be honoured with a 'treat'. When desirable and influential visitors came to Winchester, the corporation spared no expense to make them welcome and encourage their interest in the city.

By 1700 Winchester's economic transition was almost complete, and the town was settled in the path it was to follow throughout the eighteenth century and well into the nineteenth. Not all the signs of economic stress apparent in 1580 had disappeared – poverty and unemployment had been alleviated but by no means cured – but the city was on the way to recovering its economic health. Most of the external pressures which had affected Winchester, including depressions in the cloth industry, migration from rural to urban areas, and the political turmoil of the Civil War, had abated by 1700, and the city's hinterland had gained both in population and wealth. At the same time the city had completed its internal economic shift from industrial production to the distribution of goods and provision of services. John Trussell, concerned as ever about the fortunes of Winchester, had listed in the 1640s what he saw as the symptoms of decay, though in fact they were but the signs of change. 'Clothing too little used' and 'capping and many manufactures utterly left off' were part of the withering away of the city's medieval economy; on the other hand, Trussell's observations of 'taverners, innkeepers and alehouses infinitely increasing' and 'usury and malting too much practised', which he deplored, were signs of the new growth of services which were to provide Winchester's livelihood in the future.[228]

The tendency for internal trade to become concentrated in one or two towns in each county during the seventeenth century, to the detriment of other centres, had worked to Winchester's great advantage.[229] Had Southampton not been mired in decay, or had Portsmouth developed a broader range of facilities, either of those towns might have acquired Hampshire's custom, and the county was not yet rich enough to support more than one major centre. But Winchester's geographically central position, combined with its advantages as the seat of county government and ecclesiastical administration, gave it a unique combination of functions, and the custom of every level of Hampshire society was drawn to the city. Had he lived to see it, John Trussell would surely have been delighted to find his bleak picture of Winchester's old age proved wrong.

BIBLIOGRAPHY

This bibliography covers sources relevant to the period 1580–1700. Manuscripts are listed by class, with references to individual documents of particular interest.

MANUSCRIPT SOURCES

Winchester City Archives (Hampshire Record Office, 20 Southgate Street, Winchester)

1st – 7th Books of Ordinances
Proceedings of the Corporation A & B
Proposal Book 1662–1704
Book of Orders 1665
2nd – 6th Ledger Books
Chamberlains' Accounts
Coffer Accounts
St John's Hospital Accounts (3/Bx./S.J. 14–15)
Town Court Rolls (bound volumes, 58/Bk.)
Miscellaneous Court Records (57/Bx./M.C. 2)
Quarter Sessions Papers (31/Bx./Q.S. 1, 2, 10)
Proceedings in Quarter Sessions 1660–1716
Lay Subsidies (37/Bx./S.R. 1)
Tarrage Surveys (1604, c.1680, c.1700)
Charity Records (2/Bk./C.S.)
Land Tax Assessments 1703–29 (37/P/Ts 2)
Land Tax Commissioners' Minute Book 1691–1725 (37/P/Ts 6)
John Trussell, 'Origin of Cities' and 'Touchstone of Tradition'
W. H. Jacob Scrapbooks
Parish Registers
    City: St Maurice, Books A – D, 1538–1702
              St Thomas with St Clement, Books 1 – 2, 1678–1722
    Soke: St Bartholomew Hyde, Book 1, 1563–1704
              St Michael in Kingsgate Street, Books A – B, 1632–1724
              St Peter Chesil, Book A, 1597–1776
              St John in the Soke, Book A, 1595–1776

Hampshire County and Diocesan Archives (Hampshire Record Office)

Wills and Inventories: A Archdeaconry Court
                            B Bishop's Consistory Court
                            PCC Prerogative Court of Canterbury
Administrations (Adm.)
Consistory Court Deposition Books 50, 55, 62, 67, 116 (1578–98, 1633)
Visitation Books (B/2)
Churchwardens' Presentments (B/3)
Bishops' Pipe-Rolls (Eccl. 2)
Quarter Sessions Order Books (Q.O.)
Quarter Sessions Indictment Book (Q.I.)
Wriothesley MSS (5M53)

Winchester Cathedral Library

Chapter Registers
Toll-books of Magdalen Hill Fair
Survey of Dean & Chapter Lands 1649

Winchester College Muniments

Public Record Office

Assizes 24 Order Books, Western Circuit

C1–3, 5–10 Chancery Proceedings
C93 Proceedings, Commissioners for Charitable Uses
E133 Barons' Depositions
E134 Depositions by Commission
E178 Special Commissions of Enquiry
E179 Subsidy Rolls
E180 Victuallers' Recognizances
E190 Port Books
E315 Augmentations Office, Misc. Books (accounts for vacant sees)
E351 Pipe Office, Declared Accounts (Works and Buildings)
  E351/3460 Building accounts for the royal palace at Winchester, 1683–6
E407 Exchequer of Receipt, Misc. Books (compositions for knighthood)
Prob. 11 Registered PCC Wills
Req. 2 Proceedings, Court of Requests
S.C. 6 Ministers' and Receivers' Accounts (accounts for vacant sees)
SP1–16, 28–9 State Papers Domestic
St. Ch. 1–10 Proceedings, Court of Star Chamber
W.O. 30 War Office Miscellanea
  W.O. 30/48 Military survey of stabling and accommodation, 1686

British Library

Additional MSS
  Add. MS 21,922 Letter-book of Sir Richard Norton
  Add. MSS 24,860–1 Papers of Richard Major
  Add. MS 27,402 Account of Lord Ogle's career in Civil War
Cotton MSS
Harleian MSS
Lansdowne MSS
Sloane MSS
Stowe MSS
  Stowe MS 541 Expenditure on building and charity by Bishop Morley (1662–84)

House of Lords Record Office

Main Papers, 13 June 1660 (Winchester Petition and annexed papers)

Bodleian Library

Clarendon MSS
  Clarendon MS 26 Account of the siege of Winchester Castle in 1645 by a member of the
  Royalist garrison
Rawlinson MSS
Tanner MSS
  Tanner MS 140 Finances of the bishopric and dean and chapter in the 1660s
Top. Hants. MSS
  Top. Hants. c. 5 John Trussell's collections relating to Winchester, known as the
  'Benefactors to Winchester'

PRINTED PRIMARY SOURCES

'Account of the state of the Churches of Winchester, at the period of the Restoration', *Trans.
  British Archaeol. Assoc.* (1845), 105–15 (reprints a pamphlet of 1660 defending the 'new
  corporation' of the 1650s against accusations of misuse of parish churches).
Black Book of Winchester, The, ed. W. H. B. Bird (1925) (forerunner of the Books of

Ordinances, recording decisions of city government).

Diary of John Young, S.T.P., The, ed. F. R. Goodman (1928) (diary of the dean of Winchester, 1616–45).

Documents relating to the History of the Cathedral Church of Winchester in the Seventeenth Century, ed. W. R. W. Stephens and F. T. Madge (Hampshire Record Soc., 1897).

Hampshire Parish Registers. Marriages, ed. W. P. W. Phillimore (Phillimore Parish Register Series), IV, V, XI, XIII, XVI (1902–14). (Vol. IV prints baptisms and burials as well as marriages for St Swithun upon Kingsgate 1562–1812, Winchester cathedral 1599–1812, and Winchester College 1678–1861.)

Hampshire Registers, I, ed. Canon R. E. Scantlebury (Catholic Record Soc., XLII, 1942–3). (Documents on Catholicism at Winchester in the seventeenth and eighteenth centuries.)

Hyde, Henry, Earl of Clarendon, and S. Gale, *The History and Antiquities of the Cathedral Church of Winchester* (1715) (the first guide-book to the cathedral).

Map of Winchester by William Godson (1750).

Private Memoirs of John Potenger Esq., ed. C. W. Bingham (1841) (memoirs of a Hampshire gentleman, 1647–1733).

Royal Palaces of Winchester, Whitehall, Kensington, and St James's, The, ed. A. T. Bolton and H. D. Hendry (Wren Society, VII, 1930).

Thomason Tracts (British Library).

Transcripts from the Municipal Archives of Winchester, ed. C. Bailey (1856) (includes some documents since lost or mislaid from the city archives).

Winchester Settlement Papers 1667–1842, ed. A. J. Willis (1967).

NOTES

For their generous assistance over many years, I should like to thank Dr Joan Thirsk, my supervisor; Dr Derek Keene, formerly of the Winchester Research Unit; Mr Austin Whitaker, the Winchester City Archivist, and the staff of the Hampshire Record Office; and my husband, Dr Andrew Rosen.

1 HRO, Winchester City Archives (henceforth WCA), John Trussell, 'Touchstone of Tradition', f. 7v. For John Trussell and his writings see n. 85 below.
2 The origins and medieval development of Winchester are described in F. Barlow, M. Biddle, O. von Feilitzen and D. J. Keene, *Winchester in the Early Middle Ages* (1976).
3 A. B. Rosen, 'Economic and social aspects of the history of Winchester 1520–1670' (D.Phil. thesis, University of Oxford, 1975), 18–19.
4 BL, Harleian MS 595, fos. 214–16.
5 D. J. Keene, 'Some aspects of the history, topography and archaeology of the north eastern part of the medieval city of Winchester with special reference to the Brooks area' (D.Phil. thesis, University of Oxford, 1973), 54.
6 L. G. Wickham Legg (ed.), 'A relation of a short survey of the Western Counties', *Camden Miscellany,* xvi (1936), 43; see also Speed's map of Winchester in *The Theatre of the Empire of Great Britaine* (1611), 14.
7 P. Corfield, 'Urban development in England and Wales in the sixteenth and seventeenth centuries', in *Trade, Government and Economy in Pre-Industrial England,* ed. D. C. Coleman and A. H. John (1976), 224–7.
8 E.g. Canterbury and Salisbury: P. Clark, *English Provincial Society from the Reformation to the Revolution: religion, politics and society in Kent 1500–1640* (1977), 356, 400; P. Slack, 'Poverty and politics in Salisbury 1597–1666', in *Crisis and Order in English Towns,* ed. P. Clark and P. Slack (1972), 171.
9 HRO, WCA, 37/Bx./S.R. 1, no.10.

10 HRO, WCA, 2nd Ledger Book, f. 218v. For a more detailed account of cloth manufacture at Winchester, see Rosen, *op cit.*, 150–66.
11 PRO, E190/814/1 (Southampton); E190/1/4 (London, aliens); E190/2/1 (London, denizens).
12 N.S.B. Gras, *The Evolution of the English Corn Market* (Cambridge, Mass., 1915), 430–1; R. Davis, 'England and the Mediterranean, 1570–1670', in *Essays in the Economic and Social History of Tudor and Stuart England*, ed. F. J. Fisher (1961), 118–20.
13 PRO, E190/821/2 (Southampton); E190/22/3 (London): both Port Books run from Christmas 1618 to Christmas 1619.
14 *CSPD, Addenda 1566–79,* 31–2.
15 PRO, SP14/98/54; *Commons Debates 1621,* ed. W. Notestein, F. H. Relf, and H. Simpson, VII (New Haven, 1935), 252.
16 PRO, SP14/98/54.
17 *Commons Debates 1621*, VII, 252; G. W. Kitchin, *Winchester* (1890), 186 (this document is apparently no longer among the city archives).
18 HRO, Q.O./2, f. 29; see also *Seventeenth-Century Economic Documents,* ed. J. Thirsk and J. P. Cooper (1972), 38–9.
19 E.g. HRO, Q.O./1, p.196.
20 E.g. PRO, Prob.11/109 (PCC 10 Huddlestone, will of William Symondes); Prob. 11/156 (PCC 106 Ridley, will of William Bechym).
21 HMC, Portland MSS, III, 548.
22 HRO, WCA, 1st Book of Ordinances, f. 205v; 7th Book of Ordinances, f. 81.
23 HRO, WCA, 1st Book of Ordinances, fos.184, 189.
24 HRO, WCA, Coffer Accounts 1589–1627, 12 May 1620; 2nd Ledger Book, f. 279v; W. H. B. Bird (ed.), *The Black Book of Winchester,* (1925), 129.
25 HRO, WCA, Chamberlains' Accounts 22–3, 24–5 Eliz.; W. H. Jacob, 'A Retrospect of Civic Manners and Customs' (scrapbook), page B (presentments 11 June 1585).
26 HRO, WCA, Proceedings of the Corporation B, fos. 4, 6; 4th Book of Ordinances, f. 26v.
27 Lord Beveridge, *Prices and Wages in England*, I (1939), 74; C. Morris (ed.), *The Journeys of Celia Fiennes* (1947), 46.
28 Winchester Cathedral MSS, Cupboard 5, D 3, Bk. 2 (Magdalen Hill Fair toll-book).
29 A. Everitt, 'The marketing of agricultural produce', in *The Agrarian History of England and Wales*, IV, ed. J. Thirsk (1967), 496–500.
30 HRO, WCA, Proceedings of the Corporation A, fos.19, 28, 47; R. Blome, *Britannia* (1673), 109 (s.v. 'Alreston'); *VCH Hants.,* III (1908), 349, 351.
31 J. Taylor, *The Honourable, and Memorable Foundations . . . of divers Cities* (1636).
32 HMC, Var. Coll., IV (Herriard MSS), 170.
33 *Commons Debates 1621*, V, 373; C. Bailey, *Transcripts from the Municipal Archives of Winchester* (1856), 89–90; HMC, 7th Report, 179. See also n. 89 below.
34 PRO, St. Ch. 8/293/11.
35 E.g. N. S. B. and E. C. Gras, *The Economic and Social History of an English Village: Crawley, Hampshire* (Cambridge, Mass., 1930), 531–4; Winchester College Muniments 3010, 11137.
36 HRO, Adm. 1576 (Thomas Bassett); Adm. 1596 (Simon Tripp); wills A1619 (Ralph Hulton). None of the Winchester doctors identified by J. H. Raach, *A Directory of English Country Physicians 1603–43* (1962), 24, 70, 85, 92, appears in local records.
37 F. R. Goodman (ed.), *The Diary of John Young S.T.P.* (1928), 59.
38 A. F. Leach, *A History of Winchester College* (1899), 330.
39 *CSPD, 1635*, xlii; *1637*, 92; *Addenda 1625–49*, 558.
40 E.g. HRO wills B1581 (inventory of Edward White, £677 stock); wills A1623 (inventory of Ralph Moore, £73 stock); Adm. 1587 (Richard Barefote, c. £23 stock).
41 For occupations, see Rosen, *op. cit.*, 198–201; HRO wills A1624 (inventory of William

Stanley).
42 HRO, WCA, Proceedings of the Corporation A, f. 8; PRO, C2/Jas.I/G.17/2.
43 HRO, WCA, John Trussell, 'Touchstone of Tradition', f.189v.
44 J. Patten, 'Population distribution in Norfolk and Suffolk during the sixteenth and seventeenth centuries', *Trans. Inst. British Geographers*, LXV (1975), 55; the Hampshire figure has been calculated by the same methods, using the parish returns for the 1603 ecclesiastical census (BL, Harleian MS 595, fos. 214–39) and acreages from the 1851 Census. Patten's method of converting communicants (adults) to total population, by adding 40 per cent on the grounds that children constituted 40 per cent of the population, is incorrect, but the error does not invalidate the comparison between counties.
45 R. S. Schofield, 'The geographical distribution of wealth in England, 1334–1649', *EcHR*, N.S. XVIII (1965), 504.
46 J. Thirsk, 'The farming regions of England', in *The Agrarian History of England and Wales*, IV, ed. J. Thirsk (1967), 64–71; *APC*, 1586–7, 319, 362, 387; 1630–1, 120–1.
47 C. Cochrane, *The Lost Roads of Wessex* (1972), 27–9.
48 HRO, WCA, Proceedings in Quarter Sessions 1660–1716, 10 Dec. 1660.
49 HRO, WCA, W. H. Jacob Scrapbook no. 3, 24.
50 HRO, WCA, 1st Book of Ordinances, fos. 226v–7.
51 HRO, WCA, Proceedings of the Corporation A, f. 22; *ibid.*, B, fos. 1–5.
52 *Ibid.*, B, f. 89; HRO, WCA, Coffer Accounts 1589–1627, 12 Mar. 1603/4; Chamberlains' Account 3–4 Jas. I.
53 HRO, Q.O./1, 98.
54 *APC*, 1625–6, 178; HRO, WCA, Coffer Accounts 1589–1627, 27 Aug. 1625 to 20 Jan. 1625/6 *passim*.
55 HRO, Q.O./2, fos.100–25; J. F. D. Shrewsbury, *A History of Bubonic Plague in the British Isles* (1970), 389.
56 Rosen, *op cit.*, 139–42; HRO, WCA, John Trussell, 'Touchstone of Tradition', f. 237; on migration and its effects on towns, see P. Clark, 'The migrant in Kentish towns 1580 1640', in Clark and Slack (eds.), *op. cit.*, 117–63.
57 HRO, WCA, 1st Book of Ordinances, f.143.
58 HRO, WCA, 3rd Book of Ordinances, f.166v; 4th Book of Ordinances, fos.108v, 110; Town Court Roll 58/Bk. 1593–1631, f.202.
59 HRO, WCA, 4th Book of Ordinances, fos.25v–6v; 57/Bx./M.C. 2.
60 *APC*, 1586–7, 387; HRO, WCA, 3/Bx./S.J. 14, no.158; 1st Book of Ordinances, fos. 254, 256.
61 HRO, WCA, Coffer Accounts 1589–1627, 10 July 1594, 19 July 1594, 23 Dec. 1594; Chamberlains' Account 38–9 Eliz.; Proceedings of the Corporation A, fos. 35–6.
62 HRO, WCA, Coffer Accounts 1589–1627, 30 Jan. 1609/10; HRO, Q.O/1, p. 98.
63 PRO, SP16/88/56.
64 HRO, WCA, Coffer Accounts 1628–61, 10 July 1629, 4 June 1630, 9 Aug. 1630, 26 May 1637.
65 HRO, Q.O./2, f.29. Cf. Salisbury, where nearly half the population was on relief in the 1620s: P. Slack, 'Poverty and politics in Salisbury', in Clark and Slack (eds.), *op cit.*, 171–2.
66 BL, Add. MS 21, 922, fos.77, 88, 124, 143v; PRO, SP16/70/50; SP16/88/56; *CSPD, 1627–8*, 104, 106, 124, 137, 167, 181, 192, 329, 443, 471; HRO, WCA, Coffer Accounts 1589–1627, 29 Sept. 1626, 6 Oct. 1626, 29 Dec. 1626. Cf. L. Boynton, 'Billeting: the example of the Isle of Wight', *EHR*, LXXIV (1959), 23–40.
67 HRO, WCA, Chamberlains' Account 21–2 Jas. I; BL, Add. MS 21, 922, f.118v; *CSPD, 1627–8*, 407.
68 BL, Add. MS 21, 922, f. 209.
69 E.g. HRO, Q.O./2, f.144v; HRO, WCA, Chamberlains' Account 3–4 Jas. I.
70 E.g. the fragmentary list of rate-payers and recipients (a corporation document) in HRO, WCA, Town Court Roll 58/Bk. 1638–40.

71 HRO, WCA, 3/Bx./S.J. 14, nos. 153–78; 3/Bx./S.J. 15, nos.179–95. The figures have been adjusted for inflation using the Phelps Brown and Hopkins index of the price of a 'composite unit of consumables', calculated as the essential outlay of a building worker in southern England, a combination of items which probably closely resembled the necessaries of life in early modern Winchester: E. H. Phelps Brown and S. V. Hopkins, 'Seven centuries of the prices of consumables, compared with builders' wage rates', reprinted in *The Price Revolution in Sixteenth-Century England*, ed. P. H. Ramsey (1971), 40. The St John's Hospital accounts for 1621–5 do not survive.

72 *Camden Miscellany*, XVI, 50.

73 F. R. Goodman (ed.) *The Diary of John Young S.T.P.* (1928), 62, 73–4, 87; T. F. Kirby, *Annals of Winchester College* (1892), 301, 310–11, 313, 323–4.

74 BL, Cotton Titus B.v, f. 425; Cotton Vesp. F.ix, fos. 232, 250; PRO, SP12/153/24. Plans for industrial production at the London Bridewell also lapsed: A. L. Beier, 'Social problems in Elizabethan London', *J. Interdisciplinary History*, ix (1978), 217–19.

75 HRO, WCA, Chamberlains' Account 8–9 Jas. I; HRO, Q.O./1, 373–4.

76 HRO, WCA, Coffer Accounts 1589–1627, 2 Nov. 1607, 20 Dec. 1608, 27 Jan. 1608/9.

77 PRO, Prob. 11/71 (PCC 51 Spencer); HRO, WCA, 3rd Book of Ordinances, f. 184.

78 E.g. Richard Paice, a freeman since 1579 and a recipient in 1599; HRO, WCA, 1st Book of Ordinances, f. 297.

79 E.g. HRO, WCA, Coffer Accounts 1589–1627, 18 Mar. 1612/3, 23 Dec. 1625.

80 *Ibid.*, 14 Aug. 1612.

81 HRO, WCA, 6th Book of Ordinances, fos. 22–2v; Payments out of Coffer 1660–99, 12 May 1665.

82 *Diary of John Young*, 87.

83 *Ibid.*, 63, 67, 81. None of the puritan activities typically found in towns was evident in Winchester: see W. J. Sheils, 'Religion in provincial towns: innovation and tradition', in *Church and Society in England: Henry VIII to James I*, ed. F. Heal and R. O'Day (1977), 159–67.

84 Bodl., MS Top. Hants. c. 5, pp. 87, 89.

85 HRO, WCA, Trussell, 'Touchstone of Tradition', fos. 193v–4. John Trussell (1575–1648), an attorney, settled in Winchester as a young man. He became a freeman in 1606, served as mayor in 1624–5 and 1633–4, and was an alderman for over 20 years. Three manuscripts by Trussell survive: the 'Touchstone of Tradition' (a history of Winchester, and of cities in general), and the 'Origin of Cities' (a draft of the first section of the 'Touchstone of Tradition'), both of which are now in the Winchester City Archives; and the 'Benefactors to Winchester', a miscellaneous volume, now Bodl., MS Top. Hants. c. 5.

86 HRO, WCA, Proceedings of the Corporation A, fos. 25–6, 53; 1st Book of Ordinances, fos.136, 172; Bodl. MS Top. Hants. c. 5, pp. 40 (Lady Laurence), 57 (Richard Venables).

87 HRO, WCA, Proceedings of the Corporation A, fos. 31, 34–5.

88 Barlow *et al.*, *Winchester in the Early Middle Ages*, 270–1; Rosen, *op. cit.*, 195–6; Bodl. MS Top. Hants. c. 5, pp. 71–81; HRO, 102M71/P1.

89 HRO, WCA, Coffer Accounts 1589–1627, 26 Dec. 1617, 15 Apr. 1624, 24 Mar. 1625/6; Proceedings of the Corporation B, f. 38; *Diary of John Young*, 60. For the later history of the waterway, see E. Course, 'The Itchen Navigation', *Procs. Hants. Field Club*, xxiv (1967), 113–26.

90 HRO, WCA, Chamberlains' Accounts 32–3 Eliz., 2–3 Jas. I.

91 Bodl., MS Top. Hants. c. 5, p. 59; HRO, WCA, Coffer Accounts 1628–61, 10 June 1631; J. P. Hore, *The History of Newmarket and the Annals of the Turf*, II (1886), 148; L. Stone, *Family and Fortune* (1973), 148.

92 HRO, WCA, Coffer Accounts 1589–1627, 18 Mar. 1612/3, 21 Dec. 1625; *ibid.*, 1628–61, 14 July 1628, 6 Oct. 1638. For seventeenth-century interest rates, see L. A. Clarkson,

The Pre-Industrial Economy in England 1500–1750 (1971), 167.
93 HRO, WCA, Trussell, 'Touchstone of Tradition', f.194v.
94 J. S. Morrill, *The Revolt of the Provinces* (1976), 38–46.
95 Bodl. Smith newsb. e. 78(11): *A True and Exact Relation of a Great Overthrow . . . in Winchester* (1642).
96 BL, Thomason Tracts E.83. (11), p. 6.
97 *Ibid.*, E.245. (14); *Mercurius Rusticus* (1685), 144–52; P. Heylyn, *Aerius Redivivus* (1672), 441–2; Bodl., MS Top. Hants. c. 5, p. 96.
98 Bodl., MS Top. Hants. c. 5, pp. 96–7, 99; T. C. Dale, 'An episode of the Civil War', *Genealogists' Mag.*, N.S. I (1925), 66–7.
99 G. N. Godwin, *The Civil War in Hampshire, 1642–5* (1882), 55.
100 F. T. R. Edgar, *Sir Ralph Hopton* (1968), 146–8, 151, 156; Bodl., MS Top. Hants. c. 5, pp. 97–9; *CSPD, 1644*, 11.
101 Bodl., MS Top. Hants. c. 5, p. 98.
102 *Ibid.*, 100.
103 J. Adair, *Cheriton 1644* (1973), 137–45, 165–7; T. Webb (ed.), *Military Memoir of Col. John Birch* (Camden Soc., 2nd ser., VII, 1873), 11–12.
104 J. Sprigge, *Anglia Rediviva* (1647), 127, 137; J. Crofts, *Packhorse, Waggon and Post* (1967), 44–6; *CSPD, 1644*, 300, 302, 307–8.
105 HRO, WCA, 4th Book of Ordinances, f. 153; Bodl., MS. Top. Hants. c. 5, pp. 97–8.
106 Heylyn, *op. cit.*, 441.
107 Bodl., MS Clarendon 26, fos.114–17.
108 *Commons J.*, IV, 591; W. R. W. Stephens and F. T. Madge (eds.), *Documents relating to the History of the Cathedral Church of Winchester in the 17th century* (Hampshire Record Soc., 1897), 57.
109 *CSPD, 1648–9*, 57; PRO, SP28/230; BL, Add. MS 24,861, f. 44.
110 HRO, WCA, 4th Book of Ordinances, fos.162, 165v; PRO, C2/Chas.I/W.13/38.
111 PRO, C5/390/51; *Calendar of the Committee for Compounding*, 1059; *Calendar of the Committee for Advance of Money*, 761, 983.
112 PRO, C5/413/96.
113 Bodl., MS Top. Hants. c. 5, p. 99.
114 Bodl., MS Clarendon 26, fos. 114–15.
115 P. Heylyn, *Keimelia Ekklesiastika: The Historical and Miscellaneous Tracts of . . . Peter Heylyn, D.D.* (1681), xviii; cf. Dr John Speed, a physician who decided to settle in Southampton in 1667 'being acquainted with the Cavalier gentlemen of the neighbourhood': A. T. Patterson, *A History of Southampton 1700–1914*, I (Southampton Records Series, XI, 1966), 2n.
116 HRO, WCA, W. H. Jacob, 'A Retrospect of Civic Manners and Customs' (scrapbook), 13–14, 35–6.
117 *Ibid.*, 35–6, 45–6, 52.
118 T. Fuller, *Thoughts and Contemplations*, ed. J. O. Wood (1964), 108–9; see also T. Fuller, *History of the Worthies of England*, ed. P. A. Nuttall, I (1840), 51.
119 Rosen, *op. cit.*, fig. 6.
120 HRO, WCA, 5th Book of Ordinances, fos. 72v–3, 77, 103v.
121 Bodl., MS Tanner 140, f. 39v; HRO, Q.I. (Michaelmas 1659).
122 HRO, WCA, 5th Book of Ordinances, f.147; *Winchester Cathedral Documents in 17th c.* (Hampshire Record Soc.), 71, 83–4; T. Birch (ed.), *A Collection of the State Papers of John Thurloe*, IV (1742), 208.
123 PRO, Prob.11/234 (PCC 64 Alchin, will of William Phillips).
124 HRO, Q.O./3, 6–7; Q.O./4, 9, 26–7.
125 Winchester College Muniments 418; *Diary of John Young*, 177.
126 *Commons J.*, V, 535.
127 House of Lords RO, Main Papers, 13 June 1660 (Winchester Petition, annexed

statement of crimes and abuses); *CSPD, 1661–2*, 270.

128 *Commons J.*, VI, 294; House of Lords RO, Main Papers, 13 June 1660 (Winchester Petition, annexed copy of Act).

129 New groups gaining entry to town government elsewhere proved to have similarly limited aims: B. Manning, *The English People and the English Revolution 1640–9* (1976), 147.

130 HRO, WCA, 5th Book of Ordinances, fos.32, 67v, 96v–7v, 119–23v; *CSPD, 1653–4*, 287.

131 E.g. HRO, Q.O./3, 111.

132 HRO, WCA, 5th Book of Ordinances, fos.109–10.

133 HRO, WCA, 5th Ledger Book, f.120.

134 HRO, WCA, 5th Book of Ordinances, fos.106–7, 173–3v; 5th Ledger Book, fos. 73v–4; HMC, 7th Report, 93. In practice some unauthorized brewing was tolerated: HRO, WCA, Coffer Accounts 1628–61, 29 July 1659.

135 I. M. Green, *The Re-establishment of the Church of England 1660–1663* (1978), 3; HRO, WCA, Coffer Accounts 1628–61, 18 May 1660.

136 House of Lords RO, Main Papers, 13 June 1660 (Winchester Petition, annexed statement of crimes and abuses); HRO, WCA, 5th Ledger Book, f.120; 'Account of the state of the churches of Winchester', *Trans. British Archaeological Assoc.* (1845), 105–15; *Lords' J.*, XI, 130–1, 139.

137 HRO, WCA, 5th Ledger Book, f.141v; 5th Book of Ordinances, fos.177–7v.

138 HRO, WCA, 5th Book of Ordinances, f. 147; cf. Clark, *English Provincial Society*, 404–5.

139 A drawing of Winchester in 1662 by the Dutch topographical artist Willem Schellinks shows a small, almost rural town, dominated by the College, the cathedral, and the castle ruins: P. H. Hulton (ed.), *Drawings of England in the Seventeenth Century by Willem Schellinks, Jacob Esselens & Lambert Doomer* (Walpole Soc. XXXV, 1954–6), pl. 29.

140 'Account of the state of the churches of Winchester', *op. cit.,* 107–8; Bodl., MS Clarendon 26, fos.114–4v; Winchester Cathedral MSS, Survey of Dean & Chapter Lands 1649, fos. 19, 65.

141 C. H. Josten (ed.), *Elias Ashmole (1617–92)*, II (1966), 780.

142 HRO, WCA, Coffer Accounts 1628–61, 18 May 1647, March 1649, 3 Apr. 1657; G. C. Moore Smith (ed.), *Letters of Dorothy Osborne to William Temple* (1928), 163.

143 PRO, SP29/272/190.

144 PRO, E179/176/565: this is the only fully legible Hearth Tax list for Winchester.

145 Communities with a low rate of economic growth commonly showed a low mean household size: J. M. Martin, 'An investigation into the small size of the household', *Local Population Studies*, XIX (1977), 16. At Southampton in the 1690s overall mean household size was as low as 4.03, and in individual parishes it ranged from 3.69 to 4.68: P. Laslett, 'Mean household size in England since the sixteenth century', in *Household and Family in Past Time*, ed. P. Laslett (1972), 130.

146 William Salt Library, Stafford, Salt MS 33. I am grateful to Dr A. Whiteman for making her transcripts of the Compton Census available to me, and for discussion of its interpretation.

147 HRO, B/2/A, Visitation 1725, fos. 326, 364–85.

148 HRO, WCA, 6th Book of Ordinances, f.106v, and back of book (reversed); 31/Bx./Q.S. 10 (1692); Proceedings in Quarter Sessions 1660–1716, 8 Dec. 1684.

149 A. J. Willis (ed.), *Winchester Settlement Papers 1667–1842* (1967), 13, 35–40, 76, 84–5; Rosen, *op. cit.*, 142–3.

150 Kirby, *op. cit.*, 355; W. H. Jacob, 'Notes on the plague in Winchester', *J. British Archaeological Assoc.*, L (1894), 275.

151 M. M. Verney (ed.), *Memoirs of the Verney Family during the Commonwealth*, IV (1899), 135–6.

152 PRO, Cust. 48/1, p.19. I owe this reference to Peter Clark.
153 PRO, SP29/272/190.
154 *Calendar of Treasury Books*, II, 296.
155 *CSPD, 1683–4*, 391; HRO, WCA, Payments out of Coffer 1660–99, 9 Nov. 1694; for Winchester wheat prices from 1657 to 1700, see Beveridge, *op. cit.*, I, 81.
156 Rosen, *op. cit.*, table 21.
157 HRO, WCA, Proceedings in Quarter Sessions 1660–1716, 8 Dec. 1662.
158 HRO, wills A 1667 (will of Richard Dennett).
159 J. Milner, *The History, Civil and Ecclesiastical, and Survey of the Antiquities of Winchester*, I (1798), 450.
160 HRO, WCA, W. H. Jacob, 'A Retrospect of Civic Manners and Customs' (scrapbook), 19–20; 31/Bx./Q.S. 2(1672, presentation of Bennett Creed); Proposal Book 1662–1704 (reversed), f. 51; HRO, wills A 1670 (inventory of John Birch); *Commons J.*, XII, 132, 441.
161 D. Defoe, *A Tour thro' the Whole Island of Great Britain*, I (1927 edn), 189.
162 HRO, WCA, 7th Book of Ordinances, f. 58; Proposal Book 1662–1704, f.13.
163 *CSPD, 1696*, 311 ('St Cross' must be a mistake for 'St Mary Magdalen', for there was no major fair at St Cross and the note was written just after the date of the Magdalen Hill fair); HRO, WCA, Proceedings in Quarter Sessions 1660–1716, August 1713.
164 HRO, WCA, 37/P/Ts 2 (many entries are in the form 'Mr Thos Bates for his house & shops', with no indication of their exact number); for shops in the suburbs, see e.g. Winchester Cathedral MSS, Survey of Dean & Chapter Lands 1649, fos. 44–54.
165 HRO, WCA, Proposal Book 1662–1704, f. 52; 7th Book of Ordinances, f. 57v; see also J. Thirsk, *Economic Policy and Projects* (1978), 122–4.
166 PRO, W.O. 30/48, 159–67.
167 W. A. Speck, *Tory and Whig* (1970), 129.
168 HRO, WCA, 37/P/Ts 2.
169 *The Black Book of Winchester*, 157.
170 HRO, WCA, 6th Book of Ordinances, f.106; Proposal Book 1662–1704, f. 52; Town Court Roll 58/Bk. 1593–1631, f.202; BL, Harleian MS 5121, f. 18 (Peter Clark kindly drew my attention to this manuscript).
171 *CSPD, 1665–6*, 35; anon., *The History and Antiquities of Winchester*, II (1773), 206–7.
172 J. R. Western, *The English Militia in the Eighteenth Century* (1965), 397 quotes an officer's description of a 'brilliant social gathering' at Winchester in 1760.
173 Milner, *op. cit.*, I, 450.
174 Blome, *op. cit.*, 110; Defoe, *op. cit.*, I, 289–90.
175 Defoe, *op cit.*, 180–1; HMC, Portland MSS, VI, 172.
176 J. L. Wetton (ed.), *The Hampshire Seventeenth-Century Traders' Tokens* (1964); T. S. Willan, *The Inland Trade* (1976), 83–9. Tokens issued by town authorities have been omitted from this count.
177 The wide range of urban growth-rates in Hampshire does not support Dyer's argument that 'after 1560 . . . the majority of all sizes and types [of towns] grow at roughly the same rate as the countryside in which they are set . . . until 1700 at least': A. Dyer, 'Growth and decay in English towns 1500–1700', *Urban History Yearbook* (1979), 69. Norfolk and Suffolk towns showed a similar variety of growth-rates: J. Patten, *English Towns 1500–1700* (1978), 251.
178 *VCH Hants.*, III, 111; Defoe, *op. cit.*, 142, 146; J. J. Cartwright (ed.), *The Travels through England of Dr Richard Pococke*, II (Camden Soc., 2nd ser. XLIV, 1889), 164–5; Blome, *op. cit.*, 108–10, lists Havant as a disused market and fails to mention Bishop's Waltham or Fareham.
179 Defoe, *op. cit.*, 141.
180 HRO, WCA, Town Court Roll 58/Bk. 1671–94 (1692, presentments before clerk of the market).

181 R. M. Smith, 'Population and its geography in England 1500–1730', in *An Historical Geography of England and Wales*, ed. R. A. Dodgshon and R. A. Butlin (1978), 228–9, summarizes work on Norfolk, Suffolk, Hertfordshire, and Leicestershire.

182 This account of agricultural change is based on E. L. Jones, 'Eighteenth-century changes in Hampshire chalkland farming', *AgHR*, VIII (1960), 5–8; E. L. Jones (ed.), *Agriculture and Economic Growth in England 1650–1815* (1967), 9–10, 20, 36–8, 154–68; Thirsk, *Economic Policy*, 161–3.

183 N. Pevsner and D. Lloyd, *Hampshire and the Isle of Wight* (1967), lists more than 50 surviving country houses in Hampshire built in the late seventeenth and early eighteenth centuries, and many older houses which were remodelled in the same period.

184 HRO, WCA, 6th Book of Ordinances, fos. 3, 76, 109v; 7th Book of Ordinances, fos. 76, 81.

185 HRO, WCA, 31/Bx./Q.S. 2; Payments into Coffer 1660–1711, 9 May 1673, 2 Sept. 1697; Proposal Book 1662–1704, f. 9v; 6th Book of Ordinances, f. 37v.

186 HRO, WCA, Proceedings in Quarter Sessions 1660–1716, Dec. 1693, Dec. 1694; PRO, C9/136/64; C. Gross, *The Gild Merchant*, II (1890), 268–70.

187 P. Borsay, 'The English urban renaissance: the development of provincial urban culture c.1680–c.1760', *Social History*, II (1977), 581–603. The growth of a social centre for a larger region is treated by P. Corfield, 'A provincial capital in the late 17th century: the case of Norwich', in Clark and Slack (eds.), *op cit.*, 263–310.

188 For a discussion of the 'country *v.* city' theme in drama, see D. Bruce, *Topics of Restoration Comedy* (1974), 63–71. Provincial social centres were mocked as mercilessly as the countryside, notably by Thomas Shadwell in *Bury Fair* (1689).

189 Defoe, *op. cit.*, I, 186.

190 J. Macky, *A Journey through England*, II (1722), 32–3; HMC, 7th Report, 420; Cartwright, *op. cit.*, II, 114–15, 242; Patterson, *op. cit.*, I, 39–44.

191 F. J. Baigent and J. E. Millard, *A History of Basingstoke* (1889), 566.

192 HRO, WCA, W. H. Jacob, 'A Retrospect of Civic Manners and Customs' (scrapbook), 46.

193 Humphrey Bowry, bookseller (fl.1664–7): HRO, WCA, 6th Book of Ordinances, f. 20v; William Taylor, grocer (fl.1655–87): H. R. Plomer, *A Dictionary of Printers and Booksellers . . . 1641–67* (1907), 175; William Clarke, bookseller/stationer (fl.1679–1707): Plomer, *Dictionary of Printers and Booksellers . . . 1668–1725* (1922), 72; HRO, WCA, Payments out of Coffer 1660–99, 8 Jan. 1699/1700; HRO, wills A 1707.

194 HRO, WCA, 1st Book of Ordinances, f. 211; 6th Book of Ordinances, f. 76v.

195 E.g. PRO, C5/366/32; C6/229/92; C7/410/61.

196 HRO, B/2/A, Visitation 1725, fos. 370–2v; Kirby, *op. cit.*, 122, 128; C. W. Bingham (ed.), *Private Memoirs of John Potenger Esq.* (1841), 23–5; Macky, *op. cit.*, 20.

197 Macky, *op. cit.*, 14; Defoe, *op cit.*, I, 186.

198 Cf. the role played by administrative officials in modern third-world societies: J. C. Jackson, 'The structure and function of small Malaysian towns', *Trans. Inst. British Geographers*, LXI (1974), 70.

199 For Statute Merchant jurisdiction, see the Introduction to H. Hall (ed.), *Select Cases concerning the Law Merchant*, III (Selden Soc., XLIX, 1932), especially xxiv–xxvii; cf. money-lending at York: D. M. Palliser, 'A crisis in English towns?: the case of York, 1460–1640', *Northern History*, XIV (1978), 121.

200 B. A. Holderness, 'Credit in a rural community, 1660–1800', *Midland History*, III (1975), 109–10.

201 *Ibid.*, 100–1; B. A. Holderness, 'Credit in English rural society before the 19th century', *AgHR*, XXIV (1976), 105.

202 PRO, C6/229/92.

203 Macky, *op. cit.*, 41–2; on towns as marriage markets, see also Borsay, *op. cit.*, 595–6.

204 Macky, *op. cit.*, 41.

205 A. C. F. Beales, *Education under Penalty* (1963), 217–22.
206 Macky, *op. cit.*, 29; Kitchin, *op. cit.*, 208.
207 R. E. Scantlebury (ed.), *Hampshire Registers*, I (Catholic Record Soc., XLII, 1942–3), 146–9; HRO, St Thomas, Winchester, parish reg. Book 2.
208 Macky, *op. cit.*, 41.
209 HRO, WCA, 5th Ledger Book, fos. 47, 129, 341v; 6th Ledger Book, f.150v; BL, Harleian MS 5121, f.18, shows a compounder for the excise on coffee at Winchester.
210 Macky, *op. cit.*, 29–30.
211 Hore, *op. cit.*, III, 110, 133–4.
212 HRO, WCA, 6th Book of Ordinances, f.138v; *London Gazette*, 31 July 1682.
213 N. Luttrell, *A Brief Historical Relation of State Affairs*, I (1857), 215; E. M. Thompson (ed.), *Correspondence of the Family of Hatton*, II (Camden Soc., 2nd ser., XXIII, 1878), 18.
214 HRO, WCA, Coffer Accounts 1628–61, 2 May 1656; 6th Book of Ordinances, fos. 96v, 152, 154–5; 5th Ledger Book, fos. 334, 370.
215 HRO, WCA, Book of Orders 1665, f. 115; 5th Ledger Book, fos. 389–9v.
216 This account of the King's House is based on PRO, E351/3460; H. H. Colvin (ed.), *History of the King's Works*, V (1976), 304–13; A. T. Bolton and H. D. Hendry (eds.), *The Royal Palaces of Winchester, Whitehall, etc.* (Wren Soc., VII, 1930), 11–69.
217 Colvin, *op. cit.* V, 311–12; Bolton and Hendry, *op. cit.*, 43–9; *Calendar of Treasury Books*, VII, 1070; *ibid.*, IX, 1365, 1625, 1693.
218 HRO, WCA, Town Court Roll 58/Bk. 1684–5.
219 *Ibid.*, 58/Bk. 1682–4; *CSPD, 1685*, no. 392.
220 PRO, C9/101/88; E179/247/30; *VCH Hants.*, V (1912), 5; Macky, *op. cit.*, 25; B. B. Woodward, *A General History of Hampshire*, I (1861), 21 n.10; T. D. Atkinson, *A Survey of the Street Architecture of Winchester* (1934), 7.
221 PRO, E179/176/565; HRO, WCA, 37/P/Ts 2 (neither of these figures includes the large houses in the Close); Macky, *op. cit.*, 13.
222 For the rebuilding of the Close see Stephens and Madge, *op. cit.*, 135–9, 142–52, 158–70.
223 Bodl., MS Tanner 140, fos. 40, 50; BL, Stowe MS 541, fos.136–9v; A. K. Cook, *About Winchester College* (1917), 226–35.
224 BL, Harleian MS 5121, f.18; PRO, Prob.11/377 (PCC 134 Hare, will of Bishop Morley); Woodward, *op. cit.*, 93. Macky and later writers attribute the bishop's palace to Wren, but there is no contemporary evidence of his involvement.
225 *CSPD, 1670*, 138; *1689–90*, 274–5; HRO, WCA, 5th Ledger Book, f. 357.
226 *CSPD, 1685*, nos. 366, 392, 394; *1687–9*, no. 1407; HRO, WCA, Payments out of Coffer 1660–99, 18 Aug. 1676, 20 Nov. 1682, 10 Jan. 1683/4.
227 HRO, WCA, 7th Book of Ordinances, fos. 47v–8v; *Commons J.*, x, 354, 447.
228 HRO, WCA, Trussell, 'Touchstone of Tradition', f.154.
229 P. Clark and P. Slack, *English Towns in Transition 1500–1700* (1976), 31–2, 104–5; Patten, *op cit.*, 288–92.

Bath: the rise of a resort town, 1660–1800

SYLVIA MCINTYRE

Bath: the rise of
a resort town, 1660–1800

SYLVIA MCINTYRE

1 Introduction

This study is based on a doctoral thesis entitled 'Towns as health and pleasure resorts: Bath, Scarborough and Weymouth, 1700–1815', which was accepted by the University of Oxford in 1973. The original research project was an examination of three important watering places over the eighteenth century and the first years of the nineteenth. Interest in this period, which was characterized by a remarkable growth of towns, is often focussed on the great industrial and commercial centres, but the emergence and spread of the watering places, towns specifically devoted to catering for the seekers for health and pleasure, was another striking feature of the time: the eighteenth century is sometimes described as 'the age of watering places', and by the mid-nineteenth century, according to the census, their rate of growth was the highest for all types of towns. It seemed, therefore, worthwhile to look in detail at several watering places over the years when the existence of resort towns was becoming firmly established.

The towns selected for the thesis were Bath, the archetypal English spa; Scarborough, the spa which became one of the first, if not the first, seaside resort; and Weymouth, a minor port rescued from insignificance by the fashion for sea bathing. All were old chartered boroughs, governed by municipal corporations, and the thesis considered not only the economic and social factors behind the growth of the watering places, but also the ways in which the old corporations met the new challenges to local government imposed by the expansion of the towns. These challenges could be more acute for watering places than for towns of a similar size, since they had to meet not only the demands of their own inhabitants but also the requirements of an elite drawn from all over the British Isles, and one with rising standards of expectation as to the amenities of the social centres which they frequented.

The present study is a remodelling and, in some respects, an expansion of most of the section on Bath in the thesis. It examines the establishment of Bath as a spa in the late seventeenth century, and the growth and evolution of the town throughout the

198

eighteenth century, and attempts to assess the various factors which encouraged the fashion for the watering place. The growth of the watering place has not been treated in isolation, but related to the development of the town as a whole. Special attention has been paid to the activities of the townsfolk, rather than to the social life of the visitors, which has been described often enough. The occupational structure and economic life of the inhabitants has been examined as closely as the sources permit, as has the participation in the development of the town of the municipal corporation, both as owner of most of the property within the old town, including the baths and pump rooms, and as the major instrument of local government within the built-up area. In particular, it has been argued that, for the last half of the eighteenth century at least, the role of the corporation in the building (and in the centre of town the rebuilding) of Bath was far more important than is usually supposed. At the same time the corporation proved very active by eighteenth-century standards (and some nineteenth-century ones) in governing the town. The city of Bath was not only the leading watering place of eighteenth-century Britain, but also a pioneer in the acquisition of local Acts of Parliament for paving, policing and lighting the streets and public places of the town, and in providing the services required by the growing town.

2   The emergence of the spa

The history of the English watering place can be traced back to the Romans and, in local cults and holy wells, through the Middle Ages. After the Reformation, the established religion was hostile to such cults, but the sixteenth century also saw a revival of Greek and Roman doctrines on the value of mineral waters which offered a medical rather than a religious reason for using them. The first book to discuss English mineral waters was that of William Turner in 1562: he mentioned only Bath, but by 1572 John Jones had produced books on both Bath and Buxton. The Elizabethan poor law of that year also referred to the number of sick poor which resorted to those two towns. By the early seventeenth century, the search for mineral springs was well under way, so that by 1740 Thomas Short could list at least 225 spas (the name came from the 'German Spaw' near Liège), and new ones continued to be discovered and old ones rediscovered every year.[1]

The spas were perhaps always more than health resorts, and certainly more by the late seventeenth century. Even if only the sick had come, there were many who needed to be amused during intervals of treatment, and the doctors themselves prescribed diversions to ward off melancholy and provide exercise. The spas were sufficiently concerned with health to survive the Civil War and the Protectorate, though the government watched them for possible royalist conspiracies. After the Restoration, their role as pleasure as well as health resorts become increasingly important, especially when visits by different members of the royal family made them centres of fashionable pastimes, such as gambling. Medical theories were thus only one factor involved in the growth of the spas. It would, however, be a mistake to ignore them. The cure remained the excuse and, given the prevalence of disease, the reason for many visits. Fashion determined many aspects of the spas, but it was often medical fashion, as we can see in the eighteenth century change from the inland spas to the seaside resorts.

Nonetheless, the existence of mineral waters, however well 'puffed' by the doctors, did not automatically produce a prosperous resort. There were many factors which decided which places flourished and which declined after the first enthusiasm, to leave behind a pump house or a few street names. Of these, one of the most important was the location of the springs with regard to centres of population. London was the most important, but the neighbourhood of other large towns might compensate somewhat for distance from the metropolis: Lancashire and Yorkshire towns supplied visitors to the northern spas, Bristol to the southern and western. The relationship between distance from such centres and success was not a simple one. The spas near to London flourished first, but the closest proved too accessible to all and sundry, and became unfashionable. Improvements in transport over the eighteenth century tended to deprive smaller wells of their local monopoly while they benefited more fashionable ones. But though such improvements could be vitally important to a growing spa, the visitor in the late seventeenth and eighteenth centuries, who usually came for a month or more, would, if sufficiently wealthy to afford comparatively easy travel and if not seriously ill, be less concerned with a few extra miles than the week-enders or day trippers of the nineteenth century would be. Scarborough, 214 miles from London by the Humber ferry and 235 miles by the more common route through York, was too far from London to attract a national following, though during a brief period in the 1730s it drew members of the 'nobility' and 'gentry' from all over England: Bath, between 105 and 108 miles from London, according to the road, was close enough for its advantages to make it a national centre for the upper classes.

Besides access from London or other towns, the would-be spa needed an attractive setting and scope for the walks and rides which formed a part of resort life. The previous existence of a town was not essential, but was useful in offering inns and lodgings to the visitors. Given such advantage and, perhaps, a royal visit, local initiative and willingness to invest in the necessary amenities counted for much, especially in the early years, before the possible rewards for speculators were clearly revealed.

The emergence of the spas as pleasure resorts was not an isolated occurrence. In the late seventeenth century many English towns were becoming social centres for the local gentry and the 'middling' classes: county towns, cathedral towns, provincial capitals such as York, and even some industrial towns, produced assembly rooms and theatres, coffee houses and libraries, elegant streets, squares and crescents, to such an extent that the whole development has been described as an 'urban renaissance'.[2] The reasons for such an urban efflorescence are many and complicated, but it reveals the existence of a comparatively large and growing body of people with money enough to allow them long periods of leisure and indulgence in the amenities offered by the towns – prosperous gentry, substantial merchants, colonial officials and, in the later eighteenth century, manufacturers. The spas differed from other such urban centres in that they catered primarily for those who had little else to do than to amuse themselves, and who had little connection with the town itself except as a place of amusement: the provision of the various amenities was the main reason for their existence.

All these amenities were, of course, designed for those who could pay. The sick who came were, however, poor as well as wealthy. Townsfolk regarded the poor as a nuisance: even if they were really ill and not healthy beggars, the sight of them might drive away the wealthy, who were much less embarrassed then than now about expressing their true feelings on these matters. From our point of view, the poor have another disadvantage, that they appear much less frequently in the records.

But they did come, in considerable numbers, sometimes sent by their parishes, sometimes on their own, and had to be dealt with. The Bath Hospital, set up in 1738, appealed to the charitable, but it was also regarded as a means of distinguishing deserving poor from beggars, while at Buxton, the company were expected to make a small contribution to the support of poorer visitors. Nonetheless, while the history of the poor at the spas is part of the history of medical care, they had comparatively little effect on the eighteenth-century watering places themselves. It was the attraction to the prosperous of the union of medical theory with the search for amusement which caused old towns to expand and new towns to emerge, and thereby left a permanent mark on the map of England.

Without doubt, the most successful English spa was the Somerset town of Bath. The small borough of the 1660s blossomed into the pleasure capital of Georgian England, rivalling London in its attractions for the well-born and the wealthy: the population increased over tenfold by 1801, while the old city was cased in a shell of new development. Even by 1660, Bath was already becoming dependent on the visitors who came for health or pleasure. In the Middle Ages, the city was both an ecclesiastical centre and the home of a prosperous textile industry, though Leland noticed in the 1530 that it 'hath somewhat decayed'.[3] The abbey disappeared at the Reformation, though the great church remained, and the manufacture of woollen cloth declined in the late sixteenth and early seventeenth centuries with the general contraction of the cloth trade in the area. In 1622 the mayor complained: 'we are a very little poor City, our Clothmen much decayed, and many of their workmen amongst us relieved by the City.'[4] The town also suffered during the Civil War, not so much from siege as from the repeated demands of different armies for money, provisions and quartering.

A declining cloth trade was by no means peculiar to Bath in those years. The city's industry did not, however, benefit from the revival which followed the Restoration, and brought a sedate prosperity to nearby towns such as Bradford-on-Avon and Frome. Bath had no lack of water power: several mills, including at least one fulling mill, had been inherited by the corporation from the abbey. Neighbouring parishes, especially Lyncombe and Widcombe to the south, flourished by the production of wool cloth. The continued decline of the textile industry within the city limits of Bath is said to have been encouraged by the freemen's monopoly of trade within those limits and the regulations enforced by their companies. The unfree weavers could cross the river to the south, as did the tailors later, in which case the very attempts of the corporation to defend the freemen's rights contributed to the decline it was intended to prevent. Whether this in fact occurred is not clear: it was said that at the Restoration there were 60 broad looms in the parish of St Michael, outside the walls but within the city limits, and an equal number proportionately within the walls,[5] while Joseph Gilmore's map of Bath in 1692 shows the 'tenter' racks outside the walls. If the Bathonians did not take advantage of the revival of the region's cloth trade, it may not have been because they could not do so, but because they had an attractive alternative not open to the inhabitants of Bradford and Frome. Bath did not need to compete with the West Country cloth towns or the growing mercantile power of Bristol when the town could flourish by specializing as a centre for health and leisure. By the late seventeenth century, the city of Bath, after a period of uncertainty, had changed its role from a manufacturing centre to a watering place, the first such transformation in Britain.

The ability of Bath to change its role rested on the possession of the springs of hot water. These hot waters were used in Roman times, and attracted invalids through-out the Middle Ages, but the visitors were of little demonstrable economic import-ance to the medieval town. The sixteenth- and seventeenth-century interest in the curative properties of mineral waters encouraged more visitors to try the springs at a time when the decline in the cloth trade made their presence more than ever welcome: Sir John Harington remarked in the 1590s that the place was 'resorted unto so greatly (being at two times of the year, as it were, the pilgrimage of health to all saints)'.[6] The general revival of interest in mineral waters was not solely to Bath's advantage. The discovery over the next two centuries of a multitude of springs, all more or less foul-tasting, all with medicinal properties, and all potential rivals to the Bath waters, destroyed Bath's sixteenth-century position as the possessor of one of the only two English mineral waters of any note. Nonetheless, the baths of Bath were unique in the British Isles for heat and volume. They continued to attract the sick even when, from the late sixteenth century on, many doctors became enthusi-astic about drinking rather than bathing, which might make hot waters less desir-able. The warm water of Bath (and Buxton) came to be drunk as a preparation for bathing as well as on its own. The growth in the seventeenth century of the practice of cold bathing was another threat. By the opening of the eighteenth century, when Sir John Floyer published his history of cold bathing, the practice was so popular that Dr Thomas Guidott had to defend the hot baths of Bath.[7] Guidott, who practised at Bath, had good reason to do so. The baths had become more important than the looms: by the 1680s Celia Fiennes noticed that 'the town and all its accommodations is adapted to the bathing and drinking of the waters and nothing else.'[8]

Bath's medical defenders proved adequate to their task, and the hot waters contin-ued to draw the sick. The prosperous watering place needed also to attract the healthy in search of pleasure, and in attaining this goal, Bath benefited greatly from royal visits, from those of Queen Elizabeth in 1574 and 1591, to the early Stuart kings in 1613, 1615, 1628 and 1634; after the Restoration, Charles II's queen came in 1663, Mary of Modena in 1687, and Princess Anne in 1692 and, after she had become queen, in 1702 and 1703. The value of such visits to the tourist industry was recog-nized by the inhabitants of Bath, who tried with celebrations and civic improvements to encourage their royal guests to return. Where the court went, there went the courtiers, giving 'the Bath' an air of fashion which remained after the royal visitors and the crowds they attracted had left.

Visits from even kings and queens would not have sufficed, however, without other attractions for fashionable visitors. Our impression of Bath in the late seven-teenth century is obscured by the tendency of later writers to disparage the past in order to praise the present. Bath is described as having been small, poor, dirty, with inadequate lodgings, even its baths neglected until, under the spell of Beau Nash and John Wood, it blossomed into the elegant centre of pleasure as well as healing. There is no doubt that the eighteenth century transformed Bath, but if the situation in the late seventeenth century was as bad as sometimes said, it is surprising that visi-tors should have come at all.

'The City of Bath', wrote Leland, 'is set both in a fruitful and pleasant bottom, the which is environed on every side with great hills.'[9] The hills edged the valley of the Avon, which looped around the town from north-east to south-west. The town was on the Fosse Way which, after running through it, crossed the river to the south. The old town was surrounded by walls, and continued occupation had raised the level within them: 'for walking around the walls', wrote Henry Chapman in 1673, 'it is perceivable the city stands on a batch (as we call it) in the bottom from 15 to 20 foot higher than the surface without'.[10] The elevation was useful, for the river at times flooded the meadows outside the walls. The enclosed area was not large – Chapman estimated the compass at not a full English mile – and the city had begun to spread beyond the walls to the north and south along the road through the town; but in 1673 the total area was thought to amount only to about 50 acres.[11] The focus of the city's life remained within the walls, which enclosed the springs of hot water, the abbey church, the guildhall, and the market place.

The population of the city was also small. The Hearth Tax records are incomplete for Bath, but indicate for 1664 a minimum of 335 households, including 40 in the parish of Walcot, part of which was contained within the city boundaries. This suggests a population of between 1,400 and 2,000, plus the streets for which the records have been lost, which might raise the total by 100 or so.[12] Modern estimates speak of a population of between 2,000 and 3,000 at the turn of the century, apparently only by extrapolation from the Hearth Tax: the last figure is certainly a maximum for that time.

Some aspects of Bath's specialization as a resort may be seen from the Hearth Tax of 1664 (table 15). The city had the comparatively high ratio of 4.04 per household (or rather householder), 4.36 if one excludes the virtually rural parish of Walcot.[13]

Table 15   Hearth tax, 1664

A   Overall pattern

	households	hearths	estimated population (4.2 to 6 per household)
Bath city	296*	1292	1243 – 1776
Walcot	39	66	164 – 234
	335	1358	1407 – 2010
Bathwick	12	40	50 – 72
Lyncombe and Widcombe	42	133	176 – 252

B   Averages of hearths per household by location

	%
Bath city	4.36
High Street*	2.86
Northgate Street	3.85
Cheap Street	4.63
Westgate Street	4.71
Stall Street	4.8
'Bimbury' (south-west corner)	7.96
Southgate Street	2.23
Walcot	1.69
Bathwick	3.33
Lyncombe and Widcombe	3.17

Source: PRO, E179/256/16.

*The High Street section is damaged: the surviving portion for Bath city contains 285 households plus 33 hearths which, on the density of the High Street, yields 11 more households.

Moreover, many householders paid for a large number of hearths, 18 paying for 10–29 hearths and three for 30–7. Possibly some paid for several houses, but many of these substantial taxpayers are known to be the owners of lodging houses and inns: Henry Chapman paid tax on 19 hearths in one house and the Red Lion; Berkeley Carne, who paid for 37 hearths, leased a private 'bath door' from his lodging house into the King's Bath; while John Masters, who paid for 30, was probably the master of the White Hart Inn in Stall Street. Significant too is the presence of three 'Doctors of Physick' who paid for a total of 24 hearths, since the medical faculty of Bath often kept lodging houses for their patients.

These were the inns and lodgings described with such contempt in the eighteenth century. The inhabitants of the town thought differently at the time. As early as 1628, Dr Thomas Venner wrote proudly about convenient lodgings around the baths, and by 1673, Henry Chapman, a member of the corporation and probably the owner of the houses with the 19 hearths, boasted of 'such noble buildings of reception, that they appear (in respect of other places so remote from the metropolis) rather petty palaces than common lodgings.'[14] Even John Wood, despite his derogatory comparison between lodgings before 1720 and in the 1740s, admitted that improvements had been made by the turn of the century.[15] Joseph Gilmore's map, taken in 1692 and published in 1694, is decorated around the border with illustrations not only of the churches and public buildings, but also of the inns and lodgings which the citizens obviously felt were equally worthy of notice: these lack the uniformity beloved of Georgian architects, but are proud examples of pre-eighteenth-century urban buildings. Given their different points of view, the visitors' descriptions suggest that lodgings at Bath were not contemptible by contemporary standards.[16] Nor were public amenities entirely neglected. Speed's map of about 1610 shows the presence of a tennis court, and by 1700 the city also had gravel walks, bowling greens and coffee houses. If 'the Company' (the term used for the prosperous visitors) had often to entertain itself outside, even to dancing on the green, the same was true of other spas, and at Bath there was the guildhall which by the 1700s was used for balls. The streets were cramped and narrow, the city small. Nonetheless, the expansion of Bath in the eighteenth century followed upon the developments of the seventeenth century, and did not spring fully grown from the head of any one man or group of men.

3 The growth of the town

The credit for the development of Bath as a resort in the eighteenth century is often attributed to one man, 'Beau Nash', master of ceremonies from 1705 until his death in 1761. It is not surprising that legends gathered around his flamboyant figure. Contemporaries and historians tend to attribute to his influence most if not all of the improvements which followed his appointment (by the corporation, it is usually said), including the building of the pump room and the promotion of local Improvement Acts: he is seen as dominating the town and the town government as well as the Company.[17] In fact, there is little evidence for this view of Nash's importance and much against it. The corporation magistrates who organized the celebrations for the visits of Queen Anne in 1702 and 1703 may have appointed Captain Webster, Nash's predecessor, and it is not impossible that they appointed Nash after Webster's death in a duel, but neither is mentioned in the corporation minutes, which would suggest that the appointment, if any, was of a casual nature. It is equally possible that Nash was chosen as master of ceremonies by the Company, as his successors certainly

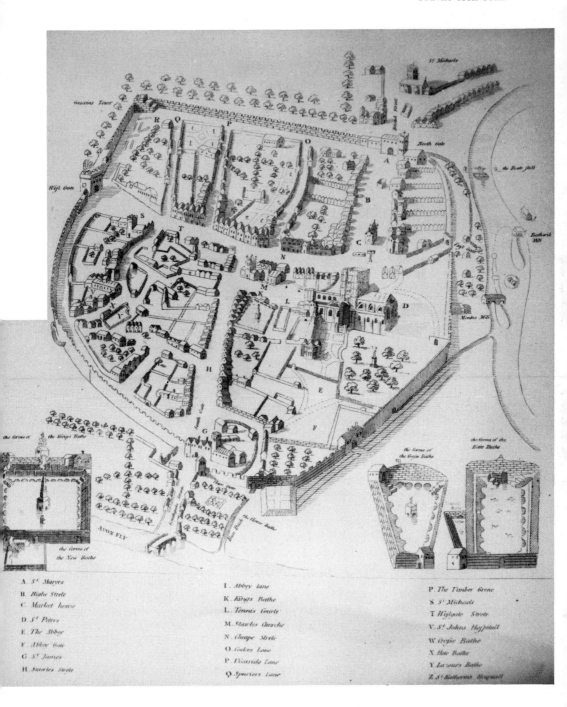

A. St Maryes
B. Highe Strete
C. Market house
D. St Peters
E. The Abbey
F. Abbey Gate
G. St James
H. Stawles Strete

I. Abbey lane
K. Kings Bathe
L. Tennus Courte
M. Stawles Churche
N. Cheape Strete
O. Cockes Lane
P. Vicards Lane
Q. Spurrers Lane

P. The Timber Grene
S. St Michaels
T. Highgate Strete
V. St Johns Hospitall
W. Grype Bathe
X. Hote Bathe
Y. La sours Bathe
Z. St Katherins Hospitall

Figure 17. Bath in the early seventeenth century (John Speed's map in *The Theatre of the Empire of Great Britain*, 1611, from R. Warner, *The History of Bath*, 1801).

were: John Wood the elder, who was resident in Bath after 1727, wrote in 1749 that the corporation 'out of high Respect to the Company resorting to the city, have not as yet attempted to make any by-laws for the better government of them.'[18] The pump room was begun by the corporation before Nash took office, persuaded, Wood thought, by the physicians of Bath, especially Dr William Oliver. Nor did Nash, as is often said, rent the pump room or appoint the pumper, whose office dated from at least 1683. It is more difficult to gauge his influence in obtaining the city Acts or other improvements over these years, but it is unlikely that a newcomer would immediately acquire authority. Nash first appears in the corporation minutes on 1 October 1716, when he was made an honorary freeman of the city, a date which probably indicates when the corporation began to consider him of importance in the town. The city government would have shown Nash, the representative of the Company, a certain deference at the height of his prosperity, and they granted him a pension at the end, but he was never dictator of the city or inhabitants of Bath.

This is not to argue that Beau Nash's reign was of no significance in promoting Bath as a fashionable watering place. In the seventeenth century, the 'master of ceremonies' was governor of court entertainments, and it was apparently in this role that Webster, at least, was appointed. The transformation of the post into the supervisor of entertainments patronized by visitors at the spas occurred first at Bath, in the person of Nash who, with his strong personality, became the master of ceremonies *par excellence*, the standard by which all others were judged. Such an officer, intended to maintain a high degree of formal organization in the social life of the spas, seemed especially necessary at places where society consisted of people unknown to each other and no longer bound by the ties which would have existed in towns where they lived and were known. It was not for nothing that the watering places were, throughout the century, pictured as the haunts of adventurers.

Nash also encouraged certain improvements to the town, though not the number with which he is usually credited. His subscription for 'the musick' in the pump room and his support for speculative ventures such as assembly rooms benefited the resort. The very gambling which Nash encouraged and by which he was supported was, in the early years at least, an attraction to many visitors, especially the aristocracy. Nonetheless, he was as much the creature as the creator of fashionable Bath.

Nash's reign covered Bath's heyday as an aristocratic resort, but only the beginnings of the physical transformation which created one of the most beautiful towns of Europe. Early improvements were on a small scale. Two assembly houses were built on the Terrace Walk, Harrison's Rooms (later the Lower Rooms) overlooking Harrison's Walks in 1706, and Lindsey's Rooms (later Wiltshire's Rooms) in 1728. A theatre was built about 1705 on the site of the Royal Mineral Water Hospital; when the building was replaced by the Hospital in 1738, dramatic performances continued in the Lower Rooms and rooms at various inns, until the building of a theatre in Orchard Street in 1750.[19] The walks near the Abbey were improved by the corporation, while in 1742 the Spring Gardens were opened across the river in Bathwick, providing yet another place of fashionable resort. Meanwhile lodging houses and inns were built and rebuilt, and standards of furnishings raised.

The baths themselves remained much as they were in the seventeenth century, three sets of hot springs feeding five baths, the King's Bath and the Queen's Bath near the Abbey, the Hot Bath, the Lepers' Bath and the Cross Bath to the southwest of the walled town. They were hemmed in by houses and inns, many of which either had doors opening into the baths or steps which allowed direct access to them.

All the baths were uncovered, so that spectators could watch the bathers from the galleries. There was, however, some shelter around the cross of the Cross Bath, or under 'the Kitchen', a wooden structure over the hottest springs in the centre of the King's Bath. The bathers might also sit out of sight on niches hollowed out of the walls, or be supported by rings around the sides, which were donated by grateful patients. The baths were entered by 'slips', covered passages where the bathers undressed and left their clothes: some, according to Celia Fiennes, had fireplaces. The baths were supervised by the corporation's two serjeants-at-mace, and patients were assisted in the waters by a number of 'bath guides', both male and female.[20]

These bathing facilities were not greatly altered until the latter part of the eighteenth century. Changes were, however, made in the methods of obtaining water for those who wished to drink. In the sixteenth century, the water was ladled out of the full cisterns in the morning before the bathers arrived, so that fresh Bath water could only be drunk once a day, whatever the doctors prescribed. By 1590, there was a 'device' erected whereby water might be obtained directly from the springs, but there was no means by which water could be easily obtained for those who drank without bathing. Pumps were introduced in the early seventeenth century, originally as an improvement on 'bucketing', the pouring of water directly on the affected part of the body: they came to be used not only to pour water on diseased heads and limbs, but also to supply those who followed the new fashion for drinking the waters. In 1673, special drinking pumps were added to the 'dry pumps' (those installed out of the baths) of the Queen's and Hot Baths.[21]

Figure 18. Rowlandson's 'The Comforts of Bath': the King's Bath in the late eighteenth century.

How successful the conduits and pumps were in supplying unpolluted water we cannot say: from Dr Jorden in 1631 to Smollett's Matthew Bramble in 1771, conscientious doctors and fastidious visitors had doubts. Most visitors were less squeamish, and drinking the waters was, by the late seventeenth century, more fashionable than bathing, especially for those whose visit was only remotely connected with reasons of health. The problem became one of supplying enough water and a place to drink it. Except for private houses around the baths, the Company had to drink in the open. The lack of facilities was disadvantageous to the city as well as the visitors, since it restricted the length of the season. Even Dr Oliver who, in 1705, argued that the hot waters might be drunk all year round, agreed that lack of shelter near the baths exposed those who drank them in winter to the danger of catching cold, 'one of the worst accidents that can happen to anybody in the course of drinking Bath waters'.[22] Aroused by Oliver's pamphlet and with the practical assistance of £100 from Dr Bettenson, another local physician, the corporation decided in 1705 to build a pump room on the north side of the King's Bath.[23] The room, finished in 1706, was a simple one-storied building: although Wood criticized it in 1749, it was at the time of its erection a considerable improvement on the facilities for drinking the waters and was not, in fact, replaced until the 1750s. The improvement made the post of pumper more valuable to the person appointed and to the corporation which appointed him.

One result of these changes to the town and its facilities, small as they were compared to those of the last part of the century, was the extension of the season. Originally the season had been a comparatively short one during the summer: in 1676 *Poor Robin's Intelligence* spoke of the state of Bath, 'where all the people live all the winter (like Nightingales) upon the stock of their summer fat'.[24] Gradually the summer season became two short seasons in autumn and spring, which expanded until, in 1762, the master of ceremonies estimated that it amounted to six full months: according to the Bath guides from 1780 on, the expensive season for Bath lodgings lasted for nine months from September to May. These tendencies were encouraged by the improvement in lodgings and public buildings, which made it more comfortable to take the waters during the winter months, so much so that in 1739 Alexander Pope drank Bristol Hotwell water in Bath, because he wanted the comforts available there in winter.[25]

It is difficult to know how many visitors actually came. A common estimate in the early eighteenth century was 8,000 at a season, while Wood recorded in 1749 that 'common fame' put the numbers which could be accommodated at once at 12,000. From its origins in 1744 the *Bath Journal* included a list of the Company who came to Bath, and though the increase in numbers results partly from increased efficiency by the paper (at least at first), it gives some idea of the number of persons of sufficient distinction to be mentioned: these rise from 510 in 1746 to 2,525 in 1760, 3,091 in 1780 and 5,341 in 1800.[26] Bath was always subject to the seasonal changes typical of a resort, but as the season became longer and the number of visitors larger, lodgings and shops were increasingly able to repay the money spent on them, and to encourage speculators to risk building more.

Improvements in transport helped to lay the foundations for the expansion of the town. The distance between Bath and London, about 107 miles, was a disadvantage to the resort, the more so as the countryside immediately around Bath was not renowned for its good roads. As Celia Fiennes remarked, 'the ways to the Bath are all difficult, the town lies low in a bottom and its steep ascents all ways out of the town'.[27] It is not surprising that attempts to mend the roads near the town began early. As Wood wrote,

> How material it was for the welfare of Bath, as well as for the country all around it, to have a good access to the city, may be conceived from the great subscription that was made in the Year 1706 for repairing a single Road of a mile in length, *viz* that which makes the ascent to Lansdown; the expence whereof was such a demonstration of the inability of the country to amend all the principal roads leading to the town, that they had just reason to apply to parliament the latter end of the new year, for the assistance of the public, to enable them to carry on a work so great and necessary.[28]

Assistance came in the form of an Act in 1708 which, among other things, set up one of the earliest turnpike trusts in England. Like the Paving Act to which it was attached, the Act dealing with the Bath roads differed from what later became the standard Turnpike Act: control was given not to a group of trustees but to any six justices of the counties of Wiltshire, Somerset and Gloucestershire, and one or more of the justices of Bath. These justices were to repair the roads leading into Bath by means of a toll. The visitors thus paid for the roads, but the city saw to it that those who left for an 'airing' on the downs had their money refunded on return.[29]

The Bath Turnpike Acts covered only short stretches of road about the city. The spa was, however, fortunate in its position near Bristol and the clothmaking areas of the West Country. Of the total 125.5 miles of the road between London and Bristol, 112.5 was turnpiked by 1730, and the whole by 1750, while other trusts took care of the branch to Bath.[30] The existence of turnpike trusts did not automatically produce good roads but, on the whole, their roads were far better than those left to the parishes. The steep hills around Bath continued to cause difficulties, but the increase in the number of coach and wagon services between Bath and London and between Bath and other provincial towns, suggests that communication had improved (table 16). The better roads, coupled with improvements in carriage building, made travel

Table 16   *Transport facilities in Bath, 1684–1800*

A   Number of services from London to Bath: journeys one way per week

1684	1		1765	27	
1740	17	summer	1768	39	
	15	winter	1770	46	
1744	17	summer	1772	46	
	15	winter	1773	42	summer
1749	17	summer		44	winter
	15	winter	1776	45	
1752	20	summer	1777	46	
	18	winter	1781	90	
1755	18	summer	1783	90	
	15	winter	1785	89	
1757	23	summer	1788	101	
	21	winter	1794	154	
1760	24		1800	147	
1763	37				

Source: London guides, 1684–1800. The figures include all forms of transport facilities.

B Number of services from Bath to provincial towns: journeys one way per week

	1755	1762	1770	1780	1790	1800
Birmingham					10	see Liverpool
Bristol	35	49	48	84	157	129
Devizes		1	1	1		
Exeter	2 (s)	3 (2s)	3	20 (7s)	21	7
					plus those to Plymouth & Falmouth	
Falmouth					6	6
Frome	1				3	3
Gloucester				5 (3s)	3 + Birmingham	see Liverpool
Gosport						6
Holyhead						3
Liverpool						3
Oxford	1	½	2 (1s)	2	12	10
Plymouth					8	2
					plus those to Falmouth	
Portsmouth					6	3 + Gosport
Salisbury	4	4	2	4	4	3
					plus those to Portsmouth and Gosport	
Shaftesbury					1	
Shepton Mallet					1	2
Sherborne	1					
Shrewsbury					3	see Holyhead
Southampton				4	see Gosport and Portsmouth	
Taunton						3
Tetbury	1	1	1		1	
Warminster	2	2	2	2		
Weymouth				9 (9s)	4 (3s)	3 (3s)

Source: Bath guides for 1755, 1762, 1770,1780, 1790 and 1800.
('s' indicates the number of journeys taken only in summer.)

much more rapid: the fastest time for the journey from London to Bath was over 60 hours before 1680, 36 hours (28 on the road) in 1750, 24 hours (all on the road) in 1763, and little more than 10 hours by the end of the century.[31] The changes made it easier for invalids and others to come to Bath, though they also reflect the demand by large numbers that they should be able to do so.

The roads brought the visitors, but for the carriage of building materials, food and coal, water transport was far cheaper. Though not itself a port, Bath was joined by the Avon to the great port of Bristol. Once navigable, the river had been blocked by weirs and mills from at least the late thirteenth century,[32] leaving only the steep and rocky roads to carry wool, cloth, and provisions. The advantages of water transport had not escaped the inhabitants of Bath: schemes for making the Avon navigable were produced in the reign of Elizabeth, and by 1619 were taken up by the corporation. A bill was introduced in Parliament in 1699, but despite the corporation's efforts in collecting petitions in its support, it was defeated by the opposition of the proprietors of the land through which it ran, the millowners, the Somerset colliers, and all who feared that improvements in carriage would lead to competition in their local market.[33] It was even argued about 1712 that the interests of the city of Bath itself would be damaged by the navigation, since 'a great concourse of people may very well prejudice the health of the Bath and the accommodation of those who have occasion to make use of their waters'. A great concourse was, however, desired by the inhabitants, and the corporation obtained its Act in that same year. The preamble argued that the navigation

> will be very beneficial to trade, commodious and convenient for the persons of quality and strangers (whose resort thither is the principal support of the said city of Bath), advantagious to the poor, and convenient for the carriage of free-stone, wood, timber and other goods and merchandizes, to and from the said cities and parts adjacent.[34]

Opinion was by that time sufficiently in favour of river improvement to ensure the passage of the Act despite 16 opposing petitions. However the corporation, to whom the Act's powers were delegated, was unable to carry out the plan, either because of continued opposition, or because its revenues were too small to meet the initial cost.[35]

By the 1720s, the popularity of Bath was enough to persuade the inhabitants to risk their money: the first step towards the expansion of the town was the improvement of the river, so that building materials might be brought in. A group of 30 men, headed by the Duke of Beaufort, and including 17 residents of Bath and three of Bristol (of which a number, such as the quarry owners Ralph Allen and Milo Smith, and the Bristol timber merchant John Hobbes, had a direct interest in the navigation), obtained from the corporation the assignment of its powers in 1724.[36]

In December 1727, the first barge moved from Bristol to Bath, while John Wood the elder, attracted by the opportunities created by the opening of the navigation, arrived in Bath in the same year.[37] Being equipped with water transport at a very early stage, the town was less affected by the 'canal mania' of the late eighteenth century. The Kennet & Avon Canal did offer the possibilities of both cheap coal and easy transport of goods to London and, as the network grew, the east and north of England, but its construction was delayed: only in 1800 could one Bath carrier advertise the carriage of goods by those parts of the Kennet & Avon which were completed.[38]

The improvements in transport, the expansion of the season, the fashion for Bath among the aristocracy, followed by gentry and wealthy middle classes, added to the increasing prosperity of the country over the eighteenth century, produced a notable expansion of the resort town. Gilmore's map of 1692 reveals a town much like that shown in Speed's map of c. 1610, still contained in its medieval walls, with a cramped street plan and gardens among the houses. Outside the walls were only two small extensions, one between the Southgate and the bridge, one outside the Northgate. By 1727, a few new streets, such as Green Street and Trim Street, had appeared, but the new town outside the walls really got under way with Strahan's Kingsmead development to the west in 1727, and Wood's Queen's Square to the north-west, begun in 1728 and completed in 1734.

Building projects were laid out and constructed on an entirely new scale, as speculators found or expected them to pay: the expansion was, of course, not continuous, but fluctuated with demand and the effects of wars and economic difficulties. On the east Wood's Parades emerged between the city wall and the river by 1748. Construction slowed in the 1740s, but revived in the mid-1750s; between 1754 and 1758, Wood's Circus rose to the north. The Seven Years War brought delays in construction, but after 1763, Bath was gripped by what Tobias Smollett called 'a rage of building'. By 1774, the Royal Crescent stretched to the west, and below the Crescent Fields, new streets appeared between the lower Bristol road and the river. With the exception of Marlborough Buildings, put up about 1790, further westward expansion was halted by the Freemen's Common,[39] but to the east of Queen's Square, Milsom Street was built after 1763. The river ceased to mark the eastern boundary of the town. Pulteney Bridge was built between 1769 and 1774, the first step in Sir William Pulteney's intended development of his Bathwick estates. The plans were delayed, partly because the corporation stopped the building of the turnpike road from Melksham to Bathwick in 1771 and 1774 on the grounds that it was both unnecessary and would damage the other turnpike trusts,[40] and partly because the property boom was slowing. The outbreak of war put another damper on such projects.

The rest of Bath also felt the effects of war. According to a local surveyor in 1794, 'from the year 1778 to the year 1783 by reason of our dispute with America, our army and navy being then on service, the seasons at Bath were so little frequented that houses in Bath were greatly reduced in value.'[41] A financial crisis added to the builders' difficulties. Once the war was over, the city expanded again, in Bathwick and to the north. Nor were the changes only at the edges of the town. Unlike the seaside resorts, where the attraction was the sea front, the centre of interest at Bath remained in the old town with the baths and pump rooms. This area had, however, become less fashionable as a place to live: a calculation based on the 1789 rate book shows that most of the centre, aside from public buildings, was filled with buildings of low value.[42] It was brought up to the new standards by the corporation: the main streets were widened, the gates taken down with most of the wall and the space thrown into the street, and new streets replaced some of the narrow lanes in the south-western and northern sections.

Charles Harcourt Master's map, published in 1794, records the peak of that wave of building. In 1793, the boom broke, for Bath was well as the rest of the country. The rising costs during the Napoleonic wars affected both builders and potential visitors, and credit difficulties brought a sudden halt to many projects. The 'overbuilding' which pessimists had been forecasting since the 1700s seemed finally to have occurred, as several Bath banks and many local builders became bankrupt. Contemporary writers spoke of 'the paralysing effects of war', and described the 'huge piles of unfinished houses' in Kingsmead fields and along the London road.[43] Bath was not alone in its difficulties: speculative ventures over the country were also hit. The wars did not end the expansion: a revival occurred in the early nineteenth century, but the grandiose plans for Bathwick shown on Master's map were never built.

The growth of the town was connected with changes in the nature of Bath. Over the second half of the eighteenth century, it ceased to be a centre for fashionable elite groups, but continued to attract, in large numbers, the wealthy 'middling' classes. The very increase in numbers altered the forms of social life. No longer could the master of ceremonies meet all the Company, or ensure that it did not break up

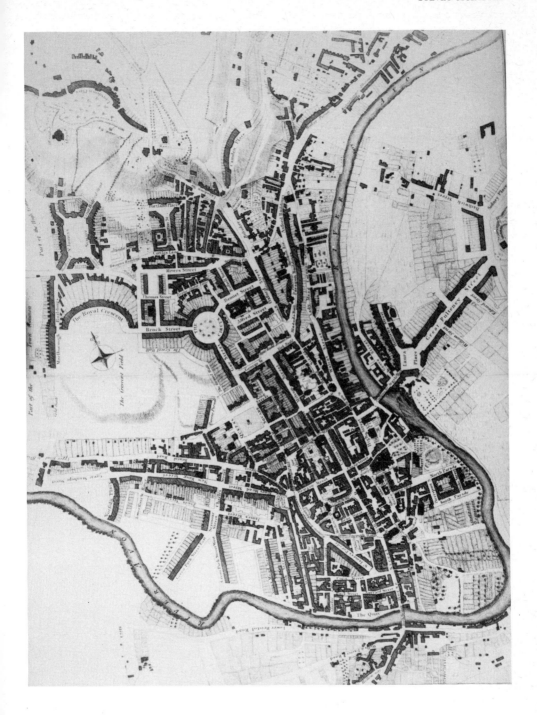

Figure 19. Bath at the end of the eighteenth century (from R. Warner, *The History of Bath*, 1801).

into private cliques. The decline of that position had begun with the suppression, not always successfully, of certain types of gambling on which Beau Nash had relied for his livelihood. His successors and imitators were more dependent on the whims of the Company. Samuel Derrick, who succeeded Nash, instituted the practice of assembly nights for the master of ceremony's benefit, a device which increased his income but reduced his status. The selection of the master of ceremonies was sufficiently important to bring the upper classes actually to blows in 1769,[44] but as the size of the Company became too large to remain one society, his role became trivial. Towards the end of the century, the visitors and the growing number of persons who chose to live permanently in Bath, often neglected the public rooms and entertainments in favour of private functions, to the disadvantage of the season. The Napoleonic wars, though they checked the building industry, may have prevented the spa's desertion by all fashionable visitors, but afterwards, when the Continent was again open to the English, Bath settled down as a sedate and increasingly unfashionable backwater.

4   The town and its inhabitants

By the time it ended, Bath's success as a watering place had produced a populous city. Wood estimated in 1749 that there were 1,362 private houses in Bath, which suggests a population of between 5,700 and 8,200, depending on the number of occupants per house: either represents a creditable increase for a town of 2–3,000 in about 1700.[45] By 1801, however, the population of the four parishes within the city limits and the 'outparts' of the parish of Walcot, had become 27,686, while the addition of the parishes of Bathwick and of Lyncombe and Widcombe, separated from the city by the Avon and in fact if not in theory part of the town, brings the total to 33,196, convincing testimony to the boom which Bath enjoyed in the second half of the century.

Table 17   *Bath: the census of 1801*

	males	females	total	houses inhabited	uninhabited
Bath city					
St James	1059	2903	3962	526	26
St Michael	1582	2118	3700	459	10
SS Peter and Paul	1051	1414	2465	310	2
Walcot	6829	10730	17559	2324	111
	10521	17165	27686	3619	149
Bathwick	1068	1652	2720	327	10
Lyncombe and Widcombe	1231	1559	2790	430	32
	12820	20376	33196	4376	191

All the city shared the increase, but not to the same extent (tables 15 and 17). The population of the old centre, consisting of the parishes of St James, St Michael and SS Peter and Paul, rose from a probable 1,200–1,350 in 1664 to 10,127 in 1801 – a considerable advance, since that area contained most of the population in 1664 and many late-eighteenth-century improvements removed rather than built houses. It was dwarfed, however, by the expansion of population in the parish of Walcot, both within and without the city limits. Walcot had an estimated population of 160–230 in

1664 and was said to contain 80 houses and two cloth mills in 1730.[46] Over the fields in this parish the new streets spread, to accommodate a population in 1801 of 17,559. Bathwick, though also expanding over unbuilt land, developed later and was therefore less affected: the 50–70 inhabitants of 1664 rose to 2,720 in 1801. The increase to the east of the river was matched by that to the south, where the inhabitants of Lyncombe and Widcombe grew in number from 170–250 in 1664 to 2,790 in 1801.

Before the end of the eighteenth century, it is difficult to extract any exact information on the occupations of the inhabitants of Bath. From 1706 to 1769 we have enrolments of apprentices to freemen which provides some indication of the most popular trades (though they may be biased by corporation pressure on certain trades to take the freedom). By 1773, the Bath guides began to list members of certain professions, doctors, artists, and attorneys, but of two directories which exist for the eighteenth century that for 1783 has only 180 names, though the *Universal British Directory of Trade and Commerce* of 1790 has 875. There is also the 'State and nature of the trade of Bath, December 1779' in Warner's *The History of Bath*, which gives the numbers involved in different trades in the parishes of St James, St Michael, SS Peter and Paul, and Walcot. Even the 1801 census describes the population in very general terms. There is, however, enough from these sources and other less quantifiable ones such as newspapers and visitors' accounts to allow certain generalizations (table 18).

Table 18   Occupations of Bath inhabitants of the eighteenth century

A   Enrolment of apprentices: occupations of masters

	1706–27		%	1728–49		%	1750–69		%
clothing and shoe-making									
clothiers and weavers	1			3					
tailors	73			55			61		
cordwainers	96			70			47		
drapers, milliners, mercers, haberdashers	17	200	39.4	13	163	37.4	22	151	29.4
others	13			22			21		
building		81	15.7		91	20.9		129	25.1
other crafts									
luxury	1			13			19		
other	46	47	9.3	26	39	8.9	48	67	13
victualling		97	19.1		67	13.1		71	13.8
professional									
medical	33			27			34		
other	1	34	6.7		27	6.2		34	6.6
services, transport and entertainment		46	9.1		49	11.2		62	12.1
miscellaneous		3	0.6						
		508			436			514	

Source: Bath Corporation, Freemen's Estate, 121.
(Retailers have not been listed separately, since it is usually impossible to distinguish between manufacture and selling.)

B Professional occupations listed in guide books

	1773	1790	1800
physicians	17	16	23
surgeons	10	13	18
apothecaries and chemists	27	25	28
dentists			4
attorneys		18	26

Source: R. Cruttwell, *The Strangers' Assistant and Guide to Bath* (1773); *The New Bath Guide* (1790, 1800).

C Occupations listed in the *Universal British Directory of Trade and Commerce* (1790)

			%
clothing and shoe-making			
clothiers	1		
cordwainers	6	154	17.6
tailors	30		
mercers, drapers, milliners,			
haberdashers	57		
others	60		
building		66	7.7
other crafts			
luxury	36	91	10.4
other	55		
victualling		252	28.8
professional			
medical	62		
clergy	24		
law	26		
banking	6		
schools, teachers etc.	25	168	19.2
brokers, auctioneers, upholders, etc.	16		
architects	3		
others	6		
services, entertainment, transport		88	10.6
other retailers		54	6.2
luxury	28		
other	25		
miscellaneous	1		
esquire	1		
	875		

Source: *Universal British Directory of Trade and Commerce*, II (1907), 97–110.

D   Locations of persons involved in trades, manufactures, and handicrafts

	1790	1799	(% of population of parish in 1801)
Bath city			
St James	148*	273	(6.9)
St Michael	149	265	(7.2)
SS Peter and Paul	180*	271	(10.9)
Walcot	209	430	(2.4)
		1239	
Bathwick	21		
Lyncombe and Widcombe	30		
unidentified	26		
	763		

Source: 1790: *Universal British Directory of Trade and Commerce*, II (1790), 97–110; 1799: R. Warner, *The History of Bath* (1801), 214–16.
*45 persons were located on Stall Street and Borough Walls: since they could be in either St James parish or SS Peter and Paul, the number has been split, 23 to St James, 22 to SS Peter and Paul.

E   Occupations in 1801 census

	agricultural	trade, manufactures, and handicraft	% population of parish	other
Bath city				
St James	2	372	9.4	3588
St Michael	1	933	25.2	2766
SS Peter and Paul	1	2305	93.6	159
Walcot	253	1935	11	15371
Bathwick	34	104	3.8	2582
Lyncombe and Widcombe	93	575	20.6	2122

Throughout the eighteenth century, as in the late seventeenth century, a large proportion of the inhabitants of Bath were involved in housing and serving the visitors. The new houses were, on the whole, financed by local speculators and erected by local builders,[47] and as the town expanded, the building trades prospered. They account for 15 per cent of the masters of apprentices in 1706–27, rising to 28 per cent by 1750–69: by 1752 they involved so many men that the corporation tried to organize them in their own companies. The 1790 directory shows only 7.7 per cent (7.9 per cent if we include the three architects), probably the result of bias in the directory, since it was published before the end of the building boom in 1795.

The renting of one or more of these houses was, over the century, a source of income to many families (table 19B). We cannot tell how many lodgings there were in the first three quarters of the century, though if the estimate of 8,000 visitors in the

1700s or Wood's suggestion of 12,000 at one time in 1749 have any reality, they must have been numerous. The first guide listing lodgings, that of 1773, names 263 persons (including 116 women) running 236 lodging houses and 38 boarding houses: by 1800, there were 300 men and 130 women running 459 lodging houses and 18 boarding houses. These numbers, which presumably include only lodgings which would attract visitors of some prosperity, make up a large proportion of the town's stock of houses: the 477 of 1800 are 11.8 per cent of the inhabited houses shown in the census a year later. These do not include the many houses advertised in Bath newspapers as let as a whole, nor those taken by what we might call 'permanent visitors' who had retired to Bath.

Table 19   Bath lodging houses

A   Lodging houses shown on Gilmore's map of Bath, 1692

Abbey House and churchyard	3
Abbey green	1
King's Bath	2
Hot Bath	1
Cross Bath	2
Stall Street	6
Westgate Street	7
High Street	2
Cheap Street and Bear Corner	3
Broad Street	1
Northgate Street	1
	29

B   Lodging houses, 1773–1800

	number of keepers			number of houses		
	men	women	total	lodging	boarding	total
1773	147	116	263	236	38	274
1780	186	113	299	288	25	313
1790	225	118	343	345	22	367
1800	300	130	430	459	18	477

C   Locations of lodging houses, 1773–1800

	1773	1780	1790	1800	% of inhabited houses in parish in 1801
Bath city					
St James*	101	85	81	73	12
St Michael	39	47	56	56	12.4
SS Peter and Paul*	63	56	24	51	16.5
Walcot	71	125	178	222	9.6
Bathwick				75	22.9

Source: R. Cruttwell, *The Strangers' Assistant and Guide to Bath* (1773), 63–72; *The New Bath Guide* (1780), 52-6; (1790), 69–72; (1800), 71–4.
* Stall Street and the abbey churchyard are in both the parishes of St James and SS Peter and Paul, and the houses on those streets are divided between the two.

In the sixteenth and seventeenth centuries, the most desirable lodgings tended to be those close to the baths, preferably with a 'bath door' directly into them. In 1692, the best lodgings, as represented by the 19 illustrating Gilmore's map, were in the Abbey churchyard, next to the King's, Hot and Cross baths, and lining the main streets, especially Stall Street and Westgate Street (table 19A). The lodgings around the baths remained until the late eighteenth century, but from the 1720s they were competing with the new and more fashionable streets outside the walls. The Bath guide books show that the four city parishes and, by the very end of the century, the parish of Bathwick, all provided lodgings for visitors (table 19c) St James and St Michael each had around 12 per cent of their houses used as lodging houses (according to the 1801 census), while for SS Peter and Paul, the figure reaches 16.5 per cent. Walcot, though containing many lodgings, had a lower proportion of its total number of houses, perhaps because houses there were rented as a whole. Of the two external parishes, Bathwick seems to have become popular for lodgings by 1800, while Lyncombe and Widcombe, across the river to the south, had, probably because of its industrial character, no lodging houses worth mentioning by the guides.

The running of lodging houses provided valuable employment for their keepers and families, though not necessarily full-time: 96 of those listed in 1773 had other occupations assigned to them.[48] To serve the visitors, there were also a multitude of domestic servants, either supplied by the lodging house keepers or hired by the visitors themselves. A large proportion of these were women, one reason for the noticeable difference between the numbers of men and women shown at Bath by the 1801 census. Other forms of service were also required by the visitors. The narrow streets of the centre of Bath, before they were remodelled in the 1790s, encouraged the use of chairs rather than coaches, especially since many chairs could take invalids directly from bed to baths and back again. The number of chairmen licensed by the corporation rose from an estimated 40 or more about 1714 to 120 in 1743, 168 in 1756 and 340 in 1800 (table 20). Hackney coaches do not seem to have been as common: the corporation, which was concerned from the 1708 Act to regulate the chairmen, shows little recorded interest in coaches until 1793, and visitors remarked on how infrequently coaches were used in the city.[49] More numerous were the porters and 'basket men and women' who could be hired to carry goods about the city: in 1767 the corporation decided to license them in order to prevent an influx of 'poor strangers' hoping to obtain a living.[50] There were also occupations peculiar to Bath, such as the 'bath guides' who attended the sick in the water.

A further source of employment lay in entertaining the Company. Coaches, though awkward in the narrow central streets, were needed for 'airings' on the Downs, as were the horses supplied by the livery stables. Theatrical performances were common, even before 1750 when the Orchard Street theatre was built. That theatre flourished under the control of the John Palmers, father and son, becoming in 1768 the first Theatre Royal in the provinces: it apparently proved profitable for the theatre patentees if not for the actors.[51] The leisured society required bookshops and the circulating libraries which developed out of them. Bath may or may not have had the first commercial lending library, but one was started by James Leake as early as 1724. That 'evergreen tree of diabolical knowledge' flourished in Bath, between five and six existing throughout the century, though not necessarily the same ones: the 1790 directory lists seven.[52] Coffee shops also catered for the visitors, though the guides do not list them on the same scale: the 1755 guide mentions only the principal two, and the 1790 directory likewise. Possibly we should include under entertainment rather than professions the various dancing masters and mistresses, music masters, writing masters and drawing masters, of whom 19 are listed in the 1790 directory. The numbers of artists listed in the 1790 and 1800 guides also suggests the attraction of the prosperous visitors to those in need of commissions.[53]

Table 20   Numbers of chairmen in Bath, 1714–99

	chairs	men
c.1714	40 or more	
1743	60 licensed	120
1744	60	120
1745	63	126
1746	61	122
1747	65	130
1748	73	146
1749	78	156
1750	65	130
1751	76	152
1752	79	158
1753	81	162
1754	81	162
1755	83	166
1756	84	168
1799		340

Source: c. 1714: J. Macky, *A Journey through England* (1714–22), 145; 1743–56; Bath Corporation, Chairmen's Book; 1799: R. Warner, *The History of Bath* (1801), 338.

One of the best entertainments, then as now, was shopping, especially for those to whom a visit to Bath was an event in a quiet country life. The money brought by these visitors supported a larger number of those providing special goods and services than might be expected for a town of Bath's size. By supplying the needs and luxuries of visitors, the town became, as Wood wrote in 1749, 'a mart to the whole Country for many miles about it, even to Bristol itself for some things'.[54] The city's markets were an outlet for the produce of the surrounding countryside, and trades connected with food and drink prospered. In 1706–27, 19 per cent of the masters of apprentices were in the victualling trades, and 13 per cent from 1728 to 1769 (table 18). These figures may underestimate the proportion of the total population: the victualling trades make up 28.8 per cent of those listed in the 1790 directory. The requirements of the Company for clothing, shoes, hats, and all sorts of toys and luxuries, attracted retailers from London and elsewhere, and encouraged the manufacture of many goods in Bath itself. 'Artificers in the most curious works', wrote Wood in 1749,

> begin to find such encouragement in the city as to induce them to settle in it; so that Bath now boasts of her painters, carvers, engravers, jewellers, builders etc . . . woollen cloth, silks and toys are some of the chief commodities sold at Bath . . . Without an exaggeration, the number of tailors and mantua makers that find employ in Bath, is a demonstration of the great consumption of the manufactures with which the body is cloathed; and the great resort of strangers to the city making it, in effect, a perpetual fair.[55]

Apprenticeship records, newspapers and directories show that 'the manufactures with which the body is clothed' remained a major source of employment in Bath: it is not surprising that Jane Austen in *Persuasion* sent Henrietta Musgrave there to buy her own and her sister's wedding clothes.

The population of Bath thus included in large proportion of craftsmen and retailers: the distinction between the two is an artificial one, since many of the inhabitants were both. Ron Neale's analysis of the 1831 census suggests that, in the early nineteenth century, the parish of St James was the home of the craftsmen, SS Peter and Paul of the small shopkeeper, and St Michael that of the bigger shopkeeper.[56] The material available for the eighteenth century is much too meagre to make such distinctions, but it is clear that, on the whole, craftsmen and tradesmen were mixed together in the city centre, though some followed their customers to new parts of town as these opened up (table 18D). Property in the three central parishes tended to be cheaper than in the new streets, and shops and workshops mingled with housing there.[57] Nonetheless, the continued attraction of the baths and pump rooms prevented the complete desertion of the centre by the wealthy, even before the area was rebuilt by the corporation. The 1801 census, in spite of its lack of information on occupations, does show that St Michael had 25.2 per cent of its population listed under 'trade, manufactures and handicraft', whilst SS Peter and Paul, in the northern part of the walled town, had 93.6 per cent of its population so classified (table 18E). Of the latter parish, Warner wrote about the same time, 'its situation renders it the focal point of the city traffic, and consequently, there is only one house (the rectory) within its precincts, which is not dedicated either to the purposes of trade or accommodation of lodgers'.[58] SS Peter and Paul, St James, and St Michael also contain a high proportion of the men classified in the 1790 directory as 'traders etc.' (which includes craftsmen and retailers as well as those providing services) when their population, as suggested by the 1801 census, is compared to that of Walcot.

Although crafts and retail trades flourished, there was little large-scale industry within the city. The market offered by the expanding town encouraged the growth of a number of industrial villages about the town, especially in Lyncombe and Widcombe across the river to the south. Before 1765, the growth of such areas was assisted by the freemen's monopoly of trade within the city: unfree tailors, for example, made clothes outside the city limits, and smuggled them in on their own bodies. The manufacture of wool cloth continued in Lyncombe and Widcombe, and at Tiverton, long after it ceased in the city. Other industries were established by the end of the century, brewing, glass, soap-making, iron-making, and even coal mining at Batheaston. The industrialization of the region around Bath did not, however, turn the town back into a manufacturing centre as it had been in the Middle Ages. When the fashion for the town declined, so did the industry.[59]

The upper classes of Bath usually lived in the northern and eastern suburbs, areas which were much more homogeneous in character than the centre. Bath had many professional men, lawyers, bankers, and capitalists, and a large number of medical men. The various medical occupations are well represented among masters of apprentices from 1706 and in the lists in the guides towards the end of the century: that for 1773 names a total of 54 physicians, surgeons and apothecaries, and the 1790 directory reveals 62, including druggists and chemists. The numbers would have been larger if they included those who had made enough money to retire from their profession: among the 'gents' and 'esquires' of the corporation were a number of former apothecaries (tables 18A, B and C, and table 21). Even so, the local professionals would not have filled the expensive housing to the north and east. Those were occupied by visitors (some 2,500 of whom were mentioned by the *Bath Journal* in 1760 and 5,300 in 1800) and also by those who had come to live permanently in Bath.

The number of outsiders who chose to live in Bath grew throughout the century. Towards the end, the city became less of a resort, more of a place of residence for persons with independent incomes who were attracted by its amenities. The lack of industry was an advantage to the navy and army officers, and to the East and West Indian traders and others who had broken their local connections with England, to members of the gentry who, like Sir Walter Elliott in *Persuasion*, were forced to find a cheaper situation but who were not to be trusted in London, and to the widows and spinsters of small or large means who made up part of the sizeable proportion of women shown in the 1801 census.

Lacking the potential of the new manufacturing towns, Bath avoided some of their social problems. Nonetheless, the independent master craftsmen and small retailers, along with their workpeople, were vulnerable during depressions, as were the workers in the building trades. Those providing luxuries and the less necessary services – dancing masters, portrait painters and entertainers – could be affected not only by depression but also by changes in fashion. Matters were made worse by the number of domestic servants brought to Bath, or attracted by opportunities for service, who could easily lose their employment. Moreover the very prosperity of Bath drew the poor from outside: in 1767, the corporation was trying to prevent the numerous 'poor strangers' from coming to pick up employment by carrying provisions about the town.[60] Hidden from sight of the visitors and ignored by the writers of the guides, slums existed in the lower part of the town, in back courts and, especially, in the areas near the river which were often flooded.[61] Periods of war produced widespread distress. In 1801 35 per cent of the population is said to have been receiving relief, exclusive of those in receipt of regular poor relief from the parish.[62] The Napoleonic wars may have been a particularly bad time, but the wars of the eighteenth century must have produced similar difficulties: in 1784, for example, the corporation decided to give £50 for the relief of the poor not receiving alms.[63] Bath had, however, the advantage of enough wealthy citizens and visitors to give relief on a considerable scale: it was partly for this reason that Bath avoided the worst outbreaks of popular unrest during troubled years.

5   The corporation and the building of Bath

One aspect of the flowering of Georgian Bath which tends to be ignored or misrepresented is the activity of the municipal corporation, which is usually shown as inert or in opposition to progressive ideas, such as those of John Wood the elder. The situation was, in fact, more complex than this. The corporation of Bath was intimately involved with the growth of the town, both as the governing body and as the owner of much property within the city, including the baths themselves. Its involvement in the eighteenth-century developments was of considerable importance.

The corporation was made up of a mayor, four to ten aldermen, and 20 common councillors. The members of the corporation were chosen by the major part of the body present from the freemen, who had no say in the actions of the corporation, but who shared in the monopoly of trade within the city limits up to 1765, and in the revenue from the Freemen's Common. Most of the corporation's income came from its property, which included the guildhall and the market place, the city wall, the baths, and much of the area within the city limits.[64] There was one large exception, the site of the Abbey in the south-east corner of the area enclosed by the walls, amounting to perhaps one fifth of the old town: except for the Abbey church, which was acquired by the corporation, this property came eventually into the hands of the Duke of Kingston. The town rulers usually let houses and lands on a fine and rent, either for 21 years absolute (42 for corporation members) or, more commonly, for 99 years or three lives. Other sources of income connected with property were the rents of the corporation water and the 'gouts' to the common sewers. The changes in the city's finances, the rents received, the expenditures on various improvements, and the bond debt so accumulated, are connected with the growth of the resort, and may be used to illuminate the town's evolution over the eighteenth century (table 22 and fig. 20).

The corporation's zeal for improving the town was affected by the interests of its members. The table of occupations of members (table 21) is useful though limited: many of them had more than one occupation, and mere description fails to indicate differences in wealth. In the late seventeenth and early eighteenth century, the corporation was made up, so far as we can tell, of craftsmen and traders of various kinds, including a large number of apothecaries. Many owned lodgings or inns: the apparent drop in the numbers doing so by 1720 is probably due to lack of evidence. Some participated in building new streets: in 1707 Trim Street was laid out on the lands of George Tryme, a wealthy clothier. All might be expected to be aware that Bath's prosperity, and their own, rested on its success as a spa. Individual private interests could, however, conflict with plans for the long-term benefit of the town as a whole, and the corporation members are often accused of putting their own advantage before that of Bath, usually on the evidence of John Wood who, though often an accurate witness, was a vigorous critic of all plans which clashed with his own.

One example is the magisterial opposition in 1708–11 to the building of Harrisons' Assembly Rooms and walks outside the city wall. Wood said of the reaction to Harrison:

> his works were soon looked upon as prejudicial to the gravel walks, and as an invasion of the liberties of the city: as such the corporation opposed them with the power of men determined by might to overcome all manner of right; and the citizens, in general, were so uneasy at the sight of every new house that was begun, that, in the utmost despair, they cry'd out, O Lord! Bath is undone; 'tis undone; 'tis undone.[65]

In objecting to Harrison making a way through the wall between his assembly house and walks without permission, the corporation was defending its own property. But if its opposition was motivated, as Wood suggests, only by the interest of some of its members, it was failing to uphold those of the town. The corporation obtained a decree in Chancery against Harrison (at a cost of £220) and ordered the wall to be rebuilt against the house. Harrison had, however, the support of the Company if not the law. In May 1711, the corporation minutes record that it was:

> reported for a certainty that the persons of quality and gentry now residing in this City have threatened and are resolved to pull down or cause to be pulled down the new wall that was erected upon the Borough Wall against Butts Garden pursuant

223

Table 21   Occupations of members of Bath corporation in the eighteenth century

1700 26 members
    1 tailor
    1 mercer
    1 ? clothier
    2 saddlers
    2 vintners
    1 attorney
    14 unidentified
    13 of the 26 owned or had owned lodg-
      ings or inns

1720 28 members
    1 clothier
    1 linen draper and mercer
    1 mercer and quarry owner
    2 saddlers
    4 vintners
    2 malsters
    1 barber
    1 milliner
    1 baker
    1 glasier
    1 distiller
    1 shopkeeper
    4 apothecaries
    7 unidentified
    3 of the 28 may have owned lodgings
      or inns

1740 30 members
    1 linen draper
    1 woollen draper
    1 saddler
    6 vintners
    2 malsters
    1 baker
    1 shopkeeper
    3 plumbers and glaziers
    1 ironmonger or tallow chandler
    6 apothecaries (1 also 'gent')
    1 postal contractor and quarry owner
    1 ? attorney
    1 upholder
    1 'gent'
    3 unidentified

1760 30 members
    1 linen and woollen draper and
      wholesaler
    1 saddler
    1 vintner
    1 ? baker
    2 plumbers and glaziers (also buil-
      ders)
    2 attorneys
    3 surgeons
    8 apothecaries (1 'gent', 1 esq.)
    1 carpenter and joiner
    1 silk weaver
    1 tallow chandler
    1 ironmonger
    1 wine cooper and land developer
    1 postal contractor and quarry owner
    1 postmaster
    1 carrier
    1 bookseller
    1 'esq.'
    1 unidentified

1780 30 members
    2 linen drapers
    1 hosier and hatter
    1 laceman
    1 silk weaver
    1 bookseller
    1 saddler
    1 carrier
    5 apothecaries (2 'gents')
    2 physicians
    6 surgeons
    2 bankers (both originally apothe-
      caries)
    3 attorneys
    1 mailcoach contractor, theatre
      owner, etc.
    3 unidentified

1800 30 members
    1 linen draper
    1 saddler
    1 brewer
    1 wine merchant
    7 apothecaries
    1 chemist and druggist
    5 surgeons
    4 doctors of physick (1 knight)
    1 surgeon and/or physician
    2 bankers
    1 theatre owner
    3 esquires
    2 unidentified (possibly apothe-
      caries)

to an order of the High Court of Chancery . . . And whereas the said Mr. Harrison has desired an accommodation and acknowledged the right of the said wall to be in the Corporation alone, [it was agreed] (to oblige the nobility and gentry) a Committee shall be appointed to be chosen out of the corporation to treat with the said Mr. Harrison for accommodating all matters relating to that Suit.[66]

Wood and others also criticized the corporation's failure to fall in with various grand plans, especially those designed for the improvement of the baths and pump room. The buildings crowded around the baths deprived them of dignity, the situation of the King's and Queen's Baths being such, said Wood, that it appeared 'as though the citizens were ashamed of the hot waters, their staple commodity'. Private property near the baths could endanger the hot springs themselves: in 1715, a man diverted some water from the Hot Bath springs and, some 20 years later, when the owner of a house near the Hot Bath was digging a cellar, 'the hot water broke in upon him in such quantity as to affect the filling of the Bath, and it was with the utmost difficulty forced back in to its usual channel'.[67]

Various plans were put forward from the 1730s, but the corporation took little action. According to Wood, one excellent plan of his for improvements to the Pump Room failed in the mid-1730s from the hostility of the mayor, whose son rented a nearby coffee house. 'He absolutely refused to put the question to his brethren, under the idle pretence that an additional chamber to the pump room would draw the Company from his son's house, and spoil the trade'.[68] In 1736 another plan by Wood, this time for the baths, was prevented, he said, by dissensions in the corporation. About this time a further plan for a covered bagnio at the baths, drawn up by Archibald Cleland, was, according to Smollett, thrown out by the influence of jealous physicians.[69] Only in 1751 did the corporation rebuild the pump room, and then not to the design or scale advocated by Wood or Smollett.

'Narrow minds will ever have narrow views', wrote Smollett in 1752:

The corporation of Bath seems to have forgot that the ease and plenty they now enjoy, and to which their fathers were strangers, are owing to their waters; and that an improvement upon their baths would, by bringing a greater concourse of company to their town, perpetuate these blessings to them and their posterity.[70]

Something, however, should be said in defence of the corporation. It was not obvious in the first part of the century that such grand projects would be successful. Although Bath was established as a watering place, no one could be certain how long its popularity would last. Even in 1763, Dr Sutherland noticed that 'nothing is so common as to hear people say, Bath will be overbuilt. Bath must be undone', though he added as consolation, 'while national debt, extravagance, indolence, or ailments continue to increase, Bath can never be undone.'[71] It is understandable and not necessarily discreditable that the magistracy should leave speculative enterprise to private individuals, including its own members. More reprehensible would have been the refusal for personal reasons to improve the baths and pump rooms, which were not only the corporation's property, but vital to the city. Episodes such as that of the mayor's son's coffee house may have occurred (we have only Wood's word for it), and the presence in the corporation of men involved in building may have prevented the body from using Wood as architect: nonetheless, an outright opposition to all improvements would have been against the interest of most corporation members. The doctors, too, though not as active as Smollett wished, were not all as hostile to change as he suggested: many exerted what influence they had over the corporation to better the drinking and bathing facilities. The main problem of the plans seems to have lain in their cost. Neither Wood's scheme for a lottery to finance his projects nor Smollett's suggestion of legislative help came to anything, so that the burden remained with the corporation.

The corporate revenue was not very large, an average of £375 in the 1690s and £531 in the 1700s (table 22). It did rise to £965 in the 1720s and £1,565 in the 1740s but expenses rose equally or more rapidly. Returns from the pumps and baths, in particular, were not great, a maximum of £230 up to 1750, and most was absorbed by maintenance and repairs. Improvements to the baths and pump rooms and their setting cost more than just new buildings: they lay in the heart of the city, and private property could only be removed from their neighbourhood by means of expensive purchases. The same was true of projects for widening the streets of the old town.

Table 22   Corporation revenue, expenditure and bond debts, 1690–1800

	average annual revenue			average annual expenditure				bond debt	
	£	s.	d.	£	s.	d.		£	s.
1690/91 –							1690/91	1,000	
1699/1700	375	3	7½	371	8	4	1699/1700	970	
(1 year missing)									
1700/01 –									
1709/10	531	11	8½	738	15	8½	1709/10	2,570	
(1 year missing)									
1710/11 –									
1719/20	701	1	1	849	12	0½	1719/20	3,640	
1720/21 –									
1729/30	965	13	4	1,003	18	4½	1729/30	5,412	10
(3 years missing)									
1730/31 –									
1739/40	1,179	10	10½	1,017	8		1739/40	3,612	10
(1 year missing)									
1740/41 –									
1749/50	1,565	7		1,506	1	6	1749/50	3,612	10
1750/51–									
1759/60	2,229	16	9	2,449	18	5	1759/60	4,812	10
1760/61 –									
1769/70	2,956	11	2	3,672	15	1	1769/70	12,162	10
1770/71 –									
1779/80	4,124	8	5	5,444	4	3½	1779/80	25,550	
1780/81 –									
1789/90	4,451	15	9	1,502	19	11½	1789/90	27,150	
1790/91 –									
1799/1800	6,220	12	10½	6,722	17	11½	1799/1800	32,600	

Source: Bath Corporation, Chamberlains' Accounts.

The corporation therefore contented itself with promoting Acts of Parliament for the roads, for the Avon navigation, and for cleansing and watching the streets. It was also active in looking after the public walks and rides about the town on which visitors could take the exercise prescribed by their doctors and show themselves to the rest of the Company: the Turnpike Acts were drawn up so as not to impede those

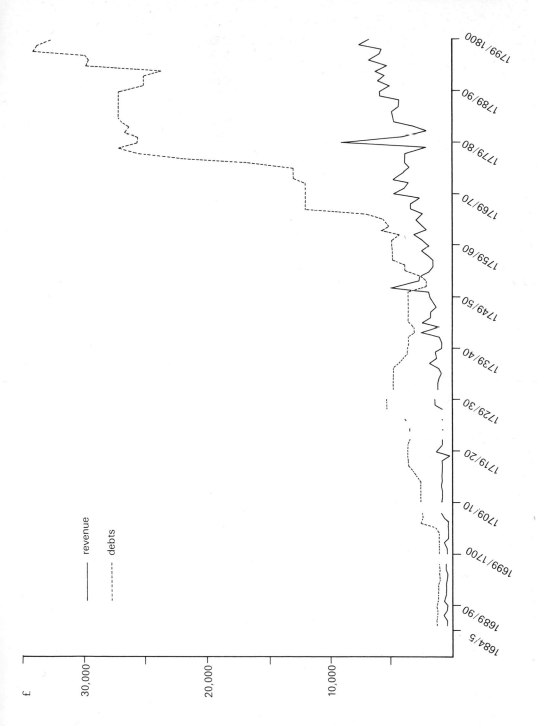

Figure 20. Bath: corporate revenues and debts, 1684–1800.

who left the town for an 'airing' in their coaches, and from 1743 the corporation paid the tenants of Claverton Down an annual rent to compensate for damage caused by its use by the visitors.[72] In managing its property, the corporation's activities were, on the whole, limited to renewing eases, checking encroachments, and looking after the public buildings. It was not until the second half of the century that the magistrates endowed with a growing revenue and infected by the 'rage of building' which gripped the town, embarked on a programme of large-scale improvements.

The corporation's interest in such schemes was encouraged by changes in its personnel (table 21). As the town increased in wealth, so did corporation members, usually the leading townsmen. According to the *History of Parliament,* the governing body in the last part of the century consisted of country gentlemen, and substantial merchants.[73] Substantial merchants there were, linen and woollen drapers, malsters and vintners, along with a growing number of professional men, lawyers, bankers, surgeons, physicians and, above all, apothecaries. There were, however, hardly any true country gentlemen. Some of the men were described as gentlemen or esquires, and some had country seats, but almost all of those obtained their position through their own or their family's success in trade, in a profession, or in speculation. The famous Ralph Allen made his considerable wealth by reorganizing the posts and speculating in the Avon navigation and in Bath stone quarries. Of the two of its own members the corporation elected to Parliament, Abel Moysey (M.P. 1774–90) was the son of a wealthy Bath doctor, while John Palmer (M.P. 1801–8) was the son of a prosperous brewer and tallow chandler, from whom he inherited his interest in the theatre: in the 1780s, Palmer also developed a system of mail coaches. Some of the men described as 'gentlemen' were or had been apothecaries, and the two knights, Sir Edward Harington and Sir William Watson, were both physicians. Not all are conclusively identified, but it is clear that there was no take-over by the gentry as happened at Southampton.[74]

As men of fortune, these corporation members were not concerned with maintaining a monopoly for lodgings and coffee houses, but rather with long-term plans. The numbers directly involved in estate development increased, including not only Ralph Allen, quarry owner, and Thomas Warr Atwood, plumber and builder, but others such as the wine-coopers Daniel and Charles Milsom, who created Milsom Street, the linen draper Francis Bennett, leaseholder of Bennett Street, the surgeon John Symons who, besides promoting improvements in the baths, was concerned in the building of Camden Place, and the banker Charles Phillott who took over Union Street from the Improvement Commissioners. Others such as Edmund Bushell Collibee, originally an apothecary, and Dr Henry Harington, supplied land for developers. Among those in the corporation who were not directly involved were men whose businesses benefited from the town's growth, or who were simply attracted to the idea of embellishing the city they governed. The best example of the latter is Leonard Coward, a wealthy laceman, who left the residue of his estate, amounting to £7,344 10s., to the Improvement Commissioners.[75] Whatever their reasons, the civic rulers of Bath were, as the century drew on, increasingly enthusiastic about major improvements.

A new interest in the potential of its property appears in the corporation's resolution in 1754 to have all its property 'planned' before being leased and even more in the decision in the 1760s to appoint official surveyors.[76] Two supervisors of bounds had always been elected annually, but the part they played in the corporation's works is unclear, though the frequent appointment of masons and builders implies that they

needed technical skills. In 1762 the chamberlain and two members of the corporation were appointed surveyors, but in 1765 the magistrates decided to appoint a
professional to plan the city works and assist the chamberlain.[77] The first such was
Richard Jones, Ralph Allen's clerk of works; he was followed by Thomas Baldwin,
clerk to Thomas Warr Atwood and a builder and architect, who was appointed surveyor in 1776 and deputy chamberlain and surveyor in 1779. Baldwin kept his offices
until 1791, when he was appointed as surveyor alone. He was dismissed in 1792 for
refusing to return the town's rentals and to submit his accounts, though 'every civil
and humane means' was used to persuade him to do so: the corporation had eventually to file a bill in Chancery. They had reason to demand their accounts. Baldwin
went bankrupt in 1793, along with other Bath builders. After these difficulties, the
architect, John Palmer, was chosen only supervisor of bounds and consulted by the
civic building committee without being officially appointed surveyor.[78] Appointment as surveyor did not mean that the man concerned automatically designed buildings erected by the city, but he had a considerable advantage over his competitors.

The building boom of the mid and late eighteenth century gave the governing
body an opportunity to improve its unbuilt properties. It did not usually initiate
schemes for new streets, but considered applications by speculators, and granted
building leases either to a number of builders, or to one man who sublet to other builders. The plan and elevation of the buildings was approved by the corporation. The
authors of these designs are often unknown but whoever designed them, they tended
to conform to what Ison calls 'the standard Palladian elevation, three stories high
and three windows wide, generally applied to buildings erected on corporate property between 1750 and 1775.'[79]

The city fathers took their first steps in developing their unbuilt property when, in
1753, they decided to let Town Acre by auction. It was taken by Daniel Milsom,
lessee of the adjoining property, to build a new street to the north of the city wall.
Unfortunately, the poor house garden lay in the way, and in 1754, Milsom, unable
either to remove the obstacle or to agree with the corporation for an abatement of
rent while the obstacle remained, decided to keep his original lease. Only after the
magistracy made, in 1760, an agreement with Charles Milsom, brother and heir to
Daniel, over the division of rents from the new street, could Edgar Buildings be
started, and only after the corporation had negotiated in October 1763 an exchange
of property for the poor house land could building leases be granted for the rest of
the development.[80] More immediately successful was the lease in 1755 of Cockney's
Gardens, on which Bladud's Buildings were erected. Thomas Warr Atwood, besides
his other activities, obtained corporation leases to the ground on which he built the
Paragon, and to the 'Hand and Flower Ground', the site of Alfred Street and Oxford
Row, which he obtained in 1773 and released at great personal profit.[81] Since the
magistrates were men of substance, it is not surprising to connect them with such projects, but Atwood, at least, seems to have behaved unscrupulously. Whoever else
profited, the corporation also benefited, as appears in the rise of revenue (table 22).

Once unbuilt land outside the walls was let on building leases, the corporation had
only to watch that the terms of the leases were fulfilled. The improvement of the old
'lower town' was more difficult. The fine streets and squares spreading over the
fields were, both in design and spaciousness, well up to the standards of the late
eighteenth century, but the centre of the town retained its cramped medieval streets
with the irregular buildings Wood deplored. Cheap Street was especially narrow:
even in 1673 it was described as 'the greatest eye-sore to [Bath's] beauty and cumber

to its accommodation'.[82] The High Street was obstructed by the town hall and the markets around it, Stall Street and Westgate Street were not very wide, and the rest of the streets inside the walls were only lanes. Here lay the King's and Queen's Baths, surrounded by houses, and the Cross and Hot Baths, accessible only through narrow passages. The old ways into the city, through Horse Street to the south and Northgate Street, Walcot Road and Broad Street to the north were hemmed in by early ribbon development. In Wood's map of 1735, the city wall still separated the old town from the new: besides four gates there were only two or three public ways through the wall. Even in the 1760s it could be described as 'almost complete'.[83] Connections between the new buildings of the upper town and the rooms and baths of the lower town were poor: the common way between Queen's Square and the baths, wrote Matthew Bramble in the 1760s,

> is through the yard of an inn, where the poor trembling valetudinarian is carried in a chair, betwixt the heels of a double row of horses, wincing under the curry-combs of grooms and postilions, over and above the hazard of being obstructed, or overturned by the carriages which are continually making their exit or their entrance – I suppose after some chairman shall have been maimed and a few lives lost by those accidents, the corporation will think in earnest, about providing a more safe and commodious passage.[84]

Making safe and commodious passages in the heart of the city was expensive. Although the town owned much of the property within the walls, it was let on long leases, which had been granted and renewed at different dates and fell into hand at different times, so that the corporation might have to purchase the lessee's interests if it wanted to carry out improvements. When the project involved other proprietors, the body had to negotiate with both proprietor and tenant. Even if the magistrates were willing to buy out the different interests, the owners, as John Symons argued in 1783, 'demand such extravagant prices for their property, when a body corporate is to pay for it, as would prove them to be very bad stewards of the public money did they agree to it.'[85] Nor were matters made easier by the fact that most other proprietors near the baths were hospitals, especially St John's Hospital, since negotiations with them could become even more complex than with private landlords.

The corporation could, however, manage many piecemeal changes. Tenants were always applying to 'drown' lives and add new ones, or to renew leases: such adjustments could be granted on condition that the fronts of the houses be set back, while part of the land might be thrown into the public street in return for abatement of fine or rent. Property which might be wanted in the future could be leased with a covenant allowing the corporation to repurchase the whole or part when needed for public works, sometimes at the price set in the lease. Pressure could be put on a tenant to sell his interest by refusing to add any lives. Tenants could stand out, refusing to sell or demanding higher prices. Nonetheless, the amount of property owned by the corporation meant that care with leases, coupled with judicious individual purchases, could accomplish much in the way of improvements.

These methods had always been available, but the corporation displayed a new energy after the middle of the century. Formerly it had striven to prevent encroachments on the city wall, and in 1741 they repaired the Southgate.[86] By 1753, however, the corporation permitted tenants to make ways through the wall on payment of a rent, and by 1765 allowed part to be taken down and thrown into the street inside the wall. In 1754, a donation of £500 by a Member of Parliament 'for some public purpose' was used to take down the north and south gates, and in the years following, the city managed by lease alterations and outright purchase to set back the houses at the sites of the gates.[87] The Walcot Road was gradually widened, almost entirely by covenants in leases, from 1753 onwards, and a similiar process improved Broad Street after 1765 and Horse Street after 1766. Within the walls, obstructions were removed in Cheap Street, Bear Corner and Stall Street. The corporation's hand was strengthened when in 1766 the new City Act granted it the right to acquire certain property, by compulsory purchase if necessary, to widen Stall Street, Westgate Street and passages around the pump room.

The most noticeable improvement during these years was that of the guildhall, said to be by a design of Inigo Jones. It was in a poor state of repair, and its position in the middle of the High Street was an obstacle to traffic, made worse by the markets near it. On 9 May 1760 the corporation decided to rebuild the guildhall in a more convenient place. The building committee was negotiating the purchase of property on the east side of High Street by 1761, and the City Act of 1766 gave the corporation the power to move the market place, make byelaws for the markets, and acquire the necessary property by compulsory purchase. Enough of the site was cleared by October 1767 to allow the butchers' shambles to be moved there, and by January 1769, almost everyone using the High Street Market was directed to move to the new one.[88]

Clearing of the market place proceeded much more rapidly than building the guildhall, which involved, as Ison notes, 'one of the most involved chapters in the architectural history of Bath'.[89] For 16 years after the decision to rebuild the town hall, the committees appointed to deal with it considered a total of six plans by five architects. The main blame for the delay seems to rest on Thomas Warr Atwood, whose own plan was accepted in 1775, over the protests of other builders. After Atwood's accidental death in 1775, Thomas Baldwin took over and finally built the hall to his own designs: by 1777 the corporation was able to consider furnishings for the new building.

The magistracy's plans, as revealed in the 1766 Act, included the enlargement of the Pump Room and the improvement of the King's and Queen's Baths. Many felt that the baths and pumps, the centre of the town's life, should be suitably adorned, while the medical men were concerned to bring continental improvements in balneology to Bath.[90] Nor was it only modern bathing techniques which were held up for imitation. The removal in 1755 of the Abbey House by the Duke of Kingston revealed beneath it Roman baths whose convenience surpassed those of eighteenth-century Bath. The excavations gave the corporation not only an example, but also competition to its baths. A hot spring was discovered on the duke's property, and though his agent worried lest the water come 'either from the Bath sewer or from the King's Bath itself, which the corporation may intercept',[91] it was used to supply a small but elegant bath whose advantages justified the high fee of five shillings: a total of 788 persons used it in 1771. By the 1780s one member of the governing body, the surgeon John Symons, was campaigning for similar improvements to the corporation baths.[92]

The Hot Bath was first to be modernized. In 1772 3, the corporation obtained at a cost of £900 the house owned by St John's Hospital and leased by Mrs Hetling, to use as pump house for these springs. The springs feeding the Hot Bath were carefully secured, and John Wood the younger was employed to build the new baths (the only time the corporation used either Wood), though the corporation – made wary by its experience over the Town Hall – postponed the start of building until they could receive suggestions for making the plan as complete as possible.[93] The resulting building, finished about 1778, was, according to Ison, 'an ingenious arrangement of dressing-rooms and small private plunge-baths, symmetrically disposed around the octagonal central bath, the latter being uncovered.[94] Symons' 'indefatigable attention' was recognized by his appointment as manager of these new baths.[95]

The Cross Bath was not ignored. In 1781, the corporation was treating with the master of St John's Hospital and his tenant Robert Clark for a house at the north end of the Cross Bath, but negotiations were delayed first by Clark's price and later by problems of title. Ison says that the Cross was taken down and the pump room built about 1784, and the bath rebuilt some years later. These changes must have been carried out by the baths committee, since nothing appears in the minutes except the acceptance in 1797 of John Palmer's plan for alterations at that bath at a cost of not more than £400.[96] Whenever it was built, the new pump room and bath formed a delightful small building, suitably displayed at the end of Bath Street.

Changes were also made at the King's Bath and the Great Pump Room. The most important of these was Baldwin's plan for 'a colonnade before the front of the great pump room' to make the room warmer and more comfortable to the Company resorting there. The colonnade, extending across the entrance to the Abbey churchyard, was finished about 1786.[97]

The cost of these improvements was considerable, and can be seen in the steady. rise of civic expenses and the amount of money borrowed by the corporation (table 22 and fig. 20). The bond debt rose from £3612 10s. in 1750 to £12,162 10s. in 1770 and £25,550 in 1780. The marked increase shown in 1766 on the graph of revenue and debts resulted primarily from the purchases of property and other expenses connected with the Improvement Act of that year, while the next great rise, from 1776 to 1779, represents the improvements of the guildhall and the baths. With all this activity, the corporation did not take full advantage of the powers of the 1766 Act, but it did not allow rising costs to divert it from improvements. Instead, urged by men like Symons who were worried lest private property around the baths should cause the hot springs to be diverted, polluted, or mixed with cold springs, and were anxious to see eighteenth-century Bath regain its Roman splendours, the city leaders took up a much grander plan for ornamenting the city.

This grand plan 'apparently beneficial to the public, and happily with it inseparably for the citizens', was drawn up by the surveyor Thomas Baldwin.[98] The great pump room was to be rebuilt, and a set of private baths erected alongside the King's Baths. The area around all the baths was to be cleared, and a number of small lanes transformed into five new streets. One of these, Union Street, joined the upper and lower town through the site of the Bear Inn (the inn so vividly described by Smollett); the other four, Bath Street, Nash Street, Hot Bath Street, and Beau Street, provided access to the Hot and Cross Baths. Minor obstacles were to be removed from several other streets. The cost was estimated by Baldwin in 1788 as £47,163 16s. 5d., though in the Act it was put at £41,169 16s. 8d. In either case, the corporation needed help in raising money. The original plan was to raise 'an annual sum sufficient to pay the interest of fifty thousand pounds by an additional toll on the turnpikes belonging to the Bath Trust', but opposition from nearby towns and the turnpike trustees forced a compromise. By the Act, passed in 1789, only £25,000 was to be borrowed, the new tolls were correspondingly reduced, and imposed only on pleasure carriages. The corporation was to give up rights to property valued at £9,006 3s. 'at least', to pay £7,163 16s. 5d. on demand, and to repay the £25,000 at a rate of £700 a year.[99]

The money was borrowed and the improvements carried out by a set of commissioners consisting of the mayor, aldermen and common council, the Members of Parliament, and 22 others. The interests of the commissioners and the corporation were not identical, but usually the commissioners acted as an extension of the select body: the corporation members were the most active commissioners, while the city surveyor, Thomas Baldwin, was appointed as the commissioners' architect and Philip George, the town clerk, as their clerk. The pump rooms and baths were built by workmen hired by the commissioners under the direction of their architect. But buildings along the new streets were erected according to the commissioners' designs either by the property owners, who contracted to set back their houses, or by builders who purchased the leases for that part of the property acquired by the commissioners which was not needed for the public street.[100]

The commissioners began promptly with the pump room and Bath Street. They were treating for the property as soon as the Act was passed, and took down houses as soon as they were acquired. By 1 April 1790 they could advertise the sale by auction of 420ft of building ground in Bath Street 'to be let in fee' according to plans and elevations exhibited in the guildhall. The plan for the colonnade to protect walkers between the pump room and Cross Bath was accepted on 16 April, and in the same month work in Cheap Street had advanced to a point where the commissioners had to close the street to prevent accidents.[101] The commissioners could not keep up this progress. Baldwin, the architect, was at this time not only acting for the commissioners and the corporation, but was also involved in other developments, especally the Bathwick estates, and the extent of his interests, plus the financial difficulties which led to his bankruptcy in 1793, delayed the work. On 28 September 1792 the commissioners stopped work at the Cross Bath 'in consequence of Mr Baldwin not having delivered his account of monies received and paid by him for or on account of the said commissioners.'[102] Baldwin protested against 'insidious insinuations' about the slow progress of improvements and the low state of the commissioners' finances. He promised a general statement

> which I flatter myself will clearly prove that had the convenyance so frequently applied for, been engrossed and sealed at the time it ought to have been, the builders would long since had had their Title Deeds, and that you could have raised Money to discharge your tradesmen's bills, and for other necessary purposes.[103]

This conveyance of the corporation's rights was obtained so that by January 1793 the commissioners could auction the fee farm rents of £260 16s a year on property in Bath Street and Cheap Street, for £6,780 10s. The purchaser, Walter Wiltshire, bought the rents 'with a view to oblige and serve this corporation' and for the protection of the hot springs, and was repaid in part by a corporation bond for £6,000, secured by mortgage on the rents. The sale did not, as Baldwin expected, end difficulties, and in June 1793 he was suspended as architect.[104] The pump room, private baths, and Bath Street were finished by John Palmer according to Baldwin's plans.

Parting with Baldwin did not eliminate the commissioners' problems. The cost of the works seems to have been greater than expected, while the war and the depression in 1793 cannot have made it easy to sell leases to local builders. The commissioners also found themselves involved in complicated disputes over rights to property they wanted, in the churchyard, on the site of what is now York Street, and at the Bear Inn, the site of Union street:[105] although the commissioners agreed with Henry Phillott for his interest in the Bear Inn by May 1791, a Chancery case halted completion of the street for ten years. The delay might have been longer had not Joseph and Charles Phillott, heirs to Henry's interest and bankers, agreed by 1802 to take over property already acquired by the commissioners, buy out the other interests, pay the commissioners £1,200 towards the completion of Burton Street (the link between Union and Milsom Street) and themselves ensure the building of Union Street with elevations acceptable to the commissioners. All ground rents over 11s. 6d. per running foot would be paid to the commissioners. The Phillotts were successful enough to allow the commissioners to sell the 'overplus' ground rents for £1749 17s. 6d., by June 1807.[106]

According to the later report of the Municipal Corporations Commission, the actual cost of the improvements, excluding interest, amounted to £64,233 and the receipts to £50,512. The gap was partly filled by the request from the corporation member Leonard Coward: by 1805, they had received £7,344 from his estate. The remainder came from the excess of the new tolls on pleasure carriages over the interest of the money borrowed, which was enough to pay the full amount, and to reduce the sum ultimately repaid by the corporation from £25,000 to £22,900.[107] Nonetheless, the cost of the 'grand plan' and other improvements carried out by the corporation alone led to increased civic indebtedness in 1795 and 1798 (table 22 and fig. 20). By 1800, the total amount was £32,600. The interest on this debt came to absorb a large part of the town's revenue: a total of only £48 10s. in 1700 and £125 3s. 4d. in 1750 had become £1663 19s. 1d. in 1800.[108]

The funds needed by the corporation were, on the whole, supplied locally. Over the first two-thirds of the century, the creditors were members of the ruling elite (or their relatives), charities (with one friendly society), a local physician and a man who was probably an attorney, a clergyman and two gentlemen with connections with the town and neighbourhood (table 23). The pattern did not change greatly in the period after 1765, in spite of a marked increase in the amount of the debt or the number of persons involved. Investors were still either from the town or, to a much lesser extent from the neighbouring parishes; only a few seem to have lived as far away as Bristol. The money was supplied by the local doctors, apothecaries, tradesmen and retailers, along with some men connected with the building trades, who seem to have accepted bonds in payment for work rather than deliberately invested. Corporation members appear in considerable numbers. This was at least partly due to civic policy: in 1775, a committee set up to borrow £3,000 was instructed to give 'the preference to the gentlemen of the corporation who shall choose to advance the same.'[109] The most noticeable difference after 1765, aside from the numbers involved, is the number of women who found city bonds a safe investment.

In remodelling the town centre and the baths and pump rooms, the corporation, with the commissioners of the 1789 Act, put one of the last important touches to Georgian Bath. Further building projects would be completed or begun after the hiatus caused by war and depression, but these only continued development at the outskirts of the town. Indeed, at the time it was actively changing the centre, the magistracy was accused of preventing such development on the edges, by not allowing building on the Freemen's Common.

Table 23   Bondholders of Bath corporation

A   Holders of bonds sometime between 1700 and 1764

professional	
apothecary	1 (C)*
clergy	1
physician	1
solicitor	?1
trades etc.	
lacemaker	1 (C)
saddler	1 (C)
tailor	?1 (C)
vintner	2 (2C)
woollen draper	1 (C)
charities	4
Charity School children	
Churchwardens of SS Peter and Paul	
Churchwardens of Swainswick	
Lady Moyer's Charity	
Amicable Bathonian Society	1
'gents'	1
country gentlemen	1
	17

B   Holders of bonds sometime between 1765 and 1799

professional	
apothecaries	7 (6C)
attorneys	?2 (town clerk and ? another)
bankers	2 (2C)
clergy	1
physicians	1 (C)
surgeons	5 (4C)
trades etc.	
carrier	1 (C)
innkeeper	1 (C)
laceman	1 (C)
linen draper	2 (2C)
saddler	1 (C)
vintner	?1
wine merchant	1
carpenter and builder	2
ironmonger	1
mason	4 } Possibly given bonds in payment of goods
plasterer	1 } rather than deliberate investors
plumber	2
timber merchants	1
charities	2
Charity School children	
Churchwardens of SS Peter and Paul	
'gents'	5 (2C)
country gentlemen	1
esquires	3
baronet	1
women	14
child	1
unidentified	5
	69

Source: Bath Corporation, Chamberlains' Accounts, 1700–1764; 'Book of account of the several sums of money borrowed by the Corporation of Bath [1765–1803]'.
*Corporation members marked 'C'.

The city fathers had, throughout the early eighteenth century, defended the rights of the freemen, especially their monopoly of the right to carry on a trade or to open a shop in the city limits. In 1714, they considered a Act of Parliament excluding unqualified traders, and in 1726, 1730 and 1736, they repeated prohibitions against 'foreigners', while at times contributing financially to the prosecution of those who disobeyed. These byelaws affected both those who lived permanently in the city and those who came to Bath 'during the seasons wherein strangers resort to the said city'. The corporation thus attempted to reserve the benefits of Bath's expansion to the freemen, but its attempt to keep the seasonal trade for its citizens must have been even more difficult than its attack on resident non-free traders. Once, at least, a compromise was reached. In 1702, strangers were allowed shops in the gravel walks for £15 apiece, while townsmen paid only £8.[110] By the 1750s, the magistracy was still active against unfree traders, though primarily with the object of forcing them to pay 20 guineas for the freedom. The advantages for which new freemen paid were, however, lost in 1765 with the Merchant Taylors' suit against William Glazeby. By this time the governing body seems unwilling to waste money attempting to defend the freemen's monopoly against the trend of the times; as a result, the building boom of the last part of the century was completely free of any restriction.[111]

One advantage which survived 1765 was the right of resident freemen to share in the Bath Commons Estate, a farm in Walcot granted to the freemen in 1619 as their share of the common lands of the manor of Barton. The common was held in trust for the freemen by the town, which found a tenant for the farm, paid for repairs, and divided the net proceeds annually among freemen living in Bath. The amounts were not large – 14s. to £2 12s. between 1770 and 1790 – but they allowed freemen to obtain higher premiums for apprentices who would share the freedom than non-freemen, even after 1765.

During most of the eighteenth century, the freemen seemed contented with the corporation's management of their estate. Losing trading rights in 1765 may have damaged the relationship between freemen and corporation. In any case, in 1789, a group of freemen petitioned to see the Commons' accounts from 1768 and, more important, brought up the question of building on the Commons:

> The buildings of this city have been gradually extended quite to the bounds of the commons, and we have lately seen an adjoining piece of ground, no more than one acre, and apparently of little value, by the judicious and well-timed conduct of its present owners, so highly improved as to produce a ground rent far exceeding the income of the commons, though containing upwards of ninety-five acres . . . ; if the whole estate may be thought too extensive to be covered with buildings, we conceive a part might be rendered much more beneficial to the freemen than at present, by being let out for gardens or pleasure-grounds.[112]

The magistracy agreed to allow inspection of the accounts, but argued that under the 1619 award, it could not grant valid building leases without an Act of Parliament. After a Chancery case in 1791, the freemen petitioned the corporation to obtain an Act, which it eventually tried to do between 1804 and 1807, at the expense of the Commons estate.

The corporation has been accused of refusing to allow building on the common in order to maintain the value of its property near the centre. The question is whether they could issue building leases, about which there was clearly some doubt, and, even more, whether they were sincere in trying to get an Act of Parliament. The two bills were lost in face of opposition by neighbouring proprietors, who objected to possible competition and wanted to keep the advantage their property had from its proximity to unbuilt land. None-the-less, some freemen felt that the city had not intended to obtain the Act.[113] Whatever the truth, the Commons remained undivided and unbuilt until an Act in 1879 paid off the surviving freemen.

It is clear that the corporation was, especially in the last half of the eighteenth century, deeply involved in the growth of the town, using its funds, especially towards the end, on a scale such as the elder Wood had wanted in the early part of the century. Unfortunately, the improvements did not, as the promoters hoped, encourage the fashion for Bath. Bath flourished in the days of Nash and John Wood, despite deficiencies in baths and pump rooms; it was becoming unfashionable as a resort while civic rulers and Improvement Commissioners were putting the finishing touches on the new town centre.

6   The corporation and the government of Bath

The corporation of Bath was concerned with the development of the eighteenth-century town not only through its ownership of property, but also through its role as the main instrument of local government, charged by its charters with the maintenance of the 'public good, common utility and good ruling of the city'. The usual instruments through which the corporation carried out these duties were the justices of the peace, that is, the mayor, the recorder, and two other justices elected under the charter of 1590. The mayor was also coroner: he or the recorder presided over the borough quarter sessions and the Court of Record, together with the other justices or the town clerk. The justices were assisted by two bailiffs and two chief constables, all corporation members, and two serjeants-at-mace. For police there were five mayor's officers and a variable number of tithingmen appointed by the corporation as lord of the manor, the latter used only in emergencies.

The jurisdiction of the Bath justices was restricted, like that of the corporation, to the city limits of Bath, which by the 1590 charter included the parishes of St James, St Michael and SS Peter and Paul, along with part of the parish of Walcot. Gilmore's map shows that in 1692 these boundaries contained the built-up area, but over the eighteenth century the town spread far beyond the city limits. The growth of Bath, tenfold over the century, increased the responsibilities of the corporation, especially since standards of amenities expected in towns, and, in particular in watering places, were rising. Any member might find himself acting on committees as well as attending the eight to 14 meetings a year, but the heaviest burden fell on the four justices who, besides the other courts, were by 1753 meeting every Monday to hear the visitors' complaints against chairmen and bath attendants. In 1773 the corporation considered obtaining an Act which would have made all aldermen who had been mayor justices for life, and in 1783 a committee was set up to discuss ways of relieving 'the daily duty attendant and inseparable from the city magistracy and its officers'. Relief came only in 1794 by a new charter, the most important of its provisions being the right to appoint up to nine additional justices from the corporation. Although the additional justices were elected each year, as were the two elected under the Elizabethan charter, the same men tended to be re-appointed, thus producing a semi-permanent bench, a belated answer to the difficulties accompanying the growth of eighteenth-century Bath.[114]

The maintenance of order in Bath had its own peculiar problems. Warner argued in 1801 that because Bath had little trade and no manufacturers:

the higher classes of people and their dependants constitute the chief part of the population; and the number of the lower classes being but small, there are consequently few whose avocations are not known, and whose person and characters are not familiar; a notoriety that necessarily operates with them as a powerful check upon all attempts at open fraud, violence, or breaches of the peace.[115]

Warner was too optimistic. The presence of wealthy visitors was itself an attraction and the waters an excuse for vagrants to come to town. Fear of increasing the number of beggars lay behind the corporation's initial opposition to the founding of the Mineral Water Hospital, and the charity was itself used as a means of social control: the rules forbade invalids to come to the hospital before they were officially accepted, and the Act founding the institution also gave the Bath magistrates special powers over those pretending to be sick. There were also the byelaws forbidding poor strangers from acting as basket men and women in the town.[116]

The well-born Company, though not given to begging, were themselves a source of trouble as well as revenue. Gambling was a major attraction of Bath in the early eighteenth century, but it brought disorder. Moreover, the Bath magistrates were legally required to suppress certain forms of gaming. How active they were in disturbing the Company is unclear. In 1739 the new Act against gambling did not prevent the season from being the most successful for years.[117] One reason may have been the popularity of the game of EO, designed specifically to elude the Act. After 1745, when that game became illegal, the justices destroyed several EO tables, though one may suspect that the lower-class gamesters suffered most from their attentions: a letter in the *London Evening Post* in 1750 applauded the suppression of the footmen's EO table, while revealing that the upper classes were playing without hindrance. Even in 1791, a writer remarked that outside London, there was no part of the world with more gaming than Bath, and the problem persisted until Bath ceased to be a centre of fashionable society.[118]

Gaming was not the only problem of keeping order among the nobility and gentry. Beau Nash assisted the corporation by forbidding duelling, though he was unable to suppress it entirely. There were also occasional outbursts of violence, such as an attack in 1747 by the Duke of Hamilton and friends on a lodging house, while in 1769, during a disputed election of a master of ceremonies, such disturbances occurred among the Company that the mayor was forced to read the Riot Act.[119] The upper classes, while expecting the Bath magistrates to prevent popular disorder, could be disorderly in their turn, and much more difficult to control.

Closely connected with keeping the peace was another duty mentioned in the 1590 charter, the 'victualling' of Bath. Failure to ensure an adequate supply of food at reasonable prices could mean riots in any town. In Bath, dependent for its prosperity on visitors, the corporation had another reason for concern. Guides to watering places noticed the availability of good and cheap meat, fish and other provisions. For this reason, the Bath justices seized large quantities of underweight butter in 1739 and petitioned in 1778 against a bill for preserving fish in the Severn on the grounds that 'the usual supply of fish would be much lessened to the great and manifest injury of the inhabitants of this city and the nobility and gentry who resort thereunto.'[120]

Although the Elizabethan charter gave the corporation the right to legislate on the markets, the power was used for only a few byelaws. The growth of the town made it necessary to expand the markets and to control them more carefully. Possibly because difficulties in the 1760s over byelaws on freemen's rights raised doubts about the validity of any byelaws dealing with trade, the corporation obtained in the 1766 Act not only the right to move the market and change the market days, but also the right to make byelaws regulating the markets, powers which it used extensively in 1767.[121]

In normal times, the corporation seems to have succeeded in 'victualling' the town: visitors and inhabitants spoke of well-regulated and well-stocked markets.[122] The corporation was not, however, able to deal with widespread economic difficulties. At various times, the justices found it necessary to swear in the chairmen as special constables in order to suppress riots over the price of food, though, except for the crisis years of the Napoleonic wars, the actual damage was slight. While discouraging disorders, the corporation supported various subscriptions for feeding the poor of the city. This interest of the corporation in the price of provisions (along with the price of coal) explains its concern with improvements in transport, apart from the interests of its members.

Bath should have had few problems with water supply, since 'the hills around abound with springs within fifty feet of their summits'.[123] Wood listed a total of seven public conduits fed by two springs, one in Walcot, the other probably on Beechen Cliff. The springs also supplied water to those houses to which the corporation granted 'feathers' of water at a yearly rent. The corporation originally treated the grant of the 'feathers' from their pipes as a privilege rather than a public service, just as they did the 'gouts' to the common sewer, giving the preference and a smaller rent to their own members. The corporation's supply was not enough in the 1730s to provide all who wanted water, though they hired a man on £2 a year to report wastage: in 1749 Wood still found that 'the scarcity of water is such that these houses are but ill supplied.'[124] By the 1750s, the corporation decided to construct a reservoir on Beechen Cliff to meet the shortage It was begun in 1756, but ran into difficulties over rights to the springs and to lay pipes, and only the 1766 Act settled these problems. Civic rulers also obtained rights to three springs in Bathwick in the 1769 Pulteney Estate Act, and as trustee for the Freemen's Estate, kept an eye on those in the commons. These changes resulted in increased water rents, to the disgust of some outside the corporation who argued that the 1769 Act 'was meant to accommodate the inhabitants, not to bring in an enormous revenue to the corporation':[125] Another sore point was the disparity between rents, which could vary from 15s. to 55s. for similar houses, according to when they had been granted. The corporation did not, however, have a monopoly of supplying water: many proprietors had their own springs and waterworks. Nor did the body make it a conditon of their leases that tenants take their water. The splitting of the water supply among a number of proprietors continued to cause difficulties, but, all in all, the water supply was, in the better-off areas at least, comparatively good for so large a town.[126]

The transformation of Bath into a Georgian pleasure resort multiplied the services expected of its rulers. For the inhabitants of Bath, the paving, cleansing, watching and lighting of their streets was desirable not only for their own comfort and safety, but also for that of the wealthy visitors they hoped to attract. The growth of the town caused by its popularity made the services still more essential. Byelaws had been passed in 1646 and afterwards to prevent nuisances and to compel householders to sweep in front of their property, and in 1702, with Queen Anne's visit in prospect, the corporation ordered ten lights to be set up by the magistrates and paid for by a poor rate, but these methods proved inadequate to meet the standards of the eighteenth century. The corporation might have used its chartered powers to regulate these matters, but it was apparently reluctant to make orders dealing with the general public. Faced with 'the complaints of the Company that resort to the city', it chose instead to obtain a Local Act at the early date of 1708. A series of such acts followed, each designed to meet more efficiently than the previous ones the needs of inhabitants and visitors.[127]

The early Bath Acts differed from later Improvement Acts in enlarging the powers of existing authorities rather than setting up new bodies of commissioners. Wood described authority under the Acts as 'vested in the corporation of Bath': strictly speaking, it was vested in the justices, with some assistance from the aldermen. The first three Acts gave the mayor, recorder and justices powers to enforce the old system of personal obligations due from householders, the paving and cleansing of the streets before their houses and, from those paying a penny a week to the poor rate, the hanging out of a candle or lamp during winter nights. The last duty could, however, be carried out by the erection of lamps at places approved by the justices and paid for by a rate, if all the inhabitants agreed. By 1752 the corporation was paying lamp rate on the baths, though in 1755 lighting by rate was still being introduced in some parts of the town. The magistrates also appointed the unpaid surveyors, and the scavengers and rakers, confirmed the rate settled by the surveyors, and appointed the collectors of that rate. Besides the magistrates' usual powers for maintaining the peace, the mayor and aldermen were given authority to license and control the chairmen, always a turbulent crowd. The night watch, first mentioned in an Act in 1739, but existing earlier, was appointed by the magistrates who both set and levied the rate of it.[128]

Wood thought in 1749 that the statutes relating to Bath 'upon a strict review will be found to answer most of the good purposes for which they were obtained . . . The citizens, even by these laws, have it in their power to make it flourish, and become one of the most agreeable towns in this or any other kingdom'.[129] The corporation which administered the laws was not so well satisfied. In 1757 it obtained the first Bath Act not tacked to a Turnpike Act, and with an elective element. The 'churchwardens and overseers of the poor and the other inhabitants' of each of the four city parishes now appointed two unpaid surveyors and two rate collectors, and as many scavengers as they thought necessary, the surveyors for each parish levied a rate for the scavengers and lighting. Householders were still expected to clean and pave before their property. The magistrates enforced the system, confirming appointments and rates, deciding where lamps were needed, setting the size of the watch and the watch rate, and judging offenders. The corporation, though it appointed the magistrates, was directly involved only as ratepayer.[130]

By 1766, the corporation regarded the 1757 Act as 'in almost every respect defective', and decided to obtain a new one which would

have the streets etc. paved by a pound Rate, to be cleaned by a daily scavenger, and to have the power of directing all matters relative to the paving, cleansing, enlightening & watching the streets etc. invested in the magistrates as before that act & not in the parish oficers.[131]

The 1766 Act treated the city as a unit rather than a group of parishes, but the 'power of directing matters' was vested not in the magistrates alone but in a body of commissioners, thereby bringing Bath into line with the usual practice. The mayor and two justices for the time being were members, along with four men elected for life by the corporation, while in spite of the civic rulers' wishes, the inhabitants of each parish also elected four men worth £50 a year in real property to act as commissioners. The Act did not specify that the corporation choose only its own members, though in fact it did, but it decreed that the parish representatives must not be members of the corporation.[132]

The 23 commissioners had the duty of looking after the streets and public places of the city of Bath. They appointed the salaried officials – clerks, treasurers, surveyors, collectors, scavengers and rakers – looked after the lights, appointed and organized the watch, and acted against nuisances. The change from requiring certain duties of householders was not complete: they were still liable to pave before their property, though if they did not do so according to the commissioners' directions, the latter could pave the streets themselves and obtain repayment through the courts. The corporation itself as still responsible for the High Street and markets, and for the old bridge. The powers of the commissioners did not cover all the city: in the streets belonging to the Duke of Kingston, to the south of the Abbey Church, they could not break up the streets or compel the householders to pave. This, with the exclusion from the property which the Act allowed the corporation to acquire for other purposes of 'the Duke of Kingston's ground behind the Burrough Walls', was the price paid by the city to avoid the duke's oppositon. The proceedings of the commissioners, which survive for 1766–82, show that though the city rulers tried to keep authority in their own hands, civic commissioners were not the most active: the parish commissioners carried the burden.[133]

The Bath Act of 1766 was more durable than its predecessors, lasting almost 50 years. The corporation and the commissioners wanted a new Act somewhat earlier, and in 1790 and 1792 petitioned Parliament, but it was not until 1814 that an Act was obtained, apparently because of opposition in the town.

The Improvement Acts, like the powers of the magistrates, were restricted to the city limits, though by the late eighteenth century the town was spreading far beyond them. The Act which in 1769 allowed the Pulteney estate to be used for the building of Pulteney Bridge also extended the city magistrates's powers over part of the parish of Bathwick and the enlarged jurisdiction was included in the 1794 charter, unfortunately, it was not exercised. Part of Walcot had been brought into the city limits by the 1590 charter which, according to Wood, left the inhabitants of the 'in-parts' faced with a double authority resulting in a 'delay of public justice'.[134] However, later Acts treat the in-parts of Walcot as under the control of the Bath magistrates, and may therefore have strengthened their hands against the justices of the hundred of Bathforum. There remained however, the outpart of the parish, under the authority of the county magistrates, and as the town spread into that area, the powers of parish and county officers proved at least as inadequate as those the city magistrates had in Bath.

For this reason, some inhabitants of the outpart of Walcot decided to apply for their own improvement act, which Bath corporation supported on condition that the Act extend its jurisdiction over the whole of Walcot. The attempt failed, apparently because the corporation had not given the required notice, and in 1792, the body duly announced its intention to apply for another Act. This proposal was also opposed; a writer to the *Bath Journal* demanded, 'Let us examine how far powers of late Acts have or have not been carried into execution before we entrust our liberties and properties to the disposal of any uniform self-elected body of men on earth'. The corporation decided it was 'inexpedient' to try for the Act, perhaps because it was then involved in negotiations over its new charter.[135]

Walcot and Bathwick were left to obtain their own Acts, Walcot in 1793, Bathwick in 1801. Each acquired a body of commissioners, not elected as in Bath but appointed by the Act with the right to fill vacancies themselves; the powers were much as in the Bath Acts. The two parishes were more fortunate than that of Lyncombe and Widcombe, which remained under parish and county government.

There was only one victory for uniformity in Bath during these years. The Walcot Act of 1793 authorized the corporation to make byelaws for hackney coaches within ten miles of the guildhall door, for chairmen within two miles, and for porters and basket women within three; in 1793–4 they made regulations covering every possible detail, including the hilly nature of Bath. Otherwise, the urban area of Bath remained divided between several jurisdictions, and under the control of at least three sets of magistrates and three sets of commissioners. The police suffered most; the situation at the end of the eighteenth century was the one described by the Municipal Corporations Commissioners in 1835:

> At present there are in the same city, practically speaking, four distinct establishments of watchmen and police officers; the mayor's officers and tithingmen, the city watchmen, and Walcot police; to which upon the same system would be added a fifth, were it not that Lyncombe and Widcombe is at present altogether uncared for.[136]

Listing the powers granted by the Improvement Acts does not show how effective they were. The magistrates and commissioners seem to have been comparatively successful in maintaining law and order, at least in those parts of the city frequented by visitors. In 1763, Dr Sutherland thought: 'Security has ever been the distinguishing characteristic of Bath. No where such opportunities for thieving. No where so few thefts'. Warner spoke in 1801 of Bath's advantages in this respect.[137] There were, of course, nests of thieves and prostitutes in the slum areas, especially those outside the city limits; the corporation itself argued in 1792 that the divided jurisdiction gave rise to 'an evil and a delay of justice, by rogues, thieves, and other disorderly persons, committing offences in one jurisdiction and running immediately into the other, and thereby frequently escaping justice, which in part destroys the welfare of the place and the morals of the people'. The beggars of Bath remained notorious, especially in the outparts of Walcot, and Widcombe and Lyncombe remained a trouble spot, outside the city's power, and with no police or lighting.[138]

Such problems were not peculiar to Bath. The maintenance of the peace, at least in the prosperous areas, was usually adequate to satisfy the visitors, though the system could not handle large-scale riots. When, in 1780, the Gordon riots spread to Bath, the magistrates could not prevent the burning of the Catholic chapel and priest's house, and were informed afterwards that many visitors would leave unless the troops which had been summoned remained. There was some feeling that the magistrates had been neglectful and should pay the rate for damages instead of levying it on the inhabitants. In fairness to the Bath magistrates, they acted with much greater promptness in calling for troops than those of London, when faced with a problem which no authority, in the absence of an organized police force, could have prevented.[139]

As for paving, cleaning and lighting, the Bath newspapers occasionally record difficulties.[140] In 1755 the manager of the Walcot lamps took them down and stored them in the vault of the church, and in 1792 the commissioners fined the lamp-lighter of the same parish ten guineas for neglect. At various times, the commissioners warned that they would be forced to repair certain paving and obtain compensation from the householders. These reports show the problems and the actions of the commissioners, but we cannot know whether matters were better or worse when the newspapers are silent: descriptions by inhabitants and visitors vary, often with their relations with the corporation. Nonetheless, the scraps of evidence available give the impression that the eighteenth century saw a general improvement in spite of the considerable increase in the town's size.[141]

The efforts of the corporation, though valuable to inhabitants and visitors, did not in the end prevent the decline of the fashion for Bath. Between 1660 and 1800, Bath had been transformed into a major city, and a centre of fashionable society, one which remains a symbol of eighteenth-century England. The 'nobility and gentry' of the reign of Beau Nash were followed by merchants, industrialists, and men who prospered from colonial ventures, annoying those who felt with Smollett that the newly rich lowered the tone of the place, but bringing considerable increase in prosperity. Individually they might spend less, but their numbers stimulated the physical expansion of the town, to an extent that the relatively fewer members of the aristocracy did not. The decision of many of the visitors to settle in the town, though adding to the expansion, accelerated the changes in the character of the community. The leaders of fashion and their imitators came to desert the inland spas for the seaside resorts, as did the newer sorts of visitor who stayed for only a few weeks or even days rather than the six or eight weeks of the season at Bath. The Napoleonic wars may have frightened those with less courage than George III from the seaside, but they would only have delayed the end of Bath's long reign as the foremost British watering place.

BIBLIOGRAPHY

MANUSCRIPT SOURCES
Archives of the corporation of Bath
The archives of the corporation of Bath provide the basic materials for this study, supplying a substantial framework to which evidence gleaned from other records, private papers, newspapers and local guides can be attached. The corporation suffered no disruption in the late seventeenth and eighteenth century, so that the succession of records was not broken: only once were those records out of the corporation's control, in 1791, when the deputy chamberlain refused to return some rentals and a Chancery case had to be brought against him. The care taken of the rentals by the corporation, and the use of massive volumes for the minutes, the chamberlains' accounts after 1733, and many other records, has kept the main series almost, if not entirely, complete.

The most useful corporation records for this study were the minutes, 1631–1800 (especially 1684–1800) and the chamberlains' accounts, in rolls from 1684/5 to 1732/3 (six of which are missing), and in volumes from 1733/4 to 1799/1800. These were supplemented by the Committee Report Book, 1794–1837, the Book of Account (Bond Book), 1765–1803, the King's

Bath book, 1774–6, the Chairmen's book, 1743–56, and the rent rolls, water rents and various corporation leases. Also valuable were the records of the Freemen's Estate, especially the enrolment of apprentices, and the papers of the other bodies concerned with the government of Bath, the Paving and Police Commissioners' proceedings, 1766–1782, and the order book and bond book of the Bath Improvement Act Commissioners, 1789–1832.

Other archives
On the whole, the manuscript materials available in other repositories only supplement the Bath archives. The Bath Reference Library has a useful manuscript collection, including papers dealing with John Wood and other Bath architects and builders, though only a fraction were used for this study. The University of Nottingham holds the Manvers papers, which contain material about the property in Bath owned by the Duke of Kingston, including the Kingston Baths.

National records
The Public Record Office provided the records of the 1664 Hearth Tax, E179/256/16, the most important document for the study of Bath's population before the 1801 census.

PRINTED PRIMARY SOURCES
One of the most important sources for the development of any watering place are the memoirs, diaries and letters of the visitors. These do exist in unpublished form, but the number which have been published, for Bath at least, and are easily accessible in the Bath Reference Library and the topographical collections of the Bodleian Library and the British Library, made it unnecessary to search the local archives of England. A. Barbeau's *Life and Letters at Bath in the Eighteenth Century* contains a list of such publications. There are also writings by medical men on mineral waters in general and Bath in particular, which often include topographical as well as medical details: a useful list is provided by W. Whitaker in L. Richardson's *Wells and Springs of Somerset*, in the Memoirs of the Geological Survey (1928). the memoirs and letters (often published soon after they were written) shade gradually into the local guides and histories by contemporaries, of which Bath has two of the best, John Wood's *An Essay towards a Description of Bath* (2nd edn, 1749), and Richard Warner's *The History of Bath* (1801). Guides and contemporary histories need critical handling – the same story is often passed unchanged from one to another – but they include valuable information on the facilities offered when they were published, such as lodgings or coach services. The guides for Bath begin in 1753, with the first edition of Thomas Boddely's *Bath and Bristol Guide,* and continue after 1762 in C. Pope's *The New Bath Guide* (after 1770 published by R. Cruttwell) at frequent intervals to the end of the century; the directories start with a section in R. Cruttwell's *The Stranger's Assistant and Guide to Bath,* and includes a section in *Bailey's British Directory* of 1784 and one in the *Universal British Directory of Trade and Commerce* of 1790.

Maps and views, either included in the histories and guides, or sold separately, provided information in another form. There is an excellent collection in the Bath Reference Library, supplemented by that in the Bodleian Library. The maps used in this study were those in John Speed, *The Theatre of the Empire of Great Britain* (1611), Thomas Johnson, *Thermae Bathonicae* (1634), and R. Warner, *The History of Bath* (1801), along with the separately published maps of Bath by Joseph Gilmore (surveyed 1692, published 1694), John Wood (surveyed 1735, published 1736), J. Basnett, publisher (1780), C. Harcourt Masters (1794), and an anonymous 'New and correct plan of the city of Bath' (1750 and 1760).

Newspapers were another invaluable source, not only for the notices of local events, but also for the lists of visitors and the advertisements of those who hoped to meet the visitors' needs. Bath had several early newspapers: the *Bath Journal,* begun in 1744, the *Bath Advertiser* (later the *Bath Weekly Chronicle*), begun in 1755, and the *Bath Herald,* begun in 1792, almost complete runs of which are to be found in the Bath Reference Library. Some London newspapers produced references to Bath, i.e., *Poor Robin's Intelligence, Hooker's Weekly Miscellany*, the *London Evening Post*, and the *Daily Post*.

OFFICIAL PUBLICATIONS

Only a few official publications were used in this study, but those few were important. The census of 1801, with all its faults, gives the first solid evidence as to the size of Bath's population and some indication of the occupations of its inhabitants. The *First Report* of the Royal Commission on Municipal Corporations, though published in 1835, contains information on Bath in the eighteenth century and before. The *Journals* of the House of Commons were also useful, especially on the background to bills and Acts of Parliament.

The Local Acts of Parliament were themselves important; those used for this study were:

6 Anne c. 42 (1708) Paving etc. and turnpike
7 Geo. I c. 19 (1720) Paving etc. and turnpike
12 Geo II c. 20 (1739) Paving etc. and turnpike
20 Geo. II c. 65 (1757) Paving etc.
6 Geo. III c. 70 (1766) Paving etc
29 Geo. III c. 73 (1789) Improvement

Walcot
33 Geo. III c. 89 (1793) Paving etc.

Bathwick
9 Geo. III c. 95 (1769) Pulteney estate.
41 Geo. III c. 126 (1801) Paving etc.

NOTES

1 For the general history of the spas see R. Lennard, 'The watering places', *Englishmen at Rest and Play* (1931), 1–79, and J. A. R. Pimlott, *The Englishman's Holiday* (1947, repr. 1976).
2 P. Borsay, 'The English urban renaissance: the development of provincial urban culture c.1680–c.1760', *Social History*, II (1977), 581–603.
3 L. Toulmin Smith (ed.), *The Itinerary of John Leland*, I (1907), 143.
4 P. R. James, *The Baths of Bath in the Sixteenth and Early Seventeenth Centuries* (1938), 89.
5 J. Wood, *An Essay towards a Description of Bath* (2nd edn, 1749), 422.
6 R. Warner, *The History of Bath* (1801), 187
7 J. Floyer, *The History of Cold Bathing* (1702); T. Guidott, *An Apology for the Bath* (1705).
8 C. Morris (ed.); *The Journeys of Celia Fiennes* (1949), 21.
9 Toulmin Smith, *op. cit.*, 140.
10 H. Chapman, *Thermae Redivavae* (1673), 3.
11 *Ibid.*, 2.
12 The missing streets would be Broad Street and Walcot Road, but they may have been included under Northgate Street.
13 Compare to 2.15 for Scarborough, 2.54 for Weymouth and 3.8 for Norwich:
S. C. McIntyre, 'Towns as health and pleasure resorts' (D. Phil. thesis, University of Oxford, 1973), 26; P. Corfield, 'A provincial capital in the late seventeenth century: the case of Norwich', in *The Early Modern Town*, ed. P. Clark (1976), 235.
14 T. Venner, *The Baths of Bath* (1628), 1; Chapman, *op. cit.*, 15.
15 Wood, *op. cit.*, 214–32.
16 Morris, *op. cit.*, 20–1; R. Blome, *Britannia* (1673), 196–7.

17 O. Goldsmith, *The Life of Richard Nash, Esq.* (1762), 29–31;
    J. Murch, *Biographical Sketches of Bath Celebrities* (1893), 83–4.
18 Wood, *op. cit.,* 411.
19 B. S. Penley, *The Bath Stage, a History of Dramatic Representations in Bath* (1892),
    17–21.
20 Morris, *op. cit.,* 18–19; for details of the baths at Bath, see McIntyre, *op. cit.,* 130–78.
21 Wood, *op. cit.,* 218; R. Peirce, *The History and Memoirs of Bath* (1693), 255–6;
    C. Lucas, *An Essay on Waters,* III (1756), 255–6.
22 W. Oliver, *A Practical Essay on Fevers* (1705), 223–4.
23 Wood, *op.cit.,* 222.
24 *Poor Robin's Intelligence,* 1–8 April 1676.
25 A. Pope, *Correspondence of Pope* (ed. G. Sherburn), IV (1956), 201–5; R. Cruttwell, *The
    New Bath Guide* (1780) and later editions; S. Derrick, *Letters written from Leverpoole
    . . . Bath* (1767), 85.
26 McIntyre, *op.cit.,* 463.
27 Morris, *op. cit.,* 17.
28 Wood, *op. cit.,* 354–5.
29 6 Anne c. 42; W. Albert, *The Turnpike Road System in England* (1972), 202; Wood,
    op.cit., 364.
30 Albert, *op. cit.,* 33, 42–4.
31 E. Pawson, *Transport and Economy: the turnpike roads of eighteenth-century Britain*
    (1977), 29–30.
32 Warner, *op. cit.,* 167–8.
33 K. R. Clew, *The Kennet and Avon Canal* (1968), 15–17; *Commons J.,* XIII, 20 Dec. 1699,
    84; 21 Dec 1699, 88; 22 Dec 1699, 92; 4 Jan. 1700, 94, etc.
34 Clew, *op. cit.,* 17.
35 Clew, *op. cit.,* 17–18; *Commons J.,* XVII; 23 Jan. 1711/12, 35; 26 Feb. 1711/12, 112;
    1 Mar. 1711/12, 118, etc.
36 J. R. Ward, *The Finance of Canal Building in Eighteenth-century England* (1974), 10.
37 Wood, *op. cit.,* 232.
38 R. Cruttwell, *The New Bath Guide* (1800).
39 See below, pp. 226–7.
40 Bath Corporation (hereafter cited as BC), Minutes, IX, 2 Feb. 1771, 179; Feb 1771,
    180–1; 28 Feb. 1774, 324–5.
41 J. R. Ward, 'Investment in canals and housebuilding in England' (D. Phil. thesis,
    University of Oxford, 1970), 181.
42 J. Barrett, 'Spas and seaside resorts, 1660–1780', *English Urban History, 1500–1780*:
    (Open University A322, 1977), 55.
43 Warner, *op. cit.,* 219 and 226.
44 Anon., *The Bath Contest* (1769).
45 Wood, *op. cit.,* 351.
46 C. W. Shickle, 'Notes on an old map of the parish of Walcot', *Procs Bath Natural History
    and Antiquarian Field Club,* IX (1898–1901), 183–88.
47 W. Ison, *The Georgian Buildings of Bath from 1700 to 1830* (1948), 29–48; R. Neale,
    'Society, belief and the building of Bath, 1700–1793', in *Rural Change and Urban
    Growth, 1500–1800,* ed. C. W. Chalklin and M. A. Havinden (1974), 254–77.
48 R. Cruttwell, *The Stranger's Assistant and Guide to Bath* (1773), 63–72.
49 Morris, *op.cit.,* 20–1; Derrick, *op.cit.* 105.
50 BC, Minutes, VIII, 25 May 1767, 327.
51 Penley, *op. cit.,* 33–49.
52 P. Kaufman, 'The community library: a chapter in English social history', *Trans.
    American Philosophical Soc.* LVII (1967), 11; *Universal British Directory of Trade and
    Commerce,* II (1790), 97–110.

53 Cruttwell, *New Bath Guide,* (1790), 76; (1800), 79.
54 Wood, *op. cit.,* 422–3.
55 *Ibid.*, 436–7.
56 R. Neale, 'Economic conditions and working class movements in the city of Bath, 1800–1850' (M. A. thesis, University of Bristol, 1963), 9–11.
57 Barrett, *op. cit.,* 55.
58 Warner, *op. cit.*, 236.
59 *Ibid.*, 214–17; Neale, *op. cit.*, 11–12.
60 BC, Minutes, VIII, 25 May 1767, 327.
61 Barrett, *op. cit.,* 55.
62 Neale, *op. cit.,* 78–9.
63 BC, Minutes, XI, 14 Feb. 1784, 43.
64 James, *op. cit.,* 12–25.
65 Wood, *op. cit.,* 225.
66 BC, Minutes III, 19 June 1710, 545; 7 May 1711, 568.
67 Wood, *op. cit.,* 264–5; J. Symons, *Two Letters from Mr John Symons, one of the Common Council of the City of Bath, to the Corporation of that City* (1783), 1.
68 Wood, *op. cit.,* 270.
69 T. Smollett, *An Essay on the External Use of Water* (1752), 32–3, 47–8; Wood, *op. cit,* 266–8.
70 Smollett, *op. cit.,* 38.
71 Λ. Sutherland, *Attempts to Revive Ancient Medical Doctrines,* I (1763), 126.
72 BC Minutes, VI, 12 Nov. 1743, 135.
73 L. Namier and J. Brooke, *The House of Commons, 1754–1790,* I (1964), 366.
74 A. T. Patterson, *A History of Southampton, 1700–1914,* I (1966), 75–7.
75 Royal Commission on Municipal Corporations in England and Wales, *First Report* (1835), 1125.
76 BC, Minutes, VI, 30 Sept. 1745, 184.
77 BC, Minutes, VIII, 28 June 1762, 56; 30 Oct. 1765, 219; 29 Nov. 1765, 220.
78 BC, Minutes, X, 23 Sept. 1776, 117; 12 Oct. 1779, 369; XI, 3 Oct. 1791, 378; 26 Oct. 1791, 380; 22 Nov. 1791, 382; 20 April 1792, 297; 11 June 1792, 400; 10 July 1792, 408; 24 Sept. 1792, 415; *Bath Chronicle*, 19 Sept. 1793.
79 Ison, *op. cit.* 153.
80 BC, Minutes, VII, 10 Oct. 1753, 81; 31 Dec. 1753, 83; VIII, 29 June 1761, 16.
81 BC, Minutes, VII, 9 April 1755, 131; 5 May 1755, 133; Ison, *op. cit.*, 159.
82 Chapman, *op. cit.*
83 George Beaumont and Henry Disney, *A New Tour thro' England* (1768), 113.
84 T. Smollett, *Humphry Clinker* (1771; Penguin ed, 1967), 63.
85 Symons, *op. cit.*, 1.
86 BC, Minutes, VI, 30 Mar. 1741, 68.
87 BC, Minutes, VII, 25 June 1753, 68; 17 June 1754, 101; VIII, 30 Sept. 1765, 213; *Bath Journal*, 3 Mar. 1755.
88 BC, Minutes, VIII, 5 Oct. 1761, 26; IX, 8 Oct. 1767, 2; 1 Jan. 1769, 73.
89 Ison, *op. cit.*, 35–7.
90 Lucas, *op. cit.*, III (1756), 262–4.
91 University of Nottingham, Manvers Papers, 4154, 24 July 1759; 4155, Lists of bathers.
92 J. Symons, *Observations on Vapour Bathing* (1766), i-iv.
93 BC, Minutes, IX, 28 Dec. 1772, 255; 2 Mar. 1773, 272; X, 30 Oct. 1775, 63; Chamberlains' Accounts, 1771/2, 1772/3.
94 Ison, *op. cit.*, 55.
95 BC, Minutes, X, 11 June 1778, 251.
96 BC, Minutes, X, 22 Aug. 1781, 462–3; XI, 10 May 1783, 13: XII, 22 July 1797, 257; Ison, *op. cit.,* 57–8.

97 BC, Minutes, XI, 3 Oct. 1785, 114.
98 BC, Minutes, XI, 31 Jan. 1788, 201; 5 Feb. 1788, 203; 18 Mar. 1788, 205.
99 BC, Minutes, XI, 21 May 1788, 211; 2 June 1789, 266. *Commons J.*, XLIV, 11 May 1789, 342; 13 May 1789, 359–60.
100 BC, Bath Act Order Book, 1 Jan. 1790, 49; 30 April 1790, 70.
101 *Bath Chronicle*, 1 April 1790; BC, Bath Act Order Book, 5 Mar. 1790, 61; 16 April 1790, 68; 26 Mar. 1790, 66.
102 BC, Bath Act Order Book, 28 Sept. 1792, 166.
103 *Bath Journal*, 1 Oct. 1792.
104 BC, Bath Act Order Book, 11 Jan. 1793, 183; 28 June 1793, 192; Minutes, XII, 16 May 1794, 5; 8 Aug. 1795, 57.
105 BC, Bath Act Order Book, 14 Jan. 1791, 103.
106 BC, Bath Act Order Book, 25 May 1791, 122; 3 Feb. 1802, 319; 14 April 1802, 327; 2 June 1802, 332; 24 June 1807, 408.
107 *First Report* of the Royal Commission on the Municipal Corporations of England and Wales (1835), 1125.
108 BC, Chamberlains' Accounts, 1699/1700, 1799/1800.
109 BC, Minutes, X, 30 Nov. 1775, 72.
110 BC, Minutes, III, 30 Mar. 1702, 333; IV, 25 Feb. 1714, 68; 28 Feb. 1726, 386; 4 April 1726, 402; V, 12 July 1730, 70; 27 Sept. 1736, 295; 27 Dec. 1731, 135.
111 For an account of the Bath freemen and the loss of the trade monopoly, see McIntyre, *op. cit.*, 68–73.
112 C. Hibbert, *A View of Bath* (1813), 12–13.
113 RC on Municipal Corporations, *First Report*, 1120.
114 *Bath Journal,* 15 Jan. 1753; T. Boddely, *The Bath and Bristol Guide* (1755), 39; BC, Minutes, IX, 27 Dec. 1773, 321; X, 21 Jan. 1783, 543.
115 Warner, *op. cit.*, 214–17.
116 BC, Minutes, VI, 12 Mar. 1739, 7; VIII, 25 May 1767, 327; Warner, *op. cit.,* 289–97.
117 *Hooker's Weekly Miscellany*, 27 Oct. 1739.
118 *London Evening Post*, 25–7 Jan. 1750; E. Clarke, *A Tour Through the South of England in 1791* (1793), 147.
119 PRO, KB1/8/1, Hilary 21 George II, Affidavits to information against the Duke of Hamilton and others; anon., *The Bath Contest* (1769), 1–66.
120 *Daily Post*, 16 Jan. 1739; BC, Minutes, X, 7 Mar. 1778, 224.
121 BC, Minutes, VIII, 5 Oct. 1761, 26; 24 Feb. 1767, 309–12; 25 May 1767, 326–7.
122 E.g., Morris, *op. cit.*, 23; G. S. Carey, *The Balnea* (2nd edn, 1799), 139–40.
123 RC on Municipal Corporations *First Report*, 1127.
124 BC, Minutes, V, 11 Nov. 1731, 130; Wood, *op. cit.,* 274.
125 BC, Report Book, 1 Oct. 1796, 19; Minutes, XI, 17 Feb. 1769, 82; *Bath Journal*, 17 Sept. 1792.
126 RC on Municipal Corporations, *First Report*, 1127.
127 Wood, *op. cit.*, 373; *Commons J*, XV, 20 Nov. 1707, 436; 13 Feb. 1708, 543.
128 F. Spencer, *Municipal Origins* (1911), 142; 6 Anne c. 42 (1708); 7 Geo. I c. 19, (1720); 12 Geo. II c. 20 (1739); BC, Chamberlains' Accounts, 1752/3; *Bath Journal*, 24 Mar. 1755.
129 Wood, *op. cit.*, 392.
130 20 Geo. II c. 65 (1757).
131 BC, Minutes, VIII, 20 Dec. 1765, 222.
132 6 Geo. III c. 70 (1766).
133 BC, Paving and police commissioners' proceedings, 1766–82; Minutes, VIII, 20 Dec. 1765, 222.
134 RC on Municipal Corporations *First Report*, 1114; Wood, *op. cit.*, 403–4.
135 BC, Minutes, XI, 22 Nov. 1791, 381; 6 Feb. 1793, 440; *Bath Journal*, 17 Sept. 1792.
136 RC on Municipal Corporations, *First Report*, 1119.

137 Sutherland, *op. cit.*, I, 129.
138 R. Mainwaring, *Annals of Bath* (1838), 335; *Commons J.*, XLVII, 16 Feb. 1792, 391; RC on Municipal Corporations, *First Report*, 1110.
139 BC, Minutes, X, 27 June 1780, 408; *A Serious Alarm to the People of Bath* (1782), iv-vi.
140 *Bath Journal*, 10 Nov. 1755; 8 Dec. 1755; 3 Jan 1788.
141 E.g. J. Macky, *A Journey through England* (1714–22), 144; Lucas, *op. cit.*, I, 245; Sutherland. *op. cit.*, 129; Carey, *op. cit.*, 139–42.

INDEX

Abingdon, 14, 27
Africa, 17, 26
agriculture, 7, 13, 16, 20, 27, 29, 36, 50–2, 104, 109, 127, 154, 174–5, 179
alehouses, 11, 19, 25, 110, 114, 122, 156, 161, 169, 172, 173, 184; *see also* inns and taverns
alien immigrants, 5, 104, 125–6, 149
Allen, Ralph, 211, 228, 229
Alresford, 151–2, 174–5
Alton, 173–5
Amsterdam, 105
Andover, 154, 173–5
Anne, Queen, 202, 204, 240
antiquarianism, 21–2
Antwerp, 149
apothecaries, 9, 106, 116, 178, 221, 223, 228, 234
apprentices, 4, 19, 60–2, 99, 120–2, 156–8, 160, 176, 236
Arden, forest of, 50, 52
Arlington, Lord, 125
artists, 21, 215, 220, 222
Ashby-de-la-Zouch, 7, 10, 13, 15
Ashford, 13
assemblies and assembly rooms, 22, 26, 27, 177, 179, 180, 200, 206, 223
assizes, 10, 21, 48, 122, 147, 152, 158, 160, 163, 171, 179
Atherall, Thomas, 9
attorneys, *see* lawyers
Atwood, Thomas Warr, 228, 229, 231
auctions, 22, 123, 233
Audley, Thomas, Lord, 67
Austen, Jane, 221
Avon, river, 18, 202, 210, 226

Baldwin, Thomas, 229, 231–3
Baltic, 12, 28, 97, 104, 106, 126
Banbury, 15
banking, 23, 24, 212, 221, 228
Barbon, Nicholas, 22
Barkham, Lady, 130
Barnstaple, 12, 14
Basingstoke, 14, 154, 173–5, 177
Baskerville, Thomas, 16, 26
Bath, 2, 14, 18, 23, 27, 30, 198–252; abbey, 201, 203, 206, 219, 223, 232, 241; baths, 27, 199, 202, 204, 206–8, 212, 219, 221–3, 225, 226, 230–3, 237; building, 206, 211–212, 214, 217, 223, 228, 229;

government of, 222–3, 237–42; industry, 201, 202, 220–1; occupations, 215–17, 219–21; population, 201, 203, 214–15; pump-room, 200, 204, 206, 208, 212, 225, 233, 237; role of corporation in development of, 20, 199, 204, 206, 222–3, 225–34, 237, 239–41; royal patronage, 202, 204; ruling elite, 223–5, 228, 229, 233, 234; topography, 202–4, 211, 212; town finances, 223, 226, 228, 229, 232–4; town surveyor, 229, 232, 233; visitors, 199, 202, 204, 206, 208, 210–12, 214, 217–19, 222, 225, 238, 243; waters, 199, 202, 206, 208
Batheaston, 221
Bathwick, 203, 206, 212, 214, 215, 217, 218, 219, 239, 241–2
Bedford, 18
Bedfordshire, 18
Berger, R., 9
Berkhamsted, 30
Berkshire, 151–2
Beverley, 75
Birmingham, 2, 15, 27, 29, 48, 50, 210
birth rate, 53, 59, 94, 96, 155, 170
Bishop's Waltham, 151–2, 174, 175
bishops, 96, 97, 146, 147, 152, 158, 160, 161, 167, 182
Blome, Richard, 89, 128
Bolton, 15; dukes of, 183–4
Book of Orders, 76
booksellers, 18, 24, 38, 152, 177, 219
boroughs, 50–1, 127, 147, 198, 201; *see also* charters
Borsay, P., 21, 22
Boston, 12, 108, 128
Botesdale, 129
bowling greens, 21, 180, 204
Bradford (Yorks.), 15
Bradford-on-Avon, 201
Bridgnorth, 6, 27
Bridgwater, 12; Earl of, 183
Brinkelow, Henry, 67
Bristol, 14, 18, 23, 30, 172, 200, 201, 209–11, 220, 234; Clifton, 27; economy, 5, 8, 11, 12, 17, 26–8, 103; hotwell, 27, 208; population, 16, 48
Brookes, Richard, 74–5
Browne, Sir Thomas, 109
Buckhurst, Lord, 125
Buckingham, Duke of, 125, 157

251

Buckinghamshire, 30, 88
building, 6, 9, 20, 22, 24, 109, 118, 130, 175,
    178, 181, 182, 200, 206, 211–12, 214,
    217, 223, 228, 229, 231–4, 236
Burton, Alexander, 107, 129
Burton-on-Trent, 27
Bury St Edmunds, 12, 14, 16, 27, 104, 129,
    130
Buxton, 199, 201, 202

Cambridge, 4, 10, 12, 108, 109, 114–15, 172
Cambridgeshire, 18
Camden, William, 48
canals, 18, 211
Canterbury, 4, 5, 9, 10, 12, 14, 20, 29
carriers, 18, 22–3, 106, 107, 124, 129
Cartwright, Thomas, 69, 73, 76–8
cathedral cities, 22, 29, 148, 158, 200
Catherine of Braganza, 202
catholicism, 46, 65, 69, 160, 163, 167, 179–80
Cecil, family, 8; William, Lord Burghley, 69
censuses, 61, 92, 160, 171, 221, 222; of the
    poor, 46, 47, 59, 60, 64, 73, 76, 77
ceremony, 22, 40, 148, 168, 184
Champion, W., 6
Chancery, 69, 74, 223, 225, 229, 234, 236
Chapman, Henry, 202–4
chapmen and pedlars, 29, 156, 172, 173
charity, 11, 14, 25, 47, 58, 65–74, 90, 126,
    158–60, 167, 171–2
Charles I, 157, 162–3, 168, 170
Charles II, 145, 169–70, 173, 180–2
charters, 89, 125, 147, 181, 237, 239, 241
Chartres, J., 31
Chelmsford, 27
Cheltenham, 30
Cheshire, 29
Chester, 8, 12, 18, 29, 179
Chichester, 28
Christchurch, 175
Church, 14, 20, 67, 68, 71, 97, 146, 152, 160,
    163, 167
Cirencester, 15
Civil War, 12, 15, 19, 27, 97, 145, 162–70,
    184, 199, 201
clergy, 74, 109, 110, 112, 113, 114, 147, 150,
    152, 158, 160, 163, 167, 171, 178, 234
Clerke, Sir Henry, 164
Clobery, Sir John, 182
clubs, 21–2, 24, 180, 234, 235
coaches, 18, 23, 114, 129, 172, 209, 219, 228
cockfights, 21
coffee-houses, 21, 27, 28, 99, 130, 180, 200,

    204, 219–20, 225, 228
Coggeshall, 104
Colchester, 5, 12, 15, 97, 104, 105, 107, 125,
    127, 129
commercial revolution, 17, 26–8
companies, see gilds and companies
conspicuous consumption, 5, 7, 9, 17, 19, 24,
    25, 117, 131, 172, 179, 220
Corfield, P., 3, 26
corn, 14, 28, 29, 36, 50, 59, 76, 104, 125, 151,
    154, 172; municipal purchase of, 128,
    157
Corporation Act, 19, 179
corporation of the poor, 25
Council of the North, 12
county towns, 3, 7, 12–14, 16, 18, 20, 22, 23,
    27, 30, 31, 48, 148, 200
courts, 23, 75, 92, 147, 152, 176; see also
    assizes, Chancery, quarter sessions
Coventry, 5, 9, 10, 12, 14, 16, 48, 50
Coward, Leonard, 228, 234
Cranbrook, 14
credit facilities, 23, 160, 162, 178–9, 184, 234
Crediton, 14
crime, 57–8, 60, 242
Cromwell, Oliver, 165, 168; Thomas, 67

Dallison, Sir Roger, 22
Davis, N.Z., 46
Deal, 28
Debenham, 104, 127
Defoe, Daniel, 26, 104, 105, 107, 128–30,
    172–4, 176, 178
Derby, 27, 179
Derbyshire, 18
Devon, 106, 149
Devizes, 210
directories, 215, 217, 220, 221, 244
disease, 4, 14, 16, 54, 64, 78, 96, 128, 155–6,
    171, 178, 199, 207; see also plague,
    smallpox
dissent, see Puritanism
distribution of wealth, 9, 52–3
dockyard towns, 16, 28, 177
Dorchester, 27
Dorset, 151, 157
Dover, 105
Downame, John, 72
dress, 9
Droitwich, 7, 15
Dudley, family, 50, 78, 79; Ambrose, Earl of
    Warwick, 50, 69; Edmund, 57, 58, 77–8;
    John, Earl of Warwick, 67; Lettice,

Countess of Leicester, 69; Robert, Earl of Leicester, 8, 50, 51, 67–70, 73–8
Dunwich, 12
Durham, 26
Dursley, 10, 13
Dyer, A., 3, 4, 6, 78, 193

Ealing, 62, 63
East Anglia, 7, 15, 26, 104, 108
Eastern Association, 15
Eastland Company, 104
ecclesiastical commission, 12
economic regulation, 7–8, 13, 17, 31, 39, 76, 120–3, 161, 176, 201, 236, 239; decline of, 19, 120–1, 167, 176
Elizabeth I, 202
Essex, 12, 18, 127
Everitt, A., 17, 29
excisemen and customs-men, 24, 112, 114, 171, 182
Exeter, 6, 8, 11, 18, 26, 27, 127, 172, 177, 210
Eye, 129

fairs, 6, 48, 53, 124, 127, 150, 151, 172, 179
Falmouth, 210
famine, 10, 14–15, 46, 60, 156, 157; see also harvest failure, subsistence crises
Fareham, 174–5, 193
Faversham, 104
Fiennes, Celia, 16, 20, 129, 151, 202, 207, 208
Fiennes, Nathaniel, 167
fire, 20, 24, 50, 152
Fisher, John of Warwick, 51, 68, 73–5, 79
Fisher, Thomas, 67, 68
flower festivals, 22
Floyer, Sir John, 202
Forbes, James, 24
Fordingbridge, 174–5
France, 5, 11, 12, 97, 108, 126, 149, 158
Fransham, 13
freemen, 6, 9, 17, 19, 90–2, 120–1, 124, 127, 147, 160, 162, 167, 180, 183, 201, 206, 221, 222, 236–7, 239
Frome, 201, 210
Fuller, Thomas, 66, 167

gentry, 7, 8, 18–23, 27–9, 50, 72, 145, 148, 150, 160, 162, 163, 166, 175–80; political influence of, 9, 50, 169, 182–4; 'pseudo-gentry', 108–9, 114, 127, 173, 177, 178; resident in towns, 8, 22, 26, 28, 50, 69, 99, 130, 166, 182, 222, 228; towns as social centres for, 2, 8, 16, 18–24, 50, 53,

130, 145, 154, 161–2, 170, 176–7, 200, 204, 206, 211
George III, 243
Germany, 14, 15, 26, 104, 105
gilds and companies: craft and trade, 7, 19, 121, 130, 176, 217; religious, 51, 66
Gilmore, Joseph, 201, 204, 211, 218, 219, 237, 244
Gloucester, 5–10, 12, 14–17, 20–4, 48, 50, 210
Gloucestershire, 10, 18, 30
Godalming, 174
Goffe, Major-General, 167
goldsmiths, 109, 150, 157, 177
Goodacre, J., 13
Gosport, 174, 210
Grandison, Lord, 163
Greenland, 97
Grimsby, 12
Grundisburgh, Suffolk, 109, 114
Guildford, 174

Hadleigh, 127
Hallamshire, 150
Hamburg, 110
Hamilton, Duke of, 238
Hampshire, 145–52, 154, 156, 158, 162, 166, 169–79, 184, 193, 194
Harington, Sir Edward, 228
Harington, Sir John, 202
harvest failure, 5, 10, 13–15, 31, 47, 50, 58, 59, 71, 73, 76, 78, 96, 128, 157; see also famine, subsistence crises
Havant, 174–5, 193
Hearth Tax, see taxation
Henley, 27
Hereford, 21; Viscount, 130
Herefordshire, 18
Hertford, 154
Hertfordshire, 18, 151
Heylyn, Peter, 165, 166
Hinckley, 7, 30
Hobbes, Thomas, 58
Holland, 26, 28, 127, 129
Hopton, Sir Ralph, 164
horse-racing, 21, 99, 161–2, 170, 177, 179–81
hospitals, 14, 47, 51, 65–72, 76, 128, 147, 158, 168, 171, 173, 201, 206, 230, 238
households, 4, 60–2, 64, 118, 192, 203–4
housing, 4, 6, 14, 16, 22, 61, 62, 64, 67, 105, 107, 118–19, 127, 155, 178, 182, 212, 217, 221–2; see also building
Howard, Bernard, 182–3

Hull, 8, 12, 19, 28, 105, 124
Huntingdonshire, 18

Iberia, 12, 180
improvement, town, 20, 31, 32, 199, 206, 212, 225–6, 228–34, 237, 239–43; Acts, 20, 124, 199, 204, 209, 211, 226, 231, 232, 239–42; dock, 19; *see also* lighting, water supplies
incorporation, 50, 67, 73, 78, 89, 147
industrial towns, 2, 16, 27, 28, 31, 198, 200
industry, 2, 4, 16, 17, 22, 27, 48, 53, 77, 221; brewing, 27, 115, 150, 169, 221; leather, 5, 13, 52, 103, 108, 150, 172; malting, 5, 27, 51, 109–10, 122, 150; metal, 5, 17, 109, 150; textile, 4–5, 12, 13, 15, 17, 26, 28, 30, 31, 48, 51, *et passim*
infirmaries, 23–4
inns and taverns, 8, 19, 22, 24, 26, 50, 109, 110, 114–16, 119, 122–3, 129, 131, 152, 154, 156, 163, 168, 173, 177, 180, 184, 200, 204, 206, 223
investment patterns, 5–6, 9, 105–7, 109, 114, 116–17, 150
Ipswich, 2, 9, 10, 24, 28, 62–4, 88–136; coastal trade, 12, 28, 88, 97, 104–5, 124, 126–9; economic regulation, 19, 120–4; finances, 92, 131; government, 89–92, 106, 127–8, 131; industry, 27, 103, 107–9, 119, 125–7; internal trade, 106, 127, 129; liberties, 89, 97, 127; merchants, 106, 116, 118, 126, 127, 130; occupational structure, 99–103; overseas trade, 12, 28, 88, 97, 104–6, 123, 125, 126, 128–9; population, 4, 88, 89, 92, 94, 96, 118–19, 126; port, 89, 96, 97, 103–5, 118, 123, 128; and region, 96–9, 127; ruling elite, 24, 106, 115, 127–8, 136; service and social centre, 23, 28, 89, 99, 130; shipping, 5, 103–6, 117, 119, 127, 128; topography, 89, 130
Ireland, 29
Isle of Wight, 168
Isham, Thomas, 20
Italy, 5, 149
Itchen, river, 146, 149, 152, 154, 161, 176

James I, 146, 163
James II, 181–3
John, King, 89
Johnson, Samuel, 27
Jones, Inigo, 231
Jordan, W. K., 11, 65, 66, 69, 71, 72

Jours, Luke, 109, 114–15
justice of the peace, 8, 76, 129, 154, 237; *see also* quarter sessions

Kenilworth, 48, 51
Kent, 10, 29, 30, 104
Kettering, 30
Kidderminster, 17
Kingsclere, 154, 175
King's Lynn, 6, 8, 12, 18, 105, 119
Kingston, Duke of, 223, 231, 241, 244
kinship, 97, 127

Lancashire, 23, 29, 108, 178
Lancaster, 15, 29
Laslett, P., 60, 61
Latimer, Bishop Hugh, 67
Laud, Archbishop William, 97
lawyers, 8, 23, 28, 34, 92, 99, 110–12, 114, 130, 147, 150–2, 160, 168, 177–9, 190, 215, 221, 228, 234
Leake, Lady, 130
lectures and exhibitions, 22; religious lecturers, 90, 96, 97, 99, 112, 160
Leeds, 2
Leicester, 6–7, 10, 14–17, 52, 172
Leicestershire, 6, 7, 10, 13, 18
leisure resorts, 2, 27–8, 30, 31, 180, 181, 198, 200; *see also* spa towns
Leland, John, 201, 202
Le Roy Ladurie, E., 46
Lever, Thomas, 67
Lewes, 27
libraries, 21, 28, 97, 99, 112, 128, 130, 180, 200, 219
Lichfield, 5, 22, 27, 29, 62, 63
lighting, 20, 128, 239–41, 243
Lincoln, 12, 15, 29
Lincolnshire, 18, 97, 179
Lisle, John, 168–9
literacy, 145, 168
Liverpool, 12, 15, 20, 28–9, 210
lodgers, 61, 64, 77, 157; lodging houses, 202, 204, 206, 217–19, 223, 228, 238
London, 5, 9, 11, 19, 21–3, 25, 27, 72, 107, 124, 125, 129, 146, 148, 151, 154–6, 163, 168, 174, 176–8, 180, 200, 201, 208–10, 220, 238, 242; Bridewell, 61, 190; population, 2, 4; trade, 8, 17, 28, 97, 104, 105, 126–8, 149, 165, 211; shipping, 103
Loughborough, 7
Love, Nicholas, 167–9
Low Countries, 97, 126

254

Lowther, Sir John, 29
Lucas, Francis, 103, 106
Ludlow, 6, 10
Lutterworth, 7, 13
Lyme, 28, 30
Lymington, 154, 174–5
Lyncombe and Widcombe, 201, 203, 214, 215, 217, 219, 221, 242
Lyons, 46, 71

Macky, John, 179, 180, 182
Maidstone, 29
Maldon, 6, 14, 97
Manchester, 2, 106
Manly, Thomas, 25
Mansfield, 27
manufacturers, 200, 243
market gardening, 25, 114
Market Harborough, 7, 50
markets and marketing, 2, 6–7, 11–13, 15, 18, 19, 26, 29, 31, 48, 76, 115, 123, 124, 127, 129, 145, 150–2, 156, 163, 170, 172–4, 220, 223, 239, 241; regulations, 6, 7, 76, 124, 128
market towns, 2, 3, 6, 7, 13, 18, 23, 30–1, 48, 148, 151–2, 173, 174, 176, 193; economy, 6–7, 13, 36; population, 13, 16, 174–5; social structure, 13
Marlborough, 163
Mary of Modena, 202
Mary, Queen, 162
Mason, Sir Robert, 182
Mediterranean, 11, 104, 149
Melksham, 212
Melton Mowbray, 7, 10
Middlesex, 151
Midlands, 2, 18, 27, 28, 30, 31, 48, 52, 54, 59
migration, 4, 7, 9–11, 13–15, 16, 25, 27, 47, 48, 53, 54, 57, 59–61, 64, 70, 94, 97, 99, 120–1, 127, 145, 155, 156, 166–7, 171, 181, 184, 200–1, 208, 219, 222; types of, 4, 156
Mildmay, Sir Henry, 168
Milsom, Charles, 228, 229
Milsom, Daniel, 228, 229
Minehead, 15
modernization, 2, 31
More, Sir Thomas, 73
monasteries, 14, 47, 50, 54, 65–9, 74, 78, 89, 144, 146, 147
money lending, 5, 23; 117
mortality rates, 4, 15, 53, 54, 59, 94–6, 119, 155, 156, 170

mortgages, 113
music, 21, 180, 206

Nantwich, 9
Nash, Richard, 202, 204, 206, 214, 237, 238, 243
Neale, J.E., 74
Needham Market, 104, 127
Newcastle upon Tyne, 11, 12, 16, 26, 28, 97, 103–5, 126-9
New England, 97, 127
New Forest, 162, 163
New Romney, 10
newspapers, 18–19, 21, 26, 99, 180, 208, 218, 221, 244
Norfolk, 18, 127, 149, 154
Northampton, 17, 20, 23, 27
Northamptonshire, 18
Norway, 105, 110
Norwich, 5, 6, 10, 11, 16, 18, 21, 26, 28, 46, 62–4, 76, 106, 107, 125–7, 160, 177, 245; diocese of, 96–7, 136
Nottingham, 16, 27, 59
Nottinghamshire, 18

Odiham, 175
Ogilby, John, 119, 130, 136
Ogle, Sir William, 164–7, 169, 183
Oken, Thomas, 74, 75
oligarchy, 91–2, 127, 128, 130, 147, 160–2
Orford, 12
Overton, 153, 174–5
Oxford, 6, 12, 14, 16, 210; Lord, 130
Oxfordshire, 18, 29, 152

Padua, 106
Palliser, D., 3
Palmer, John junior, 219, 228
Palmer, John, architect, 229, 232, 233
Parliament, 46, 211; elections and electorate, 22, 50, 74, 90, 152, 173, 182–4; members of, 22, 51, 160, 161, 168, 228, 231; Rump, 168, 169
Patten, J., 3
pedlars, see chapmen
Pembroke, 20
Penkridge, 29
Penzance, 15
Pepys, Samuel, 115
Peterborough, 14
Petersfield, 174–5
Phillips, Sir James, 166
Phillott, Charles, 228, 234

physicians, 8, 23, 27, 28, 34, 110–12, 130, 152, 177–9, 191, 199, 204, 206, 208, 215, 221, 226, 228, 231, 234
Phythian-Adams, C., 3, 14, 136
plague, 4, 10, 13, 15, 16, 19, 94, 96, 118, 119, 147, 154–7, 170, 171
players and entertainers, 22, 180, 219, 222
Plymouth, 27, 28, 210
Poole, 60
poor, 6, 9, 10, 13, 14, 24–5, 31, 35, 46–79, 107, 118, 119, 145, 150, 155, 157, 171, 184, 199, 200–1, 222; age structure of, 62, 64; family structure of, 60–1; relief of, 9–11, 16, 25, 46–7, 51, 54, 58, 65–79, 96, 128, 155–60, 167–9, 171–2, 222, 239; types of, 10, 54, 57–61
Pope, Alexander, 208
population, 16, 154, 170, 189; of towns, 3, 4, 12, 16, 47, 88, 92, 94, 96, 146, 147, 170, 203, 214; growth of, 3, 16, 26, 31, 53–4, 118–19, 170, 174, 201, 214–15; see also birth rate, mortality rates
ports, 5, 8, 12, 16, 17, 26, 28–9, 89, 96, 97, 104–5, 149, 152, 174, 198; silting in, 8, 12, 29, 105, 128
Portsea, 28
Portsmouth, 28, 152–3, 157, 163, 173–5, 177, 184, 210
post office, 30, 174
Pottery Towns, 2
Prescot, 23
Preston, 27
printing and publishing, 24
Privy Council, 76, 104, 122, 125, 155, 156
probate inventories, 5, 9, 35, 52, 53, 66, 79, 103, 105–117, 154
professions, 8, 18, 23, 24, 26–8, 50, 53, 103, 110–12, 114, 148, 177–9, 182, 215, 221–2, 228; see also lawyers, physicians
property-ownership, 50, 66–8, 211; by townspeople, 5–6, 54, 97, 103, 108, 114, 117–19, 127, 166
provincial capitals, 2, 11–12, 14, 16, 23, 26–8, 31, 47, 144, 148, 177, 200
Puckering, Sir John, 68
Pullan, B., 46
Pulteney, Sir William, 212
Puritanism and dissent, 24, 47, 72, 73, 76–8, 92, 112, 160–1, 163, 168, 190

Quakers, 92
quarter sessions, 8, 21, 23, 48, 96, 120, 121, 122, 147, 152, 158, 163, 167, 171

Reading, 14, 27, 127, 154
recorders, 50
Reformation, 11, 12, 14, 46, 51, 65, 66, 69, 71, 72, 144, 199, 201
Restoration, 19, 21, 199
Ringwood, 174–5
riots, 14, 74, 168, 222, 238, 239, 242
Ripon, 12
rituals, 62; see also ceremony
Rochester, 105
Romsey, 173–5
Rotterdam, 105, 110
Rutland, 18
Rye, 12, 28

Saffron Walden, 6
St Albans, 17, 20, 154, 172
Salisbury, 4, 5, 10, 12–16, 21, 46, 153, 160, 177, 210
Sandwich, 10, 12, 14
Savine, A., 65
Scarborough, 6, 28, 97, 105, 198, 200, 245
schools, 24, 67, 71, 99, 113, 130, 154, 171, 178, 179, 235; academies, 24; grammar, 8, 24, 97, 113, 128, 154; teachers, 24, 67, 74, 113–14
Seamer, 6
services, 2, 8, 9, 22, 24, 28, 48, 50, 110, 114, 127, 130, 145, 170, 172–4, 177–8, 217, 239
settlement: regulations, 99, 120, 121, 156–8, 171; Act of, 16, 121; see also migration
Severn, river, 27, 238
sex ratios, 60–2, 219
Shadwell, Thomas, 194
Shaftesbury, 210
Sheffield, 2, 17
Shepton Mallet, 210
Sherborne, 210
shops, 7, 15, 16, 18, 22, 24, 25, 27, 29, 106–7, 112, 115, 123, 127, 130, 131, 145, 150, 154, 157, 163, 166, 170, 172, 174, 177, 179, 208, 219, 220, 236
Shrewsbury, 5, 6, 10, 12, 18, 22, 27, 50, 179, 210
skilled artisans, 25
Slack, P., 3
Sloane, Sir Hans, 23
smallpox, 16, 23, 96, 171
Smollett, Tobias, 208, 212, 225, 226, 243
Snow, William, 166, 168
social mobility, 9, 108–9, 167
social structure, 9–10, 24, 116–19, 127

Somerset, 18, 151
Southampton, 10, 12, 28, 29, 147, 149, 152–3, 156–7, 161, 163, 173–7, 184, 191, 192, 210; Earl of, 162
Southwark, 61
spa towns, 22, 23, 27–8, 30, 198–200, 243
Spain, 97, 126
Spalding, 22
Speed, John, 204, 211
Stafford, 15, 16, 23, 29, 60
Staffordshire, 27, 29
Stamford, 9, 12, 27
Starkey, Thomas, 67
statues, 20
statutes, 16, 46, 53, 69, 75, 96, 120–2, 124, 168, 199, 209, 211, 226, 231, 232, 236–41
Stockbridge, 174–5
Stowmarket, 108, 129
Stratford-on-Avon, 27, 48, 50, 59
Stroud, 30
subsidy, see taxation
subsistence crises, 4, 10, 14–15, 62, 64, 96, 128
suburbs, 10, 62, 64, 118, 119, 146, 147, 149, 150, 155, 156, 171, 178, 203, 211–12, 214, 221
Suffolk, 12, 18, 28, 92, 94, 96, 97, 104, 105, 107, 124, 127, 154, 193, 194
Sunderland, 104, 105
surgeons, 23, 111, 112, 178, 221, 228, 231
Surrey, 151–2
Sutherland, Dr Alexander, 225, 242
Sussex, 72, 151, 166
Symons, John, 228, 230–2

Tamworth, 14
Taunton, 210
taxation, 9, 11, 14, 15, 31, 58, 62, 65, 68, 69, 71, 73–6, 78, 79, 96, 111, 118, 155–7, 162, 163, 173; Hearth Tax, 92, 99, 110, 115, 116, 118, 119, 131–3, 170, 171, 182, 203–4; subsidies, 144, 148
Taylor, John, 152
Tetbury, 210
Tewkesbury, 17, 30
Thaxted, 6
　　　es, 22, 180, 200, 206, 219
　　　ars War, 12, 15, 104, 149
　　　A.F., 71

Torrington, 15
Totnes, 28
town halls, 22, 67, 204, 223, 231, 232
towns: and country, 2, 6, 7, 17, 19–21, 23, 31, 52, 91, 96–103; elites, 6, 9, 15, 19, et passim; finances, 7, 14, 19, 47, 51, 66, 73–4, 92, 158, 159, 165–6, 170, 223, 226, 228, 229; hierarchy of, 2, 26, 148; internal economy of, 4–9 et passim; occupational structure, 7, 99–103, 215–17; open spaces in, 89, 147; political factionalism in, 22, 73–5, 78, 92, 120, 123, 168; recent research on, 3, 15–16, 144; relations with central government, 168; social zoning in, 4, 62, 118, 119, 221; urban specialization, 2, 16, 17, 26, 29–30, 51
trade, 9–10, 14, 16, 24, 59; coastal, 8, 11–12, 17–18, 26, 28, 88, 97, 104–5, 128, 129; internal, 5–7, 9, 13, 15, 18, 22, 50, 51, 97, 104–5, 106, 129, 150–2, 155–6, 165, 174, 184; overseas, 5, 8, 11–12, 14, 15, 17, 26, 28, 31, 88, 97, 104–6, 110, 128, 129, 149, 152; tokens, 174
transport facilities, 7, 17–18, 27, 28, 30, 50, 67, 124, 153–5, 161, 163, 165, 167, 174, 176, 200, 208–12, 240
Trussell, John, 146, 154, 156, 161–2, 164–6, 184, 190
Tunbridge Wells, 30
turnpikes, 18, 23, 209, 212, 226, 232

universities, 12, 65, 114–15
urbanization, 2, 193

vagrants, 4, 46–7, 54, 57–8, 60, 61, 68, 69, 73, 78, 168, 238
Venice, 46, 71
Venner, Dr Thomas, 204
Virginia, 105

wage-rates, 120
Walcot, 203, 214, 215, 217–19, 221, 236, 237, 239, 241–3
Wales, 5, 18, 26, 31, 48, 66
walks, 20, 200, 204, 206, 223, 226, 236
Waller, Sir William, 163–6
Walsall, 29
Walsingham, Sir Francis, 158
Waltham-on-the-Wolds, 13
Ward, Samuel, 97
Warminster, 210
Warner, Richard, 213, 221, 238, 242

wars, 14, 31, 157–8, 173, 212, 214, 222, 234, 239, 243; *see also* Civil War, Thirty Years War

Warwick, 2, 5, 14, 20, 27, 46–79, 160, 172; and dissolution, 50, 65–8; and Dudleys, 8, 50–1, 69–71, 75, 78; economic problems of, 48, 50–2, 73, 78; economic revival, 53; gentry in, 50, 53, 78; hospitals, 66–8; Leicester's hospital, 50, 51, 69–72; political centre, 48; political problems, 73–5, 78; poor of, 10, 11, 46–79, 160; population, 48, 53–4, 73, 78; St Mary's parish, 53, 54, 56, 58, 59, 64, 74, 76; St Nicholas parish, 53–6, 59, 69, 74; vagrancy problem, 4, 54, 57–8, 60

Warwickshire, 7, 47, 50; the Felden, 50

water supplies, 20, 124–5, 128, 239

Watlington, 29

Webster, Captain, 204, 206

Watson, Sir William, 228

Wellingborough, 30

Wells, 21, 23

West Indies, 17, 26, 29, 105

Westmorland, 94

Weymouth, 28, 198, 210, 245

Whitby, 97, 104, 105

Whitchurch, 153, 174–5

White, Sir Thomas, 126, 160

Whitehaven, 29

Willan, T.S., 18

William III, 173

Wilton, 13

Wiltshire, 5, 13, 18, 94, 151–2, 174

Winchcombe, 13

Winchester, 2, 4, 7, 15, 19, 22, 24, 27, 143–95; castle, 146, 163–6, 169, 180; and cathedral, 146, 147, 152, 160, 163, 165, 167; cloth industry, 4, 145, 147, 148–50, 155, 157, 161, 184; economy of, 7, 12, 144–6, 170–9; economic recovery of, 18, 145–6, 162, 168, 184; government of, 144, 147, 165–6, 168; industry, 145, 147–50, 170, 172; marketing, 145, 146, 150–2, 157; and national politics, 145, 157, 162–5, 169, 182–3; population, 16, 146, 147, 155, 170–1; poverty, 10, 145, 146, 155–60, 168–9; and region, 145, 151–2, 173, 174, 176, 184; royal palace at, 146, 180–2; ruling elite, 144–8, 154, 156, 160–1, 163, 168, 169, 177; services, 145, 148, 150, 170, 172–4, 177–8; as a social centre, 27, 145, 146, 148, 154, 161–2, 170, 176–7, 179–82; social structure, 144

Winchester College, 147, 151–2, 154, 158, 167–8, 170–1, 177, 178, 182, 192

Winchester, Marquis of, 162

Witney, 17

Wolverhampton, 29

Wolvesey Palace, 146, 167, 169–70, 182

Wood, John the elder, 202, 204, 206, 208–9, 211–12, 214, 218, 220, 222, 223, 225, 226, 229, 230, 237, 239–41, 244

Wood, John the younger, 231–2

Woodbridge, 108, 129

Woodstock, 17

Worcester, 5, 6, 12, 15, 21, 48, 50, 179; diocese of, 54

Worcestershire, 18, 50, 76

Workhouses, 69, 76, 158–9

Wren, Sir Christopher, 180–1, 195

Wriothesley, Thomas, Earl of Southampton, 67

Wythe, Thomas, 106, 117

Yarmouth, Great, 4, 8, 14, 16, 28, 103–5, 129

York, 4, 6, 8, 11, 14, 26, 179, 194, 200; Duke of, 181

Yorkshire, 12, 28